WHAT IF LATIN AMERICA
RULED THE WORLD?

BY THE SAME AUTHOR

Being Against the World

WHAT IF LATIN AMERICA RULED THE WORLD?

How the South Will Take the
North into the 22nd Century

Oscar Guardiola-Rivera

BLOOMSBURY

LONDON · BERLIN · NEW YORK

To Sylvia Ospina, ut pictura poesis.
To Zoe, other eyes.
To Haidy and Ceci, and the women of the Americas, Etna in one's
own home.
To Bill Swainson and Kevin Conroy Scott, mystificateurs.

First published in Great Britain 2010

Copyright © 2010 by Oscar Guardiola-Rivera

Maps by John Gilkes

Bloomsbury Publishing Plc
36 Soho Square
London W1D 3QY

www.bloomsbury.com

Bloomsbury Publishing, London, New York and Berlin

A CIP catalogue record for this book is available from the British Library

ISBN 978 1 4088 0599 2

10 9 8 7 6 5 4 3 2 1

Typeset by Hewer Text UK Ltd, Edinburgh
Printed in Great Britain by Clays Limited, St Ives plc

CONTENTS

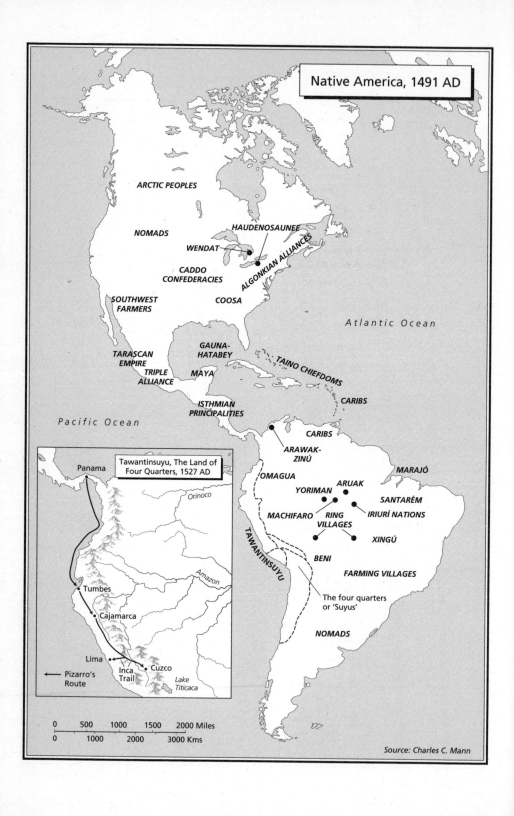

Native America, 1491 AD

ARCTIC PEOPLES

HAUDENOSAUNEE

NOMADS

WENDAT

CADDO
CONFEDERACIES

ALGONKIAN ALLIANCES

SOUTHWEST
FARMERS

COOSA

Atlantic Ocean

TARASCAN
EMPIRE

GAUNA-
HATABEY

TAINO CHIEFDOMS

TRIPLE
ALLIANCE

MAYA

ISTHMIAN
PRINCIPALITIES

CARIBS

Pacific Ocean

CARIBS

ARAWAK-
ZINÚ

OMAGUA

MARAJÓ

YORIMAN

ARUAK

SANTARÉM

MACHIFARO

RING
VILLAGES

IRIURÍ NATIONS

XINGÚ

TAWANTINSUYU

BENI

FARMING VILLAGES

The four quarters
or 'Suyus'

NOMADS

Tawantinsuyu, The Land of
Four Quarters, 1527 AD

Panama

Orinoco

Amazon

Tumbes

Cajamarca

Lima

Inca
Trail

Cuzco

Lake
Titicaca

Pizarro's
Route

0   500   1000   1500   2000 Miles
0   1000   2000   3000 Kms

Source: Charles C. Mann

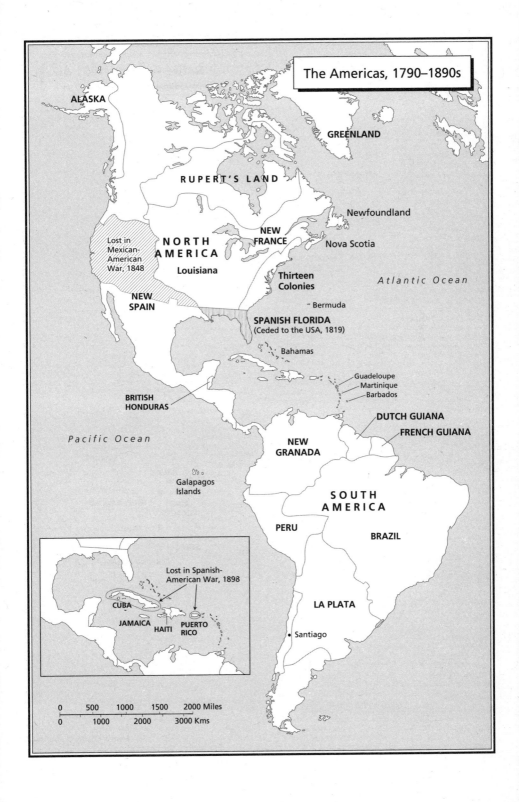

The Americas, 1790–1890s

ALASKA

GREENLAND

RUPERT'S LAND

Newfoundland

NEW FRANCE

Nova Scotia

NORTH AMERICA

Lost in Mexican-American War, 1848

Louisiana

Thirteen Colonies

NEW SPAIN

Atlantic Ocean

Bermuda

SPANISH FLORIDA
(Ceded to the USA, 1819)

Bahamas

Guadeloupe
Martinique
Barbados

BRITISH HONDURAS

DUTCH GUIANA

FRENCH GUIANA

Pacific Ocean

NEW GRANADA

Galapagos Islands

SOUTH AMERICA

PERU

BRAZIL

Lost in Spanish-American War, 1898

CUBA

JAMAICA

HAITI

PUERTO RICO

LA PLATA

Santiago

| 0 | 500 | 1000 | 1500 | 2000 Miles |
| 0 | 1000 | 2000 | | 3000 Kms |

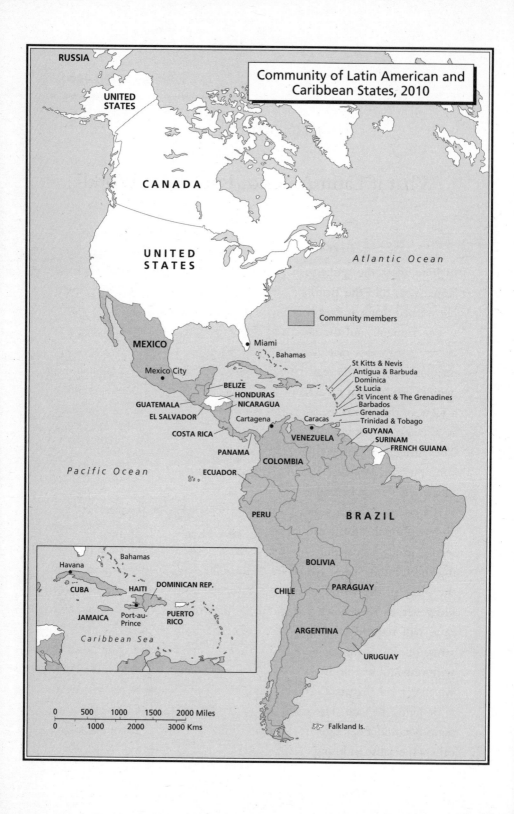

RUSSIA

UNITED
STATES

CANADA

UNITED
STATES

Atlantic Ocean

Community of Latin American and
Caribbean States, 2010

Community members

MEXICO

Miami

Mexico City

Bahamas

St Kitts & Nevis
Antigua & Barbuda
Dominica
St Lucia
St Vincent & The Grenadines
Barbados
Grenada
Trinidad & Tobago

BELIZE
HONDURAS
GUATEMALA
NICARAGUA
EL SALVADOR
Cartagena
Caracas
COSTA RICA
VENEZUELA
GUYANA
SURINAM
FRENCH GUIANA

PANAMA
COLOMBIA

Pacific Ocean

ECUADOR

PERU

BRAZIL

BOLIVIA

Bahamas

Havana

DOMINICAN REP.

CUBA
HAITI

PARAGUAY

CHILE

JAMAICA
Port-au-
Prince
PUERTO
RICO

ARGENTINA

Caribbean Sea

URUGUAY

0   500   1000   1500   2000 Miles
0   1000   2000   3000 Kms

Falkland Is.

INTRODUCTION

What if Latin America Ruled the World?

In June 2009, the spokesman of the Yanomami people of Brazil, Davi Kopenawa, told the British Parliament that history was repeating itself. He warned that a second war of conquest was coming. Across the globe, as governments and the boards of directors of transnational mining and energy companies race for dwindling resources in order to cover the needs of our highly energy-intensive, resource-hungry world, indigenous peoples are battling to defend their lands, while young people develop a view of the world less as a storehouse of valuable materials and more as a complex network of relationships that extend to the biosphere. They struggle to resolve the paradoxes caused by over-exploitation and consumerism, propelled into the uncertain future by a violent gust while catastrophes erupt behind and beneath them.

If it is true that a war is coming, and that we are witnessing the endgame of the form of globalisation brought about by the first and second industrial revolutions, then Latin America – this time also including the United States, which by 2040 will have a Latino majority – is the place in the world where the battle is most likely to be decided. However, as Kopenawa put it during his visit to London, victory this time will require something else, something more than the force of arms, or the power of economic forces. 'Governments must treat us with respect,' he told British MPs, 'we kill nothing, we live on the land, we never rob nature. Yet governments always want more. We need your help,' he said. His point was that the division of labour among nations could no longer mean that some specialise in winning while others specialise in losing.

Uruguayan novelist and journalist Eduardo Galeano once wrote that the part of the world known today as Latin America had been precocious: it specialised in losing, 'ever since those remote times when Renaissance Europeans ventured across the ocean and buried their teeth in the throats of Indian civilisations. Centuries passed, and Latin America perfected its role.'[1] A spokesman for those same Indian civilisations came from Latin America to London in 2009, donning the mantle of the prophet, to tell the west that this time things would be different. Far from fitting their stereotype as inhabitants of a region of banana republics and idealistic utopias, the peoples of South America have risen up and now stand together. They have been able to resist some of the most extreme consequences of the globalist and unfettered market policies that have wreaked havoc elsewhere in the developed world, particularly after the 2008 global financial crisis. They are now calling on the rest of the world, especially the young people of Europe, Asia, Africa and America who may choose to use their newfound consciousness of the relational nature of global space, for help and recognition, to stand together and overcome the paradox whose damaging effects we all suffer today.

Of Business and Freedom

'The more freedom is extended to business, the more prisons have to be built for those who suffer from that business.'[2] This argument, popularised in Latin America during the 1950s and 1960s, resonates with the observations made in seventeenth-century England about the link between the enclosure movement, the death penalty and imprisonment by Diggers and Levellers, and by commoner revolutionaries in New Granada, present-day Colombia, a century later. The 'prisons' referred to included forced displacement, impressment to serve in merchant and military vessels at sea, private and public debt, and indentured and waged labour as much as straightforward deprivation of liberty in dungeons and other places of incarceration. British Diggers and Spanish American commoners were conscious of the connections between the occurrence of such phenomena at home and the enslavement of poor and indigenous peoples on both sides of the Atlantic and in Africa and Asia.

They also acknowledged the role that the use of force, militarism and the limitation of liberty played in the wider context of global economic relations. A form of solidarity was born between them, based upon an emergent consciousness of the need to protect their common heritage in order to be able to create future environments for all. Contemporary native activists like Davi Kopenawa and others appeal to the associative approach and the consciousness that animated the efforts of levelling and commoner movements on both sides of the Atlantic when they say 'we need your help'. They aim not to move our sympathy and provoke charity, but to retrieve in us the deep-seated and almost forgotten memory of mutuality that long united English-speaking peoples and communities in the struggle in South America and the Caribbean. Such declarations should not be understood as appeals for assistance; rather, they contain an age-old call to action that can be heard across the globe.[3]

For years, policies favoured by the centres of power in Europe and Washington, and in the international financial institutions where their influence prevails, such as the World Bank and the International Monetary Fund (IMF) – including deregulation of financial and capital markets, privatisation of state-owned enterprises and pensions, private and public debt to sustain demand, debt conditionality, deregulation of labour markets, and trade liberalisation – compelled countries to remove obstacles to foreign investment, make labour contracts flexible and deregulate financial systems, sell everything, including most natural resources, without any consideration for indigenous rights, development concerns or environmental impact, and throw all of their efforts into raising exports to be exchanged in a playing field where players are unequal and competition unfair. All the while, these policies facilitated indebtedness, both private and public. Internal mismanagement by elites catering for their short-term interests, to the detriment of the long-term interests of the peoples they were supposed to represent, did not help.

The rationale behind such policies was that unless these countries fitted themselves with such policies as if they were a 'golden straitjacket', nations dependent on the exploitation of raw materials would never be able to join the Lexus and Samsung world. Fitting themselves with the straitjacket was thus the only path for developing countries to follow in order to succeed in the new global economy. However, the fact is that had the Japanese, Korean, Indian, Chinese or Brazilian governments followed the free-trade economists, IMF and Washington officials and their self-righteous spokespeople back in the 1960s and 1970s, or more recently in the 2000s, there would have been no Lexus and no Samsung, and no BRICs, which is how journalists and economists refer these days to the emerging countries and economies of Brazil, Russia, India and China. It is also a fact that the alleged 'only path' in the global economy led not to prosperity and success, but to the Great Recession. The emerging economies of today have responded better to the Great Recession than the 'developed' ones, not because they fitted themselves with the straitjacket and followed or imitated the 'unique path' to success, but precisely because they chose not to follow it, and distanced themselves from the recipes of free-trade economists and ideologues. Consideration of these facts in the uncertain climate of the Great Recession obliges us to set the record straight and take a closer look at the official history of globalisation.

The Official History

According to the official history of globalisation, Britain first adopted free-market and free-trade policies in the eighteenth century, well ahead of other countries.[4] By the middle of the nineteenth century it had consolidated its spectacular economic success, and other countries started imitating Britain's liberalisation or borrowed from it, together with democracy and the rule of law, through colonial channels. Everything was fine until the Great War when, in response to the ensuing instability of the world economy, countries unwisely started erecting barriers to free trade once again, such as the infamous US Smoot–Hawley Tariff Act of the 1930s. In 1932, Britain itself, the champion of free trade around the world, ceded to temptation and introduced tariffs. Only after World War II was the world economy re-established along liberal lines, this time with the United States taking over the position of global dominance vacated by Britain.

And although protectionism and state intervention prevailed in various parts of the developing world, or so the story goes, by the 1980s such policies had been abandoned following the failure of the so-called Import Substitution Industrialization (ISI) model in these countries, and the rise of neoliberalism. After the East Asian 'economic miracle' and the Third World debt crises of the 1980s, the remaining developing countries still hanging on to the ISI idea – that a backward country starts producing industrial products that it used to import and makes imports artificially expensive by means of tariffs, or gives domestic subsidies, thereby substituting imported industrial goods with domestically produced equivalents – finally embraced neoliberalism. These changes were made all the more necessary by the global integration and the possibilities opened up by new communication and information technologies 'flattening' the whole world and making it homogeneous. The crowning glory of this historical shift was the fall of communism in 1989 and the rise of the globalised world economy, hailed by the advent of the liberalising World Trade Organization (WTO), now at the centre of global governance together with the IMF and the World Bank. It was, we have been told, the end of history.

The official history is widely accepted. One of its corollaries is that in the brave new world of globalisation there is no room for rich social relations, forms of common ownership or deeper links to Nature of the kind advocated by the indigenous peoples of Latin America and other opposition movements. At best, these are relics of the past; at worst, they are dangerous and empty ideals. To speak of a 'carnal connection with goddess-mother earth' is dismissed as hippie-talk or political and economic nonsense. Moreover, when native peoples and activists use that language they demonstrate that they have no one else to blame but themselves for their backward status. 'Underdevelopment is in the mind' then becomes an acceptable slogan. And if political correctness calls for a prudent qualification of the slogan, underdevelopment then becomes a matter of faulty institutions, corruption and conflict-prone social or cultural tendencies.

Today, however, Latin American nations and social movements led by activists and native peoples in the region are resisting the pressure of neoliberalism. Furthermore, they are setting up innovative economic and environmental arrangements outside the mainstream of globalist

market strictures. Now that the Great Recession has made it clear that
a new dispensation is required, their call to set the record straight and
redefine the international monetary and economic system has become
relevant to us all.

Setting the Record Straight

Latin America's new advocates – the natives of Bolivia, Mexico and
southern Colombia, the landless of Brazil, the free associations of Chile
and Argentina, and the Latino community organisers of the United
States – together with a new generation of economists and historians,[5]
point out that the real history of globalisation includes such episodes
as: the river of silver and gold flowing between Spanish America and
Europe from the sixteenth century to the late eighteenth century; the
capture of Porto Bello in Panama by the British admiral Sir Edward
Vernon in 1739; Vernon's siege of Cartagena de Indias in 1741 as part
of the so-called War of Jenkins' Ear; the Opium Wars of 1781 and
1856 in East Asia, the Mexican-American and the Spanish-American
wars that ended with formal or *de facto* dominion of the United States
over California, Texas, New Mexico, Cuba and Puerto Rico together
with Guam and the Philippines via the Treaty of Paris of 1898; the
Anglo-German blockade of Venezuela in 1902 with the purpose of
claiming overdue debts from the South American country; and the
US-assisted separation of Panama from Colombia in 1903 that resulted
in US control of the Panama Canal until 2000. They see this recol-
lection as both a cautionary tale in relation to the War on Drugs, the
debt crisis, neoliberal globalism and the merging of development and
security that has been taking place in Latin America and elsewhere
during the last three decades, and also as a springboard for creativity
and experimentation in history.[6]

The truth is that the free movement of money, goods and people
that developed first during the 'silver and gold river' years of Spanish
and Portuguese dominion over the Americas, starting in the 1550s and
continuing until the 1850s, and thereafter during the second episode
of globalisation and industrialisation between 1870 and 1913, this time
dominated by British sea power, was made possible for the most part

by military might rather than 'free' market forces. The dirty secret of globalisation is that direct or indirect colonial relations, underpinned by force, played a key role in bringing into existence a world circuit of global trade in the late sixteenth century, and then in promoting 'free trade' across the globe in the late nineteenth and early twentieth centuries through empire, neocolonialism and unequal treaties or financial commitments. To begin with, there is little doubt that it was not until Spanish and Portuguese American exports of silver and gold began to generate large transatlantic and transpacific trade flows, that the full circle of global exchange of goods and resources was joined, making world trade a reality.[7]

There is also no doubt that the many misdeeds of empire and indirect colonialism, from plunder and the enslavement of entire populations across continents, to gunboat diplomacy and debt conditionality, cannot be justified by the argument that empire was a good thing overall because it was the cheapest way to ensure free trade, which benefits everyone. This argument, which simplifies David Ricardo's mainstream assumptions about trade and economics, and turns them into an iron-law or a consequentialist account of history, has been espoused in recent years by British historian Niall Ferguson, among others. At least Ferguson has the honesty to mention the Opium Wars, unlike most of the authors in the already long and convoluted literature on the history and significance of globalisation. However, the argument flies in the face of evidence indicating, first, that not everyone benefited, and, second, that to justify the costs from the perspective of the totality – the consequential overall and ultimate good – is both suspect and immoral.

It is suspect because such a justification depends upon the questionable assumption that it is incumbent upon thought or historical observation to uncover a reason that would prove capable of accounting for everything, including its own standpoint as observer of the totality of history up until today. This judgement calls for a reason not conditioned by any other. Only then, once the unconditioned reason of everything has been provided, could the observer survey the whole of history and conclude that the costs were necessary because they brought about something that was necessary as an overall good in history.[8] It is immoral because it justifies evil, which is a practical choice, as a necessary or inevitable sacrifice.

Checking the Facts

Did the Opium Wars in particular, for instance, or colonial relations in general benefit everyone? Evidence suggests that countries under direct colonial rule or indirect, neocolonial and unequal debts and treaties did poorly. Between 1870 and 1913, the period of the second globalisation under British predominance, per capita income in Asia grew on average at 0.4 per cent per year, while that in Africa grew at 0.6 per cent per year. In contrast, the figure for western Europe in that period is 1.3 per cent and 1.8 per cent per year for the United States. Interestingly, during the same period, the annual per capita income growth rate in Latin America rose to 1.8 per cent, in comparison to -0.03 per cent per year between 1820 and 1870. The reason? Independence was consolidated throughout Latin America only after that period, and most countries were still subjected to unequal treaties and trade relations. Once Latin America recovered tariff autonomy, things changed. Between 1870 and 1913 average tariffs varied between 17 per cent in Mexico and 47 per cent in Colombia; and yet the region grew at the same level as the United States of America.[9]

While they were busy securing free trade through colonial relations and unequal treaties, Britain and other European powers, later on America as well, kept protectionist measures for themselves. Britain only embraced free trade when its industry, the wool industry in particular, was ready – around the mid-nineteenth century. Between the 1860s and 1870s Britain featured zero tariffs and other European countries followed a similar route. Protective measures were raised again in Europe from the 1880s onwards, in part to protect local production from cheaper and technologically more advanced meat and other Latin American food industries, and also to promote emerging European steel, chemicals and other heavy industries. Competitor and successful protectionist countries like the United States, which chose to defy the advice of Adam Smith and instead follow the blueprint outlined by the first US Secretary of the Treasury, Alexander Hamilton, led Britain to rethink its path in the global economy. By the 1920s and 1930s, the United Kingdom was once more attempting to impose unequal treaties on Latin American countries, and succeeding in the case of Argentina – its main commercial partner for meat and wheat – while erecting its own barriers.

The argument of Latin America's nations breaking a new path, and that of maverick economists and historians, is that the official history of globalisation is misleading and fundamentally wrong. It distorts our understanding of how we got to where we are and where we may be heading for. After having witnessed South American countries fare better than most during the Great Recession, make their mark in global debates about climate change, or even 'take off' and assume their role as world leaders, as in the case of Brazil, the rest of the world seems ready to listen. Indeed, Latin America no longer specialises in losing.

Moving On

For Europeans and Americans, Latin America is still little more than their underdeveloped sibling, its inhabitants pitching up on its shores or struggling across the Rio Grande into the United States. It is a place of exuberant music, mesmerising football, extravagant beauty, fantastic literature, drug trafficking, caudillos, dictatorship and guerrilla warfare – in short, exotic, dangerous and exciting. However, as this book will show, by being unafraid to turn its back on some commonly held economic views that have now lost their currency, and energised by the creativity of its younger population and the collective discipline and memory of its Indian and Afro-Latin American grassroots, Latin America is making its presence felt from Brasilia to London and from Buenos Aires to New York.

In a recent conference at the Centre for International Development in London, *The Economist* editor for the Americas, Michael Reid, explained how things were changing in the region. 'Latin America has moved on,' he said. Reid was referring to the fact that the continent has left behind the years of dictatorship and widespread US intervention. Although for Americans who take pride in their nation's democratic tradition, the idea put forth by historians like Niall Ferguson that the United States may have created an 'empire' can appear repellent, most

Latin Americans would not find it surprising. Not so long ago, by backing compliant elites and militaries, the United States was able to secure natural resources and other interests in the region. In the nineteenth century it expanded its territory at the expense of Mexico, American filibusters took over parts of Central America, and the US gained *de facto* or formal control over Puerto Rico, Cuba and Panama. After World War II, America allied itself with the armed forces in South America in an effort to bolster its position in the Cold War and contain any threats of revolutionary contamination.

But recently, Latin America seems to have moved away from its stereotype as a collection of 'banana republics' and turned a critical page in its political and economic history. While US influence remains strong in much of the region, for instance in Colombia and in parts of Central America, many nations in South America and the Caribbean have taken a more independent stance, and are now playing prominent roles on the global stage. Venezuelan president Hugo Chávez's initiative to end his country's habit of pumping more oil than was allowed under OPEC quotas helped prompt a steady increase in world prices. Ecuador's Rafael Correa proposed in 2007, during the meeting of the UN General Assembly, a financial scheme that would allow oil-producing developing nations to leave their energy resources in the ground, thereby helping decisively to tackle the global problem of climate change. And as the November 2009 edition of *The Economist* reported, Brazil turned upside down an infamous trend of big loans, debts and defaults in Latin America with international financial institutions by announcing that it would now lend money to the International Monetary Fund. According to most forecasts, sometime after 2014 Brazil will become the world's fifth-largest economy, overtaking Britain and France.

What If Latin America Ruled the World?

In many ways, Brazil already outclasses both 'developed' countries and the other emerging economies of the so-called BRIC bloc. Unlike China, it is a democracy whose political and economic development model is firmly based on the respect and promotion of social and political human rights. Unlike India, it has no insurgents, no intractable ethnic or religious conflicts, and has renounced the use of atomic weapons. Unlike Russia, it has diversified its industry protection to export-oriented process industries, overcoming the possibility of sole dependence on such exports as oil and arms, and treats its neighbours and minorities, as well as foreign investors, with respect. Unlike America, Brazil does not fight wars elsewhere in the world and its 'melting pot' is, if anything, even more successful than America's. And crucially, as a society, Brazil has chosen to set a historical course to reduce the searing inequalities that have long disfigured it, and which still account for a stubbornly high crime rate, a violent police force and environmental devastation, particularly in the Amazon where the Yanomami live, thereby setting an example that is being followed throughout Latin America and elsewhere.

What counts, apart from the technical aspects and specifics of Brazilian policy, is the philosophy that is at its root. For it raises the most important issue of our time: the question of the right to social ownership of a common good, a right that by all evidence is imposing itself on the right to private ownership, or access to a common good in the form of private debt.[10] With the onset of the Great Recession after the world crisis of 2008, and in view of the transformations brought about by new technologies that are altering our sense of relations in space and time, the rationale that spawned private property relations between the seventeenth and the nineteenth centuries is beginning to fray. The result of these events is that access to common goods in the form of private debt is going to give way, increasingly during the twenty-first century, to legitimate claims to social rent and relationships in vast global networks.

Latin American countries like Brazil, Venezuela, Chile or Bolivia – in spite of their differences – are all pioneering this philosophy. And they are not alone. Among the components of the Financial Stability Plan (FSP) that is being set up in the United States by the Obama administration in order to revive America's ailing economy, the renewal of the drive to invest in health and education is being accompanied by innovative financial proposals to provide mortgage refinance funds for American families – the majority of which are Latino and African American – in order to restore value to the toxic assets that are now poisoning the world economy. The Homeowner Affordability and

Stability Plan contemplated in the FSP as part of Obama's new 'New Deal', constitutes an historical precedent on the basis of which innovative proposals such as the one referred to above could be developed in America. They share the philosophy that is being put into practice by many governments in Latin America, not as a matter of ideology, but, rather, as a matter of what is reasonable and conducive to the goal of overcoming global problems through local interventions.

For instance, Venezuela's controversial Social Mission policies, which Chávez's critics on the right and the left often describe, with more than a whiff of condescension, as proof of 'populism', could be compared to the older US vision of wealth redistribution represented by the New Deal whose memory is being recovered now in America, combined with a model of social change firmly based upon grassroots and community organisation.[11] That model is hardly unique to Venezuela, for it is similar to the grassroots mobilisation that secured Obama's electoral victory in the United States – in which Latinos and African Americans, the same constituency which must be the target of the reforms that are required to revive America's economy, featured prominently – which has also been evolving throughout the rest of Latin America for the last two decades. In so far as Latin America is pioneering political and economic efforts to turn that philosophy into a practical tool for policy and reform, and demonstrating its success in helping overcome the present crisis and create future environments for all, it shows the way in which the Global South can the take the Global North, for instance the United States and its coming Latino majority, into the next century.

A New Spirit

Michael Reid was also acknowledging a spirit of renewed confidence and maturity among Latin Americans, which sharply contrasts with the spirit of dependency that characterised relations between Latin America, the United States and Europe in the not so distant past. Having replaced British influence in the region since World War II, the United States enjoyed an unparalleled amount of leverage in South America. While US influence remains strong, many governments in Latin America are now aligned with social movements, chief among them indigenous movements and Afro-Latin American organisations.[12] Together, they defend common access to land and resources while at the same time protecting the environment for the whole of mankind, and furthering the view of a global consciousness based upon empathic attachments in global networks, in an attempt to replace the division of labour among nations with forms of mutuality, association and relationships among men and with Nature that are more appropriate to the challenges now facing mankind.

Traditionally, the majority of Latin American countries have been perceived as politically weak and volatile. They were endlessly represented by European observers, to left and right, as the last hope for a genuine people's revolt against capitalism or the site of the last battle in the war against godless communism. Between the 1950s and the 1970s, the US allied itself with the armed forces in Latin America in an effort to contain the advance of left-wing governments and insurgency in the region. It was in fact in Latin America, more than in the jungles of South East Asia, that US military, bureaucratic and intelligence personnel acquired crucial 'experience' in counter-insurgent warfare and economic development to wage the battle for hearts and minds in other parts of the world.

Three decades on, things have changed. Diminished control over the military is perhaps the most visible evidence of the decline of US influence in the region, with few and important exceptions such as Colombia. But this is by no means the only sign that a dramatic political and economic change is under way. Today, South America is a potent symbol to many in Europe, America and the so-called Third World because it has managed to challenge the prevalent form of globalisation. While it would be a gross misstatement to claim that South American countries are on their way to overturning capitalism, what must be acknowledged is the ability of governments and popular movements in the region to resist its most extreme consequences and advance a new paradigm against the predominant world view.

Since the early 1990s, schools of economic thought in Latin America had started moving away from the sort of policies which stress maximum and efficient exploitation of the region's resources, including labour and raw materials, and from the policies favoured by the IMF and the World Bank, often grouped together as 'the Washington consensus', which obliged countries to remove most regulatory frameworks on the flow of capital and credit in the global financial system. By 2003 Latin America's apparent shift away from globalism had become a political reality. That was the year when the indigenous peoples of Bolivia rose to power under the banner of a communal political organisation led by the former union member and community organiser Evo Morales, himself a native.

A new consensus has started to replace the old one, a consensus that is spreading to the United States on the back of a rising Latino population. Latinos are already the largest growing population and the largest minority group in America. They are a majority in the second biggest state of the Union, Texas. However, Latinos are poorly served when it comes to access to healthcare and education in Texas. 'This remains the most pressing issue,' says Trey Martinez Fischer, who chairs the Mexican-American Legislative Caucus, an influential group that follows the development of initiatives affecting Latinos in the Texas House of Representatives. Rafael Anchia, another House member, recently tipped by *Texas Monthly* to be the first Latino governor of Texas in the year 2018, says that the state has systematically underfunded public education and has made worse the flaws in the American healthcare system at the federal level.[13]

In this respect, and in its demographics, Texas is representative of what will happen in the rest of America. 'Texas today is what all of America will look like tomorrow,' reported *The Economist* in July 2009. Education, healthcare and economic revival, including, for instance, the provision of mortgage refinance funds for American families, as well as the intervention of the US military in missions abroad, are a racial issue as much as a class or national-interest issue, and the faces you will be watching will be, for the most part, Latino. If America does not act now, in order to reverse the possibility of a majority population with a limited skill set and no access to health and housing, it will be heading for disaster. The future of America is thus already tied up with the future of its Latino population. This has nothing to do with migration trends since, as is the case in Texas, even if you close the border tomorrow as an increasingly militant sector of America's right wing wants, Latinos would still overtake Anglos by 2034, or even as early as 2015.

This is also the case for the entire Union. According to most estimates, by 2040 the United States will have a majority Latino population. This transformation will forever change the political, economic and cultural face of America. It will also have profound consequences for the rest of the world. For instance, the steady rise of the Latino population of the US, ready to claim their right to access to common goods like health and education as a social rent, coupled with a continuous increase in their tendency to vote, means good news for the Democratic Party and helps explain the ongoing radicalisation of some sectors within the Republican Party. If the GOP continues to go the way of talk-radio hosts like California's Bill Handel (who is, by the way, a Brazilian immigrant), Rush Limbaugh or the Tea Party, it can expect a long period in the political wilderness.

In contrast, the Democratic administration of Barack Obama has overseen the appointment of Sonia Sotomayor, a Latino woman with undeniable skills and a family story to match, as the first Hispanic in the history of America to become a Justice of the Supreme Court. Obama has also committed himself to immigration reform, an issue on which the first African American President of the United States can expect to find some surprising supporters among Texas' business elite, which has historically tended to be closer to the Republicans and to George W. Bush. In April 2009, Jeff Moseley, CEO of the Greater Houston Partnership, told the US Senate that the notion that immigrants were a drain on America's resources was nonsense, that they were more likely to be net fiscal contributors, that they mostly complement rather than compete with domestic workers, and that cracking down on 'illegals' has had a perverse effect in Texas, distorting patterns of circular migration and encouraging the use of people smugglers, who tend also to be involved in drug trafficking. All the while, New Mexico's governor, Bill Richardson, the son of a Latino woman, is seen by many as one of the best reserves of the Democratic Party for a future presidential nomination. One should also watch out for people like Martinez Fischer or Rafael Anchia himself, Illinois' Gery Chico, California's US Congressman Xavier Becerra or Linda Chavez-Thompson. In any case, the United States is set to become the next Latin American country. And the rest of the world, Britain and the rest of Europe in particular, will have to accommodate that fact.

Latinos on the rise in the US and Amerindians in power in places like Bolivia are the elements of one of the most interesting stories that will unfold over the course of the twenty-first century. But the story that will be unfolding in our future will also evoke memories of times past. And it can only be understood in that context. It is fitting that Bolivia is the place that has emerged as a sign of the new times. After all, it was there that the history of globalisation started in earnest. The origins of our world lie in the sixteenth century. Our global world emerged on the back of the Spanish American silver peso. And our global consciousness owes much to those who, in order to defend themselves and their lands in the brave new world brought about by the universal hunger for silver and gold, paid the ultimate price.

The history of their dream of solidarity and connectedness may be more relevant now than ever before. For it is also our history, the history of the idea of equality. Scholars now know that the international diffusion of the Spanish American silver peso between the sixteenth and eighteenth centuries transformed it into the first truly global metallic currency. It was thanks to this transformation that a new international circuit of unequal exchanges and relations took form. It changed everything. It changed the domestic markets and societies of Europe, the Americas, Asia and Africa forever, and with them also the lives of millions of people. Those who, among them, faced expropriation and extinction, rekindled the dream of solidarity and connectedness of their forebears, and on that basis recognised what was wrong with the new world. They also understood it was not enough to have an idea of equality. They had to act on it. The point was to change the world. It remains one of the most remarkable stories waiting to be told.

The Journey Ahead

Between 2008 and 2010, I travelled between London, where I live and teach at Birkbeck College, one of the component parts of the University of London, and the Americas and Africa in order to put together the remarkable story which is about to unfold before the reader. I went to Cape Town, to Rio de Janeiro, to Lima and La Paz, to Buenos Aires and Bahía Blanca, to Mexico City, to Miami, San Francisco and New York. I travelled to an almost inaccessible Indian village near Belalcázar in the Colombian Cauca, where Victoriano Pennakwe, a young leader of the remarkable Nasa people, taught me about their community-based model of furthering political and social transformation. I saw similar models being developed and deployed in Ecuador and Bolivia, as well as in the state of Texas and in Minas Gerais.

I talked to the minister of social development for Brazil, Patrus Ananias, who explained to me the philosophy behind the social and economic programmes that have turned the 'country of the future' into Latin America's big success story. I marched in 2006 with the Latino community of the United States, and learned from them about the Latino future of the country. I studied a wealth of material, archival documents, books written by historians, sociologists, economists, anthropologists, guerrilla fighters, poets, storytellers, chroniclers and playwrights, biologists, and even cyberneticians and cognitive scientists. They were all part of the story, and helped me compose it. I also listened. I listened to many tales, long memories and stories of struggle, suffering and redemption told by common peoples from at least four continents. It has been a remarkable journey, and I hope that at the end of the book you, the reader, will agree with me.

The book is divided into three parts, which follow a more or less linear chronology. Part One comprises chapters 1 to 3, and tells the story of how the dream of the Amerindians was interrupted by and clashed with the conquerors' dream of empire. This is also the first episode in the history of globalisation, and of the development of the ideas of liberty and equality. Part Two traces the actions that between 1815 and 1970 brought about a brave new world of independent nations and republics, struggling to make slavery and dependency a thing of the past, succeeding and failing. It comprises chapters 4 to 6, and describes the second and crucial episode in the history of globalisation, its achievements and contradictions. Part Three is both a history of the present and a history of the future, charting the onset and consequences of revolutionary transformation in Latin America between the end of World War II and the 1970s, the sobering reality of crisis, and the hopeful future that has arrived in the Americas at the end of the first decade of the twenty-first century. It asks what that may mean to the rest of the world, as we embark upon the journey that will take us into the third episode of the history of globalisation, and into the next century. This is the story of how Latin America is making world history, and looks set to lead the world into the twenty-second century.

PART ONE

The Dream of the Indians

Nature

The western Brazilian state of Acre holds a secret that may change every-thing we know about the history of humanity. In 2008, after reading about them,[1] I flew over Acre in order to observe the remains of dozens of geometrical earthworks and canals reported by Brazilian researchers in 2002 when a considerable part of the thick Amazon forest was cleared for cattle ranches and logging. Their findings were similar to those described by oil company geologists and researchers in the 1960s. They observed exactly what I saw when looking at the earth from above almost four decades later: large matchstick-like, anthropomorphic figures; sets of circular mounds; collections of straight-line ridges; and, most impressive of all, zigzagging vertical and horizontal groupings of ditches and canals stretching over vast areas of land.

The first thing that strikes you is that you know you cannot have these sorts of straight lines and circles in Nature. They are abstract, and clearly man-made. The second is that these abstractions are expressions of human sensibility far deeper than the utilitarian and instant pleasure-seeking impulses that have been celebrated as the very core of human nature since the dawn of modernity, especially in the seventeenth and nineteenth centuries. I knew I had seen these things before. When I was a child my parents took me to visit the Gold Museum of Cartagena de Indias, in Colombia. The museum is dedicated to the gold art of the Sinú nation, native descendants of the Arawak-speaking family that inhabited most of the Caribbean and extended all the way to southern Brazil and the Andean-Amazon region long ago. As the gold objects in the museum reveal, their aesthetic was abstract, depicting mostly zigzagging, spiral, serpentine-like geometrical forms and dots exactly like the ones I saw from the air over Acre.

The Sinú were also well known for their amazing hydraulic engineering achievements and huge landscape interventions. In the museum there is a photograph of an enormous shell midden, one of several tightly grouped circular mounds that dot the Caribbean coast of Latin America. They are identical to the forested mounds that researchers have discovered in the eastern Bolivian province of Beni, and the ones I saw and heard about in 2008. They are thick with broken crockery. Examples of 4,000-year-old ceramics have been found in Sinú circular mounds just a short distance from Cartagena, at Puerto Hormiga and Monso. Given the large area they cover, from the Caribbean coast of Colombia to the Andean-Amazon region of Brazil and Bolivia, they seem unlikely to be the mere by-product of waste. Researchers point out that Monte Testaccio, the hill of broken pots south-east of Rome that served as garbage dump for the entire imperial city, is smaller than the Ibibate mound discovered in Beni province, which is but one of hundreds of similar mounds that dot at least half the continent. They argue that the Beni or the Grand Sinú regions surely did not generate more waste than Rome. Therefore, the ceramics in Ibibate and the Grand Sinú indicate that large numbers of people, many of them workers skilled in geometry and large-scale engineering, lived for a long time on these mounds, feasting and drinking exuberantly while dramatically changing their surrounding environment.

The third room in the Gold Museum of Cartagena de Indias, to me the most intriguing of them all, is called 'The Hydraulic Period'. It gives the visitor an idea of the enormous scale of the engineering that went on in the Grand Sinú region. At least half a million hectares of land were under cultivation with the aid of a series of zigzagging water canals and vertical and horizontal ditches. These canals are up to 4 kilometres long and about 10 to 20 metres wide. They were part of a system that also included causeways, dikes, reservoirs, raised agricultural sites, fish-corralling fences and even ball-game fields that the Indians called *batey*, which is featured in a famous contemporary salsa song in which a *negrito*, a descendant of African slaves, expresses his refusal of the individualistic and over-exploitative kind of work common to modern societies. In the song, he compares it unfavourably to the social efforts and deep empathic connection that characterised collective labour and social life in pre-Columbian America, exemplified in the football field, the *batey*, of the Arawak Indians and the hydraulic and fish-trapping constructions of their Sinú descendants. Like the games and dances associated with the *batey*, fish-trapping was not a matter of a few isolated natives with nets, but a society-wide effort in which hundreds or thousands of Arawak people built dense, zigzagging networks of earthen fish weirs among the causeways with the help of carefully woven and very resistant textiles.

These networks of water canals, dikes and reservoirs are among the largest man-made features in the Americas and dramatically transformed the landscape. The lowlands of the nearby San Jorge river, which flows into the Magdalena river and opens the environment to the Caribbean Sea, were ideal for this kind of large-scale engineering related to agriculture and fish-farming. The course of floodwaters could be redirected and stored in the canals and the reservoirs, which helped fertile sediments being deposited in the watery labyrinths instead of being flushed into the sea. When the dry season came, the natives would have access to the fish trapped in the canals and artificial lakes. They would even use their tightly woven textiles to separate salt from the sea waters as they combined with river waters and used them as part of wider systems controlling volume and currents. They would live and work in huts and orchards built on the higher ground above the canals. These still have not silted up and manage the seasonal floods as they have for centuries. As the literature of the museum states, the canals date back to around 5000 BC and were the very basis of a flourishing culture that supported a considerably larger population – much bigger than today's population in the region – for a very long time. Seen from above, the geometry and organisation of the canals, causeways, reservoirs and circular mounds of the Grand Sinú region immediately strike the observer as identical to the straight lines and circles used in Sinú gold art and jewellery, and to the abstract geometry of other similar constructions on a comparable scale along the Caribbean coast and in western Brazil and Bolivia.

These lines and circles and other abstract geometrical forms are deeply meaningful. When seen from the air they seem to leap out of the landscape towards you. They are things of spectacular beauty. When looking at them, in the museum or from an aeroplane, it is impossible not to feel closer to the peoples who created them thousands of years ago. What you feel is not mere sympathy, the idea that you can imagine yourself in the place of another and 'feel her pain', but an affective connection that is also real and extraordinarily meaningful. For these lines, zigzags, spirals and dots are symbolic. They were a code. The mainstream view of human history is that around 40,000 years ago our ancestors suddenly began to think abstractly and underwent a creative transformative explosion, which led to the stunning cave paintings that can be seen today in the Chauvet caves in southern France. On the other hand, writing, as a system of pictographic codes, dates back to just 5,000 years ago. Nobody paid much attention to the conspicuous marks that tend to appear on the side of cave paintings such as those in Chauvet. However, these signs, some of them 15,000 to 25,000 years old, turn out to be identical to the lines, zigzags and dots that the Sinú included in their gold art and used as the basis of an engineering science whose large-scale practical applications are visible from above to this day throughout the Americas and elsewhere. More importantly, these forms and symbols communicate and provoke feelings that are more congruent with another's situation than with his own situation, regardless of the time and space separating them.

In a way, these symbols both create and are the expression of a common space that is deeply affective, but also cognitive and real. The zigzags, spirals, lines and dots visible in the gold objects found in the museum of Cartagena de Indias express the collective effort required to build large-scale engineering projects such as those visible from above in the area of the Grand Sinú around Cartagena, but also create the common space that made possible both these collective efforts and the science behind them. Not only do they represent the social bond; they *are* the social bond. This is why, when you look at these objects and constructions in the museum or from the aeroplane above, you feel you share a common space with the allegedly extinct cultures that made them. You feel that you are there with them, rather than instead of them. You, the observer, project your own sensibilities on to these objects of contemplation, appreciate and enjoy their beauty, and also enter into a relation with the being of others through these objects, and come to know how they feel and think. The existence of these common objects, spaces and actual sites and constructions are the condition for this vicarious form of communication, while at the same time embodying it. Thus, these objects and constructions are neither neutral nor void of significance, but deeply meaningful and powerful themselves.

Unlike sympathy, which is more passive, these objects, symbols and constructions evoke and require from the observer active engagement: on the one hand, they evoke and require his willingness to become part of another's reality. On the other, they frame and give shape to that common reality. Thus, the phenomenon in question – aesthetic, cognitive and social – involves the very fabric of reality and may be present at its very origin and nature. One of the most intriguing facts to emerge from the work of researchers dealing with these symbols and massive humanised and meaningful landscapes, in Latin America and elsewhere, is that most of them were present in very early sites, from over 10,000 to 30,000 years ago. If the 'creative explosion' that mainstream historians and archaeologists speak of occurred and subsided around 30,000 years ago, then researchers would have expected to find evidence of symbols being invented and discarded at such an early stage, with a long period of time passing before a recognisable system appeared. Instead, it appears that by 30,000 years ago a set of symbols including dots, zigzags and spirals was already well established. This suggests we might have to rethink our ideas about the long journey and the very essence of mankind. The diversity and continuity of use of these symbols suggests that abstraction and the capacity to collaborate and create commons may have emerged in prehistory well before.[2]

Whenever they did emerge, the acceptance of symbolic representation was our turning point. For it made possible the creation of the space where we find ourselves together with others, with their differences, their plights and joys, but making their past struggles and their joy all the more valued and vicariously felt. These commons – of communication, feeling and production – are vital in the journey of human societies, past and present, towards the future. The overwhelming presence of these symbols and common representations in the art, the engineering and the myths of the Arawak-speaking peoples that were the early inhabitants of the Caribbean, the Andes and the Amazon suggests that they did not merely represent supernatural powers but were, rather, the matrix within which natural forces could be conceived and related to. By looking at them we gaze into our very souls.

That common space, symbolic but nevertheless real, may be old enough to be identifiable with what we often term human nature. The question raised by the archaeologists, anthropologists, historians, sociologists, psychologists and art critics looking at these archaic discoveries with fresh eyes concerns our human nature as much as the nature of the societies we now live in. For over half a millennia, since at least the 1500s, peoples of the world have been led to believe that human beings are flawed creatures thrown into a fallen world. Redemption would have to wait for the next one. In the seventeenth and nineteenth centuries, at various turns in the cyclical history of the relations between the west and the rest, philosophers like Thomas Hobbes and John Locke depicted human life and the human soul as 'solitary, poor, nasty, brutish and short', or as a blank slate presented by society to realise our natural predisposition to accumulate, acquire and transform the planet's vast wasteland into privatised productive property.

Their nightmarish vision, which was also a reaction to and against the dreams and powerful meanings that circulated among the natives encountered by conquerors and colonisers in the Americas, the descendants of the Arawaks of Beni and Grand Sinú, has come to be accepted in our time, especially in the most basic assumptions of sciences like economics, as the most accurate representation of our very being and ultimate mission in a fallen world. And yet, in the midst of crisis and despair, precisely when everything around us seems to confirm such nightmarish visions of a fallen world, our most basic instinct tells us that it does not have to be this way. We feel it when looking at the earth from above. On such occasions we ask ourselves: is it possible that we are not inherently envious, materialistic and self-interested, but, rather, as the archaic peoples of Grand Sinú and Beni and their contemporary descendants show, are of a very different nature?

Water

There is a chapter in the early history of the peoples of the Americas that we must remember today. Amerindian pre-Columbian cultures were persuaded of the communality of the earth and of the impossibility of dividing the body of goddess-mother Nature. Because of that they sought to realise the dream of harmony between man and world. To this end, they collaborated with the forces of Nature. Carefully, they studied such forces, gathered all the knowledge they could muster and put it to good use in order to create future environments. Amerindians from Beni in Andean-Amazonian Bolivia to the Grand Sinú on the Caribbean coast altered their landscapes and humanised them. They did not aim to keep them wild or untouched. Pre-Columbian Amerindians periodically burnt undergrowth, cleared and replanted forests, built canals and middens, raised fields, hunted bison and erected large fences to farm and trap fish with the help of carefully woven textiles. They worked on a very large scale, transforming huge swathes of land and water landscape for their own ends. They did not simply adapt to Nature; they created it. Rather than setting their sights on rebuilding or maintaining a glorified past, they concentrated on shaping a world in which to live in the future.

This view of Amerindians, the result of evidence gathered in recent years by archaeologists, geographers, historians and anthropologists who have come to accept and understand that Native Americans ran the continent as they saw fit, contrasts with the mainstream view according to which the Amazon, for instance, is a timeless wilderness inhabited by a few passive recipients of whatever windfalls or catastrophes chance and Nature put in their way. The latter is the dream of the conqueror and the coloniser. It can take two forms. It may imagine the Indians as natural creatures living in a state of innocence for many millennia, and their minds as blank slates waiting for Christian instruction and the gifts of modern technology, law and liberty. This view, which became popular in Europe and modern America through the writings of John Locke and Henry David Thoreau, dates back to one of the first Spanish conquistadors to settle in the Americas, a man named Bartolomé de Las Casas. Having witnessed the destruction caused by European greed and cruelty, Las Casas repented of his actions, became a priest and initiated a lifelong and largely successful campaign to free the Indians from slavery.

In doing so, he provided the impulse that would fire the hearts of the future liberators of the continent during the wars of independence, people like Francisco de Miranda, Simón Bolívar, Father Hidalgo or Emiliano Zapata, whose names are nowadays synonymous with the struggle for liberation and political and economic sovereignty throughout the Americas and elsewhere. But in spite of the heroic role that Indians often play in these scripts of history, in which they are inevitably portrayed as the victims, the implicit depiction of Indians as peoples who never changed the landscape from its original wild state in fact justifies the actions of conquistadors and colonisers, and provides the basis for the second image of Amerindians they created. In this second image the Indian, living in an unhistoried state, is instinctively drawn towards warfare, superstitious sacrifice and, as twice Pulitzer Prize-winner Samuel Eliot Morison put it while channelling his inner Thomas Hobbes, 'pagans expecting short and brutish lives, void of any hope for the future'.[3]

The Noble Savage and the Cannibal are in fact two sides of the same stereotype, embraced by those who hated Indians because they stood in the way of history and those who admired them because they represented a state of Eden-like innocence now prohibited to us moderns. This is how people as different as believers in the inherent supremacy of western culture and well-intentioned environmentalists often nowadays portray the balance between man and the world, body and spirit, the individual and the community that Amerindians sought to achieve and extended to all the activities of the community having an impact upon the landscapes they inhabited. However, this image of the relationship between pre-Columbian man and Nature is wrong. On the one hand, it projects upon all cultures a view of Nature as normative and of history as having a necessary purpose or a pre-determined course that is quite singular and belongs, in fact, to more recent times. On the other hand, it renders pre-Columbian man and other subordinated peoples devoid of what social scientists call agency, the capacity to be the actor in one's own history, and posits them instead as sempiternal victims, peoples at risk or vulnerable peoples in a perpetual state of dependence.

Amerindians did seek to obtain a balance between man and world, but the meaning of such equilibrium was exactly the opposite of what we have taken it to be. Its aim was not the glorification of the past, but, rather, the modification of the world for the purposes of creating a future. It did not understand Nature as normative, as a law unto itself, but instead viewed it as a common space for the interaction of natural and essentially social forces, framed by changing laws and contingency. In that respect, Nature was construed as resisting private appropriation, which only results in short-term gains and tends to sacrifice the long-term and the future. Whether it be hunting, agriculture, war, or, as in the case of the earlier water-based Amerindian civilisations that emerged in the Amazon basin, in the Caribbean and, on the Pacific Coast near the Andean cordillera, the development of large-scale projects of irrigation and canalisation, all activities were carried out with a view to preserving the equilibrium that for Amerindians was an expression of the very rhythm of cosmic creation.

This equilibrium, set by the contingency and fragility of everything that exists and is created, can be understood as the symbolic basis for richer human communication. The symbols used by Amerindians – dots, zigzags, scales, spirals – record and manifest observations about the contingency and fragility that characterises everything that exists in creation: floods and droughts, rainy seasons and dry seasons, disappearing and reappearing stars in the sky, growth and decay, death and rebirth, the rise and fall of rulers and cities. These symbols were abstractions of such natural forces and rhythms, but also contained an overall message concerning the absolute contingency that affects everything that is. If there is nothing that exists as a matter of necessity, then the only way to confront contingency and the future is to responsibly create and recreate future environments for the use of all, rather than exhausting them now. In contrast, short-term accumulation, expropriation and exhaustion of Nature's resources can only be conceived and justified if one assumes that nothing too new or too catastrophic will occur in the future, and, hence, that the way things are today will continue to be the way of things in the future.

Focusing on short-term accumulation leads to the consideration that the satisfaction of my needs today comes first, and can come first, because others in another country or in the future would do the same. Since we know nothing about the future, other than the assumption that it will be more or less the same, we might as well indulge ourselves today. A corollary of this position is that I share little or nothing with others elsewhere, in the past or in the future. There is no common space shared between us, but, rather, a series of parallel private universes – a pluriverse of self-enclosed universes – competing to maximise their inherent potential. Perhaps one could survey this pluriverse of private universes and choose among them the one that maximises a certain function, such as pleasure, happiness, utility or profit. That would give one a god-like view and the god-like power that comes with that view. That power is predicated upon the condition that those below me cannot communicate with one another, that they can only see their own advantage and not that of the whole of society. The god-like position is only a supposition, a necessary lie, for it represents nothing else but the fact that the study of one's own advantage leads naturally to that of society.[4] Therefore, not only is there no communication; there is also no unevenness in the world, no hierarchy and no unequal relation of power. There is only the pursuit of one's own advantage.

The symbolic world of Amerindians contained a very different message. It started with the observation of the contingency that frames the rhythms of creation. Then, it derived from that observation a common sense of responsibility, which the symbolic world of Amerindians made possible and communicated. The focus was on the long-term. Thus, the world view of Amerindians was acutely aware of time. Time was conceived as flowing like water, which not only takes an infinite number of shapes but also comes in cycles. Like water, it dries out and returns. The moment of drought would be seen as most dangerous and would be confronted with heightened expectation; for it may well be the case that water or rainfall would not return. It was observed that these cycles – dry season and rainy season, floods and drought – seemed to take less time. The cycles of the stars in the sky, on the other hand, which followed a similar structure of disappearance and return, seemed to take longer. These cycles could be counted and depicted as lines or circles, and observing them together would be like observing circles within circles. Like a spiral. Or like opposite and changing directions, depicted in the form of an open angle.

These abstractions – the spiral, the open angle – would also convey the message that the different counts, and the different natural phenomena they referred to, were interconnected and continuous in time and space. Rather than a pluriverse of incommunicable universes, the appropriate image for all that is created would be that of a line changing abruptly and extending into the infinite. More complex and later images and symbols such as the zigzag and the spiral seem to convey this notion of connectivity, infinity and the long-term. Observing and taking into account the complex rhythms of creation, and the effects that such observations had in altering these rhythms, led Amerindian peoples to the establishment of societies characterised by an intensified flow of material and spiritual exchanges that sharply contrasts with the deprivation and exile that characterises our materialistic and opportunistic culture.

For the Aztecs of Mexico, for instance, cutting down a tree was a serious act that required richer acts of communication to be carried out. Chronicler Pedro Ponce relates that to do that they would go into the mountains or the forest 'and before entering offered a prayer to Quetzalcóatl to ask his permission so that he would not see as disrespectful the fact that they wanted to make wood from his forest, and so he would permit them to make wood from his side'.[5] Far from being superstitious, this attitude revealed a profound sense of the impact that technological practices (construction, settlement and communication) have in altering time and space. The practices that characterised the creation of future environments among Amerindian cultures often required immense collective efforts and propelled those involved into shared times and spaces that had practical and spiritual significance, diametrically opposed to the individualistic activities that we have grown accustomed to, which tend to erect a boundary between 'mine and thine' and wall people off from one another, producing the divisions that we have come to expect and even accept in modern societies.

Today, however, after a few centuries during which the private aspect of the right to ownership was anointed as a primary form of human nature and life, we find ourselves once again in a situation in which our technological practices alter our sense and the reality of time and space in a different direction, closer to the forward-looking and long-term view of nature held by the Amerindian cultures of the past. Nowadays communication technologies quicken our innermost connection with one another, emotional as well as practical, while challenges such as climate change or the financial crisis are obliging us to reconsider the importance of common access to natural resources and collective action in relation to long-term prospects, thereby propelling us into global spaces and a new simultaneous field of cyclical time.

The result of this new situation is that to remember the sense of equilibrium and detachment from the private aspect of ownership that characterised Amerindian pre-Columbian peoples has become vital to us today. We need to remember all the areas in which the Amerindian civilisations were ahead of Europe at the time when these two parts of the globe experienced their shocking encounter: mathematics and abstraction, medicine, urbanism, the use of fibres and the forces of tension, environmental management and the use of temporal technologies such as calendars and computer-like recording systems. But we must especially remember the way in which Amerindians built their communities on the basis of forms of exchange that prioritised giving access to common goods and the creation of deep, meaningful connections within wider networks, in contrast to forms of social organisation that emphasise accumulation and short-term gains in the exploitation of natural and other resources.

The reasons for doing this are not restorative. We cannot re-establish the extremely hierarchical world of the Mexica or the Inca of Peru, or the semi-nomadic and confederate societies of desert America of the north and north-west, or of the coastal regions and the lowlands of the south and south-east – those of the Tarahumara, the Apaches, the Tupi and the Arawak Taíno or the Carib. Rather, it is because of our actual

circumstances, because the rationale that spawned private property relations and extreme individualism is beginning to fray in the wake of new
challenges and technologies – the financial crisis, climate change, the
Internet and other new communication technologies – that we need
to remember and learn from those cultures, which were almost entirely
destroyed by the dream of European conquerors and centralised capitalist commerce. It is a matter of recognition and future-oriented action
rather than nostalgia for the past.

According to the prophets of a conquering globalisation that has
proceeded apace under the auspices of centralised and monopolistic
forms of capitalist exchange, all the continents have been discovered,
all the maps have been drawn, all the ancient languages decoded and
stored in the archives of museums and university departments after their
disappearance, and all the crucial differences have been abolished. If this
is true, if all the continents of our planet have been enclosed and divided
and all of its peoples subordinated, then all we can do is turn our face
towards the past, marvel at our achievements or mourn our losses. But
this would mean that we are condemned to the fixed contemplation of
an unassailable fate, unable to remake whole what has been smashed or
plot a course amidst the uncertainty of the future while being blown
away by the storm that German critic Walter Benjamin called progress.
In such a scenario, history follows a course whose result is more or
less inevitable. In it 'the division of labour among nations is that some
specialise in winning and others in losing'.[6]

We must resist such false prophets. In the midst of the present crisis
we are in fact witnessing the birth of a new economic system that is
as different from monopolistic market capitalism as the latter was from
the systems of exchange that characterised feudal city-states and agrarian or nomadic communities. And it is not just a matter of finding new
managerial or regulatory formats to upgrade the conduct of business
within the same economic system. It is the present market exchange
and financial mechanism that is becoming outmoded. In the present
market system buyers and sellers come together for a short period of
time to exchange goods and services for money, then part. Nothing but
flattened human discourse and relations can emerge out of such chance

encounters. The result is not simply isolation and alienation, but also social weakness and political paralysis given that strong collective mobilisation, needed to overcome crises, requires thicker social relations. Also, the lapsed time between such passive exchanges represents, on the one hand, lost productivity and added cost, and, on the other, the sort of unequal relations that tend to characterise global trade and financial speculation. Eventually, these make markets obsolete.[7]

New information and communication technologies allow for shared virtual spaces and long-term continuous activity. This means that conventional start-and-stop property exchanges, dependent on margins, credit and transaction costs – that is to say, private ownership – can be replaced and are increasingly being replaced by continued network relations over time – that is to say, access. This can be seen today in the examples of music industry providers versus retail stores, or in the transformation of the publishing and car industries from goods producers and retailers into service providers. But this process of transformation also entails the legitimacy of raising once again the question of social ownership and the possibility of claiming certain forms of access to common goods as social rents rather than private debts. This is precisely where the contemporary activism of native and other subordinated peoples around the world, especially in Latin America, is being concentrated. Their focused action is helping transform the way we see the world. In that sense, their age-old dream of water-like flows in equilibrium and harmony between man and the world, and body and spirit, seems more relevant nowadays than the homogenising dreams of conquistadors, colonisers and conqueror globalisers.

French writer J. M. G. Le Clézio, who won the Nobel Prize in Literature in 2008 and lived in Mexico and Panama with the Emberá natives, reminds us that 'for the Indian nations of middle America, water was the most precious of goods, the divine element which sustained life on earth. It was water that engendered the sacred liquid – blood – which men offered to the gods in exchange for the fertilisation of the land.'[8] Put another way, the Indians of the Americas considered water as a common good, central also to their accounts of cosmic and natural destruction and creation, the rhythms of the whole of creation. The Aztecs believed that

'Atonatiuh', which means 'sun of the water', ended the world by a flood and an inundation 'where all men were drowned and all things created perished'.[9] For the Chichimeca, the Toltecs and the Maya, as well as the Aztecs, the very origin of the gods was water, for they were believed to have have come from the sea, like Quetzalcóatl, also known in later retellings of the story as the prophet of the Mexican rainforest. Paradise was *tlalocan*, the realm of the Tlalocs, gods of rain 'of the greenery and of freshness', according to Spanish chronicler Bernardino de Sahagún, which welcomed those whose death was associated with rain or water: being struck by lightning or drowned or affected by drought.

The water principle was portrayed among the Maya by the cross, whose centre represented the heart of the world. These images and conceptions fitted societies gathered around water, which flourished on the basis of diets, technologies and large-scale projects related to the use of water resources, such as hydraulic engineering, textiles and vertical architecture, whose notions of time and social relations were based on analogies with the sea and flowing rivers and conceived of events radically changing the course of history.

A Storm Is Coming

Latin America no longer specialises in losing. Back in 1989, for instance, after a major international campaign supported by public figures such as Prince Charles and rock celebrities such as Sting, the Amerindian Yanomami people who live on the border between Brazil and Venezuela scored a notable victory when the Brazilian government finally recognised their land rights on the eve of the United Nations Earth Summit. The story of their triumph resonated around the world. It helped usher in a renewed sense of power and identity for indigenous and subordinate peoples all over the globe.

It resonated, for instance, with the peaceful opposition that the Ogoni people led against the presence of oil companies like Shell in the Niger Delta, particularly after the execution of writer and human rights activist Ken Saro-Wiwa in 1995. The Ogoni accused Shell of complicity in the assassination. In 2006, the oil giant had been ordered to pay $1.5 billion to the Ijaw people but managed to escape the fines. In 2009, Shell agreed to pay £9.7 million to the families of the Niger Delta to settle out of court the case the indigenous Ogoni had brought to the jurisdiction of that state.

The example of the Yanomami resonated also with the claims made by the native peoples affected by new laws opening their ancestral lands to international mining in the Philippines during the 1990s. After a visit in 2007, Claire Short, former UK international development secretary, said she had never seen 'anything so systematically destructive. The environmental effects are catastrophic, as are the effects on people's livelihoods.' More recently, the UK-based Working Group on Mining in the Philippines, which Ms Short serves as chairperson, reported that 'mining generates or exacerbates corruption, fuels armed conflict, increases militarisation and human rights abuses, including extrajudicial killings'.

A similar situation has been denounced and opposed by indigenous peoples, ethnic minorities and peoples of Asian and African descent in Russia, Canada, China, Cambodia, India, Mongolia, Papua New Guinea, the United States, Europe, and with particular intensity throughout the whole of Latin America. What appeared to be merely isolated incidents of tribal and traditional peoples standing in the way of states and corporations are now becoming major conflicts, as government-backed companies move deeper into the lands of peoples long ignored as unproductive and backward. These, in turn, respond to the enclosure of their lands, to the idea that everything is for sale, and to their depiction as merely disposable peoples with increased awareness and sometimes even force. 'A massive resistance movement is growing,' said Claire Short, 'but the danger is that as it grows, so does the violence.'

In Arizona, the Navajo nation is fighting uranium mining through the US courts. Similar projects are being opposed in Australia, India, Canada, Niger and Botswana. In Colombia, as oil and mining companies move into the western Amazon and the south-eastern Pacific coast, indigenous and Afro-Colombian peoples find themselves trapped in the crossfire between the state, guerrillas and supposedly demobilised paramilitary forces. The operations of the latter have driven a massive land grab in the marginalised regions of the country. However, the prospects of returning such lands to their ancestral occupiers are very poor. The government conditions compensation and land return to the setting up of 'economically viable projects' that comply with its aims concerning the 'inevitable' internationalisation of the economy. And although the affected communities have become better at using the courts, legal frameworks are often limited and there is still collusion at the highest levels in judicial and policy-making centres to ignore land rights when they conflict with the economic interests pursued by governments. In the case of Colombia, in fact, the forced displacement of indigenous peoples and other so-called minorities by paramilitary forces, now acting under other names, continues to play a decisive role in the pursuit of such interests, placing unarmed indigenous and other communities in an untenable position. Similarly, in Guatemala, thousands of indigenous peoples have been forced to move and make way for development projects. Death squads have re-emerged.[10]

A battle is taking place for natural resources everywhere. It involves rich nations as much as poorer ones. As mining and oil firms based in the rich world race for land and dwindling resources, around the globe peoples who have been identified and talked about as belonging to a time different from the people who talk about them, either as vicious barbarians in a state of chronic warfare or as noble savages, find themselves in the middle of a clash that could result in their extinction and that of the environments they have long engineered, managed, and protected.[11] For them, to lose this battle would not only entail the loss of their lands, lives and dignity, but, moreover, a loss for the whole of humankind and the planet we all inhabit.

Clashing World Views

'This is a paradigm war taking place from the Arctic to tropical forests,' says Victor Menotti, of the California-based International Forum on Globalisation. As countries and international banks increase spending on major projects, and governments strive to expand infrastructure into lands long ignored as wild and unproductive but now considered central to the purposes of internationalisation, or to sell whatever they can to counter the effects of economic crises, the conflicts will grow. The clash for land and natural resources is now global.

But it would be a mistake to understand the paradigm war that Menotti speaks of in terms of a clash of civilisations, as readers of

American internationalist Samuel Huntington might have us believe. Certainly, it is not a confrontation between the past and the present, between ancients and moderns, or between identities – one fixed, the other changing. 'It is a battle,' Menotti says, 'between industrial and indigenous world views.'

Does this mean that 'our' world view must confront 'theirs' in mortal combat and come out victorious? When we put it this way, we fail to recognise the significance of the presence and coexistence of these 'others': indigenous, ancestral, subordinate. We are also repeating history. Rather than acknowledging that to recognise all others as our partners in communication is a condition for interaction in the community, hence of participating in the sort of social-cultural practices that characterise all forms of life in common – a common planet, a shared world view, the very basis for perpetual peace – we recreate the conditions that made imperialism and empires possible in the past.

History teaches us that to imagine these others as 'lazy, childlike, and cruel', too narrow-minded to take time out of fighting to grow crops, or living in a permanent state of prelapsarian innocence, is central to the claim that their lands have always 'stood empty of mankind and its works'. Thereafter, it takes but a small step to argue that 'the story of Europeans in the New World', for instance, 'is the story of the creation of a civilisation where none existed'. It seems justified, then, to act in consequence.[12]

The link between the threat of extinction and the enclosure of land and resources plays a key role in the long history of subaltern and indigenous peoples around the globe. It also provides an appropriate starting point to tell the story of the crucial relationship between Britain, the other European powers and the Americas. Latin America in particular has long been the place where Britain, and later on the United States, could project and examine the anxieties prompted by their own transformation into imperial powers. Signifying nothing, Latin America could be made to mean to signify just about everything.

The World's Least Discovered Continent

One prominent result of Latin America's relationship with the cultural and economic imperatives of the English-speaking west has been the loss of the continent's own history and that of its people. In the early nineteenth century, for instance, Britain's model of political, economic and industrial modernisation captured the imagination of earlier proponents of independence in the Americas. Among them were 'disaffected Spanish Americans from all regions of the [Spanish] empire' who visited London on many occasions soliciting financial aid, political recognition or military assistance and searching for generals, politicians and radical thinkers or activists. They took time to visit Jeremy Bentham, the dissenting parish of Newington Green, Robert Owen's model farms and factories and discuss the merits of the abolition of slavery with Thomas Clarkson and William Wilberforce. When they made their way back to the Americas, it was their vision of Britain as a free society of liberal thought and radical debating, of 'law, order and material progress', that exercised a lasting influence over the forging of Latin American republics after independence.[13]

By the 1820s, revolution in the Spanish Americas had become a source of immense interest in Europe, but beyond the press and the coffee houses neither the interest for the continent nor its struggle for independence created between Britain and South America the sort of deeper connection that would exist between Britain and India or other imperial possessions. The relation between Britain and India gave rise to a series of practical considerations of government, economics, mores and religion that forced an extension of British cognitive and cultural boundaries. But in Latin America, while the British had extensive resources and potential trade relations to exploit and profit from, they had no people to govern. Hence, the British had no reason to involve themselves with the locals and their cultures at any deeper level beyond the exercise of influence and commerce. And therefore no need to expand their settled patterns of thought and tradition 'to make room for the challenges posed by contact with Latin America or its people'. While Latin America remained merely a commercial interest in the eyes of the British, 'their established perceptions of it and the prejudices they fed could survive undisturbed'.[14]

The specific nature of British and European relations with Latin America, particularly during and after independence, was determined by the primacy of commercial interests, ownership and the need to secure such interests, but with the exception of Spain, without assuming the 'invidious burden' of direct past or present colonial rule.[15] Furthermore, the consolidation and expansion of the British Empire in the early nineteenth century coincided with the rapid expansion of the revolutionary independence movements of Latin America. As the British were coming to terms with the realities and moral dilemmas arising from extensive dominion across the globe, people in the Americas and the Caribbean were in various ways and with varying degrees of success liberating themselves from, and questioning for the first time in human history, the yoke of empire, while at the same time asserting in the most radical way the rights of free men. The decisive event in this respect was the overthrow of the slaveholding regime in the French colony of Santo Domingo by insurgent slaves and their free allies and the establishment of the black republic of Haiti in 1804, which embodied the spirit of the Indians. Native peoples and commoners had been resisting the yoke of colonial government and ownership since at least the sixteenth century and continued to do so until the eighteenth century, from the Andes of South America to the Yucatán Peninsula in Central America. Their struggles and those of the Haitian slaves contained an explicit affirmation of rights, titles and capacities that were truly universal and extended over to the domain of the common ownership, management of and carnal relationship with Nature. This contributed to a reawakening of the memory of the commons and of liberty before the enclosure of the land and the privatisation of social relations, also among the wider public in Britain and elsewhere.[16]

This return of a repressed memory – expressed, for instance, in the writings of Thomas Spence and Thomas Paine, or Mary Wollstonecraft, Anna Barbauld and Olaudah Equiano – was perceived as a threat to the consolidation of British global dominion and also as a splinter in the developing modern psyche of Britain and Europe. As a result, Latin America and the Caribbean became inextricably intertwined with a range of efforts to understand, justify or transform the invidious burden of empire. Latin America and the Caribbean furnished an ideal space in which the symbolic world of the commons and a deeper relationship with Nature could impose itself on or be vanquished by the new order of ownership and empire. In this sense, Latin America and the Caribbean are the splinters in the mind of modern Europe and therefore the narrative of modern Europe – its history, consciousness and fiction – can also be understood, among other things, as an effort to weld these seemingly opposite world views together or to disguise their contradiction.

As a consequence of this, on the one hand the narrow understanding of British and European relations with Latin America, 'and the distorted vision of it that this has fed', explains why until 'as recently as 1989 South America remains the world's least discovered continent'.[17] On the other hand, it is in Latin America and the Caribbean where the buried reality of the costs and consequences of the privatisation of social relations led by Europe's imperial affirmation across the globe 'could be exhumed and held up for examination'.[18] The point that has been made before by European and North American observers, though more often by Latin Americans writers themselves, such as Octavio Paz, Frantz Fanon, Carlos Fuentes or Gabriel García Márquez, 'labouring under the condescension conferred by the English-speaking west's self-interested responses to the continent'.[19] Thus, a history and a story of Latin America and Latin Americans coexist with the imaginations of modern English-speaking peoples on their way to becoming global powers. In aiming to tell that story I do not intend to describe what Latin America really is; for this is a story of communication and debate about what is common. It is a crucial chapter in the history of the formation of the common world view of mankind.

In this conversation, when I speak of what is common, I refer not just to what is valued and employed only to the extent that it helps celebrate or redeem the imperilled homeland, or of the imaginings and portrayals that result in the representation of Latin America – or any other region of the planet – as a lost world that remains so. First and foremost I refer to such commons as air, water, natural resources and land, but also to knowledges and cosmologies, which are treated by globalism and neoliberal economics as commodities to be enclosed and traded. This is the point being made by native peoples and other advocates of a richer social texture in today's world. In order to understand the position of indigenous and other opposition movements in Latin America and elsewhere, and their rise to centre stage in global affairs, it is crucial to acknowledge that their world view represents a paradigm founded in largely traditional land and ecological systems that firmly oppose complete commodification and marketisation. This paradigm resonates strongly with the memories and traditions of English-speaking western peoples, anxious about the path taken by their own communities and wary of its consequences for the future of the planet. The next section will be dedicated to exploring the tension between our responsibility to create future environments and the short-term imperatives of markets and exchanges, as a crucial part of the common history of peoples on both sides of the ocean.

A Short History of Common Life

The link between extinction in the long term and land enclosure, made by the indigenous peoples of the Americas, strongly resonates with the dissenting tradition represented in British history by the likes of John Lilburne and the Levellers, or Winstanley and the Diggers. In the late 1640s they observed how kingly power 'hedges the weak out of the Earth, and either starves them, or else forces them through poverty to take from others, and then hangs them for so doing'. In 1649, the author of the abolitionist tract known as *Tyranipocrit Discovered* denounced the slavery being developed in America, of both poor people and Indians, following a similar line of reasoning: 'The idle rich commanded others to labour, the thieving rich commanded others not to steal, and together they made thieves by Act of Parliament and hanged them. Yet God was no respecter of persons.' On 29 March 1649, one day after the Leveller leadership was crushed by the arrest of John Lilburne and others, Oliver Cromwell, soon to become England's Lord Protector, took charge of the expedition to conquer Ireland. The seizure of land and the deployment of Irish dispossessed labour across the Atlantic following the defeat of antinomians at home and the conquest of Ireland, opened the way to imperialist contest and war against the Dutch and the Spanish, to the seizure of Spanish Jamaica and to the establishment of a broader system of slavery in the Atlantic, from West Africa to the West Indies and the rest of the Americas.

Just as Cromwell's army debated in the Putney Debates whether or not the law of God legitimated unbridled private ownership and the reduction of considerable parts of the population to the status of brutes of labour, so the Spanish debated in Valladolid in 1550 whether or not the natives had a soul and the capacity to govern themselves, and thus what was the legitimacy of appropriating their lands. Similarly, Cromwell's Army Council explored whether 'to eradicate the natives' or merely 'to divest them of their states', in the wake of the conquest of Ireland. After the 1652 Act of Settlement had decided the issue, and 'increased agricultural labour replaced subsistence strips and environmental egalitarianism', Sir William Petty's Down Survey of the 1650s merely repeated in Ireland the mapping and surveying techniques used by the Spanish colonial administrators of the Council of the Indies in the case of the Americas. Crucially, in both cases these cartographic and surveying techniques served not only to amass a considerable amount of information for purely functional purposes, but also to expropriate knowledge and to suppress or negate what was considered irrelevant or deemed dangerous. Here we are confronted with another example of loss and denied history.

In the case of the Americas, a fundamental cognitive pattern that connects cosmos, earth and human territoriality got lost in the maps and surveys erected by colonial administrators. Contrary to colonial maps, territorial conceptions among the natives of the Americas encompassed both natural resources as well as the memory of the communities' history. These depictions were less preoccupied with providing a precise delimitation of geographic boundaries, but, rather, as is the case with similar traditions found among the Navajos, the Incas, and ancient Chinese, Jewish and Christian cosmologies, with a specific model for territorial ordering and memory, for the sharing of time and of everything that takes place within time and the language that contains it.

A mere two decades before the defeat of the Levellers' and the Diggers' views on freedom and land enclosure in the context of the English Revolution, Massasoit, a leader of the Wampanoag, asked the Plymouth pilgrims and colonists: 'It cannot be the earth, for the land is our mother, nourishing all her children, beasts, birds, fish, and all men.

The woods, the streams, everything on it belongs to everybody and is for the use of all. How can one man say it belongs only to him?' That fundamental connection between memory, language, territorial order-ing and the use of natural resources, which involves issues of coexistence and sharing (if you prefer, in a word, *time*, or the challenge presented to us by the fact that we must reshape our past in order to live the present and prepare future) resonates in the long history and the story that concerns this book.

Such a story runs from the Arawak-speaking people who created one of the largest, most ecologically rich environments on the planet, extend-ing between the lowlands of Beni in present-day Bolivia, throughout the Amazonian basin in Brazil and Venezuela, the heights of the Andes in Peru and Colombia and the coasts of the Caribbean, on the one hand; and, on the other, to the Yanomami, Evo Morales and the indigenous government of today's Bolivia, the Afro and indigenous communities of south-eastern Colombia, and the several thousands of Awajun and Wambis Indians who fought the Peruvian government to prevent them from allowing free access to exploit oil and timber from the northern Amazonian frontier in June 2009. The story includes Massasoit and the Levellers, abolitionists and veterans of the English Revolution, spread throughout the Atlantic and leaving a lasting legacy still alive during the cycle of Caribbean, indigenous and commoner, or *comunero*, rebel-lions in Latin America more than a century later (between the 1730s and 1780s) through the American and Haitian revolutions, the liberation of Spanish America and a renewed wave of abolitionism in Europe, to the contemporary rise of indigenous consciousness to power in Bolivia – represented by the government of Evo Morales – and the increased centrality of Brazil, Ecuador or Venezuela in their defence of the resources of the Amazon against the interests of declining empires and powerful corporations.

A Matter of Life and Gold

The Andean-Amazonian region of Latin America, better known to its inhabitants since pre-Columbian times as Tawantisuyu, the Land of Four Quarters, encompasses a staggering twenty of the world's thirty-four main ecosystems. To go from the rainforests of upper Amazonia in Bolivia to the deserts of the Peruvian or Chilean Pacific coast, the traveller must move through almost every imaginable type of terrain and endure some of the hardest conditions known to man. Those who have tried – archaeologists, adventurers, explorers and British television presenters – can tell you how gruelling the experience can be. It seems difficult to imagine that this was once home to the greatest empire on earth.

'Bigger than Ming Dynasty China, bigger than Ivan the Great's expanding Russia, bigger than Songhai in the Sahel or powerful Great Zimbabwe in the West Africa tablelands, bigger than the cresting Ottoman Empire, bigger than the Triple Alliance (as the Aztec empire is more precisely known), bigger by far than any European state,' explains American science writer Charles C. Mann. Against all apparent logic, millions of people not only insisted on living in such seemingly inhospitable conditions – over ten or even fifteen thousand feet above sea level – but also thrived in them.

In fact, they thrived *because* of them. Geographer and ecologist Jared Diamond postulates that the first large-scale human communities tended to arise where geography 'provided a wide range of altitudes and topographies within a short distance'. One such place was the Fertile Crescent between the mountains of Iran and the Dead Sea, which brackets the Tigris and Euphrates river systems and gave place to Sumer and Assyria, well known to many as cradles of civilisation. Another was Upper and Lower Peru, which encompassed parts of what are now the countries of Bolivia, Peru, Ecuador, Chile, Colombia, Argentina and Brazil. Here too emerged one of the world's cultural wellsprings, between the Amazon basin and the high peaks of the Andes.

Verticality characterises such places. Fittingly, the Inca homeland is uniquely steep, high and diverse, but also uniquely narrow. 'The distance from the Pacific shore to the mountaintops is in most places less than seventy-five miles and in many less than fifty,' says Mann. As he explains, it was such diversity of conditions that made the Inca extraordinary. 'If imperial potential is judged in terms of environmental adaptability, the Inca were the most impressive empire builders of their day,' says historian Felipe Fernández-Armesto. Combining the products of many ecosystems – fish and shellfish from the coastal areas, beans and cotton from the river valleys, maize, quinoa and potatoes from the foothills, wool and meat from llamas and alpacas in the peaks – Andean and Amazonian cultures enjoyed a better life than most other cultures anywhere in the world. In fact, by the time the Spanish arrived in Peru, the inhabitants of the region had solved for themselves the problem of famine. To survive, they specialised in the management of ecosystems.

'For thousands of years, we have run the Amazon forests,' said Servando Puerta, one of the leaders of the indigenous protests against oil and timber exploitation in the Bagua Grande region of Peru in June 2009. His statement is no exaggeration. It contains a more profound truth: for thousands of years, Indians and Paleo-Indians have learned how to manage the different ecosystems of the region – the forests, the coastal areas, the heights – because they created them. This region is an ecological treasure, but one designed and executed by human beings. When geography doctoral student William Denevan flew over Beni in 1961, he contemplated out of the windows of his DC-3 a sight that could forever change our view of indigenous peoples and their relation with the environment. 'I knew these things were not natural. You just don't have that kind of straight line in nature. It's a completely humanised landscape,' he told Charles Mann. Denevan was referring to the building mounds, raised agricultural fields, canals, dikes and zigzagging networks of earthen fish-corralling fences fashioned more than a thousand years ago by hundreds, perhaps thousands, of people among the causeways of the naturally flooded savannah in eastern Bolivia.

Although much of the landscape is the result of flooding, the Indians maintained and expanded the grasslands by setting fire to huge areas. As Mann observes, 'over the centuries the burning created an intricate ecosystem of fire-adapted plant species dependent on indigenous pyrophilia'. The practice still survives and is seen with suspicion by many conservationists. To them, regions like Beni should be left untouched, as close to wilderness as possible, while to others such areas should be developed into economically viable projects. For both, the presence of indigenous seems to be an obstacle. Would conservationists approve of large-scale burning in the Amazon? Can governments stop development projects in the name of pristine Nature or indigenous traditions? Indians, like Servando Puerta, propose placing control of the land into their hands, or, more accurately, point out that in fact it is they who have ruled these lands for many years, both in the sense that they have created them and in a sense that comes close to the west's idea of government.

Forms of government may have existed on both sides of Peru – to the east in Beni and to the west in Norte Chico – long before the Inca ruled the greatest empire on earth. If the evidence unearthed by a new cohort of scholars now working in the Americas and their hypotheses prove correct, it may be the case that forms of government emerged autonomously in these regions out of the society-wide efforts that went along with the refashioning of the terrain and were driven by a sense of common economic good rather than, say, security or common defence.

Evidence in archaeological research often comes from looking at two questions: 'where do societies come from?' and 'what is their food supply?' Crucially, in both cases the food supply is fish. Society-wide efforts, including fence-building, burning and farming (of cotton needed to make nets, as was the case in the Norte Chico region) had their foundations in modes of sustenance and exchange based on the great fisheries of Andean-Amazonian rivers and the sea. Archaeologists Susan deFrance at the University of Florida and Daniel Sandweiss at Maine explain that evidence coming from bone analyses of Pleistocene coastal foragers shows that they got '90 per cent of their protein from the sea – anchovies, sardines, shellfish and so on', a pattern continuing for thousands of years and confirmed by dig after archaeological dig. It may help connect in history the 3500 BC mounds and irrigation channels found in the mouths of the four rivers of the Norte Chico region in Peru with those found on the other side of the Andes, in the causeways of Beni in eastern Bolivia, which date back as far as three thousand years ago.

A new generation of archaeologists, including Clark Erickson, deFrance and Jonathan Haas, has put forward an image of pre-Columbian America that radically challenges our most comfortable intuitions. Not only because it throws into disarray some deep-seated notions in a variety of disciplines (for instance, the idea that Andean civilisations have maritime and river foundations has been critiqued as an economic impossibility) but also because it profoundly questions what we believe is politically possible.

For a long time, philosophers, political theorists and international-ists have argued that governments emerged out of the need for secu-rity and protection. Defence against common enemies and expansion requires the setting-up of highly centralised structures organised around the single figure of a warlord or an army. That is to say, a Leviathan to command and control the multitude, with religion as its ideological sidekick. In turn, the maintenance of armies for defence and occupation requires taxation or large-scale resource extraction, and the latter can only be sustainable if work and production are organised, labour divided and discipline forcibly imposed. The case of the Americas, backed by evidence found in Peru's Norte Chico and elsewhere, suggests some-thing else: a form of government and exchange that seems to have arisen from collective and spiritual good, made concrete in society-wide efforts to create and sustain the commons, rather than to defend ourselves from others and from one another. The former is a matter of riches, of gold, silver and oil; the latter is a matter of life.[20]

2

The Dream of the Mountain of Gold

Driving while thinking about matters of life,
matters of writing, and listening to Iggy Pop.

The Pan-American Highway extends some 29,800 miles, from Prudhoe Bay in Alaska to the town of Ushuaia in the province of Tierra del Fuego, in Argentina. It passes through all imaginable – and some pretty unimaginable – geographical landscapes and climates, from glaciers to coasts, from deserts to mountains. It links all the mainland nations of the Americas, and according to *The Guinness Book of Records* it remains the longest motorable road in the world.

Writing in 2006, *Harper's* chronicler Jake Silverstein called it 'a system so vast, so incomplete, and so incomprehensible it is not so much a road as it is the idea of Pan-Americanism itself'.[1] To people like Silverstein, the highway evokes all that is whimsical about the Pan-American utopias dreamt up by the likes of the Haudenosaunee Indians of North America, authors of one of the first constitutions of the Americas, now known as the Great Law of Peace; by Túpac Amaru, two of them in fact, both leaders of indigenous rebellions that, in the case of Túpac Amaru II, connected the traditions of the English Revolution still alive in the Caribbean with the spirit of Latin American independence; or by Simón Bolívar, liberator of the Americas and frustrated proponent of a Pan-American Union in the nineteenth century. In contrast, rather than evoking the grey political pragmatism that Silverstein's comment represents, driving down the Pan-American Highway has always reminded me of the perils and the arrogance of our modern ideas of progress and god-given command over Nature. That, and the need to recover a deeply felt sense of passion for life in our times.

Back in the late 1990s I attempted to recreate Francisco Pizarro's historic navigation from Mexico's Pacific shore to Peru by driving along the highway, except that for fifty-four miles the thick rainforest of the Darién between Panama and Colombia makes it impossible. The layout of the highway through Central and South America corresponds to the navigational advice given by Pizarro's pilot in the sixteenth century: 'sail south along the coast until you no longer see trees. Then you are in Peru.' After having driven all the way from Mexico City to Yaviza in Panama, along the Pacific coast, I continued southwards from Turbo in Colombia, listening to music by Iggy Pop & The Stooges. Then I drove to Cali in the Cauca river valley and from there to Quito in Ecuador. Ascending to the foothills of Chimborazo, where I stopped to read aloud Pablo Neruda's *General Song*.[2] Finally, I drove along the coastline to Peru where the dense forests of the River Cauca, the tributaries of the Amazon and the Andean foothills and heights disappear out of view and are replaced by the most dramatic desolation.

A desert it is. The average annual precipitation is about two inches. If you continue driving along the Chilean shore you end up in the Atacama Desert, reputedly the driest place in the world. Atacama is unlike most other deserts, the Gobi or the Sahara. Rather than sand dunes, immense flatbeds and scorching sun, there are impossible drops from the Andean cordillera directly into the sea, rivers that bring Andean snowmelt at incredible speeds to the coast, fog during the winter months and, according to the latest archaeological finds, evidence that this is one of two places in the world where mankind actually invented sophisticated forms of social organisation and government.

Researchers argue that since the environment did not favour intensive agriculture, the people of the valley used the fast-running rivers to create irrigation channels, shaping the landscape and making it fit for one main purpose: growing cotton. Two out of the four domesticated kinds of cotton that exist worldwide come from the Americas, and South American cotton was most likely grown first in domesticated form near the mouth of the Amazon river or one of its many tributaries falling from the Andes. This was the soft but firm basis of all ancient Andean civilisations, from Norte Chico to Cuzco and Beni, and from the earlier fish-farming societies of Huaricanga in Peru to the tree-farming Arawak-speaking ancestors of the people now called the Mojo and the Bauré in Bolivia and Brazil, to the later Inca centralised union.

Cotton was crucial to trade. According to archaeologists such as Jonathan Haas, inland centres settled around the rivers and channels such as Caral and Huaricanga had irrigation-produced cotton, fruits and vegetables, and controlled most of the exchange, while coastal settlements like Aspero provided vast quantities of sardines, anchovies and so on. Evidence found in both settlements indicates that they swapped one for the other. 'Cotton was needed and easily stored, which made it useful as a medium of exchange or status,' says Charles C. Mann, citing the work of Haas and others. Warehouses were built for storage and security, big public monuments and ceremonial structures erected for the encouragement and reward of the builders' workforce.

'What was it like to build these first great structures?' asks Mann in his fascinating account of the Americas before Columbus. In apt form, he replies in this manner: 'In June 1790, a year after the French Revolution swept away a corrupt and ineffectual monarchy, thousands of Parisians from every social class united to create the enormous Champ de Mars as a monument to the new society. Working in heavy rainfall without coercion or pay, they dug out the entire enormous space to a depth of four feet and then filled it up with enough sand and gravel to make an outdoor amphitheatre suitable for half a million people. The whole huge effort took only three weeks. Something analogous – an awed, wondering celebration of a new mode of existence – may have occurred at the Norte Chico.' His description fits well with the sort of collective action, without payment or coercion, that to this day is central to the lives, and, we might say, regained political power, of thousands of Indians in Latin America. They call it *la minga*.

By the time Francisco Pizarro arrived in Inca-ruled Peru, the textile-, cotton- and maritime-based foundation of Andean societies had become more sophisticated. Textiles, for instance, had become record-keeping media, and were also used as tools for number-crunching. They were called *quipus*. Making and reading *quipus* required the kind of tactile sensitivity that we tend to relate to music and rhythm, and to certain forms of painting, which is missing from the more mainstream forms of indirect construction, such as dictation or denomination, which we now associate with the act of writing. The textile-based societies that Pizarro encountered in South America viewed the direct construction of memory as a form of weaving or making; as a way of putting things together, like composing a piece of music or building the Champ de Mars in common,[3] rather than as a form of abstract conversation. Making and reading records in a *quipu* were acts of direct creation, of bringing something new into the world.

In his 1590 *Historia Natural y Moral de las Indias* the Spanish chronicler José de Acosta acknowledged the non-figurative character of the Peruvian textiles and *quipus*. 'The Indians of Peru,' he wrote, 'had no sort of writing, not letters, nor characters nor ciphers nor figures, like those of China and Mexico.' For a man of letters like Acosta it was possible to separate, on the one hand, the pure functionality of letters, ciphers and figures – their potential as substitutes for something else; in fact for everything else, all the other objects of the world, which they denominate, communicate and transform – from, on the other, the solid surface of inscription. The first is a pure form, an active principle or form relative to an absolutely social function (exchange). The second was conceived as a mere vessel, an artefact to be used, and, after the event, disposed of. Or, even worse, as fetishes.[4]

Acosta's sixteenth-century conception of writing already contained a number of distinctions that allowed him to place people, the Inca people in this case, on the other side of a demarcation line separating the civilised from the savage when deployed upon their objects. Chief among them were ideas of exchange and value. What attracted Acosta's attention to the textile *quipus* was not their material appearance, but, rather, what the Incas did with them.[5] Hence the kind of analogy he makes between these textiles and the letter-based systems of writing he was familiar with. He sees them as rule-based forms of circulating differences among people belonging to the circuit or circle. 'And in every bundle of these,' he writes referring to Inca textiles, 'so many greater and lesser knots, and tied strings; some red, others green, others blue, others white, in short, as many differences as we have with our twenty-four letters, which *we weave together, relate and organise* in different ways so as to obtain an *infinity* of words; so did they, with their knots and colours, draw forth the innumerable *significance and value* of things.'[6]

Acosta recognised the functionality of these objects as square or circular spaces of organisation within which things and events could be located and given value, within which they circulate and may be communicated. In short, as mnemotechnic devices, modes of conservation and retrieval of 'memory of ancient lore', which allow the Inca to provide 'accounts of all their affairs of peace, war, and government'. Thus, he also understood them as social systems for the placement of value and identified them with the possibility of holding on to such value. In this way, he projected on to the textile *quipus* his own conceptions of memory and writing, which already in the sixteenth century were intimately associated with the activities of record-keeping proper to an expansionist, world-trade-based and gold-lusting society. In doing so, he misunderstood the more profound and ancient meaning evoked by the Latin term *textum*, and still alive during the Middle Ages, which, by the time of conquistadors like Pizarro and chroniclers like Acosta, had faded from the vocabulary of Europe.

In Latin, *texo* meant 'to make' and more specifically 'to weave', as Duke University semiotician Walter Mignolo points out. 'It was also used in the sense of "joint or fit together", to interlace or to intertwine. Hence, *textum* invoked the idea of something woven or made into a web. Like a net, or music,' he told me. I can't say whether or not Mignolo knows about the discoveries of archaeologists working in the Norte Chico of Peru, where they have unearthed evidence of earlier Andean societies (if the settlement at Aspero in the Norte Chico region turns out to be older than now thought, it might earn the title of the world's oldest city in history) based on fishing, cotton net-weaving, and music-making for the purposes of the political positive reinforcement of communal spirit; or if he knows about the debates around the 'maritime foundation' hypothesis. But his observations on the materiality of writing among the Inca, its aesthetic associations with rhythm and a tactile sensitivity that begins in the 'pulsating environment of the unborn child far in advance of the development of other senses', fit very neatly with the evidence and the hypotheses put forward by the latest archaeological research. Together, they help us gain a more complete picture of what is at stake when world views collide. They may also provide us with a better basis for understanding what was lost when a form of exchange and government, profoundly invested in lusting after life, was replaced by a form of exchange based upon a seemingly insatiable lust for gold.

Lust for Gold: How Globalisation Was Invented in Latin America
'Gold is a wonderful thing! Its owner is master of all he desires. Gold can even enable souls to enter Paradise.' These words, attributed to Christopher Columbus's letter from Jamaica, dated 1503, sum up the world view that collided with Andean civilisations in the sixteenth century. That world view distinguished between symbols and their places of inscription. Gold, for instance, became the universal incarnation of value. Holding on to gold meant being able to transform everything else into a valuable relation. The whole world could then be mapped in such terms, as more or less valuable. Thereafter, things, places and peoples had no significance of their own but only relative value. This principle, which sees the objects of the world merely as a set of relative values with no significance of their own, had assisted the transit from textuality to alphabetic writing in the post-Ptolemaic map-making, book-worshipping, money-hoarding societies of Renaissance Europe.

The same principle operative in the act of writing and the making of maps was at work in the establishment of a form of wealth always ready to be held and used. Maps, tables and circles, it should be remembered, not only refer to geometrical or technical concepts, but also have social connotations 'as a circumference containing people who share certain goods, certain kinds of information, or interest . . . The "circle" calls up another concept crucial in understanding objects: Objects may, as commodities, circulate within "spheres" or circuits by which they are determinated (valued) and which they determinate.'[7]

This point can be generalised to the case of alphabetic writing in the context of the massive changes occurring within European and Andean societies, and perhaps accelerated if not prompted by their encounter in the sixteenth century. In this respect, it can be useful to pay closer attention to the connection, or contradiction, between writing and monetary value, on the one hand, and *textum* (including textiles and textuality) and community, on the other.

The suggestion that spatial distribution, taxonomic classification and anthropological speech and writing, what may be called 'the "scientific" collecting of objects', has always been entangled in a complex net of purposes, practices and processes, not the least economic and expansionist purposes whose common denominator was the emerging form of market relations and commodity exchange, seems particularly apt to the story of how globalisation was invented in Latin America during the sixteenth century, on the back of the appearance of the first 'world money': the silver peso.[8]

There are countless tales of the greed of conquistadors and colonisers, and their lust for precious metals and territorial power is well known. You can begin with the Spanish and Peruvian chroniclers themselves, writing early on after the defeat of the Inca, such as the critics of empire Bartolomé de Las Casas and Felipe Guamán Puma de Ayala, the rebellious commoners, or *comuneros*, of eighteenth-century New Granada (in present-day Venezuela and Colombia). You can continue through Robert Southey's epic poem *Madoc* in the English-dominated nineteenth century, to the fantasies projected on to the continent by Winston Churchill (*Savrola*, 1897), R. B. Cunninghame's history of the Jesuit missions of Paraguay (*A Vanished Arcadia*, 1901), and Joseph Conrad's subtle but ultimately contradictory vision of Caribbean Latin America (*Nostromo*, 1904). And you can end with the equally subtle condemnations written by V. S. Naipaul or contained in the historicised fiction of the younger generation of Latin American writers either recently translated into English or pending translation, such as J. G. Vásquez's *The Secret History of Costaguana* (2010) or William Ospina's *Ursúa*. But only rarely is the important question of the reasons for such lust posited, let alone put to rest.

Only with the possibility of keeping hold of socially produced value, and with the extension of commodity circulation, is it that 'the lust for gold awakens'.[9] When value, place, difference and significance can be abstracted and inscribed on a solid basis, it can be transferred and accumulated in the form of wealth or information. This procedure also permits the subordination of objects corresponding to other forms of communal organisation and exchange misunderstood or experienced as dangerous or archaic. Out of this procedure to circulate abstractions emerges the potentially infinite circulation of objects within circuits of value and their transformation into signs, one of which is money. The latter can take the shape of coins, or, later on, squares of paper with graphic signs printed upon them.

In this respect at least, we must understand that from here onwards there is more than a family resemblance between money, books and maps. Indeed, circles, tables and squares also call up another concept crucial to the understanding of modern societies characterised by the incessant movement of objects around the globe (what we now identify loosely with 'globalisation'): coins, money, the gold fetish, the silver peso, coexisting side by side with orbs (also known as 'circuits'), maps, tablets and thereafter legal systems and fixed international borders. They all belong to the category of things being placed by means of signs and symbols that we, like yesterday's conquistadors and the first ethnographers, mistake for wonders.

On 5 August 1495 Christopher Columbus received a peculiar but extremely important letter from the Royal Cosmographer, Jaume Ferrer de Blanes. The letter, addressed to the Admiral of the Ocean Sea and discoverer of worlds, came at the request of Her Catholic Majesty Queen Isabella of Spain. The Spanish crown was anxious about the apparent lack of progress so far, in the enterprise of the Indies delivering the desired profits, and no one was better placed than Ferrer to take up the issue. The Catalan was one of Spain's foremost geographers and cosmographers, having proposed to the crown a method for establishing the longitude of the meridian drawn in mid-ocean by the crucial 1494 Treaty of Tordesillas, an achievement recognised today as an example of mathematical and geographical genius. It helped solve a major dispute between Spain and Portugal, the two most powerful navigational powers of the age, which the legal document addressed, concerning the distribution of the New World after Columbus's momentous discovery.

Crucially, always the Renaissance man, he was almost as good at conducting business trading gems, gold and silver in the Levant as he was applying his mind to intractable cosmographical problems. During his dealings in the region he had learned from 'Indians and Arabs and Ethiopians' that precious metals and stones and all manner of good things often 'come from very hot regions whose inhabitants are black or dark brown'. His observation on the unique nature of place, climate, peoples and the goods to be found in each different location,was to have momentous consequences for Andean civilisations, and for the world at large. A tragedy for the former, it would give rise, in the case of the latter, to a modern history characterised by crises; the short and long cycles that we often refer to as 'history repeating itself'.

After expressing his belief in the connection between 'great and valuable things' and 'hot regions inhabited by darker skinned peoples', Ferrer addressed Columbus: 'and therefore, in my judgment, until Your Lordship meets such peoples, You shall fail to find an abundance of such things'. He concluded that Columbus should head south, 'at the turn of the equator', as the learned cosmographer put it in his letter. Columbus's biographers and most reputable experts in all things relating to Columbus tend to agree that the steep turn towards the equator that led him to discover South America during his third voyage was urged upon him by the sort of observations contained in Ferrer's letter. In his *Historia de las Indias*, a damning account of the war of conquest unleashed by the conquistadors upon the Indians, and written on the basis of his examination of primary documentary sources (among them Columbus's diary, now lost), Bartolomé de Las Casas wrote of his experiences after arriving in the Americas on the same ship as the future vanquisher of the Inca empire, Francisco Pizarro. Columbus, having experienced the doldrums off equatorial Africa, 'and suffering the heat he thought was in danger of setting his crew and ships ablaze', included an observation in his diary according to which 'under that parallel of the world more gold and things of value are found'.

In a previous entry dated 21 November 1492, Columbus expressed his mistrust of the latitudinal readings of his quadrant in north-eastern Cuba, reasoning that the great heat he and his men were experiencing there was evidence that he could not be as far from the equator as the instrument suggested. From this observation he concluded 'that he was venturing into one of the richest gold-bearing regions of the globe'. Years later, in the *carta-relación* of the fourth voyage, dated 7 July 1503, Columbus repeats once again his line of argument and establishes its premise: 'gold is generated in sterile lands and wherever the sun is strong'.[10]

These certainties pervaded Columbus's observations as much as, at the time, they pervaded and informed the minds and actions of explorers and conquistadors like Pizarro and others. In his letter to Columbus, the connection made by Ferrer between heat, an abundance of precious metals and the dark skins of peoples in southern equatorial regions therefore appears to obey an ancient commonplace that scholars of Columbus nowadays call a 'cosmography of riches'.

The term is appropriate, for it refers not simply to a set of navigational problems related to what experts understand by the notion of latitude, the north–south degrees of separation between any given place in the globe and the equator, or, approximately, the angle between the zenith and the sun at an equinox. Rather, it refers to a philosophical problem involved in the question of Columbus's and Pizarro's journey to the south. Few men, among them Bartolomé de Las Casas and later the cosmologist and adventurer Alexander von Humboldt, have made this problem explicit. It concerns a certain ambiguity between deeply held ancient (cosmological) assumptions concerning the nature of places and the peoples inhabiting them, on the one hand, and emerging modern ideas about the movement and circulation of things, including commodities, on the other. Both the tragedy of Andean civilisations and the repetitive nature of the history of modern globalisation can be understood as consequences – geopolitical consequences – of that ambiguity.

Geography and politics have always been closely allied. They were twin disciplines in the ancient cosmological tradition 'that imagined the orderly workings of the geocentric universe as *machina mundi*, the machine of the world', explains Brown University historian of science Nicolás Wey Gómez. As he observes, the idea of place was a crucial part of the tradition that witnessed the encounter between Europeans and the native peoples of the Americas. At a crucial moment in the history of mankind these conceptions about the nature of the lands, climates, and peoples – and also, critically, of the goods circulating within such places and the manner of their circulation – became an integral and explicit organising principle not only of the enterprise in the Indies but also of the reordering of the entire world.

It informed an emerging, newer sense of the accumulation of wealth, as well as the connection between such accumulation and the distribution of races north and south of the globe; crucially, it also shaped arguments concerning the capacities for self-government of such races. In the minds of people like Columbus and Pizarro, geography was not merely a tool for 'locating, describing or reaching' the various parts of the inhabited or supposedly uninhabited parts of the world. It also justified waging a war of races. This was to have enormous political consequences for the peoples invented by European discoveries as 'Indians', 'Americans' or more simply as 'savages'.

The contradictory geopolitical distinctions projected upon the southern latitudes soon took the form of arguments justifying the subjugation and enslavement of the peoples of the Indies, rehearsed during the sixteenth-century debates between the apologists and creators of modern imperialism, claiming legal titles to overseas colonies, on the one hand, and, on the other, humanitarian opponents of empire like Bartolomé de Las Casas or Felipe Guamán Puma de Ayala, himself a descendant of the native peoples of Peru. In the process, sometime between 1539 and 1550, what we now call international law was invented, together with the very idea of nations (which the Dominican friar Francisco de Vitoria divided into 'perfect' and 'perfectible' communities, in a way echoed today by our distinctions between 'developed' and 'developing' nations) and that of a republic of the whole world, thereby preparing the ground for a genuine global political philosophy.[11]

Following French astrologer and cosmographer Pierre d'Ailly, the enterprise of the Indies was designed and executed in accordance with the view that had long prevailed in the Latin west concerning the distribution of land and the arts of mankind in the planet. In his view the three main continents – Europe, Africa and Asia – constituted a single landmass isolated in the upper quarter of the globe, and the part of the world filled with mankind and its works was supposed to form a narrow 'temperate' and, thereby, 'civilised' corridor 'within this geographical system, besieged to the north and to the south by the extreme cold and the heat of the "wild" Arctic and tropics'.[12] Sub-Saharan Africa, also known as 'Ethiopia', and the lands on the basin of the Indian Ocean, or 'India', soon to include all other lands that shared similar conditions because of their similar latitudinal placing, or 'the Indies', were thus contradictorily imagined as more or less uninhabited fringes where merciless temperatures forged the much coveted metals silver and gold, while at the same time harbouring a truly vast realm, wealthier than anything Europe had seen before, precisely because such lands stood 'in the part of the sun'.

'Most unfortunately,' writes Nicolás Wey Gómez, 'while longitude may speak to a technical feat that many of Columbus's contemporaries deemed impossible, latitude speaks to a geopolitical process that Bartolomé de Las Casas called "the destruction of the Indies", *la destrucción de las Yndias*.' Indeed, Columbus's and Pizarro's southing, their drive to sail south and uncover the wealth lying at the turn of the equator, would spell the end of such immensely rich civilisations as that of the Incas, their cultural wealth squandered or destroyed in the seemingly unstoppable search for silver and gold.

The Destruction of the Indies . . .

It was Friday 15 November 1532, and Francisco Pizarro and his men had just negotiated the pass over the green valley of Cajamarca. These men had climbed nine thousand feet from the coast, having sailed south from Panama and followed it until the trees disappeared. As he looked down on the canals and the terraces thick with maize and cotton, Pizarro recalled the hardships endured during the first two attempts, and, thinking of the riches lying ahead, considered it all worthwhile. These were, after all, men of Extremadura, individuals used to the trials of poverty and seemingly composed of the same material that covered the arid plains of western Spain. They were tough and unsentimental, and, when necessary, they could set aside what few scruples they had and be as brutal as the circumstances demanded. Having grown up destitute and apparently condemned to a life on the fringes of an extremely hierarchical society, these people would stop at nothing to achieve their dreams of power, status and wealth.

They were less an army than a makeshift group of armed entrepreneurs. The older, more adventurous meaning of the word 'filibuster' (relating to piracy and hijacking) immediately comes to mind. When Pizarro was fifteen he heard of Columbus's fantastic journey to the 'New World', and understood that El Dorado would be the place to realise his dreams and gain a name for himself. By 1524, three years after another *Extremeño* named Hernán Cortés hijacked and killed Moctezuma, the head of the Aztecs, bringing an end to the Aztec empire, he had formed a company with fellow partners Diego de Almagro and financier Hernando de Luque. Their economic model, recently originated in Europe, portended an extraordinary future. These were armed men, self-financed and single-minded, who felt entitled to a share in any future spoils, the rivers of silver and gold that, according to the information gathered during their peregrinations along the Colombian and Peruvian coasts, lay ahead in the south. By 1528 Pizarro had arrived in Tumbez. There, he witnessed the military campaign of pacification that followed the rise of the Inca in the region named after their original settlements in the valley of Cuzco and the River Pirú, or Perú, as the Spaniards pronounced it. Now, Francisco Pizarro and his fellow Spaniards, accompanied by some black slaves, a Dominican friar, a few natives from Central America and several slave women of Muslim descent, were ready to take their place in history.

Just a few miles beyond Cajamarca lay the camp of the Inca ruler Atahualpa, son of Wayna Capac. He was still savouring the recent victory of his army over his brother Huascar, which would allow him to enter Cuzco, the city of his youth and heart of the empire, and claim it as its undisputed lord. Little did he know that the power struggle he had just won over his brother would play him into the hands of his future conquerors, the Spanish, just as the invisible germs of measles, smallpox and pneumonic fever (which had probably killed his father) had done in the previous months and years. Knowing that Atahualpa was aware of their presence, and fearful of his army, yet hopeful of exploiting whatever divisions remained in what looked, every step of the way up the

Andes, like the final throes of a bloody civil war, Pizarro and his 167
men, 62 of them on horseback, continued to ascend the Inca road.

Pizarro was now fifty-four. Glancing to one side of him, he exchanged
a look of complicity with the dashing young Hernando de Soto, future
explorer of Florida, Georgia and Arkansas, and the first European to
set eyes on the Mississippi river. The thirty-two-year-old De Soto
was something of a dandy, given to wearing form-fitting clothing and
often stylishly adorned with an assortment of earrings. He was also an
Extremeño. The two of them made quite the couple. It was De Soto
who led the advance party on horseback along the labyrinthine roads
connecting Cajamarca with the camp where the ruler of the greatest
empire on earth awaited them.

The Spanish chronicler Francisco de Jerez described the scene that met
the eyes of De Soto and his men as a circular formation on the flank of
a small hill with cotton tents extending three and a half miles, and some
thirty thousand lancers guarding Atahualpa's bathhouse at the centre.
There on a stool sat Atahualpa himself, covered in gold jewellery and with
a scarlet headband across his head and shoulders, 'as the Turks and Moors
are accustomed to sit. He projected such majesty and splendour as had
never before been seen . . . surrounded by all his women, and with many
chiefs near him'. De Soto rode right up to the Inca ruler and looked down
on him from a height of fully nine feet. True to form, Atahualpa kept his
eyes fixed on the ground and listened to the speech that was being translated for him by one of Pizarro's native interpreters, a man from Tumbez
they named Felipillo, disgusted by the Spaniard's ill manners and the way
in which the native rendered De Soto's words in a most corrupted form
of *runasimi*, the Quechua language of his Cuzco ancestors.

The interpreter knew almost nothing about the theological smoke
and legal mirrors employed by De Soto in his speech, which would have
been unintelligible to him anyway, even spoken properly and within a
shared frame of language. Thus, having listened to what sounded like
little more than a stream of nonsense, Atahualpa perfectly well understood the truth about these men who talked to their white pieces of
cloth and supposedly ate gold and silver. Wanting to finish his last day
of ceremonial fasting, and having seen first hand the barbarous ways of

these foreigners, Atahualpa signalled to one of his chiefs to make his excuses to the visitor; his part in the performance was over.

At that point Francisco Pizarro's younger brother, Hernando, rode into the camp and introduced himself to the Inca. Having understood him to be the brother of the leader of the foreigners, Atahualpa stood up, and, reaching with one hand, took an iron collar from one of his chiefs and threw it at the feet of the Spaniards. 'This is proof that you have mistreated my chiefs and put them in chains,' he said. 'My chief Maizabilica from the River Zuricara sent to tell me this is what you do. How dare you? He sent me this collar, and also said he has killed three of you, half-men, half-beasts, who cannot walk up the mountain and instead attach themselves to giant llamas, who, unable to read a *quipu*, stare and talk to pieces of cloth, eaters of silver and gold, who do not observe any of our uses and rules.'

De Soto and Pizarro were startled by the fury of his accusations, which they knew to be true. Three Spaniards had indeed been killed while crossing Puna to reach mainland Peru a few months earlier; the Spaniards had retaliated, killing an unknown number of natives. To forestall another attack, and acting on rumours (what we might now call 'intelligence') concerning a plot near Tumbez, Francisco Pizarro had organised a pre-emptive strike, seizing, chaining and later on burning alive a chieftain along with his principal men. It was all part of what we would now term 'psychological warfare'. Not knowing how to respond to Atahualpa, the Spaniards decided to raise the stakes. Hernando retorted that Atahualpa's information was based on misinformation. 'Your chieftains are scoundrels. They lied to you,' he said. 'Maizabilica could not kill a single Christian, neither could any of his men. We would not have mistreated them unless they attacked first, for this is our law and such our Christian values. We treat well those who wish to be friends, and destroy those who wish to attack us, down to their last man. They are chickens. Let Pizarro give you ten of his men on horseback,' boasted the young Hernando Pizarro, 'and you will see how they are enough to destroy any of your enemies.'

At that moment, as if on cue, Hernando de Soto, who had remained on horseback, as had the other Spaniards, dug in his spurs, turned the animal around and suddenly charged straight at Atahualpa's seemingly fearless warriors. He pulled up at the last moment, and, backing up his horse, made it rear up on its hind legs and neigh very loudly. Atahualpa's elite guards lost their composure and, terrified out of their wits, fell over one another in a desperate attempt to escape. Later that day, Atahualpa, who had remained calm during De Soto's display of horsemanship, had them executed, but now he ordered refreshments to be offered to his visitors. Women, chosen from among the prettiest daughters of his chieftains, came wearing precious gems and silver and gold earrings, beautifully woven green, red and yellow cotton dresses, and silver pectorals that embraced and showed off their small but perfectly formed breasts. They brought golden goblets filled with chichi, the fermented drink made out of Mexican-imported maize and reserved only for the elite. The Spaniards drank, their eyes still fixed on the beautiful women. Then everyone drank. De Soto noticed that Atahualpa's goblet had been fashioned out of a human skull, presumably that of one of his enemies. In fact, it belonged to General Atoq, one of the chieftains loyal to Atahualpa's brother Huascar. De Soto's heart was filled with terror; or perhaps, he may have thought, this was the effect of the firewater burning down his throat. 'Tell Pizarro,' Atahualpa said, 'that tomorrow I will lodge in the Great Chamber on the square of Cajamarca. Then he will be allowed to be in the presence of the Sun-god, ruler of the Inca.'

As night fell upon the valley, Atahualpa withdrew into the shadows. He had made a decision to seize the arrogant foreigners and castrate them. He would kill most of them and oblige the others to teach them how to mount their giant llamas. He had seen how effective they were at instilling fear in the hearts of the enemy. Politics and war were, after all, less a matter of sheer military might than a question of being able to stage the most spectacular and terrifying performance. That was the point of the corpses the Spaniards had seen hanging from knotted cords all the way up to Cajamarca. That was the point of the beautifully clad women, the silver and gold, the claims about being a descendant of the Sun-god, the point of the very architecture of the city with its temples, monuments, roads and Norte Chico-style sunken plazas, the massive number of troops amassed in one place, their steely composure and the majesty of the Inca. It was all a display, a masterful game of smoke and mirrors, shock and awe.

And it had worked. Hernando's obvious boasting had given them away. Atahualpa knew the Spaniards were bluffing. He may have understood very little of the speeches made by De Soto and Hernando Pizarro but he gathered that these were soldiers sent by another chief, and a chief with so few soldiers to send would no doubt belong to a small and less powerful dominion. Their fate rested in his hands. And yet he had his doubts: why had they been so foolish as to come within striking distance of his many thousands of lancers? He had witnessed his most experienced chieftains running like little children when De Soto's horse had charged at them. He had not seen a display like it before. Had he made a tactical mistake in allowing them to progress all the way to Cajamarca in the first place? And then there were their manners, their boasting and arrogance. These men were clearly unimpressed by the majesty of the descendant of the Sun-god of Cuzco.

Atahualpa had made a crucial observation. He knew well the stories about the origins of his people and their rise to power. In about 1450, Capac Yupanki rode to Cajamarca on the orders of his brother Pachakuti. There, he ambushed Minchacaman, the eleventh ruler of the Chimor dynasty based at Chan Chan, famous for its exuberant construction plans and a sense of razzle-dazzle that almost guaranteed imperial ambition. The people of Chan Chan, in turn, had combined the organisational sense of the Wari with the taste for the spectacular of the Tiwanaku, whose legacy they perfected. Until the fifteenth century the Inca had been a less well-known and fairly insignificant group established on the shores of Lake Titicaca. But when Capac Yupanki and Pachakuti put an end to the Chimor rulers at Cajamarca, they made their centre the courtly magnificence of Chan Chan. Crucially, they took with them the gold, silver and gem craftsmen and artists and instructed them to transform Cuzco into an even more impressive Chan Chan. Their rule and extensive dominion, like those of the Tiwanaku in 300 BC, were thus based on a cross between a flow of exchange directed by kin and government rather than market forces, and a sense of awe and spectacle directed at collective organisation (but also intimidation) carefully orchestrated in the shape of a state-based religious order. Fearful of a priesthood in control of supernatural powers, and awed by the magnificence of courtly manners, local rulers and potential opponents tended to subject them-selves to order. State religion and what social scientists and students of geopolitics call 'ideology' performed much the same work as military armies of conquest at a fraction of the cost. Mired in doubt, Atahualpa hoped his gods were more powerful than those of the strange foreign-ers he had just met. Exhausted, he went to sleep, only to be visited by powerful nightmares.

. . . and the Birth of Money

Had Atahualpa been able to understand De Soto's speech he would have concluded quite quickly that the Spaniards would fall neither for the magnificence of his court nor for the mysteries of the power-ful Sun-god. His priests traded in such secrets in order to maintain the political unity of the Inca empire. But the Europeans had gods of their own, and they were equally powerful. First was the aggressive Christian god who seemed to justify killing and waging wars in his name against peoples who had never heard of him before – precisely because they had never heard of him before. This was a god whose laws could be discovered, fixed and read on the book of Nature. Therefore, Nature being normative, there was no need for mysteries. Everything could be explained and justified in this sphere of existence. The rules of this world and everything within it could be established, for it was a *machina mundi*, a machine set in motion by the creator and presented as a gift to man, His creature. Second – and here the order does not necessarily describe the correct hierarchy – were silver and gold; a gift from the creator to those clever enough to discover and use the rules of Nature to pursue it and gain its use.

When Hernando Pizarro and De Soto returned to Cajamarca they went straight to the lodgings where Francisco Pizarro resided and described in detail the immensity of the riches they had seen in the camp of the Inca lord, his stature and majesty, measured in the enormous quantity of objects in silver and gold that he possessed, and described to the Governor (as they addressed Pizarro) how they had been offered a potent transparent drink in golden goblets so heavy they had to use both hands and all their strength to swallow the liquid without spilling a drop or falling from their horses. They also told Pizarro about the accuracy of Atahualpa's information about their expedition, and the size of his armies.

They mentioned as well how they had managed to scare some of his warriors. 'Atahualpa made an offer of alliance,' said Hernando Pizarro; 'our troops and his would march together and wage war on a provincial chieftain who persists in disobeying him.' 'It looks to me more like he was testing our hand,' interrupted De Soto, a more experienced soldier than the younger Pizarro. Eager to impress his older brother, Hernando continued: 'I told him no matter how many men he and his chiefs had, a few of us on horseback would be enough to kill any number of them.' 'And he laughed at the very suggestion,' interrupted De Soto once more. 'I had to impress him by mounting a mock attack on horseback,' he said. 'That scared a few of his soldiers, but the Inca remained solemn throughout. He demonstrated the majesty of a king. He was angry about the natives we killed. We should choose our path carefully here. If we had any doubts about the size of his empire before, they have been well put to rest today,' he concluded.

Annoyed at the constant interruptions of De Soto, whom he secretly hated, and sensing he could exploit the latter's emerging admiration for the Indian prince, Hernando Pizarro went on the offensive and described to his brother a rather grim scenario, spiced with the promise of riches galore. 'We only have two options,' he said; 'either we flee and let the savages know we fear them, or we join forces with them, as their Lord suggested, drink more firewater out of his golden goblets and enjoy his women, at least for the moment. Then, after amassing a small fortune out of the many objects of silver and gold we saw in his camp, having gained information about his mines, and having pleased ourselves to satisfaction, we wait for the right moment to turn his chieftains and enemies against him, as Cortés did in Mexico. Then we strike. Besides, there are at least forty thousand men camping out there. Do you really think we can run fast enough? I say we cheat him, earn his trust and then wait for the right moment to kill him and all of his most trusted men. The others will then fall in line with us, and you, my brother, will be the new ruler of El Dorado.'

'There is another alternative,' said De Soto. Reminding Francisco Pizarro and the other captains how the cunning Ulysses had vanquished a much bigger army by entering Troy in a wooden horse, he proposed setting a trap. 'Let us station the cavalry in three groups of around twenty men, hidden inside the buildings surrounding the plaza. At Pizarro's signal they will attack at the same time through the many doorways. Governor Francisco will be in the building at the entrance to the plaza with some foot soldiers and a few horsemen. Their job will be to seize Atahualpa, like Cortés did, as Francisco suggested, and make sure no harm comes to him.' Hernando Pizarro nodded his head, flattered by De Soto's acknowledgment of his strategic genius. 'But what do we gain from your scheme?' asked Governor Pizarro. Pleased with the cunning of his young captain, he wanted him to persuade the others by explaining that a bounty would be forthcoming and their lives spared. He was no stranger to the manoeuvre proposed by Hernando de Soto – they had used it together many times in the past, capturing lesser chiefs with varying degrees of success. 'A dead emperor would be useless to us, and might provoke the Indians to kill us instantly. We do not know if another one of them will take his place immediately. We shall keep him alive and ask for ransom. We will free him once we reach the coast of Tumbez and have sailed safely back to Panama. In this way, not only can we guarantee safe passage for ourselves, we will also make each other immensely rich.' The scheme seemed to put to rest some of the doubts expressed by the captains, and the promise of gold captivated them, but in their hearts the soldiers and financiers of this private army could not contain their fear. Not knowing what to expect from Atahualpa and his men, they, too, starting with Francisco Pizarro himself, were visited that evening by nightmares.

On the morning of 16 November 1532, Pizarro distributed his men, together with four cannons and nine old harquebusiers, in accordance with the plan. The firing of the artillery would be the signal for the all-out attack. While the Spaniards waited nervously in their hideouts, in the Inca camp the lancers and chiefs were also busy making travel preparations. Only the day before Atahualpa had been informed of the capture of his brother Huascar in the south. As soon as he dealt with the foreigner bandits he could head back to Cuzco and celebrate his victory in earnest. Decades of peaceful rule and expansion lay ahead. The spies he had sent to Cajamarca early in the morning had come back and reported that the Spaniards were hiding in the stone houses out of fear. 'Many urinated themselves without noticing it, out of sheer terror of the Sun-god,' they said. Atahualpa smiled. He was pleased. The strategy taught him by his ancestors had worked out once more. Wearing a soft vicuña-wool tunic and the golden garments of war, he climbed on to his litter and headed towards Cajamarca. Ahead of him, the Spaniards saw what looked like phalanxes of Spartan soldiers in golden armour, sending shining rays of light against the midday sunshine.

Having entered the main square surrounded by thousands of his brightly attired soldiers, the ruler of the Inca called out to the Spaniards, ordering them to show themselves. Two of them, a friar and the native translator of the day before, came out of their hiding places and made their way to Atahualpa's litter. In an almost uncanny repetition of the events of the previous afternoon, an unintelligible formula called *requerimiento* – a legal-theological summons which called for the Indians to submit to the divinely ordered authority of the King of the Romans and of Spain – was read to Atahualpa by the friar from a small book decorated with something that looked remarkably like the Southern Cross that was visible in the night sky, followed by an invitation to meet Pizarro inside one of the buildings (where, the friar knew, it would be easier to capture Atahualpa) and another atrocious translation by Felipillo. Intrigued, the Inca asked for the book to be shown to him. These men, who did not know how to read a *quipu*, shouted at bound pieces of white cloth inscribed with small black symbols. Unimpressed, he threw the Bible on the floor and responded to the friar's *requerimiento*: 'I will not leave this place until you return all that you have stolen. Do you think I don't know how you have behaved on the road? I welcome you gracefully and allow you to climb up the Inca road. How do you respond? By killing my chieftains and robbing their storehouses of their cotton and their temples of their gold and silver. You shall return it all to me, or you shall pay!'

With a gesture, Atahualpa ordered his men to prepare for battle, while the friar, Vicente de Valverde, ran back to Pizarro's quarters urging him to proceed with the attack. 'These are not men, but dogs who reject the things of God!' he shouted at the soldiers, clutching his crucifix. Pizarro signalled to the artillery to open fire. The roar of cannons and harquebusiers, and the sight of bodies, stone and metal flying through the air, stunned Atahualpa's warriors. Calling on St James, as they had done when expelling the Muslim infidel from the Iberian Peninsula, Hernando de Soto, Hernando Pizarro and the other captains directed their horses at the phalanxes of lancers. Suddenly, having believed he had the foreigners cowering in a few buildings, Atahualpa realised he had fallen into a trap. Meanwhile, Pizarro and his twenty men, arming themselves with shields and angling their steel lances and daggers in an attacking formation similar to that adapted by Roman legions, advanced towards Atahualpa's litter. Pizarro himself abandoned the thick coat of armour and, brandishing his sword, slashed, stabbed, beheaded and hacked his way through until, at the foot of the Inca's litter, he reached out with one arm and in the name of St James pulled Atahualpa out and rushed him back to one of the buildings, helped by De Soto's cavalry. Like so many horsemen of the Apocalypse, the other captains continued to pursue their foe down the valley and killed as many natives as they could, after one of the walls in the central square gave way under the pressure of thousands trying to flee and save their lives or to mount a counter-attack.

The counter-attack never came. Instead, the next day the Spaniards received an offer: 'Give me a year,' Atahualpa told his hijackers, 'and I will give you a room full of silver and gold.' At that point Hernando de Soto and Hernando Pizarro, who had been sent to explore the camp of the escaping Inca army, came back with an astonishing treasury of objects of silver and gold: 'monstrous pieces, large and small dishes, pitchers, jugs, basins, and large drinking vessels and various other pieces, which Atahualpa said came from his table service, and that his Indians who had fled had taken a greater quantity more'. All in all, more than eighty thousand pesos of gold, seven thousand pesos of silver and a dozen emeralds the size of a clenched fist. The sight of such treasure amazed Pizarro and his men, and confirmed to Atahualpa that these eaters of silver and gold would spare his life and go away if he managed to satisfy their hunger.

But Atahualpa did not understand that the thirst and hunger of these men was insatiable, for it could last forever. A Mayan tale has it that when men were first created, unlike all the other animals they had a hole where a heart should have been. Nothing could ever fill this hole. In hindsight, the story seems to prophesy the coming of men from the emerging nations of sixteenth-century Europe. They liked Atahualpa's tableware not because it was shiny, luxurious and impressive, but, rather, because everything else could be transmuted into the materials the goblets and plates were made of, and this process could go on for ever, or at least for as long as people continued to believe in the seemingly supernatural powers of money.

It is no coincidence that Atahualpa's tableware happened to be made of exactly the same rare materials from which money was made in the Old World. Silver and gold could take the place of all the things that, in the form of commodities, moved through the ever-expanding circle of trade driven by market forces – from the ports of Canton in China and Calcutta in India, to the Levant and the capitals of Europe – now also in the Americas. Silver and gold are special commodities because they function as a measure of value and therefore also as a medium of the perpetual movement of all other commodities in the circle of exchange. This movement is perpetual because the alternating flow of sale and purchase can first be represented in the minds of those who participate in it as a sign or an abstract symbol, and then inscribed, incarnated or represented in the incessant turnover of solid silver and gold serving as money.

It is like alphabetic writing or language: we represent our exchanges with the surrounding environment and other people in a series of abstract signs that by themselves would perhaps mean nothing, but acquire their proper significance once they are set in relation to all other symbols, and then inscribed on solid surfaces. Just as Pizarro had understood little of the

size and communal bonds uniting the Inca empire, so Atahualpa failed to
grasp the secret behind alphabetic writing, remembering and conveying
information by looking at symbols inscribed on a solid surface. To him
it all seemed like crazy talk, the mad performance of uncivilised, bearded
men, incapable of using the *quipus*, who instead spoke to themselves by
looking at white pieces of cloth filled with doodles, traces and scratches.

The very idea that such traces were graphic signs that, inscribed upon
a solid surface, shared significance and value, the fruit of men's common
efforts, and which it was then possible for someone to hoard or accumulate, was completely alien to Atahualpa. Similarly, he could not understand that the materials of which his tableware objects were made formed
the basis upon which the men and women of Renaissance Europe fixed
common value. He could not fathom that such materials were the site
of a veritable transformation, not unlike an alchemical transmutation or
a metamorphoses, by means of which the movement of commodities
becomes an end in itself, rather than merely the means to satisfy certain
needs, and therefore potentially infinite.

Accumulation made possible a new historical age in world economic
evolution. The discovery of gold and silver in Latin America, the
enslavement and entombment in mines first of the native population
and then of black peoples commercially hunted in Africa, and the beginning of the conquest and plunder of the Orient, attended its birth. As
the treatment of all of earth's resources – gold, silver, sugar, dyes, water,
oil – turned them into commodities which could be traded from hands
in which they have no value to hands in which they have value, the
product of one region of the world replaces that of another. This change
requires money, not only in its material aspect – silver and gold that we
can use to exchange for another commodity, a precious metal we see
and touch, and hold on to – but also its formal aspect, the social fact that
the other commodities, through their prices, relate themselves to gold
and silver while the latter embodies that social connection, which can
then be held on to, privatised, and accumulated.

With the extension of commodity circulation to the Americas, Africa,
India and China, aided and abetted by the extension of the money economy, the world became one. It also became one and the same story of

invasion, plunder and misery, repeated without end, for the original peoples of Latin America and elsewhere. They became the wretched of the earth. The unequal distribution of forces that attended the wars of conquest between the invaders and the invaded in the battlefields of North and South America served as a prelude to the inequality of exchange and rent distribution among the peoples and nations of the earth. But it is difficult to say which inequality, used as a weapon, caused more misery. As the Lakota chief Red Cloud put it to the head of one of the reservation agencies in nineteenth-century America: 'of all the weapons you have mobilised against us, you are the ones we have always feared the least'.[13]

American peoples were conquered and colonised within a process driven by Europe's need for gold and silver. To keep the money in circulation it was necessary to stimulate world capitalism 'in the hour of its birth'. A new class of men took control of the cities, founded banks and corporations, and cut down the size of the world to fit their expectations. Many of these men, Spanish, Dutch, British, who dreamt of El Dorado and went on to realise that dream, acquired their vision and the capital to make it happen in the silver mines of the Americas and in the circuits of illegal and legal trade that the flow of silver and gold helped create in the Caribbean. These same men, the first bankers, investors and financiers, produced and exchanged merchandise, conquered new markets and established new states, often with the help of private armies.

Among them was Francisco Pizarro, conqueror of the Inca empire, who first heard of the legend of El Dorado while accompanying the Spanish explorer Vasco Nuñez de Balboa in the first sighting of the Pacific Ocean by a European. Almost immediately he deduced that to cross to the Pacific from the Atlantic and sail south held the promise of untold riches. He founded a company under the auspices of the Spanish crown, struck silver and gold, and together with his small group of armed entrepreneurs created a kingdom of his own – perhaps the first truly mercantile capitalist state in history. He built this kingdom upon the ruins of the Inca civilisation he helped destroy. Later on it was the turn of William Paterson who, in the eighteenth century, heard of the legend while making his fortune in the Caribbean as a smuggler. He too had the vision of a crossing between the Atlantic and the Pacific in Panama, as the key to becoming master of the universe. He too set up an investment company with which to finance a small band of colonisers, grab and occupy an extension of land in what is now the border between Panama and Colombia, and realise his grand scheme. As we shall see in the next chapter, although the play did not go in accordance with the designs of its author – plays rarely do – he laid the groundwork for the complete reordering of the world in centuries to come. Rising from apparent failure in Panama, Paterson went on to found the Bank of England, and was central to the consolidation of Scotland and England into a united kingdom.

Following in the footsteps of these men, and modelling their own schemes upon their forerunners', often without knowing it, bands of armed entrepreneurs known at the time as filibusters would set out from the American south and eastern coasts to Panama and other places in Latin America. Usually with the financial support of railroad or shipping tycoons and other investors from the east, they would move west and south, in and around Indian lands and emerging polities in North, Central and South America, giving shape to a new country – the United States – in the process, and to a new chapter in world history. It would be based on the notion that a manifest destiny would drive the former colonial settlement to the position of global power enjoyed by Spanish and British colonisers in previous centuries. That notion accompanied the march of filibusters to what are now Mexico, Honduras, Nicaragua, Panama and Colombia, and gave rise to the doctrine named after US president James Monroe and its corollaries. It provided confirmation, in the eyes of the recently formed Latin American republics, of the Liberator Simón Bolívar's grim prophecy about a nation 'there in the north, at the head of this continent . . . very hostile and capable of anything'.[14]

What started as private enterprises, away from, and sometimes even against, the strictures of state policy – as was the case of the conquistadors' mistreatment of Indian populations, Paterson's adventurism, or US filibusterism in the Americas – quickly became identified with it. This is because the basic mission of such pioneers, adventurers and bankers was to open the gates to the flow of resources so that their emergent

European nations could accumulate them. In the process the economic structure of the former Spanish colonies was subordinated to an external market where profit and geopolitical power were being concentrated. At work were the dynamics of supply and demand in the emerging world money economy.

From the sixteenth century and until at least the early nineteenth century, the flow of Latin American silver and gold was nearly constant and was of consistently high quality. High-quality silver and gold coins were in extraordinary demand among several groups that were coming together at the time – merchants involved in long-distance trade, international merchant bankers who sought profits from the arbitration of differentials in silver/gold ratios, states that needed precious metals for their own minting and for payment of armies, and producers of commodities with high international demand. Silver mines in central Europe were very productive until the early sixteenth century, and, in Asia, Japan provided India and China with most of the silver they needed until 1640. But Latin America produced more silver, of higher quality and for longer periods of time, than any other region in the world. Those sources were under the control of the Spanish crown from the sixteenth century onwards until the end of the first third of the nineteenth century. Because of this, and given the financial needs of the administration of the Habsburg Empire in Spain, Flanders and Germany, which were highly cyclical during the sixteenth and seventeenth centuries, mainly as a result of the financial requirements of European wars, the share of the metropolitan state increased over time.

For instance, during the Thirty Years War in Europe, between 1616 and 1648, the transfer of Peruvian silver to Spain – and hence to Spanish armies in Italy, Germany and Flanders – was, according to the calculations made by economics historians, 'truly astonishing'.[15] At the end of the eighteenth century, when the Spanish crown became involved in successive international wars against Great Britain (1763–7, 1779–83, 1796–1803), France (1793–5, 1808–14) and also in southern Italy and the Philippines, the demands of the Madrid treasury increased, and colonial administrators were instructed to remit as much fiscal surplus as possible. 'Bourbon Mexico alone was obliged to send 250 million silver pesos of net fiscal surplus abroad between 1760 and 1810,' writes historian Carlos Marichal.

To these transfers connected to imperial competition and warfare one must add the shipments and private remittances of silver and gold from Latin America to Europe and elsewhere tied to international trade, imports paid in silver and gold, 'which in turn became the chief exports of the colonies for three centuries', as Marichal points out. The *flotas* from Seville and Cádiz included manufactured goods and luxuries from Italy, France, Flanders and England, as well as from China and India. A smuggling business emerged parallel to the more legal trade and competition for sea power in the Caribbean, led by British, Dutch and French adventurers and navigators, pirates and naval officers working for the state or private companies and contrabandists. It is estimated that by 1680 France provided some 40 per cent of the products that circulated in the Caribbean region, followed closely by Britain and Holland. Significant flows of silver pesos and gold went to the islands of the Caribbean, and were actively sought after by English and French pirates from the early seventeenth century onwards. Men like Francis Drake, Edward Vernon and William Paterson made their fortunes and laid the groundwork for their political and military carriers in such environments.

Finally, the existence of a dual monetary system that reflected the stratification of the economy and the society in the colonial settlements of Latin America helps to explain why Spanish America, and in particular the popular sectors, suffered the consequences of the emergence of a vast, global money system. On the one hand were small but powerful miners, great merchants and large landowners in control of labouring populations, highly monetised and with their eyes firmly set on the metropolis rather than on the development of the places they inhabited. On the other hand was most of the rest of society, living on the fringes of the monetary economy, getting by, participating extensively in barter and persisting forms of pre-Columbian exchange, and often falling into debt peonage. This made for low levels of local savings and capital.

Latin America supplied in precious metal exports at least four times the value of slaves, textiles and all the other manufactured and luxury goods it imported. In the process, international and internal divisions were created, marred by inequality of rent extraction and control over resources. Each region became identified with what it produced, and each produced what Europe wanted of it: Peru, Mexico and Bolivia were silver, Brazil and Colombia were gold, Venezuela became cacao, Chile was identified with copper and the Caribbean with sugar. Each product became 'a vocation and a destiny'.[16]

3

The Dream of the Conquerors

The Mountain that Eats Men

When Atahualpa promised Pizarro a roomful of gold, he also disclosed crucial information about the extent of the Inca dominion and the existence of mountains of silver and gold to be found further inland. He thought this would satisfy the thirst and hunger of these gold-eaters, who would then leave for good and allow him to govern his empire in peace. He was wrong. For once silver and gold serve as money, accumulation becomes potentially infinite. Silver and gold money appear thus not only as mere signs but also as wonders. Christopher Columbus put it this way when he wrote in a letter of 1503: 'its owner is master of all he desires'. With the possibility of keeping hold of value, embodied in gold and silver, controlling the sources of these precious materials, and the workforce needed to maintain the sources of high-quality metals in constant production, all of the requirements for the existence of a truly global monetary system were in place. Atahualpa did not see it, but his people would soon understand that this had been the subject of his nightmare. Not even a mountain would fill the hole in the hearts of the eaters of silver and gold.

When Francisco Pizarro first arrived on the coast of Peru, around 1528, a powerful leader named Wayna Capac ruled the vast swathes of the Land of Four Quarters. Having refined the spectacular displays and forms of political control first used by the Chimor dynasty of the older city state of Chan Chan, the Inca people had transformed their remote settlement, located on the shores of Lake Titicaca into a vast centralised union. The Inca 'empire' brought together a wide variety of communities into a territorial unity that became known as Tawantisuyu – the land of four quarters.

They had achieved all this in a mere sixty years. According to the evidence found in numerous archaeological digs, around 9000 BC the ancestors of all these peoples had become domesticated and were cultivating potatoes as far inland as present-day northern Bolivia. They farmed little and relied mostly on fish brought to the shores of South America by what we know today as the Humboldt Current, while developing a symbiotic relationship first with communities that did farm in the lowland valleys, and then in the uplands, using irrigation canals and terraces, which they devoted mainly to cotton. Some time around 3000 BC they were building sunken plazas, celebratory monuments, carving staff gods, and possibly even genetically engineering potatoes, and engaging in massive engineering projects that transformed the landscape, from the Amazon to the Andes, and from there to the plains of North America, into a man-made, sustainable environment that could also serve as the basis for a thriving population. All this is evidence of an organised civilisation that grew accustomed to engaging in cooperative efforts, reinforced by government-led forms of positive incentivising that required and developed a deep sense of memory – demonstrated, as we have seen, in the primitive computer-like recording system based on textiles known as *quipus* – but also a sense of the mysterious and the spectacular.

The sense of the mysterious and the spectacular found in the use of metals such as silver and gold both an appropriate base and a vehicle. It is said that around 1520 Wayna Capac left the capital, Cuzco, in order to seek relief for his poor health. While travelling to the thermal springs near Cantumarca, his eyes lit upon the perfect cone of the Sumaj Orko – the beautiful hill – which commoners also called Ccolque Porco – the generous hill – because of the considerable amounts of silver discovered in its surroundings. He was not concerned with hoarding or using these metals as a means of payment. He preferred his craftsmen to hammer them into thin sheets or threads, to form these sheets around moulds, and weave the threads as if they were cotton so as to create fine ornaments and jewels, tokens of power and signs of affiliation.

In modern terminology, it was all about bling. And as every West

Coast rapper, New York socialite and East LA gang leader knows full well, if a piece of jewellery is to proclaim your status and the power of your clan, it had better be lustrous and shiny. Luminous gold and silver, which seem to resemble the sun and the moon and thus have the power to turn the wearer into the son of the sun or the daughter of the moon, are therefore preferable to dull tin, iron or copper. Craftsmen and gold- and silversmiths in the Andes developed techniques to strengthen soft gold and silver by mixing them with these other metals, mainly copper, heating the alloy and pounding it with mallets. In this way, they would make the shiny, thin pieces of alloy that formed the goblets from which Pizarro and De Soto drank, or the armour of the golden armies that Francisco Pizarro's men saw approaching Cajamarca. Mastering the forces of tension, these craftsmen were able to create strong sheets and ever finer threads of metal that would glitter, and allow artists to create impressive objects, from pectorals and masks for the women and men, to staff gods, and a full body of armour made out of gold and silver for a higher ranking officer and the ruler's personal army. One such suit of armour can be seen today on display in the Gold Museum of Bogotá, the capital of Colombia.

Wayna Capac was as awestruck by the sight of the Sumaj Orko as visitors to Potosí are today. The city has lost most of its colonial grandeur, and the few tourists who come here do so in order to contemplate the mountain or to participate in one of the many rituals that take place at night within the bowels of the mountain in order to placate its anger. The perfection of the Sumaj Orko suggested to Wayna Capac that here too luminous metals might be hidden. 'Climb the hill,' he ordered his men, 'and probe it carefully, using your stone and wood and flint tools.' His miners had barely begun to open the veins of the mountain when a frightening noise came from the inside. 'Stop at once!' said the god of the mountain. 'You do not rule down here. Perform the rituals each time you descend into the mountain. Only then will you know whether the forces of the gods who live in the caves will join yours,' said the voice. Then it warned them: 'but bear in mind that when you break the inside of this mountain, it will ask for sacrifice and retribution. The more you take, the more it will take in return. Take care of the mountain so that it will also provide for your children and their children. If you do not, if you take everything it guards, I shall curse your generations. Spare yourselves that horror and leave it to others, who will come here from afar after your people have gone. The silver of this hill and its damnation is destined for those other masters.'

The voice of the god of Ccolque Porco sounded like thunder. Wayna Capac listened. He renamed the mountain *Potojsi*, which indeed means thunder. His miners took what they needed for the craftsmen, but no more. Strict limits on what to take, when to take it and how to do so were set down and followed. Rituals were performed each time the miners descended into the bowels of Ccolque Porco, and payment was made. The tradition continues to this day.

The silver obtained was used only in the works and arts of the crafts-men, which revealed to all the magnificence and majesty of the sons of the sun and the daughters of the moon. And the mines continued to be used for this purpose, most of the mountain remaining almost untouched until the Spanish arrived in 1546, renamed it Cerro Rico Potosí, the rich hill of Potosí, and intensified mining operations with the intention of using the metals for another purpose altogether: the making of money.

It is said that an Indian named Huallpa was looking after his flock of llamas and had to spend the night at the foot of the hill. It grew very cold at night and Huallpa went into one of the caves where he lit a fire. Immediately, the walls of the cave shone like the tears of the moon goddess. He had found a vein of pure silver. When news of the discov-ery reached Spanish ears, rivers of silver followed. The event would forever change the global landscape, giving the world its first monetary system.

Only eleven years after Huallpa's discovery, Potosí celebrated the coronation of Philip II of Spain with a month of festivities which cost approximately eight million silver pesos. According to the German scientist and explorer Alexander von Humboldt, total silver production in Latin America, most of it coming from Cerro Rico Potosí, was esti-mated to have reached more than four billion pesos. A more recent esti-mate by economics historians Denis Flynn and Arturo Giráldez suggests that 'Spanish America was the source of approximately 150,000 tons of silver between 1500 and 1800'.[1]

Such a staggering level of production was due not only to the fact that the mines in Bolivia (and also those in Mexico) were among the richest in the world, but also that there were few labour constraints in the development of the mines. The mine of Ccolque Porco produced large quantities of precious metals in the sixteenth century, exploited some 13,000 forced labourers. Working in mines situated at over 12,000 feet above sea level was exhausting and working conditions, which involved the use of poisonous materials like mercury for the purposes of amalgamation, were very poor. Even in the eighteenth century, according to evidence carefully collected by economics historian Enrique Tandeter, approximately half the workers in the mines of Potosí were forced labourers, enslaved by Spanish officials through the colonial system of collective work known as *mita*. The visitor to present-day Potosí might find that the situation has not changed much over two centuries. Once called the beautiful mountain, the hill of Potosí became the mountain that eats men.

Rivers of Silver

The flow of silver to Seville and other European ports increased between 1550 and 1630, and then again between 1670 and 1810, and was sustained by a massive influx and sacrifice of labour. By the late sixteenth century the silver peso had become the most widely circulated currency in the world, and had found a place in the monetary language of most European nations. It was referred to as 'pieces of eight', stukken van achten, pièces de huit réaux, pesos Fuertes, piastres and patacones.

Confidence, quality and stability in production improved merchants' confidence, and so it was not long before the Spanish Habsburg Empire, which included the Americas, most of Europe and the Philippines, proclaimed the silver peso to be the very standard of measurement. In Antwerp, in present-day Belgium, then under Spanish control and possibly the most important port and financial centre in northern Europe of the age, the arrival of ever increasing amounts of American silver and gold was central to the success of the stock market. These metals served as the basis for the first international market of securities, among them the debt bonds of the Spanish monarchy called *juros* that were floated with increasing success from as early as 1553. They financed the military expansionism of Charles V, Philip II and Philip III, thereby becoming the money of armies on the march through northern and central Europe and decisively transforming in a relatively short period of time the political alliance between the kingdoms of Castile and Aragon into the leading power of Europe and truly the first world empire.

No less important for the history of globalisation is what occurred with private remittances tied to international trade after the introduction of the silver peso. Every year maritime convoys known as *flotas* would leave the ports of Seville and Cádiz for the Americas. Their cargo would include textiles from Italy, France, Flanders and England, but also silks and other goods originating from such far-flung places as the port of Canton in China. The famous Manila Galleon would also bring Chinese and other luxury Asian products directly to the Peruvian port of Callao via the Pacific route. In turn, the shipments that arrived in the Philippines in the Manila Galleon brought approximately two million silver pesos a year from Peru and Mexico, and from the Philippines to Canton. This exchange remained virtually unaltered until the early nineteenth century. Historians and economists calculate that over the course of the eighteenth century approximately five hundred million silver pesos entered China either via the Manila and Indian Ocean routes or through Europe. More or less a third of the total production of Mexican and Bolivian silver in that century ended up in Chinese coffers.

In the case of India, cotton and silk from Madras, Bengal and elsewhere was sent to Europe and also to other markets in the Levant and other parts of South East Asia. Many of these products were then re-exported from Manila and other places to Spanish America. And the majority of them were paid for with silver coins and gold from Mexico, Potosí and Colombia. The Dutch East India Company would send cargoes of silver pesos to Calcutta in order to pay for local cloth, which was then re-exported to South East Asia in exchange for pepper and other spices. Historian Carlos Marichal comments, based on the work of economics historian Om Prakash, that India's hunger for Spanish American silver is explained by the need to keep up production of cotton textile goods in Mughal India, much in demand in Europe before the industrial revolution. Unsurprisingly, silver and gold were also used as currency among Indian merchants and merchant bankers, for ornaments, and for the decoration of temples, just as in Catholic Spain. Tourists today look at the magnificence of the Catholic temples of Seville, their walls and altars almost entirely covered in silver and gold, without realising that all of it came from the mines of Mexico and Bolivia.

In India and China, silver was hoarded by a considerable percentage of the population as a secure way of saving money in an economy where savings and deposit accounts were largely absent. Given the size of the population in both countries, it is hardly surprising that the market effects led to a considerable and durable demand for silver. Such a demand remained constant and continued into the early twentieth century.

A New World Emerges

The case of the British colonies that later became the United States is no less intriguing. As we saw in the previous chapter, trade in the Caribbean was oiled by the flow of silver pesos. Smuggling circuits extended from Caracas to Cartagena, from Veracruz to Havana, from Potosí to Panama, and from there to San Juan in Puerto Rico to Florida. The Spanish Viceroyalty of Mexico, for instance, directly financed with silver pesos the administrative apparatuses of Cuba, Santo Domingo, Puerto Rico, Trinidad and Florida. French, British and Dutch contrabandists, smugglers and others traded within a circuit that connected the coastal areas of Latin America's mainland with the islands of the Caribbean and the south of the present-day United States.

The steady network of exchange quickly extended north of the coast of Florida and into the thirteen colonies of North America. People and ideas, not just silver and luxury goods, circulated within such networks. When in 1741 the British-held Fort St George, then the most prominent building in the city of New York and a key British military garrison in the north-east, was blown up, among the conspirators were two Spanish-speaking 'Latino Negroes'; they were possibly runaway slaves from Cartagena who expected war to be declared between Britain and its imperial enemies, France and Spain in particular. The conspirators were counting on the Spanish American Armada in Cuba, or the French, to attack British positions. They would assist them in taking the city. That would give them a better chance of freedom.

It was widely known at the time that the Spanish king had promised liberty to the slaves of English masters through royal decrees, or *cédulas*, in 1733 and 1740. Such legal documents promised both limited and full freedom to anyone who escaped from an English settlement to a Spanish one. Spanish American officials in New Spain, as Florida was then known, had complied with His Majesty's demands by establishing a village for runaway and freed slaves in the northern part of their colonial settlement called Gracia Real Santa Teresa de Mose. Hundreds of runaways, mostly from the Carolinas, settled there and created a buffer zone against English attacks from the north. Stories circulated in the ports of Anglo-America about the Spanish encouraging the Maroons of Britain's Caribbean colonies, chief among them Jamaica, to revolt against the British colonists. 'It was an accident of history, though a fateful one, that Afro-Cubans and Afro-Jamaicans conversed about freedom in New York in 1741,' according to Marcus Rediker and Peter Linebaugh. Furthermore, historical accounts state that Spanish officials deliberately planned to use agents such as Hispanic sailors to foster slave revolt in English possessions in North America in the 1740s. Historians relate how Juan Francisco de Guemes, Governor-General of Cuba, wrote to Manuel de Montiano, his counterpart in Florida, about an imminent military action involving some three thousand Cuban soldiers against North or South Carolina between April and June 1742, unleashing a force of 'negroes of all languages' to 'filter through the countryside, promising land and freedom to the slaves of English masters and inciting revolt throughout the province' that, hopefully, would extend all the way up to New York.[2]

'At the heart of the New York Conspiracy of 1741 lay a love story,' write Rediker and Linebaugh. It involved John Gwin, an African American slave, and Margaret Kerry, a twenty-one-year-old Irish beauty. Margaret lived at John Hughson's waterfront tavern, where her lover, John, who was rumoured to work for his owner at Fort St George, joined her on many a night. Eventually she bore his child, 'whose colour was a matter of considerable gossip and debate around town'. Some said it was white, others insisted it was black. It was at Hughson's where the scandalous couple plotted what was later called 'the most horrible and destructive plot that was ever yet known in these northern parts of America'.

John and Margaret did not act alone. With them were Antonio and Juan, two Afro-Hispanic sailors quite knowledgeable about incendiary substances long used in the plundering and burning of cities through-out the Caribbean. They and a dozen others set fire to Fort St George on St Patrick's Day 1741 – the day on which the abolition of slavery is celebrated in Ireland. The fire extended to the governor's mansion, the chapel, the army barracks and the office of the general secretary of the province. No fewer than thirteen more fires would terrorise the inhabit-ants of the city in the weeks to come. The Afro-Hispanic sailors spoke constantly of an imminent attack by Spanish or French forces. These were the days when the merchant Robert Jenkins waved his severed ear before the members of the British Parliament, after his merchant vessel *Rebecca* was boarded by the Spanish ship *La Isabela*, commanded by Julio Fandino, who accused Jenkins of piracy and cut off his ear as punish-ment after threatening to do the same to the English king if he dared to show his face in Spanish waters. Affronted by such an insult, Parliament declared war on the Spanish Empire (the War of Jenkins' Ear, 1739–48). In 1740, the settlers of the colony of Georgia launched an attack on the Spanish province of St Augustine in Florida, supported by British naval forces. The attack failed, and the British forces, commanded by James Oglethorpe, withdrew to Georgia and began to prepare for a retaliatory Spanish assault.

But by far the largest action in the course of the so-called War of Jenkins' Ear was the attack launched by British admiral Sir Edward Vernon in March 1741 against the port of Cartagena de Indias on the Caribbean coast of present-day Colombia. Vernon was already famous for having captured Porto Bello, a silver-exporting town on the coast of Panama. Like Balboa and Pizarro before him (and as William Paterson and Theodore Roosevelt after him), Vernon had seen that the occupation and control of the isthmus would give whoever controlled it a decisive commercial and military advantage. An attack would severely weaken Spanish finances and defences, and, if sustainable, it would give Britain the key to the gates of the Pacific and insurmountable sea and trade power. Vernon had overcome the city's poor defences in twenty-four hours and destroyed its fortifications, port and warehouses, but not before he had acquired for the British crown a sizeable fortune in Spanish American silver and gold. In 1740, at a dinner in honour of Admiral Vernon's marvellous achievement, the anthem 'Rule, Britannia!' was performed for the first time, and what is now one of the most popular streets in London was named after his victory.

The Battle of Cartagena, though, was an entirely different affair. The invading fleet was one of the largest in history (and remained so until World War II), numbering 186 vessels and almost 24,000 men under the command of Admiral Vernon and George Washington's half-brother, Lawrence. Like other American colonists, Washington had volunteered, lured by Vernon's promises of mountains of gold and silver, and perhaps a new expedition to take definitive control of the Isthmus of Panama. The battle against three thousand Spanish colonial soldiers and an unknown number of Indian and black sailors, defending the city from within the heavy fortification of San Felipe de Barajas under the leadership of the experienced, one-legged, one-eyed Spanish naval commander Blas de Lezo, lasted sixty-seven days and ended with the British fleet withdrawing in defeat, thanks in no small part to widespread yellow fever, dysentery and starvation. Not much remained of the occupation of Cartagena and the Panamanian dream of El Dorado after Vernon's defeat. News of the event was prevented from reaching the public, and Lawrence Washington renamed his Virginia plantation Mount Vernon in honour of his commanding officer. And for the members of the New York conspiracy, and New Yorkers in general, it was proof positive that a major conflict involving the Spanish and the French was inevitable. This was the backdrop against which they could carry out their plans.

But the conspiracy failed. The promised foreign assistance never materialised, and the uprising of Africans, Irish and Hispanics – which sought to turn the world upside down – died out. On six evenings in

July more than thirteen people of colour and four whites were hanged, among them John Gwin and Margaret Kerry, whose romance lived on beyond the gallows in local lore and legend. Others were exiled to Santo Domingo, present-day Haiti, and other parts of the Caribbean. The 1741 New York Conspiracy set the precedent for the series of riots, rebellions and disorder that plagued the thirteen colonies, and resonated with similar uprisings in the Caribbean and on the Latin American mainland – including the commoners' rebellion of New Granada in 1781, and the rebellion led in Peru by the descendant of the Inca rebel Túpac Amaru – all the way to the years leading to the American War of Independence and the Latin American wars of liberation.

The merchants, shippers, runaway slaves, commoners and sailors of the thirteen Anglo-American colonies created very stable and constantly active channels of commerce and exchange that reached the Caribbean and extended further into the Latin American mainland. Not only goods travelled such routes. When in 1781 the revolutionary commoners, or *comuneros*, of New Granada, today's Colombia, reached the village of Palos in the south of the country, they declared Túpac Amaru their leader, and called a constitutional convention which in form and result shows clearly the exchange of ideas and inspiration – as well as the actual efforts of people – that extended from Anglo-America in the north, through Panama and the Caribbean, and now well into the Andes. A kindred spirit of revolutionary freedom already united the inhabitants of the three Americas, and informed another variation on the dream of El Dorado: not power and riches, but the dream of Pan-Americanism. It is no coincidence that when, later, in 1824, the liberator of South America, Simón Bolívar, wrote a letter to the governments of the emerging republics asking them to meet and discuss the possibility of Pan-American union, he designated Panama as the most appropriate site for the reunion.

The activities of such Anglo-American merchants and sailors increased after the revolutionary war, and independence in 1783. Spanish Americans were in fact directly involved in some of the skirmishes and large-scale military actions that took place in West Florida and elsewhere. Bernardo de Gálvez, the energetic governor of Spanish Louisiana, for instance,

gained complete control over the lower Mississippi river by capturing
Fort Bute and forcing the surrender of British troops at the Battle of
Baton Rouge. Leading an army of Spanish American soldiers, Gálvez
sailed from Havana on 13 February with the aim of taking Pensacola.
Together with the reinforcements of a combined Spanish–French fleet,
by 1 May he had taken control of the entire British West Florida.

As a result of increased relations during and after the American
Revolution, silver pesos circulated more widely and soon became the
most important metallic currency in many of the thirteen colonies. During
the revolution the government of the Confederation of the United States
adopted the silver peso as the metallic reserve for its new paper currency
of dollars. In fact, the first issue of paper money made it clear that the
bills were to be measured against 'Spanish milled dollars', which of course
meant Mexican and also Bolivian silver pesos. After independence, the
monetary law issued by the US Congress on 2 April 1792 established that
the metallic currency known as the silver dollar would be equal in value to
the Spanish American silver *peso de ocho reales*, the famous pieces of eight.
Thus ended the story of the Spanish American origins of the nascent US
economy. The silver peso remained legal tender in the United States until
the first part of the nineteenth century.

Dreaming of El Dorado

The idea that rivers of silver and gold could be found by traversing the
narrow strip of land now known as the Isthmus of Panama is responsible
for some of the most remarkable events in the history of the Americas,
and indeed the world, as well as some of the darkest. It turned the strip
of land between the Atlantic and the Pacific Oceans into a transit zone,
a zone of colonising schemes and low-to-mid-intensity warfare, of invasions – Spanish, British, American – into a virtual non-place where
big dreams dissolve and everything that is solid vanishes into thin air.
The story of Panama, which in many ways sums up the history of the
modern world, is thus connected to the many attempts of interested
parties – Spanish, British, French, Americans, Latin Americans and now
the Chinese – to take advantage of a geographical feature turned, by dint
of magic and geopolitics, into a wonder.

This is the dream. The American Dream. But also the dream of Pan-Americanism. The dream of El Dorado, first conceived by Balboa and Francisco Pizarro. Nations have risen and fallen because of it; empires emerged while others crumbled and were consigned to history, either as memory or as aspiration. Men made their fortune there and lost it. All in pursuit of the same great idea: the dream of crossing from the Atlantic to the Pacific and heading south, establishing ports on both coasts, and transferring cargo between them to ignite a circuit of trade on a scale never before seen. It would save European ships the long and treacherous voyage around Cape Horn and the Indian Ocean that was necessary to reach the ports of India, China and the Philippines.

And as if the small distance between the oceans in this part of the Americas were not enough, the strip was already criss-crossed by communicating lines, swamps and rivers. British coastal raiders, most of them sailors, pirates and smugglers who had befriended the Indians or used Maroon slave villages as hideouts, which also doubled as trade entrepôts, had spotted a part of the isthmus where almost no accident of geography impeded the transit from one sea to another and where, to quote one of them, 'broad, low valleys [. . .] with no mountain range at all' extended from coast to coast. You could easily envisage a chain of boats passing people and goods from river to river or across the swamps, as the local Indians already did. The area could be fitted with a system of carriages, bridges and roads; you could imagine, in time, the building of a waterway. The result would be a series of truly global trading posts connecting north and south, east and west, which would rival any in the world. Whoever controlled the isthmus would possess 'the Gates to the Pacific and the keys to the Universe'.

This was the language used by William Paterson as he touted his grand investment scheme around England, Scotland and Europe. A businessman and an entrepreneur, Paterson, as well as founding the Bank of England in 1694, was also influential in the setting up of the Bank of Scotland. His 'Great Idea', as he called it, predated the construction of the Panama Canal by more than two centuries, and correctly charted the course of history for years to come. However, he was not the first to entertain the idea. In 1510, the Spanish conquistador Vasco Nuñez de Balboa ventured inland from the Caribbean coast and founded the settlement of Santa María La Antigua del Darién, following in the footsteps of his compatriot Alonso de Ojeda, who had established a nearby post at San Sebastián de Urabá, in what is now Colombia, a year earlier. Balboa's settlement proved more successful. The soil there was more fertile and the Indians less warlike. The colony prospered; alliances were made and agreements brought different peoples together. The place seemed destined by God to become a hub of global diplomacy. In the following months, the settlers and their allies saw the establishment of the first form of 'modern' democratic government – in the shape of a municipal council – anywhere in the Americas.

In 1513 Balboa travelled further inland into the Quaregua region, defeating or befriending the indigenous peoples of Careta, Comagre, Ponca and Tumaco. According to the account of Italian chronicler and member of His Majesty's Council, Peter Martyr d'Anghiera, it was here that Balboa became outraged by the carefree sexual practices he witnessed at the local chief's court. In his *De Orbe Novo* ('On the New World') Martyr described how 'Vasco discovered that the village of Quaregua was tainted by the foulest vice. The king's brothers and a number of other courtiers were dressed up as women and according to the accounts of the neighbours, shared the same passion. Vasco ordered forty of them to be torn to pieces by dogs.'[3]

The episode, involving cross-dressing and homosexuality among the Indians, became immortalised in one of the most widely reproduced images of the conquest. It can be seen nowadays by visitors to the New York Public Library; Balboa is portrayed setting his dogs upon terrified Indians, practitioners of what is now known among many indigenous peoples throughout the Americas as 'two-spirit' love. *Two-spirit* individuals – a contemporary term that harks back to the past and reclaims the respect these men and women were given by their peers among such pre-Columbian peoples as the Navajos, Cheyenne, Aztecs, Mayans, Quechuas, Moches and Tupinambá – were given the choice by their parents and elders to follow that path. If they accepted, they would grow up learning the customs and manners of the gender they had chosen. Often would become shamans, healers, matchmakers or soothsayers, revered as having powers beyond those of more ordinary medicine men and women. But for Balboa and most other Europeans of the Christian faith these were *berdajes*, an offensive term that meant little more than male prostitutes, and loose-living women, *de mala vida*. Certainly not all indigenous peoples held their two-spirited fellows in such high esteem, but nothing like Balboa's homophobic brutality seems to have existed.

It was from one of Comagre's two-spirit seers that Balboa learned of the existence of 'another sea' where untold riches were to be found. Upon observing the Spaniards squabbling over the quantities of stolen gold ornaments they were being allotted, the seer, who may have been Comagre's first son, Panquiaco, knocked over the scales used to measure gold and shouted at them: 'if you are so thirsty for gold that you leave your lands in order to wreak havoc in those of others, I'll tell you how to get to a place where you can quench that thirst'. He then added an ominous warning addressed to Balboa himself, 'as for you, you will die before realising your dream, killed by one of your own men. He will enter the city of the people who use gold powder to cover their faces, drink from golden goblets and eat from silver plates, not you.'

Among the men who accompanied Balboa during their first crossing of the isthmus, and one of the first Europeans to see the Pacific Ocean, was Francisco Pizarro. Over the next five years Pizarro would become a close associate of Pedrarias Dávila, who in December 1518 instructed Pizarro to arrest Balboa personally and bring him to stand trial. On 15 January 1519, Balboa was duly sentenced to death by decapitation. Since then, Indians and locals have spoken of *el fukú del conquistador*, the damnation of the conquistador, and the lure of the isthmus, a curse handed out to each and every man who comes to the region with the intention of bridging the land between the two coasts, and opening up the way towards the seas of silver and gold that flow from the other side.

And if the life story of William Paterson and those who succeeded him is anything to go by, the power of the Indians' *fukú* is beyond doubt. An adventurer almost by nature, Paterson travelled widely, risked his life in exotic locations and specialised in devising grand schemes that often translated into profit and political gain not only for himself but also for the British nation. He was born in the small hamlet of Skipmyre midway between Dumfries and Lochmaben, in Scotland. Like Balboa and Pizarro, he was the son of farmers. At seventeen he left home for Bristol and from there he went on to the Bahamas. It was in the West Indies that he fell for 'the lure of the isthmus', the cursed venture to cap them all. While he thought of ways to bring his latest grand scheme to fruition, Paterson involved himself in the bountiful commerce that took place between the Caribbean islands and the colonies in North and South America. He was part of a new race of men, born in the wake of the English Revolution and the Restoration, who were preparing the world for the onset of industrialisation and empire.

From the 1640s to the early 1650s, England's new coming men had been taking steps to extend and consolidate their commercial and military power in the Atlantic. It was quickly understood that the two often coincided. The Navigation Act of 1651, intended for the merchant shipping industry, and the Articles of War of 1652, addressed to the Royal Navy, both of them reaffirmed by the Restoration government after 1660, signalled England's intention to challenge the French and the Dutch, and ultimately the Spanish Empire, for maritime and commercial supremacy in the Atlantic. But if Cromwell must be seen as the founder of the modern English maritime state, and Charles II and William III as the bearers of its promise, it was men like William Paterson who realised it.

He, and others like him, did so by carving up and inhabiting a grey area between ambition, patriotism and lawlessness that became a concrete space beyond the mainland, in places like the Caribbean, the Isthmus of Panama and elsewhere. Small wonder, then, that among the founding fathers of political arithmetic, or economics, as we now know it, one often finds men of the sea. William Petty, for instance, who wrote the *Political Anatomy of Ireland* for Charles II, was once a cabin boy and also served in England's conquering army in Ireland. As a cartographer of confiscated lands in the Down Survey of 1654, he observed the crucial importance of what was later called 'the Holy Trinity' by one of his followers: land, labour and international connections. Upon this insight, early economists converge with the magical wisdom of indigenous Bolivians, Peruvians and Ecuadorians. In turn, William Paterson, who also worked as a cabin boy on ships bound for the Caribbean, learned in the West Indies that the relative freedom of the offshore paradise would serve the ambitious adventurer ready to take his place in the new network of global connections.

To expand them would immediately increase profits everywhere. 'Do open these doors,' he would later tell the Parliament of Scotland, 'and trade will increase trade, and money will beget money, and the trading world shall no more want work for their hands, but will rather want hands for their work.' With these words, Paterson prefigures the thoughts of Adam Smith and David Hume. In the early 1690s he wrote *A Brief Account of the Intended Bank of England* for William III; in July 1694 the Bank of England was established by Royal Charter and Paterson became one of its Directors. He was removed a year later as a result of some financial scandal.

Always a patriot, William Paterson saw the connection between his own interests and those of his country. As far as he was concerned they were one and the same. In many ways then, he is the prototype of the men of destiny and progress who drive modernity and capitalism in all corners of the planet. He anticipates Ferdinand de Lesseps and Teddy Roosevelt. In fact, all three shared the same dream even though only one of them would accomplish it. They are characters in a play whose lines are repeated again and again, often without the knowledge of its actors. In this respect, Paterson also prefigures our contemporary over-lords and masters of the universe, the bankers, financiers and entrepreneurs, both in the size of their ambitions, which know no bounds, and in their capacity to wreak havoc on a scale previously unimaginable. Patriots they may be, but their only true home is Utopia. These are the true citizens of the world. Their life stories read like the abridged history of the planet, often condensed into one and the same place. One such place is Panama. It was here that the west was won. And it was here that the west won the rest of the world.

Paterson struck gold when the Scottish Parliament, not yet formally united with the English Parliament and often jealous of the new riches flowing to the English from the Atlantic trade, passed an act encouraging new settlements and actively calling for entrepreneurial investors and adventurous recruits to establish trading posts in the Caribbean and elsewhere. He rushed to Edinburgh, and, as Oxford historian Matthew Parker puts it, 'paraded his knowledge of the Americas and hinting that he possessed a great secret'.[4] The great secret was a location not far from where Pizarro and Balboa had unleashed their dogs upon those they saw as savages; Paterson told them that near the Isthmus of Panama were cities whose inhabitants drank from golden goblets and ate from silver plates. As always happens, there were those who objected, pointing out the lack of evidence and resources to undertake an enterprise of such a scale; but all this was to no avail, the government was sold on it. The Act of the Scottish Parliament establishing the 'Darién Company of Scotland trading to Africa and the Indies' was passed in June 1695, barely a year after the establishment of the Bank of England. They should be seen as bedfellows.

Up to that point everything seemed to be going quite well. But then, as so often happens in Latin American soap operas, the fine art of lobbying for special interests got in the way. William III, who in principle had supported both Acts, later recanted under pressure from the East India Company's lobby in the English Parliament. The latter firmly opposed the Scots' scheme, citing as reasons the protection of English monopoly and the threat of war with Spain. This meant that the important funds for investment raised in London and Hamburg, more than £300,000, were withdrawn. What followed was a story to be repeated by the French who, later in the 1880s, fell for the charms of Ferdinand de Lesseps, and turned the whole thing into an expression of nationalistic pride. The dream, first translated into a fraud, later becomes national interest. Scottish investors saw English rejection as an insult to the nation and the scheme as a matter of reinstating pride in the face of this and other adversities. Money came pouring in afterwards from all quarters and all levels of society. Without any difference of creed or class, craftsmen, servants and small traders, as well as merchants and aristocrats from places as far afield as Inverness, Inverurie, Kintore and Aberdeen raised £400,000 and committed themselves to taking part in the adventure. By now, it had become a national adventure in more senses than one: about half the country's available capital and a good number of its people had now invested in the scheme. The very future of the country was at stake.

On 26 July 1698 almost the entire population of Edinburgh took to the port to wave goodbye to the twelve hundred men and women from all over Scotland who embarked on the ships *Unicorn, St Andrew, Caledonia, Endeavour* and *Dolphin* bound for the land of plenty Paterson had promised. These large vessels were loaded with some of the finest goods produced in the country, mainly woollen cloth, shoes, slippers, stockings, hats, wigs and over twelve hundred leather-bound bibles printed in English. The passage was taxing. Around forty would-be colonists died before the ships dropped anchor off the coast of the Panamanian isthmus on 3 November 1698. They named it Caledonia Bay. Like Balboa's men, the Scots were pleased to find themselves among less warlike indigenous peoples; they should have known better. 'They're very free and not at all shy,' goes one account; 'they got drunk and lay on board all night'. The description is reminiscent of Columbus's account of his fourth voyage, which brought him to the Gulf of Urabá, not far from Caledonia Bay. Columbus also described how the 'not at all shy' indigenous peoples came on board, among them a group of barely pubescent girls who got the sailors drunk and danced for them half naked. Then, when the crewmen were insensible, the women and some warriors took them prisoner and ate them. Most contemporary readers acknowledge that Columbus's invention of cannibalism among the Indians of the isthmus has more to do with his own grievances and troubles with the Spanish crown than with the local inhabitants themselves. But it may have served the unsuspecting Scots with a warning of things to come. For the real cannibal in these lands was the mosquito.

After an auspicious beginning, things started to go badly wrong when many of the men and women contracted malaria and died. Among them was Paterson's wife. Initially, however, the settlement, baptised New Caledonia, and standing just opposite the shallow valleys allegedly connecting one coast to the other, thrived on the strength of alliances with the local peoples who saw the Scots as potential allies against their brutal Spanish masters and their plundering of the wealth of natural resources. 'The country is healthfull to a wonder,' wrote a settler to a friend in Boston, in a letter cited by Matthew Parker. 'The Weather is temperate,' it continues, 'if Merchants should erect factories here, this place will soon become the best and surest Mart in all America.' In that same document, the settler points out that there was one small problem: '. . . little Trade as yet; most of our Goods Unsold'.

By the time the Scots landed in the New World, the rebellious culture of 'free trade' whose emergence Paterson had witnessed had already developed into a collection of fully established and well-protected merchant monopolies. Trading routes were well patrolled by Spanish and British navies and their more shadowy allies, bandits and corsairs, the rude inheritors of Pizarro's band of armed entrepreneurs and precursors of the late nineteenth-century American filibusters and today's irregular armies or private security contractors. Monopolies, as the Scots learned to their dismay, were enforced at cannon point. Put another way, the more democratic diplomacy and solidarity that had gathered together merchants, adventurers, pirates, sailors and freed slaves was well on the way to being replaced by 'gunboat diplomacy'. A modern parallel might be the twenty-first-century drug barons and financial schemers working in the shadow of studiously indifferent states, protecting their monopolies over more or less the same routes, the same points of contact, and the same trading points and banking systems.

As soon as the Scots reached Latin America, they started to make enemies: the Spanish, the English merchants, the Dutch, the Indians, you name it. The English crown had issued orders to its governors in Virginia, New York, New England, Jamaica and Barbados forbidding them to trade with or supply provisions to the Scottish colonists. In addition to that the locals, who became the only alternative partners of the Scottish settlers, had little use for leather-bound bibles or wool and little time for anybody unwilling to help them stand up against their Spanish oppressors. From then on it was all downhill: food became scarce, yellow fever became widespread and took many lives, internal division and strife became rampant. In May, the rainy season filled swamps and marshes, and the mosquitoes multiplied a thousandfold. On top of it all, the Indians brought news of an impending attack by Spanish forces from the nearby San Felipe garrison in Cartagena. It was all over, and it was not long before the Scots recognised the gravity of their situation.

On 20 June 1699, after only seven months on the isthmus, the Scots abandoned the settlement at New Caledonia and left for New York. In the preceding months nearly four hundred colonists had died of hunger, yellow fever and dengue fever. No attempt was made to venture inland in order to find the shallow passage overland to the other sea and on to the land of untold riches on the other side. In fact, no such shallow passage existed – only marshes and swamps and clouds of mosquitoes. Two more attempts were made by the Scots to colonise Darién and open up the passage between the oceans to a whole new world of trade. They, too, failed, one as a result of an act of God, the other thanks to the King of England. When the third expedition arrived, the newcomers found some of their countrymen living among the indigenous peoples, who were still half naked but apparently much less inclined to follow their allegedly barbarous ways.

Less fictive was the strong will of the Spanish, determined to protect their supplies of gold and the route to Cartagena. By now convinced that the King of England would not send his navy to protect the colonists, the Spaniards made their move. The Armada made its appearance in Caledonia Bay. Divided and initially hesitant to abandon the strict puritan ethic that forbade war, the Scots at last found it in themselves to take the fight to the Spanish forces, which included a considerable number of mulattoes, zambos, negroes and mestizos. This was a truly global conflict, with peoples from virtually all corners of the world fighting on both sides. In hindsight, it may be seen as a sign of much interracial strife to come. For now, the Scots made some advances against their combined enemies and for a moment it seemed as though the tide had turned. Victory was short-lived, however. On 30 March 1700, the Spanish governor of Panama and Cartagena, after mobilising his naval fleet against New Caledonia and deploying forces from Panama City and Santa María del Darién, offered honourable terms of capitulation and gave the Scots fourteen days to leave. Some of them did; others stayed in the area, mingling with the local inhabitants or escaping to the *cimarronajes* or *palenques*, the Maroon villages set up by escaped slaves deep inland. On the journey north, most of the original vessels were wrecked and only 360 of the 1,300 who had arrived in the isthmus with the third expedition survived. Others were dispersed around the Caribbean. Paterson's grand idea ended up unleashing a catastrophe of hurricane-like proportions upon Scotland. His bold banking schemes had cost over two thousand lives and at least half of the savings of the entire nation. 'So many men and women died; everybody lost their lifetime earnings around here,' I was told by Sheila Scott, a domestic worker from a long line of domestic workers (once they would have been called servants), employed these days at Keith Hall House outside Inverurie, in Scotland, the magnificent family seat on what was formerly the estate of the Laird of Kintore and now belongs to bankers and oil companies. 'And yet, those who invented the whole thing bounced back in no time. It's all the same nowadays,' she said. Indeed, Sir William Paterson returned to Scotland to become a member of the Scottish Parliament, where he advocated union with England in exchange for a loan that could be used to compensate the otherwise disenchanted populous, or at least secure the support of those needed to pass the Act. Paterson proved to be not only a cunning businessman and negotiator; he also recognised the political power of money and its capacity for reinvention. Knowingly or not, he paved the way for the populist leaders of Latin America and elsewhere. His last banking scheme, a merger, became a reality with the Act of Union 1707. It is perhaps by sheer chance – or perhaps it is an example of something extraordinary – that the strip of land on the border between Panama and Colombia became the single most important cause of the creation of the United Kingdom. The moral? Beware of bold banking schemes.

Gold Rush

'So, am I to eat this mango on its own?' I ask Héctor. 'No way, *compadre*,' he replies, closing down his position in the market. I like that: 'his position in the market' sounds grand and sophisticated, as if we were in the City of London, on Wall Street or in one of the many investment banks that occupy the buildings in the upmarket parts of Panama City. 'Let's have a couple of rums at Diego's place,' he suggests. I grab today's newspaper. On the first page there is a picture of Sir Allen Stanford surrounded by the Stanford Superstars in Antigua, and another of his helicopter touching down at Lord's Cricket Ground in London. According to the paper, he has given himself up to the authorities after been accused of mass fraud. 'Which baseball team is that one?' asks Héctor. 'It's not baseball, it's cricket,' I say, as if I know the first thing about cricket. To make matters worse I try to explain: 'cricket is almost exactly like baseball, only you can score over a hundred or even a thousand runs'. 'I like it then,' he says. 'Yeah,' I say, 'you score by hitting a ball with a bat while the other team fields the ball trying to prevent you from scoring and puts your batting men out.' 'It's just the same,' says Héctor. 'But the fielders are not allowed to wear gloves,' I retort. 'Ah,' he says, 'it's like they used to play in Massachusetts.'

Now I know I'm in trouble; if he knows about the 'Massachusetts game' that means he's a real connoisseur and my bluff has been called. To divert Héctor's attention, I show him another picture of Stanford in the paper. In this he is laughing, surrounded not by the all-black Superstars but by an all-white troupe of very young and very good-looking women. All of them are looking at him. It is like the frontispiece of Thomas Hobbes' *Leviathan*. One of them is sitting on his lap. 'That's the wife of an English player,' I inform Héctor, 'like in the *telenovela*, they all go for the rich gringo; it says here that although he was married he fathered no fewer than five children by three women other than his wife.' Héctor replies: 'It's not that simple, *chico*. It's the same with the kids here getting into drug trafficking and all that. You get the money, the women, and the helicopter and everybody respects you. It's not just the money, it's the status.' I stand corrected. 'What I don't understand is that he's Texan but he likes cricket rather than baseball. How's that?' Héctor sees a story coming.

'Well,' I say, 'it all began with a great idea.' Stanford's first business was a chain of upscale gyms in Waco, Texas, not far from George W. Bush's ranch in Crawford. It didn't take off, so he went back to flipping burgers at a joint he had set up with his family. But that went bust, too. The money came from Allen's father, James, who owned an insurance company; nothing big, but enough to give him a head start. He lived with his mother, Sammie, who wrote a gossip column for a local newspaper south of Dallas. Like George W., he stumbled through education;

unlike him, he did not end up in some Ivy League university. He graduated in 1974 from Baylor, in Waco. He worked with his father at the company and married a pretty dentist named Susan. So far there is nothing remarkable about the Allen Stanford story. What is remarkable is how similar this story of humble origins is to that of so many bankers and their ilk. Like William Paterson, like James Cayne, the disgraced CEO of Bear Stearns, like 1980s trader Ivan Boesky, whom many believe was the inspiration behind the character Gordon Gekko in Oliver Stone's *Wall Street*, like David Murcia Guzmán, the Colombian financier whose story runs parallel to Allen Stanford's not only in terms of their common origins but also in time and space. 'Like your Pablo Escobar,' interrupts Héctor. I nod half disapprovingly.

'How did somebody go from Total Fitness Center to being a knight in the Caribbean? Jesus Christ! But, hey, you know, this is America. Anybody can be anything, I guess.' This is K. Paul Holt, a Waco businessman who had met Allen Stanford in the early days, cited by Bryan Burrough in an article in *Vanity Fair* in June 2009, just before Stanford handed himself over to the FBI. He's half right: it's not just America. What men like Paterson, Stanford and Murcia Guzmán have in common is the same geographic area. Paterson had the Bahamas and his Scottish investors in Panama; Stanford had Antigua and his Latin American investors; Murcia Guzmán had Panama, once again, and a considerable number of Latin American (mainly Colombian) investors perhaps not as rich as Stanford's but no less so than the Scots who invested in Paterson's scheme. That is the other thing they all had in common: the venture to cap all ventures. What do you do if you want to make big money and all that comes with it? Forget charisma and personality, or knowledge of highly sophisticated financial operations. Those things may help, but they are neither sufficient nor necessary. Like Paterson, Stanford and Murcia Guzmán, and Pablo Escobar as well, you go to the Caribbean. Then you become a pirate. Why the Caribbean? By now we know that is not mere geography. In addition to that there is also an X-factor, the dream that takes on a variety of names – 'gold rush', perhaps, or 'grand idea' – and transforms this place into a springboard for all sorts of enterprises. And yet, ultimately they all seem nothing but variations on the same theme:

Paterson had his 'grand idea' when he moved to the Bahamas. There he heard stories about rivers of silver and gold waiting for adventurous men to discover and exploit them. There were mountains of silver and rivers of gold in Bolivia and the Pacific coast of Colombia. But the real flow was the movement of goods and pieces of eight through the illegal circuits of banking and trade that emerged throughout the Caribbean and connected the islands with the coastal mainland in the north and the south, as minor European powers competed to skim the cream off the bounty appropriated in Spanish America. This is what transformed the Caribbean into an offshore paradise. And just as Paterson heard of it while stationed in the Bahamas during the late seventeenth century, so Allen Stanford had his epiphany in the late twentieth century, while taking a long vacation in the Caribbean during which he supported himself by giving scuba-diving lessons.

'It was beside a resort swimming pool,' writes Burrough, 'that Stanford met a charming European expatriate named Frans Vingerhoedt, who dazzled him with stories of the easy money to be made operating a bank in the Caribbean.'5 'My only flaw is that I dared to dream', said David Murcia Guzmán to a *New York Times* journalist during an interview at La Picota prison in Bogotá: 'what is criminal about dreaming?' he added. Murcia Guzmán's epiphany came to him as he stood atop a waterfall in central Colombia, contemplating suicide after his personal life and early business enterprises shooting wedding videos and casting aspiring actors – himself among them – came crashing down. He moved to a flophouse in the coca-growing southern region, where he was inspired by the autobiographies of Donald Trump, Warren Buffet and Arizona-born billionaire Rex Maughan. Like Stanford, he then set up a health and beauty outfit selling Maughan's Forever Living brand products. Following in the footsteps of the Mormon Arizona entrepreneur, he promptly established his own brand, DMG (his initials), which operated by dint of employing an army of independent contractors who were persuaded that they could also get rich by selling some 'sophisticated' financial products; this was exactly the same line used by Stanford to explain his operation to potential customers. And, just as in Stanford's case, therein lay the catch: as prosecutors in the cases of both Stanford and Guzmán have pointed out, a sales or investment network becomes a fraudulent one when it relies mainly on attracting new victims whose investments are used to pay off earlier investors, as in a Ponzi scheme.

According to one former employee of DMG, 'none of this would have been possible without the allure of and the cover provided by offshore porous financial systems and easy-to-get banking licenses'. 'And there is no better place to be introduced into such networks,' this employee said, 'than the coca-growing regions in the south of Colombia. Where do you think these people send their money? The idea that it gets buried underground like in some children's pirate tale is utterly ridiculous. Why would you do that when there are so many friends in Panama, Antigua or Montserrat you can count on?' The story went, he told me, that it was beside a swimming pool in the Pacific port of Buenaventura (celebrating the launch of an operation similar to his earlier 'solidarity selling network') that Murcia Guzmán first met a charming broker with connections in Panama and Belize who dazzled him with stories of how money could be multiplied tenfold by operating through the countries' porous licensing systems and weak financial regulations. 'There was talk of setting up an insta-bank,' he said.

Stories like this are difficult to verify, since they usually appear as a typical mix of fact and half-baked rumour; nevertheless, there are similarities with other stories, like those of Stanford and Paterson before them. These places are notoriously shady; and the reason for this isn't simply down to almost non-existent regulation, given that the latter is called for, almost encouraged, by the very principles that made 'free trade' a reality in this part of the world before it took over the entire planet. One can try and distinguish these cases from the 'normal' operation of the market, and, most certainly, since the market is a social creation, there is nothing in it that remains a fixed necessity; new and stronger regulation can be introduced, and calls for a renewed ethic of transparency and discipline against greed, arrogance and mendacity can be made. And yet, who can say that a strong, almost narcissistic, personality and laser-like focus on ambition, combined with the 'right' environment for profit-making and a crucial measure of freedom, are not precisely the way the market should operate? If there is such an alternative way of doing things, it seems not to exist either here, in the 'offshore' paradises of Panama or Montserrat, or anywhere else in the world. In fact, these places seem more like the very embodiment of the 'alternative', parallel to, and sustaining the more normal markets of, London and New York.

Montserrat is a British colony, Panama was a *de facto* American colony; some Panamanians, like Héctor, would actually challenge my use of the past tense. But the real point is that, as transit zones, these places give concrete form to the illusion of perpetual mobility – of goods, riches and people – that has become the only universal truth left standing in our world of manifold differences. Geography in and of itself is no guarantee of the importance of places like Panama or Montserrat as part of a world-wide network of transit. As the history of the isthmus shows, the flow of peoples and riches varies with changes in trading and navigation policy, and mainly as a consequence of struggles resulting from competition and differing degrees of productivity. In the case of Panama, after the failed colonial endeavour of the Scots and the successful attacks by the English in places like Porto Bello, Spanish navigation policy shifted back to the Pacific and the southernmost parts of the continent. The revolutionary wars of independence in the early eighteenth century briefly revived Panama's importance as a transit zone, inaugurating a series of counter-points between Mexico and Panama that would play a pivotal role in the failure of the Liberator Simón Bolívar's dream of pan-American integration, but on the whole the isthmus would have to wait until the end of the nineteenth century, after the announcement of the discovery of gold in California started an altogether new gold rush, to reclaim its position as the centre and potential capital of the world.

PART TWO

4

The Dream of Revolution

You Say You Want a Revolution

In order to keep the river of silver and gold flowing into Europe, slavery was revived in the New World. Of course, Africans did not choose to come to the New World. African rulers and European merchants who enslaved them, bought them and sold them, and the shipowners who transported them across the Atlantic 'Middle Passage' made that decision for them. Africans and Afro-Spaniards, including enslaved Muslim women, accompanied the first explorers and conquistadors to the Caribbean and the Andes in the 1490s and 1500s. Later on, when Spanish and Italian entrepreneurs established the first sugar plantations on the island of Hispaniola, and thereafter in Mexico, New Granada (Colombia), Venezuela and Peru, and sought to replace the dwindling indigenous populations working in the mines, their numbers increased sharply.

Planters and miners in Spanish and Portuguese America initially relied on Indian workers to provide labour for the plantations and the silver and gold mines. In the major centres of mining in the Mexican and Peruvian highlands most of the work was not carried out by African slaves. But the discovery of smaller yet significant gold deposits in Hispaniola, Cuba, Central America, Colombia and Venezuela, and the shortage of Indian workers, led to the use of African slaves more familiar with gold-mining techniques during the 1500s. Between 1500 and 1550, excessive labour, enslavement and new European diseases almost wiped out the native population. In Brazil, for instance, one-third of the Indians living in Jesuit missions in sugar zones died of smallpox and measles during the 1560s. The Portuguese started importing Africans to replace them.

From the early 1500s onwards, slavery became the backbone of the emergent world economy. The world's most important producers of silver and gold relied on work gangs of slaves in Brazil and in the Pacific coastal regions of Colombia, and on Indian forced labourers in Mexico and Peru, often managed by Indian, free black or mulatto overseers working for European masters who could not tolerate the intensely hot and humid conditions or the thin air of the highlands. And as the export-oriented economy diversified into a wider variety of economic activities, slaves participated in almost all of them alongside waged workers. A transport service industry developed alongside the export of primary goods, with slaves working as muleteers, porters and stevedores in rural areas, ports and cities, or as sailors, fishermen or oarsmen ferrying passengers up and down the Chagres river in Panama or the Magdalena river in Colombia. They were prominent in construction and manufacturing, too. Meat salting and drying factories in southern Brazil and Argentina, food-processing establishments in Lima, comb, furniture and hat factories in Buenos Aires and glassmaking industries in Rio de Janeiro made heavy use of slave labour. They also worked in artisan workshops producing shoes, clothing, leather goods and other items, some of them even rising to the level of master artisan and thus constituting a visible presence in the skilled trades, but also, prominently, in domestic service and street commerce. As such, slaves became a basic feature of Latin American family structure and the urban landscape. Slaves worked as cowboys, or gauchos, on cattle ranches in Argentina, Uruguay, southern Brazil and in the Venezuelan and Colombian plains, or *llanos*.

The more integrated into the international export economy a local economy, and the less available to meet local demands Indian labour, the greater the demand for African slaves would be. This explains why Central America or Chile imported fewer African slaves than Cuba and Santo Domingo; why in Mexico local slave owners imported an estimated 86,000 Africans as the native population fell from twelve million to one million between 1520 and 1620 and then, as the Indian population began to recover, slave imports fell despite rapid economic growth and demand for workers. It also explains why African slave populations tended to be located in regions associated with specific forms of work

– sugar cultivation and gold mining in the Caribbean or the Pacific coasts of Mexico, Colombia, Peru and Argentina, and urban slavery in Cartagena, Quito, Lima, Potosí, Buenos Aires and Montevideo – in countries where the bulk of the economic burden fell on Indians and Euro-Indian Creoles or mestizos. The centres of the African slave trade and labour were export-oriented colonies that had insufficient, or dwindling, Indian labour to meet local demand.

These places, where Indian peoples under threat of extinction would come into direct or indirect contact with growing African slave populations in specific moments of global economic expansion, would be, for that very reason, the local focal points and engines of world transformation and revolution. Early in the 1500s, the Dominican priest Bartolomé de Las Casas had pointed out that '[Arawak Indian] slaves were the primary source of income for the Admiral [Christopher Columbus]. With that income he intended to repay the money the Kings were spending in support of the Spaniards on the island [Hispaniola, present-day Haiti and Dominican Republic]'. The Arawak-speaking natives were taken by force to mine for gold in the island, or captured and sent back to Spain as loot or payment to investors and funders of Columbus's expeditions. As a child, Las Casas himself had been given a native Arawak-Taíno youth as servant when his father returned from Columbus's second voyage in 1498. He renamed him Juanico. Master and servant were together until Juanico was returned to Hispaniola with other surviving enslaved Indians by order of royal decree in 1500. The deep relationship that was formed between the two was as crucial to Las Casas's later revolutionary statements against the slavery of the Indians as it would be, further down the line, to Simón Bolívar's epoch-changing espousal of the cause of freedom and American independence. This was encapsulated in his love for the black nurse Hipólita, a slave from the city of San Mateo in Venezuela, who became a mother and father to him after the death of his parents when he was nine.

The depth of Bolívar's relationship with Hipólita is shown in an episode that took place later in his life. When the liberator of the Americas asked his sister to care for Hipólita, he referred to her in loving terms: 'her milk has nourished my life and she is the only father I have known'.[1] Close relationships with those at the lower levels of the burgeoning global economy, like Hipólita or Juanico, taught Bolívar and Las Casas a lesson about the nature of progress. Progress was paradoxical: on the one hand, it brought diverse peoples together, heightening empathy and human consciousness. On the other, it made some people into mere tools, part of the storehouse of resources whose intensive and extensive use and exploitation was required for the advancement of civilisation. To Las Casas and Bolívar, this insight found substance, firstly, in the real threat of extinction of those peoples obliged to work in order to secure just that progress and advancement – Indians and Africans since the fifteenth century – and, secondly, in the subsequent extension of such a threat to us all.

Las Casas and Bolívar understood that the plight and suffering of the Indians and the African slaves was a local or regional problem – one of becoming mere 'brutes of labour' – which actually illustrated the global paradox. Throughout history new energy regimes have converged with new exchange and communication revolutions. For example, the tall ships, while capable of harnessing the power of the winds and sea currents and thereby facilitating the European discovery of the Americas and the emergence of the global circuit of exchange, bringing people together and enhancing our sense of humanity, were responsible for the ever greater consumption of the earth's diversity, energy and other resources, and thus for the deterioration of the planet as a whole. In the transformation of Indians and Africans into mere commodities – 'brutes of labour' – is contained a threat to the very existence of all of us.

Those whose vision is limited to the short term would not care much for the sacrifice of the Indians and the Africans as long as their gains and profit are guaranteed; they might consider it a 'necessary evil' or an unintentional albeit disastrous consequence, and even make a sympathetic call for the amelioration or prevention of such consequences. But for those who choose to contemplate the long term, no short-term gains or preventive policies can justify or ameliorate the consequences of such sacrifices, because, in the long run, the consequences are catastrophic for everyone. These long-term visionaries would point out that people who conjure up catastrophes and then call for their amelioration or prevention tend to bring about the very thing they seek to avert in the act of announcing it. Furthermore, such a tragic outcome becomes farcical when those who suffer the consequences are recast in the role of barbarians, infidels and backward peoples who are themselves responsible for their suffering, and the perpetrators recast themselves as saviours.

History, the long term, does not respond to the imperatives of short-term gains, or to the interests of some, and thus new forms of being in common and collective organisation are required in order to defend the interests of all. From that perspective, the sacrifices of the many in the interests of a few is unacceptable and therefore it is justified that the many – for instance, the working masses of the Americas, both Indian and African – stand up to the interests of the few in the name of the interests of all. This is precisely the argument that Bartolomé de Las Casas developed in the course of his lifelong struggle against the slavery of the Indians and the destruction of their homeland, always in connection with the practices of resistance and rebellion of the Indians themselves, and in sharp contrast with the practices of the conquerors and merchants, whose exploits benefited the Spanish crown, and the financiers of Genoa, Venice, Antwerp and London.

Later on, following the example set by Las Casas, Simón Bolívar would expand this insight into a justification of revolution and a call for regional and global unity against all empires, present or still in the future, addressed to the subjects of the British Empire as well as to the peoples of the Americas, in his famous *Letter from Jamaica*. The *Letter from Jamaica*, written to a British merchant from exile in a British colony, may well be one of the most important foundational documents in Latin American history. In it, Bolívar seeks to set the historical record straight about the central role played by Latin America in the emergence of global trade and the modern world. He rejects the farcical assumptions that led to the subordination of Indians, Africans and others, and of Latin America, into 'a state even below slavery'. Having dismissed the perception of Latin America as a submissive, child-like creature of the European mother country, Bolívar presents the tragedy of Latin America in the transformation of its first Indian inhabitants, Africans and Latin Americans into 'brutes of labour' or, at best, simple consumers who have only 'the bowels of the Earth to dig for gold, the plains where we could breed cattle, wilderness to catch wild beasts for the sake of their skins, and the soil to produce indigo, grain, coffee, cocoa, sugar and cotton. All this to satisfy the needs of that avaricious nation', Spain in particular, Europe in general.[2]

Bolívar takes the long-term view favoured by Las Casas and the Amerindians and from that standpoint he justifies the right to revolution of those whose future has been hijacked and sacrificed for the short-term gains of those who benefit from an unequal state of affairs. The initial inequality of this state of global affairs meant that in order to recover their capacity to create future environments, Indians and slaves would have to 'tilt the playing field' in their favour. The relationship between people like Hipólita and Juanico and people in the position of Las Casas's father or Bolívar's family, exemplified this wider truth about the nature of the relationship between imperial centres and peripheral colonies. The global system of exchanges had emerged on the back of the labour of Indians and African slaves in the mines and plantations of the New World but it discounted them as much as their capacity to create new and autonomous environments in the long term. To recover that capacity, Indians and slaves in peripheral colonies would have to stand up against such a system of relations and transform it. To do so they would have to stand together, withdraw from existing relations and create new ones in which their initial position of inequality is taken into account and corrected. This is not just a matter of compensatory justice, but also concerns the possibility of creating new environments for all.

In this spirit, Bolívar calls for a league of the independent nations of the Americas and elsewhere, capable of standing up, through unity and empathy, to the might that sustains such an unequal system in world affairs. Rather than announcing a coming catastrophe in order to avert it, he follows the example of Las Casas: having stared into the abyss, contemplating the catastrophe that has taken place already, he projects into the future the image of a world united in order to realise it. By taking the long-term perspective and taking into account the need to revert the existing situation, *Letter from Jamaica*, written in the nineteenth century, repeats and perfects the symbolic world of the Amerindians,

heavily invested and focused on the long term and the fragility of everything that is created, as well as the prophetic vision developed by Las
Casas in the sixteenth century. This is why, in order to understand the
call to revolution that came from the Americas and shook the world to
its foundations, one must start precisely where the *Letter from Jamaica*
starts, with the example of Bartolomé de Las Casas.

The Prophet of the Mexican Rainforest

Las Casas emigrated to Hispaniola in 1502 as part of the expedition of
Nicolás de Ovando, who in 1503 established on the island the *encomienda*,
a trusteeship labour system by which the Spanish crown granted a person a
number of natives as wards. Technically, Indians entrusted to Spaniards as
wards were free men who remained in control of their land and had to pay
tribute in return for instruction in the Spanish language and the Catholic
faith. It was a form of indentured labour that made possible the settlers'
acquisition of the land and became central to the economy of the colonies,
even more so than that of silver, gold and other natural resources. In 1574,
for instance, the Viceroy of Peru, Diego Lopez de Velasco, estimated that
out of the 32,000 Spanish families living in the New World at least 4,000
had *encomiendas*, and there were 1,500,000 natives paying tribute.[3]

By 1516, after listening to Father Antonio de Montesinos preach a
fiery sermon in which he asked the colonists: 'tell me by what right of
justice do you hold these Indians in such a cruel and horrible servitude?
Why do you keep them so oppressed and exhausted, without giving
them enough to eat or curing them of the sickness they incur from the
excessive labour you give them, and they die, or rather you kill them, in
order to extract and acquire gold every day?' Las Casas petitioned to be
allowed to form a settlement at Cumaná, in northern Venezuela. There,
the Indians would be paid, have hospitals and churches and be instructed
in agriculture along with the Spaniards. That early experiment in coexistence and freedom ended badly, when neighbouring Carib Indians
attacked the settlement after being raided by colonists, against Las Casas's
orders, who were looking for slaves.

His lobby campaign for legal reform on behalf of the Indians was
more successful. In 1542, the New Laws were passed abolishing the

encomienda and prohibiting the enslavement of the Indians. Their enforcement by the first Viceroy of Peru, Blasco Nuñez Vela, led to the revolt of Spanish conquistadors and colonists under the leadership of Gonzalo Pizarro, the younger half-brother of Francisco Pizarro, who declared Peru independent of the Spanish king and imposed the will of the *encomenderos* by force of arms all the way to Panama. A much-watered-down version of the New Laws was issued in 1552, after Las Casas's brilliant defence of the abolitionist viewpoint during the 1550 Valladolid Debates, called for by Charles V of the Holy Roman Empire, in order to enquire into the legitimacy of the occupation of the Americas and the nature of its natives, and the publication of his *Short Account of the Destruction of the Indies*, dedicated to the then Prince Philip II of Spain. The latter has value not only as a descriptive piece, which may or may not be as exaggerated or as accurate as his critics and hagiographers would like to think, but also as a vision of the future. Its apocalyptic imagery of destruction is linked with a concern for the political future of the Americas.

This is made clearer in his later works. At the age of eighty, Las Casas argued against a proposal made by owners of Peruvian Indians to be able to buy Indians from the Spanish crown in perpetuity. He did so in two treaties known as *The Treasures of Peru* and *Twelve Doubts*. These are no mere diatribes but works of institutional design and political imagination. In *The Treasures of Peru*, he expresses his opinion that 'the future is always at the consideration of men', and wonders why the societies that emerged in the Americas after the conquest resulted in a profound disequilibrium between government and the governed, as opposed to the equilibrium between the rights and interests of individuals and the common good, based on common laws, and what the future consequences of such an imbalance might be.

Las Casas acknowledged that the actions of the Indians, explicit or otherwise – from pretending to obey and follow commands, or appearing to assimilate while actually undermining the status quo, to straightforward rebellion – meant they never gave their consent to Spanish rule and that therefore it was a tyranny. Thus, the empire neither invalidated Indian sovereignty nor dispossessed them from their lands and liberties.

This allowed him to argue for a kind of Pan-American confederation, comprising free, independent Indian kingdoms under their native rulers, or *Incas*, attached to but autonomous from the Spanish crown in much the same way former British colonies and other territories came to form a commonwealth.[4]

Both Las Casas's writings and the New Laws he helped establish can be considered to be the origins of international law and human rights. In chapter fifty-eight of his *History of the Indies*, Las Casas concluded that 'all the nations of the world are human, and of each and every human it is the correct definition that they all have equal will and understanding, all have senses, and all prefer what is good and find pleasure in what is appetising and alluring, and reject that which is evil, unsavoury and harmful'.[5] When the French National Convention decided to abolish slavery on 4 February 1794, Georges Jacques Danton praised Las Casas; his conception of liberty, he noted, according to which 'liberty is a right inherent to man by necessity and derived from the principle of his rational nature',[6] both provided fertile ground for and went beyond the declaration of liberty made by the French republic in the Declaration of the Rights of Man debated between 20 and 26 August 1789, the Constitution of 1791 and the Declarations of May and June 1793, which Danton thought 'egoistic' in comparison to Las Casas's position on the issue of liberty from slavery. The Universal Declaration of Human Rights states in Article 1 that 'All human beings are born free and equal in dignity and rights. They are endowed with reason and conscience and should act towards one another in a spirit of brotherhood,' while the preamble recognises the inherent character of liberty and human rights.

Many commentators have observed the common links between Las Casas's conception, the French Declarations and the UN Universal Declaration of 1948, yet few have pointed out the one between these documents, models of excellence in mankind's great journey, and Simón Bolívar's *Letter from Jamaica*, written on 6 September 1815. Their experiences early in life seem to have provided both Las Casas and Bolívar with a singular vision and profound empathic sensibility to the causes of abolitionism and anti-slavery, as well as with actual examples of mobilisation against slavery and resistance set by those who suffered the consequences of the new global system.[7]

The Most Magnificent Drama in the History of Mankind

In 1581, Philip II of Spain told the administrative council, or *Audiencia*, of Guadalajara that at least a third of the Indians of Latin America had been wiped out. Those who survived were legally free under the reforms introduced by the 1512 Laws of Burgos and the New Laws of 1542, which put an end to the labour system known as *encomienda*. Under that system, the Indians were wards entrusted to investors, entrepreneurs of conquest, and, in very few cases, to indigenous nobility serving as subordinate officers of the empire. For the most part, only Spanish *peninsulares*, those born in Iberia, and their descendants or relatives, like Francisco Pizarro and his brothers Hernando, Juan and Gonzalo, could become *encomenderos*. The latter did not own the land on which the natives lived. The Spanish crown administered the lands of the natives, which were to remain in their possession. This is why *encomiendas* were supposed to revert to the crown after two generations. But few *encomiendas*, if any, were ever reverted. In Mexico, for instance, it would take until the 1910 revolution for the system to be abolished.

In other parts, the *repartimiento* and the *hacienda* came to replace the *encomienda* system during the seventeenth century. As in the previous system, no land rights were given under the *repartimiento* (also known as *mita*) and Indian workers, often belonging to communities located in the proximity of colonial settlements, were directly allotted to the crown, which would assign them through local officials to work for settlers. Many would leave their communities or attempt to dilute their identity by seeking intermarriage with Spaniards or Creoles and challenging their status in court; others would abandon their tribes and seek paid labour, all this in order to escape the *encomienda* and the *repartimiento*. In time, this led to the severe weakening of Indian identity and ancient traditions. By contrast, *haciendas* or privately owned estates did give land rights, as they originated in grants given to Spanish minor nobles, first, and then to their descendants born in America, known as Creoles, *criollos* or mestizos.

These land grants often included power of life and death over every native in their domains. The *haciendas* aimed for self-sufficiency, often combining various economic activities: mainly the growing of crops such as sugar, cacao, tobacco or coffee, but also cattle for the export market, sometimes mining, and little or no manufacturing. Having no court of appeal and no other real authority than that of the *patrón* – the owner of the estate who often became involved in local politics or competed with officials directly sent from Spain for control over local businesses and politics – *haciendas* also aimed for political self-sufficiency, to become societies in their own right, or, at least, to avoid interference from state officials often completely foreign to the local setting given their provenance (only *peninsulares* could become state officials).

Apart from the landowner, the *patrón* and his small circle at the top of *hacienda* society, their eyes (and coffers) forever set on gaining status *vis-à-vis* their metropolitan masters, the remainder were *peones* (pawns or serfs), mounted ranch hands or *vaqueros* or gauchos, and the Indians – now completely dispossessed of their lands and rights, even in the purely legalistic sense of the Laws of Burgos and the New Laws – their numbers fast dwindling, were on their way to becoming peasants or landless *campesinos*.

As King Philip put it to the *Audiencia* of Guanajuato and Guadalajara, the surviving Indians were compelled to pay the tributes of the dead. They were still being raided, bought and sold. Their communal bonds were severed, and their identities came under threat. No wonder mass suicide became commonplace among the natives, and Indian mothers killed their children to save them from the torture of the mines, from destitution and from the meaningless life of peasant estate workers.[8] But despite his furious Catholicism, in his response to the *Audiencia* the king attended not only to the arguments of his Dominican and Jesuit priests but he was also profoundly concerned about the part he played in the Spanish American bounty. He had inherited from his father, Charles V, an empire in great debt. Despite its immense dominions, Spain produced little, raised few taxes, spent hugely, had an enormous annual deficit (about one million in gold money), and owed Genoese and Dutch bankers over thirty-six million in gold money. Faced with bankruptcy, the economy of the kingdom depended more than ever on the flow of gold and silver coming from the Americas. The sharp decline in the number of Indians available to work in the mines and on the estates was fatal. At the same time, growing sympathy for the Indians in Europe and unrest in the Americas – native revolts initiated right after Atahualpa's death continued in earnest until the eighteenth century – made the mistreatment of Indians sinful, illegal and politically unsustainable.

But every time the two religions of Europe – Christianity and gold – clashed the latter seemed to gain the upper hand. At the same time as one decree after another came out of the Spanish court in order to protect Indian land tenure and shield them from abuse, Philip II, like his father, and thereafter his successors, ordered the *encomienda* system to be continued or renewed under new titles. Sometimes the results were positive. In New Mexico, for instance, the community land grant of the Spanish included common pasture lands and preserved the system of pueblo communalism in water irrigation and riparian rights.[9] But in Mexico, land grants dating back to the time of Hernán Cortés, conqueror of the Aztec Confederation, gave place to the big estate, or *hacienda*. The newer land systems seemed much better placed to suit the new economic realities fast replacing quasi-feudal institutions. The evolution of the *encomienda* system into the *repartimiento*, and then the *hacienda*, should be read as three stages in the story of how Indian land was stolen and privatised.

The fourth chapter in the story was the forced migration of Africans into the New World. Over what amounted to almost four hundred years of the slave trade, from the late fifteenth to the late nineteenth centuries, about 12.4 million souls 'were loaded on to slave ships and carried through a "Middle Passage" across the Atlantic to hundreds of delivery points stretched over thousands of miles'.[10] Visiting one such point in South America, Santafé de Antioquia in north-eastern Colombia, American historian Marcus Rediker explained to me that along the dreadful way 1.8 million of them died, 'their bodies cast overboard to the sharks that followed the ships', while most of the 10.6 million who survived were sold in markets like the one we were standing on in Colombia's Antioquia, and 'thrown into the bloody maw of the killing mine and plantation systems' in places like nearby Urabá, or mines on the Pacific coast, or in the *haciendas* that started to appear in valleys and mountains all over the region, along the Cauca valley, in Peru, Ecuador, and to the north in Venezuela, the islands of the Caribbean and elsewhere. Often, such large estates were bought with the riches of the gold mines, and the labour force of Indians and Africans was put to the service of the diversification of the economy as the latter transited from the more feudal-like settings of earlier colonialism to modern ones, better fitted to supply the needs of the bourgeoning export and money economy.

American scholar, campaigner and champion of the Back-to-Africa movement W. E. B. Du Bois referred to the enslavement of Africans and their forced migration to the Americas as 'the most magnificent drama in the last thousand years of human history. The transportation of ten million human beings out of the dark beauty of their mother continent into the new-found El Dorado of the West. They descended into hell.' When it comes to establishing the exact number of Native Americans who died during the conquest of the continent, anthropologists, political scientists and statisticians distinguish between so-called High Counters and Lower Counters. The former tend to place the figure in the tens of millions, the latter are sceptical about such figures or even the feasibility of such counts. Bartolomé de Las Casas is considered the patron saint of High Counters. A High Counter like Las Casas estimated that 'more than twelve million souls, men and women and children' were wiped out in the first five decades after Columbus's arrival. Twenty years later, he raised his estimate of Indian deaths to over forty million. A Lower Counter like David P. Henige – who questioned the debates and estimates over the initial population of the Americas based on colonial sources in his book *Numbers from Nowhere* – argues that 'perhaps 40 million throughout the Western Hemisphere' is a 'not unreasonable figure'. As Charles C. Mann observes, 'it is the same figure provided by Las Casas, patron saint of High Counters, foremost among the old Spanish sources whose estimates Henige spends many pages discounting'.[11] All in all, it seems true, as Simón Bolívar put it in 1815, that the majority of Americans occupied 'no other place in society than that of brutes for labour'.[12]

Latin America's Station

Modern slavery cannot be understood if separated from the land grabs of the five centuries since the arrival of Columbus and the ensuing extermination of the Indians. Both slavery and the struggle against slavery, including the establishment of a right to revolution, must also be set in the context of the paradox that world connectivity and resource-intensive globalisation ride on the back of what sociologist Jeremy Rifkin calls 'an escalating entropy bill', an account of destruction that threatens the whole world. This paradox was identified early on by people like Las Casas and Bolívar and is well represented in the quantitative figure of the millions of Indians who were exterminated in the process of conquest and colonisation of the Americas, which was the first episode of globalisation.[13] Human traffic was offered and accepted as an alternative to their extinction and the enclosure of their lands. Conversely, abolitionism and independence in the Americas cannot be divorced from the question of land redistribution, the construction of a commonwealth and the ability of our species to survive on this planet and create future environments. By the nineteenth century, when Bolívar wrote his *Letter from Jamaica*, these questions were inseparable from the global nature of merchant capital.

As already suggested, the point of Bolívar's letter was to set the historical record straight and describe the destruction of the independent future of Latin America as a result of the reduction of its inhabitants to the status of brutes of labour, or at best mere consumers fated to exploit and deplete its energy-resources and other raw materials. 'All this to satisfy the needs of that avaricious nation', Imperial Spain in particular, but also the rising British Empire and its actual or potential competitors in Europe and North America. This is why, he said, 'the position of the inhabitants in the Colombian hemisphere has been, for ages, without parallel. We were in a state even below slavery, and consequently suffered great difficulty in raising ourselves to the enjoyment of liberty.'[14] Rising to the enjoyment of liberty from slavery both requires and justifies the exercise of a right to rebellion and revolution, aimed not only at the abolition of slavery in the more particular sense of the term, describing the institution of human trafficking, but also at the overturning of an unequal system of global economic and political relations.

This can only be achieved if, after independence, autonomous nations gather together in a league or a community that defends their interests before those of powerful empires and neocolonial forces, and presents such autonomous interests as the interests of all. Ultimately, in accordance with the *Letter from Jamaica*, the aim is to resolve the paradox between growing empathy and world interconnection on the one hand and, on the other, the escalating destruction or 'entropy bill' that threatens our very existence, thereby passing the test of our species' ability to create future environments. 'I hope that some day we shall have the happiness of installing the representatives of republics, kingdoms, and empires in one august congress [. . .] This sort of body may very possibly occur during some happy stage of our regeneration. Any other expectation is impractical,' says Bolívar, in a specific reference to a proposal made at the time by the Abbé de Saint-Pierre to set up a European Congress that would decide the fate and interests of the nations of Europe. Commendable as that proposal may have been, it was inadequate because it discounted from the very outset the participation and concourse of the autonomous nations, once subordinated by Europe, which nevertheless provided Europe with the very means with which it could defy the world. It was also inadequate because the interest at stake was neither purely national nor simply that of the powerful players of a region, but, rather, both local and global at the same time. In so far as the *Letter from Jamaica* attempted to describe and seek a solution to the paradox of global connectivity and destruction, and rose to the task of confronting the most critical test of our species on this planet, it must be considered as important as the Putney Debates or the Federalist Papers, and the various declarations of human rights.

Gold and silver from the mines and crops from the plantations of the Americas were now translatable into money in the global market. The plantation owner had thus become a cosmopolitan. But Indians and Africans were no strangers to that global flux, no matter how local their memories and attachments to the land may have been. Both parties therefore confronted each other as cosmopolitans. But there is a crucial difference: the former appeared in the new cosmopolitan space as commodity owners, the latter as commodities themselves. The distinction is not, therefore, between the 'haves' and the 'have-nots', given that Indians and Africans, who comprised the majority of Latin America's population at the time of the wars of liberation, cannot confront the subjects of the global economy (rich or poor) as such, but rather only as commodities. We must think of them as a third category, one 'below' the mastery of the rich and the slavery of the poor of the nations of Europe. Thus, the slavery of the nations of Latin America was of a specific kind, albeit not a singular or exceptional one.

'The position of the inhabitants in the Colombian hemisphere has been, for ages, without parallel. We were in a state *even below slavery*,' Bolívar argued. His point was not that Latin America is placed in exceptional isolation in (or outside) history. Rather, he contended that, politically speaking, Latin America had been left 'in a sort of permanent infancy', deprived even of 'active tyranny, because we are prohibited from serving it as functionaries'. This was in keeping with the appearance of the vast majority of the inhabitants of Latin America in the cosmopolitan space of commerce as 'at best . . . simple consumers' but mostly as 'brutes of labour', as he put it; that is to say, as commodities. And the one thing owners and commodities have in common in the global economy is money. They can confront one another only in such terms. In the case of Latin America, however, British producers and consumers confronted Latin Americans, for the most part, as 'brutes of labour'.

This explains the ambiguity of the British and other Europeans in relation to Latin America, the movement between sympathy and indifference, which has been a constant since the nineteenth century. Appearing as mere commodities, Latin Americans mean nothing; being nothing, they can be made to appear as just about anything. I contend that this explanation is much better than the elegant but ultimately over-imaginative descriptions of Latin America as a melancholic 'land of solitude' or an 'uncomfortable self-reflection of empire'. The majority of Latin Americans were not possessors of money but were, actually, exchangeable for money. They were below humanity, they were noth-ing, *even below slavery*, as Bolívar put it. Slaves can be the object of sympathy, that soothing spirit which tames feelings of lust, hunger for power and military ambition and is thus never too far from economic self-interest. But mere commodities leave us bland, indifferent: can a soldier still sacrifice himself or others for a piece of cloth on a pole? Is there room in the age of universal commerce for a knight to fight for a lady's glove?

Perhaps it is better to acknowledge that when money becomes the only universal symbol, we take signs and symbols for wonders and, blinded by the allure of money and the accumulation of value, lose our sensual connections with other things and with the world, including our own products. In principle, the soldier knows that behind the flag is the nation, and the lover knows that the glove, the letter or the text message relates to the hand of the object of his affection. But when the glove, the letter, the text message and the flag – their specific substance, their singular allure, their difference and value – become universally translat-able into money, these objects do not return us to the lover and the nation. We remain with money, and start to believe that the accumula-tion of value in money is what really matters. The result is an impover-ished world in which we can only be, at best, simple consumers and, at worst, 'brutes of labour', exploiting and depleting our resources, thereby bringing about the very disaster we are trying to avert. Given this state of affairs, evident to cosmopolitan men of the nineteenth century as much as to the black sailors who roamed Europe, Africa and the Americas, it became clear to Bolívar that Latin America had only two options: either to confront the rest of the world as mere consumers, or to do so as noth-ing more than a reserve of commodities and resources.

He quickly realised the latter was the most likely option: 'At best we are simple consumers, clogged with repressive restrictions. For example, the prohibition of cultivating European crops, the King's monopoly of a wealth of products, the prohibition of manufactures which the Peninsula itself does not possess, the commercial restrictions on even basic neces-sities, the obstacles placed between provinces to keep them from inter-course and commerce,' Bolívar said. He concluded: 'In short, if you wish to know our station, we had the bowels of the Earth to dig for gold, the plains where we could breed cattle, wilderness to catch wild beasts for the sake of their skins, and we had the soil to produce indigo, grain, coffee, cocoa, sugar, and cotton. All this just to satisfy the needs of that avaricious nation.'[15]

But that situation would mean, in all likelihood, a repetition of the history of destruction that Bartolomé de Las Casas had described in the case of the Indians of the past. The only difference being that now, in the nineteenth century, direct administration and the costs of sustaining an army of occupation would be considered excessive. Commercial prevalence and indirect rule could do the same job, at a fraction of the cost. And even then, a debt default or a serious threat to the interests of a producing nation could be met with the sound of cannons being shot from a gunboat on the shores of, say, Panama or Venezuela. This being the case, faced with the dilemma of choosing between the past (the extermination of Indian memory, the taking of the land, the plundering of resources) and the present (extermination, land grabbing, and plunder under the 'new' rules of commerce – the use of irregular armies or armed entrepreneurs, less accountable than state ones; client governments or political factions; trade sanctions; ultimately, gunboat diplomacy), Bolívar concluded that the two options were in fact not options at all. Then he had to consider the true question facing him: what can be done when there is no option?

Latin America as Prophecy: Bolívar with St Paul

When faced with unpalatable choices, refusal becomes an option. Given the world historical position of the Spanish colonies in the nineteenth century, Bolívar seems to have concluded that to choose neither the past nor the present had become the 'irrevocably fixed' destiny of Latin America. He expressed this conviction in memorable terms: 'neither Indians nor Europeans.' In trying to prevent history repeating itself, Bolívar himself becomes an example of such repetition. In rapid succession, the body of the Liberator is possessed by ghosts of the past. Las Casas in Mexico,[16] the Indian kings of America,[17] St Paul in Imperial Rome – 'I consider the present state of America as similar to that of

imperial Rome when it was decaying . . . there is one remarkable difference, which is that in Europe the dispersed tribes re-established their
ancient customs . . . But we hardly preserve a vestige of what we were,
being neither Indians nor Europeans.'[18] Could we read instead 'neither
Jews nor Romans'?

In the case of St Paul, the statement has been taken to mean the advent
of a new universal after the fragmentation of the Roman Empire, or
kairós, an overturning.[19] It is thus a sign of an end and a new beginning,
of repetition and revolution, of the one who chooses the future over
the apparent compromise between the past and the present to iterate a
history of tragedy in the register of farcical crises: credit crisis, ecological
crisis, the crisis brought about by an excess of fiscal expenditure (four
years after he wrote the *Letter from Jamaica*, Bolívar would witness the
first money credit crisis in the history of capitalism), political crises. In
the case of Bolívar, after having invoked in all but name the spirit of
militancy against the first Roman Empire (he was witness to the decadence of the second – Spain became the Holy Roman Empire during
the rule of Charles V), and just a few lines down from his evocation of
the language of prophecy, we find this most peculiar line: 'We were [in
the Colombian hemisphere, Latin America] in a state *even below slavery*.'

'Neither Indians nor Europeans', 'neither Jews nor Romans', but
rather 'in a state *even below slavery*'. If this is a prophecy ('it would take a
prophet to predict what policy America will finally adopt,' he says) it is
a strange one. He prophesies not the cosmic race but, rather, something
low, lower than low. The complete sentence reads thus: 'We were in a
state even below slavery, and consequently suffered greater difficulty in
raising ourselves to the enjoyment of liberty.'[20] He produces an image of
verticality, like the latitudinal trajectory of Columbus or the geometry
of the Incas, but one in which the ascent takes place from the lower-
than-low to the higher-than-high. In an attempt to explain the situation of the Americas and justify its irrevocable destiny of refusal and
revolution to the British, Bolívar seems to discover a third element that
disrupts the synthesis of two (rich and poor, east and west, producers and
consumers, even capital and labour) organised by the system of global
commerce. Incidentally, this structure is repeated in his description of

the constitutional designs for Colombia and Venezuela, and later in life in his constitutional proposal for Bolivia. But what does Bolívar's prophetic phrase mean?

His observation may also have been intended as a reference to the sentiments of sympathy and benevolence that certain circles in Britain and France cultivated in respect to the cause of the abolition of slavery. The nineteenth-century Scottish philosopher Adam Ferguson referred to such sentiments when he wrote that 'love and compassion [are] the most powerful principles in the human breast'.[21] This elevated air of benevolence and humanitarianism was present in the clubs and coffee houses of London and Paris, and was expressed in the pages of the most influential journals of the time, such as *Tatler* and *The Spectator*. To feel deeply and sincerely about the destinies of such distant others as the Africans forced to take the Middle Passage was a matter of imagining oneself in their place, of allowing oneself to be touched by their suffering, as depicted by the press or expressed in the speeches of the abolitionist William Wilberforce before Parliament and the sketches of his collaborator Thomas Clarkson. And yet, such sentiments were in fact subordinate to and dependent upon the kinds of symbolic exchanges that were taking place in the global money economy – which they both responded to and rejected. The political destiny of Latin America had more to do with such symbolic exchanges, and could hardly be founded solely upon sympathetic sentiments.

That at least is the message that Bolívar's *Letter from Jamaica* seems intended to convey to its British reader. Crucially, sentiments like sympathy and benevolence were often in nineteenth-century Europe translated into the language of friendship, as in the case of the French *Société des amis des noirs*, for instance. Bolívar himself used this language in *Letter from Jamaica* when he referred to Las Casas as 'that friend of humanity'.[22]

Although psychology is only beginning to shed light on the neural underpinnings of such sentiments, which allow an infant, for instance, to imitate its parents' facial expressions, it is well known that sympathy operates as a mirror-like relationship in which objects and other people are reflected back at us. A spontaneous mimicry takes place between the other and us: the other wants to be like us, while, from our perspective, we recognise in the other what is already familiar to us. That is to say, we imagine ourselves in its place, and in that sense at least we and the other become interchangeable. We can stand in its place, and stand up for it. Bolívar is no doubt appealing to the benevolence of his British reader, and, through him, that of the British public. He wants them to stand up for the cause of Latin American independence. He also wants them to be the representatives of the cause of Latin American independence in Europe, just as Wilberforce and Clarkson were the representatives of the cause of the African slaves.

In the process, he also emulates the British, and thus he describes the political future of Latin America (at least in the case of Venezuela and Colombia) in terms that would be familiar to anyone with a certain knowledge of the British political arrangement: a sort of constitutional monarchy with two parliamentary chambers, each representing one of the two leading sectors of society – aristocratic landowners and common-ers – and an autonomous, quasi-monarchic Executive.[23]

But he may also be pointing out something else: that the apparent similarity or sympathy between Britain and Latin America, their mirror-like relationship, is always in danger of being undone by the unexpected emergence of a third term in the relation, represented in this case by the situation of the majority of the inhabitants of Latin America, Indians and Africans. They appear in the global space of commerce – which is the stage of history in the nineteenth century – neither as producers nor as consumers, but, rather, as he says, as 'brutes of labour', by which he means as commodities themselves.

This means that in one sense Indians and Africans represent the whole of Latin America, since they are in the majority (a quantitative fact with political consequences, at least in the case in which Latin America estab-lishes some form of Republicanism, even if contained within a consti-tutional-monarchic arrangement). But in another sense, the economic sense, they stand for nothing; or, more precisely, for no one – no politi-cal subject – since they are nothing but commodities. They are neither 'high' – like the aristocratic landowners, Bolívar's family, for instance – nor 'low' – like the commoner artisans, traders and wage earners of the *haciendas* – but 'lower-than-low'. And since they stand for the whole of Latin America as well, the latter is also lower-than-low. As Bolívar puts it, 'in a state *even below slavery*'.

This places Latin America 'in a most extraordinary and embarrassing dilemma', as he says, both at home and on the international stage. At home, it means that while the 'top' – the landed aristocracy – and the 'bottom' – the artisans and wage earners – remain in place, represented by the two houses of an imagined unitary Parliament, the unity of such a compromise (an imaginary or specular unity) will be broken by the unexpected irruption of the third (lower-than-low) element. Abroad, it means that Latin America does not confront Britain and the rest of Europe (as well as the newly formed United States if, as Bolívar predicts, the former British colonies realise their potential as a commercial power-house) as an equal, as a producer or a consumer, but, rather, as a reserve of commodities. Put in that situation, Latin America can only appear in the eyes of Europe as the object (or the set of objects – gold, cotton, sugar and, in the end, money) that drives its economic interests. And thus, as the present situation of Indians and Africans demonstrates, Latin America appears once more in the eyes of Europe as the site of a repetitive cycle of extraction, extinction and destruction. This is the limit of an ethics of sentiment and benevolence, such as that which animated the efforts of European abolitionists. A rigorous reading of this most important of Bolívar's texts seems to show him delineating a certain realism: to recognise the repetitive nature, a certain necessity, of the drive to destruction that has characterised the history of Latin America since the arrival of Christopher Columbus.

The Laws of Credit: Bolívar's Baroque
Psychology of International Relations

The specular or mirror-like relationship between two seemingly opposites is often called 'emulation'. Psychologists call it 'the imaginary stage' and point out that it is an important part of what makes us human. They observe how children tend to imitate the expressions and behaviour of their parents, and how the latter are delighted to see themselves in their children. Adult friendships and relations follow a similar pattern.

Psychologists also argue that if we remain in this imaginary and particular stage at least two things may be lost: on the one hand, that 'emulation' and exchangeability means not only friendship but also envy; and on the other hand, we misunderstand how resistant we can be to the idea and the real possibility of radical evil. Confronted by it, we tend to look away. This may help explain the ambiguity of our attitudes towards those distant others with whom we feel strangely intimate and at the same time entirely foreign. It can also be an important element in our exploration of the relationships between nations in contexts of encounter, crisis and fragmentation. The case in point is the position of Latin America *vis-à-vis* Europe in the wake of the fall of the Spanish Empire in the nineteenth century, as seen through the eyes of one of its most important protagonists, Simón Bolívar.[24]

The imaginary (sympathy, friendship) resists being translated into rational or comparative terms, for instance the terms of exchange and commensurability, which are central to the practices that characterise the global market. Crucially, it also resists the realities of war, repetitive violence and the possibility of radical evil caused by envy, the illusion of self-propelled limitless expansion, and, ultimately, by the fact that the recognition of the existence of real others is never far from catastrophe.

In contrast with the feel-good humanitarianism prevalent in nineteenth-century Britain, and manifested in the sympathies marshalled by abolitionists like William Wilberforce, Bolívar may have implied that the cause of independence in Spanish America marshalled only some sympathy, or *could not* have marshalled anything but a little sympathy in Europe or the United States (as shown in the case of the 1801 Haitian Revolution) precisely because such sentiments could only develop as an imaginary extension of the moral sentiments felt among the well-off towards the situation of the poor, as Adam Smith had shown in Britain.

Imaginary globalisation and imaginary cosmopolitanism were thus always fraught with, haunted by, the possibility of catastrophe (extermination, genocide, land grabbing). The establishment of true empathy and a worldwide sociality, together with its rules, empathic institutions such as a league of autonomous nations and global peacekeeping mechanisms, emerges from that possibility as a solution to the challenge it posits, to 'contain' it and/or to realise the promise of a truly global civilisation. In that sense, political cosmopolitanism of the kind proposed by Bolívar in his 1815 *Letter from Jamaica*, the kind that aims at achieving 'perpetual peace', is always opposed, by definition, to the limitless expansion of exchange, envy and empire. This is the realm of 'practical reason', of realism, which is absent in the imaginary stage.

Such realisation also explains why sympathy, commendable as it may be, is not enough. It is one of the limits of imaginary ethics that the drive to feed, as it were, on death, and to profit from it (as well as from crises and catastrophes), along with the notion of unmotivated evil, seems well-nigh inconceivable. In their (evangelical) appeal to inner feelings, sentimentalists and benevolentists like those who expressed sympathy with the cause of abolitionism and humanity in the pages of *Tatler* or *The Spectator*, or British eighteenth-century classical economists like Adam Smith or Francis Hutcheson, cannot accept that any human being could lack sympathy for his fellow man. Thus, they could not concede the grounds upon which Bolívar and other Americans attempted to justify their call to revolutionary war.

Such grounds could be found in Las Casas, as Bolívar makes clear at the beginning of the letter to his British correspondent, and included the 'barbarism' and 'horrid crimes', past and present, committed by Europeans 'under the influence of a sanguinary frenzy'. However, at least in one important aspect of Bolívar's reasoning seems to have gone beyond anything Las Casas might have contemplated: the connection between such crimes and violence, on the one hand, and the economic realities of the nineteenth century, on the other, and the consideration of the potential for the repetition of such crimes under present and future conditions.

On one side, Bolívar acknowledges that 'contemporaries had refused to believe in these barbarous stories [the accounts of the conquest], seeing them instead as fables which fell so far below the depravity of human nature that they could not be credited'.[25] On the other, he urges his British reader to confirm such wickedness and horrors by reference to Las Casas and 'the tyrant's own secret documents' and to accept that 'the destiny of America [revolutionary war] is irrevocably fixed': 'we are fighting for our liberty'. In this way he points out the limitations of humanitarian sentimentalism and imaginary ethics. He also finds a way out; literally, he sees light at the end of the tunnel. 'We are threatened by death and the most terrible dishonour by a disgraced wicked stepmother!' he says.[26] In such darkness, with no other options, out of 'desperation', as he puts it, 'the veil has at last been cast off', 'we have seen light.'[27]

Let us call it a different kind of enlightenment, a Baroque Enlightenment, if you will. Or is it Romantic, Gothic perhaps? For Bolívar then proceeds to introduce Latin America as a protagonist of the drama of world history in the guise of a monster. It is no coincidence that at this precise point the language of the letter becomes prophetic.[28] If Bolívar wanted to gain the support of the British for the purposes of revolution, and at the same time warn them about the consequences of not giving support, then, as can be seen, an appeal to their sympathy (as in the case of the abolitionists) was not enough. First he had to elevate Britain beyond sentimentality, and he could only do that by reducing the level of Latin America to that of a monster, below that of humanity, *even below slaves*.

Only from that perspective – viewed either from very high up or from very low down – would it have been possible to contemplate the realities revealed to the protagonists by the global economy (the symbolic stage of exchanges), the relationship between monetary and sacrificial exchange (embodied in the character of Indians and Africans as mere commodities), and to conceive the possibility of purely unmotivated malevolence and profit from death. And then, perhaps, do something about it. Only then does revolutionary war, the last resort, become the *only* resort. Are we speaking of a stage in Bolívar's thinking in which revolution became not only a duty but *a right*? Be that as it may, it becomes vital for us to understand that morality, the object of international relations, which is one of the most urgent of exercises of our capacities for practical reasoning, has nothing to do with feel-good sentiments or compassion in the face of distant suffering. In relation to this aspect of international relations, Indian economist and Nobel Prize-winner Amartya Sen, by no means a champion of armed struggle, has argued, correctly, that 'behaviour based on sympathy is in an important sense egoistic, for one is oneself pleased at others' pleasures and pained at others' pain, and the pursuit of one's utility may thus be helped by sympathetic action'.[29]

The German philosopher Immanuel Kant recognised in 1784, only three decades before Bolívar wrote his letter, that the realistic grounds for what he called perpetual peace – the cosmopolitan society, which for him involved the establishment of a world commonwealth that would prevent the extermination and plundering of one nation by another – were the inevitability of commerce and the money economy, leading to a world of winners and losers. Bolívar too arrives at his proposal for a World Congress to be based in Panama, after having presented the situation in which Latin America found itself as that of a nothingness made into a monster ('*even below slavery*'), refusing to be sacrificed at the altar of global economic exchange. The proposal entails the displacement of our monstrous drive to profit from death and catastrophe on to a commonwealth of happiness comprising the four corners of the world. He regards such an achievement, unsurprisingly, as 'sublime'.

'How sublime it would be if the Isthmus of Panama should become to us what Corinth was to the Greeks. I hope that some day we shall have the happiness of installing the representatives of republics, kingdoms, and empires in one august Congress, and of treating and discussing great and interesting questions of peace and war with nations of the other three parts of the globe. This sort of body may very possibly occur during some happy stage of our regeneration.'[30] There is no trace of idealism in his proposal: 'Any other expectation is impractical,' he says. He then compares it to the suggestion made by the Abbé de Saint-Pierre concerning a European Union. He calls it a 'commendable delirium'. Although such proposals may have seemed crazy to many at the time (as they seem to many in *our* time), the alternative was simply unreasonable world war, the repetition of imperialistic competition and its consequences at home and abroad. Seen from the perspective of the twenty-first century – from that of the proverbial angel of history, looking down in mid-flight upon the past and contemplating only ruins – delirious proposals such as Bolívar's seem not only commendable, but the very definition of sanity. His realistic assessment of the internal difficulties that beset the establishment of republics in post-independent Latin America arises from similar considerations.

Anglophilia and Latinmania

For Bolívar, the assessment of the political situation in Latin America at a moment of crisis must begin with the recognition of the sublime characteristics that gold and silver – as world money, and therefore, Indians and Africans as 'brute force' involved in the extraction of such metals in the mines, and labouring in the plantations – acquired at the dawn of industrialised society. To speak of the 'sublime' nature of gold and silver in the age of the Baroque, when the Spanish Empire was at its height, and during the Enlightenment is, however, to refer to an entirely new kind of fetish: not merely the gold of Atahualpa and the silver of Potosí, but the gold standard of Britain and the laws of credit. If in Las Casas's sixteenth century the crucial differences between Europe and Latin America – between, say, Pizarro and Atahualpa – were of Christian and pagan, or hoarding and idolatry, by the time of Bolívar's *Letter from Jamaica* those differences have become between usurer and debtor – say, Shylock and Antonio, whose merchant ships, the reader will remember, were stranded in Mexico.

Latin America is first mentioned in the great literary tradition of modern England in a speech by the calculating Shylock, who mentions Mexico when he weighs up Antonio's creditworthiness. At the beginning of Act 1, Scene 3, of Shakespeare's *The Merchant of Venice*, Shylock and Bassanio discuss the matter of the soundness of Antonio's investments. Latin America then enters the world stage: 'Ho, no, no, no, no,' replies Shylock to Bassanio, 'my meaning in saying he is a good man is to have you understand me that he is sufficient. Yet his means are in supposition. He hath an argosy bound to Tripolis, another to the Indies. I understand moreover, upon the Rialto, he hath a third in Mexico, a fourth for England, and other ventures he hath squandered abroad.' The intimation is that the enterprise is risky, and thus that Antonio 'shall become bound'. Throughout the play, our views of the familiar and the foreign are shaped by monetary terms.[31]

The Merchant of Venice (1598) is as much a product of the age of expansionism and gold lust as Bartolomé de Las Casas's *Short Account of the Destruction of the Indies* (1552), but only in the former does sacrifice cease to be understood in terms of a primal economy centred in the body (of the Indians for Las Casas, that of their victims in pagan rituals of sacrifice for Juan Ginés de Sepúlveda, his opponent during the 1550 debates in Valladolid on the legitimacy of empire). It begins to be considered in terms of monetary exchange. By the time Bolívar wrote to his British correspondent describing the majority of the inhabitants of Latin America as 'brutes of labour,' and its calamitous circumstances as 'even below slavery', the monetary notions he used to frame the relationship between Britain and Latin America were well established in the minds of its intended audience. It had become clear to them that in the new sacrificial setting of the merchant economy, all the vagaries of world history seemed to follow the laws of credit.

Las Casas's most famous denunciation of the atrocities against the Indians had been available to English readers since 1583 under the title *The Spanish Colonie*, in the context of Spain's attack on the Confederacy of Northern Provinces (present-day Netherlands). But it would only acquire more global connotations around 1656, when it was rendered as *The Tears of the Indians* by John Milton's nephew, John Phillips, in support of Oliver Cromwell's campaign against Spain in the Caribbean. In contrast, Milton's *Paradise Lost* seems to fall on the side of an extension and further secularisation of Las Casas's arguments against the political mechanisms of a gold-based society. After Adam envisions Moctezuma, Atahualpa and El Dorado, his next vision is that of the murder of Abel by his brother Cain. Envy and repetitive warfare follow the contemplation of the kingdoms of gold. This subdued form of human sacrifice (rather than its abolition, which, from Ginés de Sepúlveda and the retelling by Spanish chroniclers of the legend of the prophet of the Mexican forest to Mel Gibson's *Apocalypto*, has served to justify imperial expansionism) would remain as the mark of temporal history.

At the same time that Milton turns the world (and Renaissance sacrificial epic) upside down, John Dryden infuses new life into English theatre with an Englishman's portrayal of Spanish Catholic expansionism in

The Indian Emperour (1665). Set in Aztec America during the conquest, it portrays the impact of a modern culture based on the use of signs (both numeric and alphabetical) upon another one in which all signs are supposedly absent. Crucially, one of the most important contrasts is that between money-based and alternative systems of exchange, 'while showing how they reach the same consummation in human sacrifice'.[32] This is the time of the revolution in the way things are calculated and the revolution in navigation technology that would allow distant lands to become part of a global network of commerce in which products and bodies – like the body of Atahualpa in Cajamarca, that of Moctezuma in Dryden's *The Indian Emperour*, or that of Africans and Indians in Bolívar's *Letter from Jamaica* – can be traded for gold.

In such a world, global dominance depended upon sea power, unimpeded access to land suitable for planting crops and establishing trading ports, and control over cheap and plentiful labour. The British had recognised the connection between the revolutions in calculation and the navigation early in the seventeenth century, and sought to reorganise themselves as a sea power or a maritime state. It did not take them long to realise the importance of the slave trade – bodies traded for gold – in the brave new world of global economic exchange.

By 1649 the post-revolutionary government of Oliver Cromwell and the Commons in Parliament had made 'the terrifying discovery that they had only fifty naval vessels with which to defend their republic against the monarchs of Europe, who did not look happily upon the severed head of Charles I'.[33] Almost overnight the new men of Britain dedicated the shipyards at Chatham, Portsmouth, Woolwich and Deptford to the production of the necessary ships. Laws were passed to provide enough labour to undertake the enterprise and extend Britain's commercial and military influence by sea. From the very outset the idea was to displace the Dutch and the French as primary carriers of the transatlantic trades and open up the monopolies established by the Spanish in the Atlantic.

Aided by the revolution in the way things were mapped and calculated by men like William Petty, Oliver Cromwell's cartographer and surveyor during the campaign in Ireland, the British government could gather statistics and use them to predict the outcome of its policies.[34]

Lands, items and people became terms in equations 'whose solution takes centuries', thereby allowing Petty and others to draw maps of the future, or at least to divide it into a future that was assured and one that was not.[35] Historical teleology, an idea derived from classical philosophical geography and the cosmography of exploration that imagined the world as a machine, according to which there is an order and orientation inherent to the workings of history and geography that can be predicted and perhaps even manipulated, became equation-driven. Such equations and statistics seem to leave no room for doubt as to the scale of the British achievement: in the space of a mere sixteen years, between 1673 and 1688, the amount of cargo shipped by English merchants tripled and the shipping industry expanded at a rate of 2 to 3 per cent per year. Great Britain was on its way to becoming a dominant sea power.

The experiences of men like Sir William Petty and William Paterson as shipmates on the Atlantic gave them a precise understanding of what had to be done: bodies suitable for labour had to be mobilised through trade routes, and British labour policy had to become transatlantic because of the nature of far-flung lands. Petty, for instance, advocated shipping felons and other 'insolvent' populations to plantations overseas. He soon realised the increasing importance of the slave trade to all other international demand and supply networks, and to the ongoing expansion of British interests in Ireland and the Caribbean initiated by Cromwell in 1654. On the back of his experiences in the setting up of plantations in Ireland and elsewhere in the early eighteenth century, he observed that 'the accession of Negroes to the American plantations (being all Men of great labour and little expence) is not inconsiderable', meaning that the possibility of trading bodies suited to labour at a cheap price, and removing them to America to work in mines and plantations, would be crucial to the development of a global exchange economy useful to British interests. Having in mind the Middle Passage, and the connection between producers and consumers, Petty concluded that 'the Labour of seamen, and freight of Ships, is always of the nature of an Exported Commodity, the overplus whereof above what is Imported, brings home money'.

The correct meaning of the concept of 'overplus' is exactly what William Paterson had in mind when, upon returning from the Caribbean in the 1690s, he spoke of 'money that begets money' while explaining his scheme to potential investors for the establishment of a Scottish trading port in Panama. This was also the process that Simón Bolívar witnessed almost a century later throughout the Caribbean. That experience served as the basis for his communication to the British public, marvelling at the possibilities opened up by commerce, while at the same time warning them of its darker side, exemplified in the plight of Africans as much as in the destructiveness and frequency of wars of imperial competition among Europeans.

One example of such a conflict was the so-called Nootka Sound Incident. In the late 1780s Nootka Sound, one of the bays carved out of the coast of Vancouver, in present-day Canada, had become a centre for trade in fur and fisheries between indigenous peoples, Russian, French, American and British traders. These developments did not please the Spanish crown, which claimed sovereignty over the whole continent and monopoly over its trade routes and posts as a result of the 1494 Treaty of Tordesillas. The Treaty of Tordesillas had divided the entire continent between the two main naval powers at the time, Spain and Portugal, leaving little or no room for the other emerging European powers. In 1789, Spanish troops entered Nootka Sound. In an effort to enforce the treaty, Spanish soldiers seized four vessels belonging to Captain John Meares, a British adventurer with trading interests in the zone.

In response, the British Prime Minister William Pitt dispatched the Royal Navy, eager to recover some of the momentum he had lost as a result of the American War of Independence and growing unrest throughout its colonies in the Caribbean and Latin America. This was not simply a matter of saving face after the American Revolution. The possibility of a spillover of the cycle of Caribbean rebellions threatened Britain's commercial interests as much as the flow of Latin American gold it had secured when Portugal had signed the Methuen Treaty in 1703. The treaty was the final result of a series of concessions and privileges granted by the Portuguese to British textile manufacturers and merchants. The latter provided fine linens and clothes, which the former paid for with Brazilian gold. In the process, Portugal ruined its own textile industry and was never able to place its products – wines, for instance – in good positions within the British market. In addition, following the example of Spain, Portugal banned the establishment of any kind of manufactories in Brazil: sugar refineries remained banned until 1715, local looms were prohibited in 1785.

Until the eighteenth century, Spanish America and Brazil produced much more silver than gold, and much more as a percentage of world production. During the sixteenth and seventeenth centuries the gold production of Latin America represented only between 10 and 20 per cent of world totals. The situation changed dramatically during the eighteenth century. For more than fifty or sixty years, between 1720 and 1780, Brazil was the one of the world's largest producers of gold. Between 1730 and 1770, it was the world's largest producer and exporter of gold, 'providing close to 60 percent of global totals'.[36]

This explains Queen Anne's proclamation of 1704 establishing the gold standard in the British colonies of the West Indies, and the introduction in 1717, by Sir Isaac Newton, then Master of the Royal Mint, of a new mint ratio between silver and gold which drove silver out of circulation and effectively put Britain on a gold standard. Brazil's gold boom brought a host of Portuguese merchants, traders and officials to Minas Gerais, thereby stimulating imports of manufactured products from Britain, and at the same time providing the means to pay for them. Just as in the case of Spain and Potosí, Portugal quickly became an intermediary in the transit of gold to European bankers, most of whom were located in the City of London. When the Portuguese Marquis de Pombal attempted to change the direction of the gold flow, he had to resign himself to recognising that 'the English had conquered Portugal without the trouble of conquest . . . and that British agents controlled the whole of Portuguese trade'.[37]

It is thanks to 'historical graciousness' that Britain could use Brazilian gold to pay for essential imports and concentrate on investments in the manufacturing sector. Thus, Britain's industrial revolution may owe as much to Brazilian gold as it does to William Petty and Adam Smith's division of labour. In addition, the financial centre of Europe moved from Amsterdam to London, where it remains to this day. Brazil's gold boom was crucial to the early formal adoption of the gold standard by Portugal and Britain between 1816 and 1821, switching from the silver standard, ahead of all the other naval and industrial powers, and one of the main factors behind British foreign policy in Latin America and the Caribbean.

Small wonder, then, that when the Spanish sent troops to Nootka Sound, Britain responded by redoubling its efforts to provoke further destabilisation in the already disintegrating Spanish Empire. To this aim, the so-called Precursor of Independence, Francisco de Miranda, was summoned. Miranda responded, and from 1789 to 1792, and then again between 1801 and 1805, he brought his 'continental consciousness-raising campaign' to London. He had travelled all over Europe meeting the most important minds on the continent, from Diderot to the German-Jewish philosopher Moses Mendelssohn, and romancing the most important and beautiful women, including Catherine the Great of Russia.

Now he was seeking to turn his home at 27 Grafton Way in London's Bloomsbury into one of the most important centres of modern world history. The list of visitors to his house reads like a who's who of world revolution and the Enlightenment: Adam Smith, Jeremy Bentham, William Wilberforce, John Adams and his wife Abigail, Adams' son-in-law Williams Stephens Smith, the French leader of the Girondist movement Jacques-Pierre Brissot, and religious Dissenters; in addition, there were also the future Protector of Chile Bernardo O'Higgins, Venezuelan intellectual Andrés Bello, the Mexican Fray Servando Teresa de Mier (who wrote one of the most important documents in the history of Latin America not far from there), the father of the Argentinean nation José de San Martín, Bernardino Rivadavia and, of course, Simón Bolívar himself. And when the aforementioned made their way back to Latin America, they took with them a vision of Britain as a 'free society of law and progress' that profoundly influenced the destiny of the future republics. If Vilcabamba was the guerrilla capital of the world in the sixteenth century, in the nineteenth that title belonged to Haiti, on one side of the Atlantic, and London on the other.

The crisis initiated by the Nootka Sound Incident quickly subsided when a new cycle of political crises rose up, precipitated by the onset of the Peninsular War in Europe. The French advance across Portugal and Spain, designed to tighten the trade blockade of Britain already in place, set in motion a chain of events that would have a long-lasting impact on the course of liberation and independence in the Americas: the defeat of Napoleonic forces at the hands of the Haitian revolutionary army of black slaves that then set out to establish the first black republic in human history in 1804 and decisively extended the inherent universalism of rights to the question of slavery; Miranda's campaign in Europe and the Americas between 1806 and 1812, which sought to find enough support, financial, military and political, to launch a revolutionary war against the Spanish Empire; the fall of the Bourbon monarchy in Imperial Spain brought about by Napoleon's forces, which in turn brought about a crucial if short-lived wave of republicanism in Spain between 1807 and 1814, symbolised in the 1812 Constitution of Cádiz and mirrored by the white Creole elites of Spanish America in the 1810s, which, in spite of its ultimate failure, did give Latin American elites a taste of the liberty that the subordinated classes had already consumed and were fighting for; the relocation of Portugal's imperial throne from Lisbon to Rio de Janeiro thanks to the intervention of the British, who provided the vessel in which King João VI, his son Pedro and his family reinstalled the imperial family in Brazil in early 1808. This crucial period culminated in the defeat of Napoleon by the allied British and Prussian forces under the Duke of Wellington and Blücher at the Battle of Waterloo on 18 June 1815.

Bolívar refers to the ensuing crisis of imperial legitimacy in Spanish America during the period in his 1815 *Letter from Jamaica* in the following terms: 'When the French eagles destroyed the impotent government of the Peninsula, stopping only at the walls of Cádiz, we Americans were left in the state of orphans. We had first been delivered over to the mercy of a tyrant [Napoleon]. Then we were flattered with a semblance of justice, and mocked with hopes, always disappointed. Finally, from a situation of uncertainty as to our future destiny, we threw ourselves into the chaos of revolution.'[38] He describes the crisis that followed the clash between Europe's imperial powers – old, new, rising – in terms of a sacrificial drama that explores the unintended consequences of unwilling perpetrators and of the exposed victim, at the expense of the system in which they are forced to participate and which blinds them in relation to the future. In that situation, revolution is not yet a duty or a right, but merely chaos, just as in sacrificial dramas the exploitative system is frequently sustained by the insanity of a collective 'delivered', 'mocked', 'thrown', into abject passivity.

A crucial distinction then: the scapegoat-pursuing mob (first delivered into the hands of a tyrant, then offered a semblance of justice – scapegoating – finally throwing themselves into abject passivity and chaos), on the one hand, and the enlightened, faithful group, on the other. 'But the veil has at last been cast off . . .We have been free but our enemies want to enslave us once more. We are fighting defiantly for our liberty, and desperation seldom fails to bring victory in its wake. We should not lose faith in our destiny just because our successes have been partial and incomplete thus far.' If the former acts 'from a situation of uncertainty', for the latter the future is no longer a matter of calculation, but a matter of choice. In such a situation, the probabilities of success, or lack thereof, no longer count. As in the then popular novel *Les Incas* (1778) by the Encyclopédiste Jean-Francois Marmontel, we are given an account of social evolution: the coming civilisation (which in the novel, as in Bolívar's text, evokes Rome) will consummate the movement away from the condition of sacrificial mob to one in which the sacrificial body (the body of Indians and Africans) is no longer erased by the blinding forces of the system (of crises, imperialist competition and warfare).

This narrative involves the establishment of a direct relation between crisis, great-power competition and warfare, on the one hand, and racial and political conflict on the other. Ever since Bolívar's childhood, keeping slaves and former slaves under control – keeping them down, lower-than-low, *damnés* – has been *the* central issue, both for economic and political reasons. Now he makes the naked bodies of slaves and Indians stand (stand in, stand up) for the whole of Latin America. In 1791 slaves had revolted in the French colony of Santo Domingo (present-day Haiti) following a string of rebellions in just about every coastal colony and island, from New York to Jamaica and Bahía, in Brazil. In 1801 the Haitians, as they now called themselves, had abolished slavery and declared the island a free republic, the first of its kind in human history; afterwards they issued a constitution declaring universal equality. In 1802, when Bolívar and his then-wife Maria Teresa tried their hand at running a plantation, the air was heavy with talk of rebellion. But it was not politics that ended the dream of these young lovers. Maria Teresa contracted a tropical fever and died in Caracas in 1803. His heart broken, Bolívar set sail for Europe, where the most crucial debate of all time awaited him.

Britain and France were the scenes of increasingly bitter debates prompted by abolitionists, radicals and benevolentists concerning the plight of slaves, commoners and other forcibly displaced peoples. Among those debating the issues was Thomas Spence, born in 1750 in Newcastle. In 1775 he gave a famous lecture before the Philosophical Society calling for the equal restoration of land to all the people. He was thrown out of town, moved to London and opposed patenting while praising the agrarian communalism characteristic of the Indians of the Americas. His actions resonated with the formation in the 1790s of various reform associations and 'friends of the people' who in their meetings and debates linked Magna Carta to the memory of the English Revolution, while at the same time alluding to the Waltham Black Act by calling for 'a speedy abolition of the slave trade and game laws'. Thomas Clarkson, a central figure in the Abolitionist movement of Britain and a close associate of William Wilberforce, wrote of the Abolition Bill of 1807 abolishing the British slave trade that it was a 'Magna Carta for Africa in Britain'. He may as well have extended the territorial jurisdiction of his Magna Carta: to Haiti; to the commoner town of Silos in present-day Colombia where, in 1781, the *comuneros* abolished slavery; and to the Caribbean.

These debates were directly connected with the events unfolding in the Americas, and with the impact that such events could have in the European metropolis. These were not merely theoretical or fairly remote preoccupations. The rebellious energies the adult Bolívar would seek to harness for the cause of independence were more often than not those of peoples of the 'lower races', the lower-than-low who were already rising up against an increasingly exploitative system. That system he identified with colonialism, with imperial competition and repetitive warfare, with the extermination of Indians, the enslavement of Africans and the systematic plundering of Latin America's resources (its transformation into a reserve of commodities to satisfy the needs of avaricious nations). Thus, like Miranda and others before him, Bolívar took back home a vision of Britain as a 'free and progressive society' that resonated with the views and arguments of those – abolitionists, benevolentists, friends of the people – who recognised in Britain and elsewhere the immense cost involved in harnessing the forces of power. Those who paid the highest price were, of course, the peoples of the 'lower races', Indians and Africans, and the nations of the Americas that were even below slavery. Nowhere else was this as visible as in the commercial centres of the Americas and the Caribbean: in Jamaica, in Cartagena, in Haiti, in Brazil, and in Venezuela.

In turn, after Napoleon's surrender and exile to Elba in 1814, Britain increased its involvement in Latin American affairs, seeking to affirm its interests in Brazil and the West Indies while capitalising on the opportunity to extend its influence at the expense of its erstwhile ally, Spain, in the Napoleonic Wars. When Ferdinand VII reclaimed the throne of Spain and launched a counter-revolutionary attack in Venezuela, Colombia, and Peru, those who had looked to Britain for spiritual inspiration now asked for material support. The timing of Bolívar's *Letter from Jamaica* was thus particularly propitious. The end of the Napoleonic Wars had left a considerable number of unemployed troops in Europe, and many newly discharged soldiers joined the Latin American cause. On December 1817, the first vessel carrying British recruits left London for the ports of Venezuela. In the next three years, more than eight thousand men went to fight in the revolutionary armies of New Granada, Chile and Peru.

By the 1820s, British newspapers and magazines 'were full of news, opinion and optimistic forecasts about the future of South America'.[39] And yet, in spite of the apparent mania for Latin America, a very different influence was attempting to justify British intervention in Latin American affairs in terms of a 'civilising mission': the extirpation of native backwardness, expressed in the oft-used image of human sacrifice, would be the principal theme of Robert Southey's *Madoc* (1805). In it, the British win the hearts and minds of the naïve native peoples of North America at the expense of their crueller Aztec conquerors. At the end of the epic poem, the Aztec are forcibly sent into the exile that will take them south of the Rio Grande and into the great lake that existed where Mexico City stands today. Exactly in the way that Napoleon's expansionist campaign was justified, so here the advance of civilisation – calculative, driven by material progress – permits the sacrifice and forced displacement of a whole people.

Ten years after Southey's *Madoc* was published, Bolívar concluded the *Letter from Jamaica* with yet another take on the Aztec of Mexico. This time, the discussion is prompted by a proposal to win the hearts and minds of the peoples of America made by his British friend. 'Consider, Sir,' he says, 'what effect would be produced by the appearance of an individual among them [the Americans], who would exemplify the character of Quetzalcoatl, the Buddha of the Mexican rainforest, of whom other nations have said so much? Do you not think it would incline all parties to unite?' Bolívar's response is in sharp contrast to Southey's view of the Mexicans as a barbarous people. 'The general belief,' says Bolívar, 'is that Quetzalcoatl was a divine legislator amongst the pagan tribes of Anahuac, of whom the great Moctezuma was the Emperor, and that Moctezuma derived his authority from Quetzalcoatl.' Rather than the vision of an uncivilised society based upon the barbarous practice of human sacrifice, Bolívar describes a civilised nation based on the respect of an order given by an original legislator. Perhaps the historical reference behind the legend was the figure of Deganawidah, the Peacemaker, and giver of the Great Law of Peace to the Five Nations north of the Rio Grande.

As in the story of the Buddha of the Mexican rainforest, the various traditions among the Indians of North America agree that Deganawidah was not a member of the Five Nations, that he arrived on a boat from the north, and delivered a message of peace in what was once a place of constant violence. Over the years, he persuaded the various tribes to form an alliance instead of constantly fighting. Two leaders, Tododaho and Onondaga, continued to refuse. In a parley, Deganawidah took a single arrow and invited Tododaho to break it, which he did easily. Then he bundled together five arrows and asked Tododaho to break the lot. He could not. In the same way, Deganawidah prophesied, the Five Nations, each one weak on its own, would fall into darkness unless they all banded together. He then laid out the Great Law of Peace. Similarly, Quetzalcoatl symbolises internal political structures and contrasts with the War Serpent. The bundled five arrows can still be seen in the coat of arms of the United States of America.

For Bolívar, the story of the Buddha of the Mexican forest retains all its value as a moral and political lesson. It applies to the case of Latin America: 'Union is certainly what we need most in order to complete our regeneration. However, our division is not surprising, for this is the distinguishing feature of all civil wars formed between two parties: the friends of the status quo, and the reformers. The first are usually more numerous, because the empire of custom generally produces obedience to constituted authorities; the last are always less in number, but more arduous and enthusiastic. Thus it happens that physical power is balanced with moral force, and the contest is prolonged while the result is uncertain. Fortunately, in our case the people have followed the intelligent cause.'

5

Independence: An
Exterminating Thunderbolt

Sparagmos

On the evening of 5 April 1815, a loud explosion was heard in the east of the Indonesian archipelago. At first it was thought the thunderous sounds, which continued all night, were cannon fire. Following rumours that one of the neighbouring villages was under attack, Governor Sir Thomas Raffles, stationed in Jakarta, deployed his regiments. However, they failed to spot any invading party, any filibusters, as the small armies of mercenary soldiers at the service of private companies and competing imperial interests were known. Raffles ordered two boats to sail in search of enemy ships or a vessel in distress. He had good reason to fear a filibustering invasion as he himself had organised one when he had seized control of Java from Dutch hands earlier in the Napoleonic Wars. Before hostilities had ceased, Lord Minto, then Governor-General of India, appointed him as Lieutenant-Governor. He had been born in Jamaica, in the West Indies. Destiny, luck, providence – what forces had brought him to the other side of the world?

Wondering what turn of fate awaited him this time, he summoned his second-in-command, Lieutenant Phillips. The sound of explosions could still be heard in the distance. The sky had blackened. 'We found no trace of the invaders, Governor, Sir,' said Phillips, 'no enemy corvette, no cannon carrying ship.' Instead, Lieutenant Phillips informed Governor Raffles that he had sailed to the west of the island, passing the villages of Bima and Dompo. What he saw had filled him with terror. 'The villages were completely deserted and the houses and trees burnt and fallen down,' he said. 'In Bima there were no animals. No birds ever flew over our ship. It is as if they all vanished in thin air. In Dompo the horses were dead. Nearby we found untold misery and the remains of hundreds, perhaps thousands of disinterred corpses. They were torn apart. I have seen *sparagmos*, I have seen bodies torn apart,' he said, 'I have seen the wrath of God.'[1]

News of a giant tsunami came from Sanggar on the evening of 10 April. On the same date, just before midnight, a wave 4 metres high hit the coast of east Java and laid to waste the Moluccan Islands. Thus the East Indies' lucrative spice trade, which had been one of the driving forces of the world economy since the end of the Middle Ages, came to an end. When the Ottoman Turks took Constantinople in 1453 and the Byzantine Empire was no more, the search for spices had driven the Portuguese and the Spanish to forge an empire. The Portuguese had been the first to round the Cape of Good Hope, off the southernmost part of Africa, and to sail across the Indian Ocean to the south Indian city of Calicut. The wealth of the Indies was now open to Europe.

It was during this time that men working for the Portuguese and Spanish crowns, and for their Genoese and Venetian bankers, had set foot in the New World. First Christopher Columbus landed in Hispaniola in 1492, and then Pedro Álvares Cabral, while attempting to repeat the voyage of his Portuguese compatriot Vasco da Gama to India, was blown westward and into Brazil in 1500. They, and the Spanish and Portuguese explorers who followed after them, introduced the first African slaves into the New World. Some, West Africans and Afro-Spaniards, came accompanying their expeditions. When Spanish and Italian entrepreneurs established the first sugar plantations in Hispaniola (present-day Haiti and the Dominican Republic), Mexico, New Granada, Venezuela and Peru during the 1500s, their numbers shot up. Then, between 1530 and 1600, the Portuguese and Italian merchants who had developed the sugar industry of the Atlantic islands off the coast of Africa moved their ventures to Bahía and Pernambuco, in northern Brazil. Soon these two regions accounted for over a half of the world's sugar production.

When the same genocide that had wiped out the Indians of the Caribbean and Peru was turned on the Indians of Brazil in the 1560s, the Portuguese started importing Africans to replace them. Over half a million Africans arrived in the Portuguese colony during the 1600s and 1.7 million more during the 1700s. By 1800, 2.5 million Africans had been forcibly displaced to Brazil, compared with just over a million brought to all of the viceroyalties and captaincies of Spanish America. In the late 1650s, the English took Jamaica and Barbados from the Spanish, promptly displacing Brazil as the leading sugar producer and slave importer in the Americas. Thomas Raffles had been born on a boat, just off the coast of Jamaica. At fourteen, he joined the British East India Company, the trading company that shaped Britain's overseas conquests and would shape his fate. In 1811 he mounted a filibustering expedition against the French and the Dutch, the success of which provided him with the Governorship of Indonesia. Once installed, he moved to regulate the opium and slave trades, which he effectively stopped, much to the chagrin of the Company. He even had time to engage in the conservation of monuments and to become a naturalist. News of the destruction caused by the 1815 disaster in the Indonesian archipelago affected him deeply. His wife had died the year before, and now everything he had fought for and had come to love lay in ruins. The next year he would return to England to continue his efforts to acquire Singapore for the British.

Only when a thick cloud of ash began to darken the skies above Borneo, Sulawesi and the Moluccan Islands did it became clear exactly what had happened: Mount Tambora had blown, in what was to date the largest volcanic eruption in history. The explosion in eastern Java was heard as far away as the island of Sumatra, some 2,000 kilometres distant. It completely devastated the vegetation of the islands, sending shattered, uprooted trees into the sea, covered in dark grey pumice ashes. These trees formed rafts of up to 5 kilometres across that travelled as far as the port of Calcutta, in India, causing sailors to spread the rumour that a fleet of boats carrying the dead souls of African slaves was on its way to announce the end of the world. Indeed, after the rafts were sighted, the torrential rains of the delayed summer monsoon helped cholera to spread from Bengal to Moscow. In China, summer never arrived and the chill killed trees, rice crops and water buffalo, and floods that destroyed most remaining crops and brought about the worst famine and destitution in a long time, overwhelmed the Yangtze valley.

Longitudinal winds spread the volcanic ash from Mount Tambora, in the east of the Indonesian archipelago, all the way to Europe. Pink and orange sunsets were visible in London at the end of 1815, and in the following months a persistent fog over the north-eastern coast of the United States, that neither rain nor gales could disperse, blotted out the sun. The dimmed sunlight made it possible to see the black spots of the sun with the naked eye. The entire northern and western hemispheres suffered the most extreme weather conditions between the end of 1815 and the first half of 1816. Incessant rainfall during the uncongenial summer of 1816 was followed by red snow falling over Italy, Hungary and Switzerland. Crops failed, animals died, plague took thousands of lives, industries came to a grinding halt and food riots brought Europe to its knees. The violence was severe in the United Kingdom and France, where grain warehouses were looted, and worse in Switzerland, where the government had to declare a national emergency. It is estimated that, by the end of 1816, close to 200,000 lives had been lost in Europe. It was as if the world had ended. Some called it 'the year without summer'. Others spoke of a curse that had befallen the imperial powers of Europe and the North American colonies because of the trade in human beings. 'Europe has brought this curse upon itself' went a story carried word of mouth by sailors, slaves and 'talkee' women throughout the north-eastern coast of the United States and the British and Spanish colonies of the Caribbean; 'it is payment for the pact they had signed with the devil.'

Darkness

In June that same year, in the Villa Diodati near Lake Geneva, Switzerland, Lord Byron, the Shelleys and John Polidori amused themselves with the composition of a series of stories that could capture the sense of impending apocalypse: 'I had a dream, which was not all a dream. / The bright sun was extinguished, and the stars / Did wander darkling in the eternal space [. . .] And war, which for a moment was no more, / Did glut himself again [. . .] The world was void, / the populous and the powerful was a lump / Seasonless, herbless, treeless, lifeless / A lump of death / A chaos of hard clay [. . .] A fearful hope was all the world contained,' wrote Byron, capturing the apparent lack of all divine purpose in his poem 'Darkness', written in July 1816. For him, the present disaster was merely the final link in a chain of events that included lifeless slavery, fear, war and the dehumanisation of life and work through the extended use of machinery.

A few years earlier, on 27 February 1812, he had addressed the members of the House of Lords on the so-called Frame-Work Bill then being put before Parliament, a law that proposed the death penalty for Luddites. The workers degraded as a result of mechanisation, known as Luddites, protested by direct and violent action against the means of their slavery, smashing the machinery that turned them into lifeless clay in the hands of the powerful. They perceived such means as no different from the use of the *owba coocoo*, as West Africans called the dreaded slave ship, in the enslavement and trade of human bodies across the globe. For these men, the cause of anti-slavery and their own suffering were one and the same. 'You call these men a mob,' said Byron, 'desperate, dangerous, and ignorant; and seem to think that the only way to quiet the *belua multorum es capitum* is to lop off a few of its superfluous heads.'

Byron intimated that the monstrous creature their Lordships looked upon with fear and disgust was their own creation. 'It is the mob that labour in your fields and serve in your houses, that man your navy, and recruit your army, that have enabled you to defy all the world,' he said. But now that the many-headed beast moved itself into action, Byron contended, the landed gentry and the new class of wealthy industrialists readied themselves to let loose upon it 'your dragoons and your executioners'. Calling them 'a multitude of heads' (*belua multorum capitum*), Byron reminded his fellow Lordships that the multitudinous beast was capable of reflective judgement and action.[2] In doing so, he invoked the recent memory of the last three dark decades: the Gordon Riots of 1780, when Newgate was besieged under the leadership of former African American slaves Benjamin Bowsey and John Glover; the burning of the Albion Mills by protesters in Lambeth in 1791; the challenge of Sheffield workers petitioning Parliament to put an end to slavery in 1791, which, like the Luddites, the cuttlers of Sheffield saw as akin to their own destitution, brought about by mechanisation, the loss of commons and the cost of imperial efforts abroad. The next year would see the formation of the London Corresponding Society (LCS), similarly committed to equality among all 'whether black or white, high or low, rich or poor'; the transatlantic consequences of the Haitian Revolution – a shock to planters, slave traders and landowners, an inspiration to those condemned to half-life in the abodes of world production – inspired and carried out by black slaves and freed brown workers or *pardos* on the Caribbean island in April 1792; the Irish Rebellion of 1798; the Despard Conspiracy of 1802; the impact of 'Spence's Plan' on the popular culture of the 1790s and the first decade of the 1800s, modelled upon the example of the Indians of the Americas and rebellious slaves, including its call 'to look backward to the medieval commune and forward to the withering away of the state'.[3]

Byron's voice was not a lone one. William Blake had referred to the Albion Mills, the first steam-powered factory in London, when he famously questioned in the preface to his epic *Milton, a Poem*: 'And was Jerusalem builded here / Among these dark Satanic Mills?' He had also taken part in the Gordon Riots of 1780. The factory was located just down the road from Hercules Buildings, where Blake resided. A few yards from it was a public house called the Oakley Arms. Blake left London during the famine of 1800, but by then he was well acquainted with the people and arguments that circulated around the same streets and often converged on the Oakley Arms, individuals like Thomas Spence, and fellow Spenceans such as Edward Despard, Ottobah Cugoano and Robert Wedderburn, all of them political radicals and the latter two former slaves.

He knew Ottobah Cugoano, an African servant in London who had arrived from the Caribbean and become a preacher and writer. Between 1787 and 1791, Cugoano wrote a tract called *Thoughts and Sentiments on the Evil of Slavery*. In it, he uses the literary motifs of light out of darkness and justified action out of desperation, words and metaphors used by Byron in his 1812 speech before the House of Lords, and present also in the letters written by the former slave Robert Wedderburn in London to his half-sister Elizabeth Campbell, based in Jamaica, and in Bolívar's 1815 *Letter from Jamaica*.

Cugoano defended the Indians of the Americas, whom he had known and worked with during his time as a plantation slave in the Caribbean; he opposed the expansion of the death penalty, repeatedly referred to his 'fellow creatures' and invoked the languages of friendship, the human race and the world turned upside down. Like Byron and Bolívar, he spoke of his fellow Africans and the American Indians as the leftover of a vast system of transatlantic exchange and empire: a monstrous 'creature' made up of the severed limbs, rotten corpses and half-dead bodies left after the Middle Passage. The monstrous creature, he contended, was neither African (nor Indian) nor European. It could only be both, or neither, or perhaps something, someone new whose appearance in this world could not be predicted, only anticipated. A violent apparition, a spectre recovering possession of the body it had once owned. In any case, no longer the end result of avarice, stock-jobbing, and private property.

Lightning

For Cugoano and Wedderburn, as well as for Bolívar and others like Byron and Despard, an end to such tragedy could only come about through an assembly or a confederation of the many diverse peoples: 'the human race'. While Bolívar spoke of such an assembly in terms of legal and political design, mixing the language of philosophical radicals like Jeremy Bentham and James Mill with the Indian and African metaphors of divine wandering and return from the wilderness and the darkness of the underworld, Cugoano used the language of the 'everlasting gospel' and preached that 'church signifies an assembly of people; but a building of wood, brick or stone, where the people meet together, is generally called so'. This language, theological though it may be, has as much modern political significance as the Utilitarian constitutionalism of Bentham and the radicals who published in William Cobbett's *Weekly Political Register* or in Francis Jeffrey's *Edinburgh Review*, founded in 1802. In hindsight, we could call it a nineteenth-century Liberation Theology.

However, unlike the jargon of Utilitarian constitutionalism and the literary and political articles of the *Edinburgh Review*, which were known to the predominantly white Creole leaders of Latin American independence, the Jubilee gospel of Liberation Theology was hugely popular among those with whom people like Bolívar grew up, worked with and fought with (for and against) in Caracas, Cartagena de Indias, Jacmel and Kingston. 'And should the people be frightened away by the many abominable dead carcasses which they meet with,' wrote Cugoano, 'they should follow the multitudes to the fields, to the vallies, to the mountains, to the islands, to the rivers, and to the ships.' The language of 'abominable dead carcasses' and 'multitude' of *sparagmos* and terror, is more common to Equiano, Bolívar and Byron, than to the less baroque and unromantic Utilitarians, with whom, nevertheless, and in spite of important differences, they also shared a kindred spirit of enlightenment.

'Are we aware of our obligations to a mob?' asked Byron in the House of Lords in the 1812 Parliament. They, he said, 'who have enabled you to defy all the world', can also 'defy you when neglect and calamity have driven them to despair!' In the space of a few lines, the gentle idea of the masters' and civilisers' sympathy and obligations to the conquered, the poor and the enslaved (the beastly mob) turns into its opposite: the militant right of the many to defy their masters, always the few, when catastrophe and disaster push them into exodus – to the mountains, islands, rivers and ships, as Cugoano says – and thus into a position of desperation. Light out of darkness, defiance justified by despair, the recourse to exodus from slavery and oppression; together, these motifs constitute the conceptual and rhetorical pillars of a veritable right to revolution, seemingly pulled out of a hat through a sleight of hand (or, rather, tongue) by a twenty-four-year-old Byron.

'It lives!' seems to shout Byron at their Lordships and the wealthy industrialists gathered in Parliament: you have created this monster, used it in your pursuit of glory and power, and after all is said and done you seek to discard it, dispatching your dragoons and executioners to do the dirty job for you. But it lives, it talks, it acts. Moreover, it can do so, it *can* defy you, it *will* do so; 'it' has the right to defy you when catastrophe has driven 'them' to despair. In the process, 'it' becomes 'them', the people themselves. 'You may call the people a mob,' said Byron, 'but do not forget that a mob too often speaks the sentiments of the people.' A similar fire burns within the pages of Cugoano's *Thoughts and Sentiments on the Evil of Slavery* and Bolívar's *Letter from Jamaica*. In the latter, the anxieties of the planters confronted by their slaves are set in contrast with the rhetoric of slave 'defiance out of despair'. Together with the link between Afro-Indian and Christian gods and prophets on the one hand, and on the other, the literary motif of the rise from the darkness down below to the light – not just the light of calculating reason but actually an exterminating bolt of lightning – this rhetoric becomes an argument for liberation, revolution and exodus from colonial oppression. This places Bolívar, Byron and Cugoano in a category of their own, which distinguishes them from other radicals of the time like Bentham or James Mill, with whom they otherwise appear to have much in common.[4]

Another participant of the 1780 Gordon Riots in Newgate was the Jamaican-born Robert Wedderburn. The son of a Scotsman, the owner of a sugar plantation in Jamaica, he would play a central part in the events of the decades leading to Byron's parliamentary address and the wars for freedom in the Americas. He met the English commoner Thomas Spence, collaborated with the veterans of the London Corresponding Society, and embodied in his own person the connection between the practices of slave revolt widespread in the Americas during the 1760s and 1770s, on the one hand, and the rising tide against 'man-stealing' and slavery, on the other, often expressed in Britain and the Americas through the religious language of John Wesley and the political-theological traditions of the Jubilee, John the Baptist (a militant figure displacing pacifist readings of Christ) and the apocalyptic language of Ezekiel and Isaiah.

He was merely one among a considerable number of like-minded people, men and women, operating through the same transatlantic circuits that made possible the actions of Bolívar, Francisco de Miranda and other leaders and collaborators of pro-independence movements in Spanish America such as José de San Martín, the Scot Robert Sutherland, the Cochranes, the Ecuadorian J. M. Antepara or the Mexican Xavier Mina. From the 1780s onwards, many of them communicated dissident views to the poor congregations of Britain, the Caribbean islands and the coasts of South and North America. A growing number of them were

African Americans: Moses Baker, George Liele, Moses Wilkinson, John Marrant, Thomas Swigle, Richard Allen, Absalom Jones, John Jea and George Gibb. Others were based in the islands of the Caribbean, such as Robert Wedderburn's correspondent Elizabeth Campbell, his half-sister and a Maroon or *pardo* former slave in Jamaica. Yet others – like the Haitian sailors and soldiers who served in the navy of the republic of Cartagena de Indias in 1812 – moved in and around the coasts of South America.[5] Besides the good news of the everlasting gospel, rumours of emancipation decrees supposedly issued by the imperial powers, and stories about the American Revolution, British abolitionism and Spanish reformism, together with French reformism and Abolitionism, and, crucially, the Haitian Revolution in Santo Domingo, helped form in slave and coloured communities of Spanish, Portuguese and English America a culture of expectation that helped bring about revolution.

An Exterminating Thunderbolt

These circuits of communication included radical London. Elizabeth Campbell wrote to Robert Wedderburn from Jamaica informing him that from the early nineteenth century 'the free Mulattoes [were] reading Cobbett's Register, and talking about St. Domingo'.[6] Her reference was to the media and the message that accompanied the wave of revolution that had been rolling through the Atlantic world since at least the 1740s. Beginning in 1741 with the New York Conspiracy and culminating in the events of Santo Domingo, in the 1790s and 1800s, slaves and abolitionists pursued the same aims and developed the same strategies everywhere in the Americas and the wider Atlantic. Those goals included autonomy from their owners, acceptable living and working conditions, an end to undue and cruel punishment and ultimately the cessation of work, debt forgiveness, land redistribution and freedom from bondage. The strategy followed in all cases involved a radical form of syncretistic modernity – ideological as well as practical – realised through a variety of means, scenarios and engagements: bargaining, litigation, petitioning, striking, exodus or flight and rebellion. This plan of action and the tactics employed smote the Atlantic world with the force of an exterminating thunderbolt.

In other terms, faced with a catastrophe comparable in scale only to the most devastating natural disaster, Africans, Indians and those who identified with their cause responded collectively. Collective action by enslaved Africans and Indians may hardly be surprising given the conditions under which they lived, but the way in which it altered slavery, this most basic of the political and economic institutions of the modern world, remains a cause of wonder and a historical lesson that resonates down the centuries. As a lesson it is particularly relevant in times of crisis, such as we are experiencing now, when pressing circumstances are made more challenging by our inability to think and act together. At least in that respect there is much we can learn, and much that Africans and Indians, and their descendants in the Americas, continue to teach us.

Take the hybrid, radically syncretistic nature of the modern context of Africans, Indians and mestizos – ideological as well as practical. Elizabeth Campbell, herself a Maroon and a mulatto with mixed European and African ancestry, a freed woman living in the early 1800s in Kingston, Jamaica, and a slave owner, describes in this way the thought process and the actions of her fellow Caribbean and Afro-Latin American brethren since the early 1800s to her brother Robert Wedderburn in London. In her letter, she informs him that the members of the Afro community in Jamaica and the wider Caribbean have been 'reading and discussing' the contents of the most widely read paper by the middle and lower classes of London, a broadsheet that followed and published the debates of the reformists in Parliament, as well as the radical strategies and tactics of the British mob (Byron's 'people'),[7] side by side with the recent developments in Santo Domingo, the stormy night of voodoo in the Bois Caiman that launched the Haitian Revolution, and the popular Christian motifs, political as well as theological, of Jubilee and 'Kingdom Coming', spread throughout the Caribbean and the rest of the Americas by preachers, exhorters and *obeah*, or 'talkee', men and women of African and Afro-Indian descent.

A similar mixture was basic to the embracing of Christianity by slaves visible throughout the Caribbean and Afro-Latin America in those years. Importantly, such enthusiastic embracing did not imply their abandonment of African religious traditions. While Iberian Catholicism and mainstream forms of Protestantism demanded rigid orthodoxy, most of the African religions required no such exclusivity and instead allowed for the investment of Christian figures with the attributes of African gods – chief among them the Virgin Mary, which Yoruba slaves, for instance, linked to Yemayá (the *orixá* or 'embodiment' of the Sea) in Cuba, Colombia, Venezuela, Mexico and Brazil.[8]

The rite of spirit possession, which still sends 'God-fearing' souls like American televangelist Pat Robertson, for instance, into a frenzy of panic, bridges 'one of the most deeply held of all slave aspirations: the desire not just to rest from hard labour but to "re-create" themselves through African music, song, and dance'. As historian George Reid Andrews observes, music and dance were healing on almost every level, 'a balm for body and mind'. As he put it, 'the graceful movements of dance, movement done purely for pleasure and enjoyment, were the antithesis and direct negation of the pain and exhaustion of coerced heavy labour'.

Moreover, when performed collectively, as they usually were, African music and dance not only removed, at least temporarily, the degraded status of slavery and caste, but also created politically crucial sentiments, symbols and actual existing forms of strength and subjectivity that could be opposed to the fantasies of their planters and colonial masters as much as to the intolerable present situation. Thus, a dance by six hundred slaves in the streets of Montevideo during the Christmas season of 1827, a drum-led dancing and singing session in Rio de Janeiro in 1808, and the celebrations during saints' days in Mexico or Buenos Aires were actual forms of social and political organisation, as well as consciousness-altering and spirit-enhancing vehicles for transformation and spiritual manifestation.[9]

One of the central and most enduring messages of African music is 'that rhythm lifts us out of the daily grind by transforming conscious-ness, transforming time, transforming and heightening our experience of the moment', of the present as well as of the future. It is no surprise that most planters and slave owners were profoundly uneasy about the foreign nature of the music and the dance and wary of the political dangers involved in allowing large joyful religious gatherings. In the 1790s, an observer in Bahía, Brazil, noted, 'it does not seem politically wise to permit throngs of negroes, of both sexes, to have their barbarous war drum dances in the streets and squares of this city. They dance in a lascivious fashion, sing heathen songs, and speak in strange tongues.' The dances, known as Batuques de Negros, were banned several times in Portuguese America, and viewed with suspicion by the town councils and authorities of Buenos Aires, Cartagena de Indias and Kingston.[10]

Hybrid and syncretistic religiosity, music and dance, together with intellectual and literary engagement, were part of a revolutionary enlightenment that united the streets of Buenos Aires and Rio de Janeiro with the Methodist churches of Jamaica and the public houses of London. They were no less important for radicals and slaves in availing themselves of their rights and protections already established under royal laws – to change owners, to complain against mistreatment, to have access to the *Defensores de Esclavos* or court-appointed attorneys, and even to express their ideas about equality – or posited as matter of course and a universal condition of possibility for the existence of 'the human race'.[11] Such was the case with prescribed notions of equality, not in the abstract sense, but in the concrete sense of land and freedom. In this respect, the syncretistic strategies of Afro- and Afro-Latin American slaves converged with those of Indians in the Americas and radicals or commoners elsewhere.

For instance, Cobbett's *Register*, which Elizabeth Campbell refers to as being widely read and debated by free mulattoes in Jamaica since the early 1800s, had published 'Spence's Plan'. Named after the English commoner Thomas Spence, whose activities and ideas were well known to the British public between 1755 and 1814, the plan devised and defended a strategy to create a day on which the inhabitants of each parish in Britain would meet 'to take their long-lost rights into possession'. He called that day Jubilee, invoking the call to action inherent in the biblical and oral tradition shared by Robert Wedderburn, Elizabeth Campbell in Jamaica and many slaves and Indians in the rest of the Americas. It involved the restitution of land, the manumission of the bonded, the remission of debt and the cessation of work. Understood in this sense, the language of Jubilee was a call to action that overcame the dualities of religion and secularism by bringing together radical religious notions (Christian, Dissenting and otherwise) and Thomas

Paine-like republicanism, racial dichotomies between white (Creoles or Europeans) and black (slaves) or Indians fighting for revolution, but also the broken memory of Native Americans and African Americans in what they might contribute to a worldwide movement of independence and liberation (as evidenced by Spence's 1794 short story *The Marine Republic* and the dialogue of his 1796 *The Reign of Felicity*) and point towards a future free from all forms of slavery.

Spence knew of and sold Thomas Paine's *Rights of Man* in his book-stall located in London's High Holborn, together with his own *The Real Rights of Man*. By then he had taken a particular interest in the affairs of the Americas, like many other radicals and dissenters at the time. He focused with particular zeal on the way in which the example of sailors, Indians and freed Africans might attract the slaves and all disenfranchised labourers and castes created by European imperialism and help lead them to independence and liberation.[12] Caribbean activists and campaigners for abolitionism like William Davidson and Robert Wedderburn were drawn to his political group and called themselves 'Spenceans'. By 1802, the year of Despard's failed conspiracy to overthrow the monarchy in England, seize London and declare a republic, there was scarcely a wall in London that did not have chalked upon it, in the manner of nine-teenth-century graffiti, the slogan 'Spence's Plan and Full Bellies'. This is the time when the plan appeared in Cobbett's *Register*.

How Not to Turn the World Upside Down

William Cobbett was an outspoken political journalist and a lifelong campaigner for electoral and parliamentary reform intended to root out bribery, corruption by private interests and monarchic influence in Parliament. Two years after his return from Philadelphia in 1800, he established his *Weekly Political Register*, which was soon turned into a broadsheet and quickly became the most widely read publication among the middle and working classes of London. From 1806 onwards, he asso-ciated himself with a Scottish naval officer whose exploits in command of the ship *Flying Pallas* had brought him instant fame. His name was (Lord) Thomas Cochrane. Lord Cochrane's uncle, Rear Admiral Alexander Cochrane, was commander of the British naval fleet stationed in the

West Indies. Early in 1806, Admiral Cochrane agreed, of his own will (or perhaps persuaded by the pragmatic arguments presented to him by his brother and his brother's friend, the merchant John Turnbull) to provide ships and materiel in support of a filibustering expedition, a privately funded military attack on Spanish Venezuela, led by Venezuelan agitator and abolitionist Francisco de Miranda. Turnbull was a close associate of Miranda and an advocate of the commercial opportunities that a free Venezuela would represent to English merchants like himself. On several occasions he had used his influence on key players within or close to the British government, men like Sir Home Popham for instance, in order to sell Miranda's schemes in Britain. In America, William Stephens Smith, the son-in-law of the second President of the United States, John Adams, also provided crucial materiel and financial support from New York, mindful of the fact that President Jefferson and his Secretary of State, James Madison, had decided not to involve themselves or their nation in any explicit form with Miranda's plan.

While Miranda waited for the promises of support of his British and American friends to materialise, other forces, new protagonists on the stage of transatlantic politics, and the changing political destinies of England and continental Europe, then embroiled in the Napoleonic Wars, were already at work trying to undo his plans. On 15 July 1806, the British Cabinet led by Lord Grenville sent instructions to Rear Admiral Cochrane 'highly disapproving of his having taken upon himself, without instruction, to assist general Miranda by the employment of ships under his command, and even to conclude a treaty with him, and that he should be directed to take no steps by which His Majesty can further be committed in that enterprise'.[13] While discussions in London continued, Miranda spent his time recruiting soldiers in New York and the Caribbean for an imminent attack on Venezuela. The attack was launched in August 1806, before the assistance promised by Admiral Cochrane materialised.

Miranda, an abolitionist and a *pardo* himself, sailed from Jacmel, in free Haiti, where he unveiled for the first time the tricolour flag of what was to become the Great Colombia. At first he was successful, landing in the Bay of Coro on 3 August, and raising the flag for the first time on

Spanish American soil. But the wealthy planters and inhabitants of Coro, who had no intention of abolishing slavery and plenty to fear from a brown *pardo* arriving from dreaded Haiti, left the city and did not join the revolt. Miranda sent off for reinforcements from his British friends. In response, Admiral Cochrane offered only neutrality and a promise of secret assistance to keep enemy vessels in the area at bay. On 13 August, deserted and vulnerable to an attack by the approaching Spanish troops, who had the support of the planters and of Venezuela's elites, who had from the outset looked down upon Miranda and his Canarian *pardo* family, sailed off to the island of Aruba. There, he learned from Admiral Cochrane of the British government's loss of heart about the prospects and the convenience of a South American revolution.[14]

Miranda's filibustering expedition had been planned to coincide with another 'private' expedition into Buenos Aires, led by his friend Sir Home Popham, a close associate of the merchant John Turnbull and of Admiral Cochrane's brother, who had also lobbied the British government on Miranda's behalf. Popham was at the time stationed in the Cape of Good Hope. In those days, affairs concerning the southernmost parts of Spanish America were considered to fall under the jurisdiction of the offices of the British Empire established in South Africa. On 8 June 1806, still unaware of William Pitt's death in January of that year, and of the changing priorities of the new government, Sir Home Popham assembled a filibuster army in the Cape and sailed across the South Atlantic with the initial intention of seizing Montevideo, in present-day Uruguay. Instead, having learned that the city of Buenos Aires in the estuary of the River Plate lacked defences and was now a repository for Peruvian silver, he landed his men in the Argentinean capital named after the Virgin Mary (Our Lady of Buen Ayre), taking control of it and of its handsome bounty.

From there, he wrote to Miranda communicating his conviction that 'the Ministers would accede to your propositions and send you here, that your plan [to attack Venezuela and free Colombia] would take as well from this side as from the other'. Popham's filibustering adventure had finally forced the hand of an indecisive government but the response of Grenville's Cabinet of All Talents proved slow and inept. Mired by difficulties and the many conspiracies and schemes concerning the fate of South America after the advance of Napoleon's armies in Europe, the Cabinet of All Talents collapsed. Its instructions in support of Popham's filibustering adventure were tardy and convoluted; the British occupation of Argentina was in the end short-lived. Popham was nonetheless presented with a sword of honour for his efforts to 'open new markets' while Miranda wandered the British Caribbean for a year, waiting for British aid that never materialised.

George Canning had entered the Duke of Portland's Cabinet after the fall of the Cabinet of All Talents as Secretary of State for Foreign Affairs. His counterpart at the War and Colonial Office was Viscount Castlereagh. Canning thought little about the failed attempt to secure Buenos Aires, and instead concentrated his efforts on responding to Napoleon's intention to add Denmark and its naval fleet to his resources and remove Portugal and its Brazilian gold from the British sphere of influence. When Napoleon invaded the Iberian Peninsula and ordered his troops into the Portuguese kingdom, the British fleet appeared before Lisbon, removed the imperial family and transported it to a new imperial throne in Rio de Janeiro. With British commerce excluded from all the ports under Napoleon's control, a new mercantile existence was forced upon England. On the horizon were plans for an alternative economic and imperial arrangement, one that could meet the challenge of economists and commentators like Adam Smith and Jeremy Bentham, who were warning against the mounting costs of direct imperial occupation, while also taking into account the looming possibility of further involvement in the European conflict.

In that context, a renewed scheme for an enterprise in South America could provide an alternative. Short of occupation (whose inconvenience had been shown by Popham's failed Argentinean adventure), the continuation of contraband trade and the establishment of independent monarchies in the place of Spanish viceroyalties seemed a viable strategy. On the one hand, such a strategy would put a halt to the contamination of Jacobin and radical principles throughout the Americas; on the other, it would attract the loyalty of the Creole populations already fearful about the prospects of a re-enactment of the events of Haiti in

Spanish America and lower the costs of British intervention. From then onwards, the role of Britain would only be that of a beneficent auxiliary. The plan explicitly excluded support for fully-fledged independence and its corollaries, abolition and land redistribution, in Spanish and Portuguese America.

This was the course advocated by Viscount Castlereagh in his memorandum of May 1807, composed after consultation with Sir Arthur Wellesley. This was also the course followed by Wellesley's brother, Richard Colley Wellesley, the former Governor-General of India, when the latter became Britain's Foreign Minister after the infamous pistol duel between Canning and Castlereagh, their resignation and the fall of Portland's Cabinet in 1809. The Foreign Office thought that 'by use of the bond of allegiance to Ferdinand [Spain was now an ally following Napoleon's invasion, and Wellesley would not risk upsetting that relationship] England may preserve her colonies to Spain yet compel Spain to alter her commercial system [in England's favour].'[15] The first Marquis of Wellesley met Bolívar and the other members of the Venezuelan diplomatic mission of 1810 privately at his home in Apsley House. One result of the conversations was deadlock; the Venezuelans obtained only informal expressions of sympathy and protection against France. Britain was more concerned about placating Spain and containing Napoleon's influence in continental Europe, while preserving its own commercial interests in the West Indies, than with the prospects of Spanish American *afrancesados* (abolitionists and rebels similar to the popular radicals at home, perhaps even Francophiles) taking charge of their own destinies.

Another result was the confirmation of the conviction in the minds of Bolívar and Miranda that to identify independence as a worthy cause was not sufficient, that another strategy and different tactics were necessary. The new strategy included transatlantic solidarity, friendship of humanity, freedom, and a newly developed concept of 'the human race'. The latter would be embodied in the sort of confederation or 'league of nations' that Bolívar would propose in 1815. The thoroughly revolutionary character of such a proposal at the time should not be underestimated. As a result of the establishment of an international body like that, predicated upon the solidarity of the former colonies, the sheer force of the big imperial powers could be contained, perhaps even brought under the 'sublime' notion of a Corinth-like place, which he located in the Isthmus of Panama, where the newly established 'republics, kingdoms and empires', big and small, more powerful and less powerful, could gather, under conditions of equality and freedom from coercion, under the same law or institutionality, 'in one august congress', as he put it, in order to treat and discuss 'great and interesting questions of peace and war with nations of the other three parts of the globe'. The immediate consequence would be the radical transformation of the shape and content of international relations, nothing less than a reordering of the world under completely new terms: equality, freedom and the right to revolution. The sort of effect that the existence of the General Assembly of the United Nations and the system of international law based upon the notion of a right to self-determination, as a pillar of the discourse and practice of human rights, however precarious it may be, actually has on the privileges of veto-holding, economically and militarily powerful nations.

Both the strategy and the tactics were closer to those already discussed and advocated at the time by popular movements and activists on both sides of the Atlantic. Given that the new line followed by the British ministry meant the cause favoured by Miranda and Bolívar was lost, it was time to look for resources and inspiration elsewhere. In the following weeks, Miranda arranged a series of meetings at his residence in Grafton Way to introduce the members of the delegation to his friends and acquaintances, and into London's wider public sphere.

Some of London's public voices were more radical, among them those of abolitionists like William Wilberforce or Thomas Clarkson whose activities were sustained and encouraged by the black population of Britain's capital, among them the Igbo slave and sailor Olaudah Equiano, who had had experience in the sugar economy of the Caribbean, and had contacts with Dissenters and Antinomians in both England and the West Indies. Like Afro-Latin Americans, he too developed a concept of human rights. He quoted Milton's *Paradise Lost*, and his words 'are you not hourly in dread of an insurrection?' addressed to the rulers of England, were echoed by Lord Byron in his 1812 speech before the House of Lords.[16] These radical voices construed Spanish American independence as a vector of revolution that travelled westward into the Atlantic and southward to the Caribbean and what we now call Latin America, in a relation of identity around common issues such as the rejection of expansionism, slavery and the sacrificial economy of short-term winners and long-term losers that was establishing itself as dominant across the globe, in the name of a new understanding of rights and humanity.[17]

Others construed Spanish America and Britain as being united through their shared victimisation by illegitimate power, via an identification between France and Spain, or paired, as a matter of strategy, by Spanish America's need to build a sound pre- and post-war economy based on free trade, and Britain's need for war-time trade. Names associated with Miranda's Grafton Way circle such as James Mill, William Walton and William Burke, as well as Jeremy Bentham, made that case in their writings and in the pages of the *Edinburgh Review*, the *Quarterly* and the *Morning Chronicle*. Mill portrayed Spanish America's patriots as lovers of British constitutional monarchy and aristocratic advocates of reform. Perhaps he was thinking of someone like the British naval hero and aristocrat-turned-radical-politician Lord Thomas Cochrane, popular in Westminster electoral circles and among readers of Cobbett's *Weekly Political Register*, upon whom he could model these South American patriots without making them, or himself, appear like unpatriotic *afranc-esados*.[18] Mill contended that these Latin Americans could comfortably respond to the conservative maxim according to which 'as much as possible should be done for the people – but nothing by them'.[19] In fact, the forced abdication of Ferdinand VII of Spain in the face of Napoleon's invading army added credence to this portrayal, since it could allow Creole patriots to say exactly what the British government wanted to hear: that they were fighting to preserve the rights of the Spanish monarch, 'making *de facto* independence a return to tradition rather than a disruptive break with the past'.[20]

Though it was not without risk to endorse any rebellion in these years – reactionaries of all kinds were recoiling in horror on both sides of the Atlantic at the sight of the potential consequences of the American,

French and Haitian revolutions – people like William Burke, James Mill and the translators of the Jesuit Juan Pablo Viscardo's *Letter to the Spanish Americans* (1799–1808) found an ingenious way to dispel from the minds of merchants, planters and rulers on both sides of the Atlantic the spectres of terror in France, bloodshed in Haiti or brutal loyalist reaction at home. They could support the cause of Spanish American autonomy without fear of being perceived as radical revolutionaries, or hide their politics of contestation behind a thick veil of patriotic bluster and exotic tropical scenery. Within this safe space writers like Robert Southey or the reformist Whig parliamentarian and playwright Richard Brinsley Sheridan could appeal to the same audiences that followed the cause of independence in Spanish America by presenting it as similar to Britain's opposition to France, as Sheridan did in his popular play *Pizarro*, in which the conquistador stands for the villainous Napoleon.

Quite different, however, were the impact and enduring legacy of more radical voices, like those of Equiano, Wedderburn, Barbauld and others. Their cause was given impetus by a series of debates that took place between 1790 and the early 1800s. These debates were transatlantic in scope. Their focus was freedom from slavery, the vindication of Nature and natural rights before the interests of trade and accumulation, independence and revolution. At stake was the call made by those thrown out of their lands and put down below the main deck of slave ships, the families displaced from their English rural commons and thrown into barracoons, dungeons and factories in the big cities, or into the bloody maw of the mine and plantation systems. They sought to invent the words, the metaphors, the language with which to express their desire to walk away from the dark abodes of the global triangular system and into the light of a new world brought about by their own actions.

One of the starting points in the creation of such a language was the publication in the 1790s of Thomas Spence's *The Real Rights of Man*, a version of his 1775 address to the Newcastle Philosophical Society, *On the Mode of Administering the Landed State of the Nation as a Joint Stock Property*, in which he proposed that 'the country of any people ... is properly their common', and argued that 'the first landholders were usurpers and tyrants', as were their heirs. Also related was the delivery in 1789 of *A Discourse on the Love of Our Country* by the Dissident theologian and moral philosopher Richard Price, a man close to both Anna Barbauld and Mary Wollstonecraft, the first salvo in the ensuing pamphlet war known as the 'Revolution Controversy' in London, which brought to a head differing views about revolution in France and the Americas, popular unrest at home and the connections between these events and the sentiments of the people, in particular the middle and lower sectors of society, concerning liberty from slavery and self-government.

Price's sermon provoked the well-known response by Edmund Burke, *Reflections on the French Revolution*, published in 1790, in which the British parliamentarian, always with an eye on the increasing tide of domestic radicalism, warned his compatriots that the popular uprising in Paris could only lead to war and tyranny. In turn, Burke's tract provoked not one but at least three famously hard-hitting rebuttals by people closely associated with Price, and to whom the wider public lent a ready ear: Thomas Paine from Norfolk, Mary Wollstonecraft from Spitalfields and Newington Green, London, and Anna Barbauld from Leicestershire and also a member of the Newington Green Dissenting community.

In their rebuttals, Paine, Wollstonecraft and Barbauld extended Price's ideas on the egalitarianism inherent in the spirit of the revolutions. Paine's *Rights of Man*, published in 1791, clearly expressed the notion that all men have equal rights in Nature and therefore the right to equal participation. In 1792 Paine was elected to the National French Convention and was welcomed by the Girondists, the party of French abolitionist Jacques-Pierre Brissot and the Venezuelan Precursor of Independence, Francisco de Miranda, as an ally. Like Miranda, Paine was arrested by Robespierre's *Montagnards* in December 1793 but released soon afterwards. By the time *Rights of Man* was published and available in London, Paine had spent twelve years in America where his political writings, especially his 1776 *Common Sense*, were much admired and were partly responsible for the Declaration of Independence of the same year. Like Spence, Paine was deeply impressed by the ability of Native Americans, the Five Nations of the Iroquois Confederation in this case, to live in harmony with Nature while achieving a democratic form of political organisation that did not require the presence of a monarchic figurehead and purposely avoided the appearance of a single point of power and accumulation within the community. Like Spence, Price, Despard, Bolívar, Wollstonecraft, Barbauld and Wedderburn, he opposed slavery, and like Spence he thought long and hard about the way in which private landownership separated the majority of the people from their natural inheritance (for instance, in his 1795 *Agrarian Justice*).

In turn, Mary Wollstonecraft, a congregant in Price's parish in London's Newington Green, which also included dissenting preacher and moral thinker Joseph Priestley, whose influence upon philosophical radicalism was acknowledged by Jeremy Bentham, extended the egalitarian arguments of her friend and mentor to the position of women in society. This served as the basis upon which she denounced the rhetoric as well as the premises of Edmund Burke's attack on Price and the visionary ideas, looking forward to the coming of an equal society, espoused by the radicalised sectors of British society, and the transatlantic circuit. In her 1790 pamphlet *A Vindication of the Rights of Men, in a Letter to the Right Honourable Edmund Burke; Occasioned by His reflections on the Revolution in France*, Wollstonecraft directed her attack at the sentiments of contempt for the people that underlined the language and attitude of fatherhood, masculinity and chivalrous sympathy used by Burke, which were the very nature of elitism. For her, Burke's rhetoric justified a society founded on the subordination of women, on opulence and corruption, and on the inhumane treatment of the poor and the enslaved.

While elitism, personified in Burke himself, is backward-looking, the stance that calls for action in order to abandon a situation of darkness and oppression to enlightenment and freedom, personified by Richard Price, has, as Wollstonecraft says, 'an orientation toward the present and the future, and the rejection of power and riches'. Along the same lines, she rejected inheritance and echoed the claims made by Spence, Paine, Wedderburn and others that the problems of the present were rooted in the inequity of property distribution. She also noted that the tenor of Burke's arguments 'settles slavery on an everlasting foundation'. As she put it, in accordance with Burke's advocacy for a backward-looking view of history 'we are to submit to the inhuman custom [slave traffic], and term an atrocious insult to humanity the love of our country, and a proper submission to the laws by which our property is secured . . . And to this selfish principle [security of property] every nobler one is sacrificed.'[21] Of course it is not just abstract principles that are sacrificed, but millions of people. She advocated revolution.

Burke's book sold 30,000 copies in two years, an astonishing number at the time, Thomas Paine's *Rights of Man* sold a staggering 200,000 copies or more, and the first edition of Mary Wollstonecraft's *A Vindication of the Rights of Men* sold out in the space of a mere three weeks. These numbers are an indication of the impetus such publications gave to the reformist cause of radical politicians like Cobbett and Cochrane, but are also a reflection of the new climate encountered by advocates of revolution in Spanish America such as Simón Bolívar or J. M. Antepara after their arrival into London in 1810. They were not strangers to such a climate, or to the revolutionary language invented by the radicalism of the time in order to justify its actions and make sense of international political developments. And they did not have to wait to come to England in order to discover and equip themselves with such language, or the arguments and ideas to which it lent a proper voice.

A Gathering Storm

Whereas commentators like James Mill, Robert Southey or the reformist R. B. Sheridan identified Britain with Latin America through their shared opposition to monarchic Spain and Napoleonic France, other writers like Anna Barbauld 'used Spanish America to expose the uncomfortable similarities between Napoleonic Europe and Britain'.[22] Barbauld used the anti-Spanish language of the Black Legend in order to condemn Britain's commercial interests and expansionism as no better than Spain's, as in the verses 'the Golden tide of Commerce leaves thy shore / Leaves thee to prove the alternate ills that haunt / Enfeebling Luxury and ghastly Want'.[23] She portrayed Spanish America 'not as the Romantic correlative of British patriotic virtue, but instead as the last refuge of liberty after the moral and financial collapse of Europe'.[24] At the same time she saw the 1803 purchase of Louisiana by the United

States, the British-American War of 1812 and the Spanish-American wars for freedom that began in 1810 as the three component parts of the same historical and geopolitical puzzle.

The first, the Louisiana Purchase by the United States from France, was prompted by the Napoleonic fear of slave revolts in the Caribbean, specifically Haiti. The Louisiana Purchase encompassed most of fourteen existing US states, around 23 per cent of America's territory today, and two Canadian provinces. It doubled the size of US territory, guaranteed unimpeded American access to the trade port of New Orleans and initiated the expansionist drive of the US westwards and southwards. Napoleon himself acknowledged the importance of the event when he stated, upon completion of the deal, 'this accession of territory affirms forever the power of the United States, and I have given England a maritime rival who sooner or later will humble her pride'. Without taking into account the importance of the Louisiana Purchase, Barbauld's expansive vision of the future Anglophone world would be difficult to conceive. With it, the United States redefined itself by becoming a continental power. That single event would unleash forces, positive and negative, as a consequence of which the destiny of the Americas and that of the rest of the world would change forever.

The second component is no less important for America's redefined identity; even the national anthem of the United States comes from the 1812 British-American War. The crisis between Britain and America originated in the 1809 Orders-in-Council issued by the British government authorising British ships to impress deserters from the Royal Navy taking refuge in American ships. Britain's claim was similar to the contemporary doctrine according to which a country that harbours terrorists or terrorist suspects, who may be nationals of the countries claiming to be under threat of attack, may itself be considered terrorist, and thus allows for the use of force against it by the countries that claim to be under threat of attack by such terrorist suspects. In the process of enforcing that claim, which Americans at the time correctly read as a neocolonial claim, many Americans were bagged. This not only reasserted the continued British claim to the illegitimacy of American identity. Just as important was the fact that sailors, among them many former slaves, understood the practice of impressment – kidnapping seamen and forcing them to work – as a form of slavery.

The 1812 war had often unnoticed Spanish American dimensions. The coasts of Chile, Rio de Janeiro, Tierra del Fuego in Argentina, and Galápagos, off the coast of Ecuador, saw action. The 1806 filibuster intervention by Home Popham to take control of Buenos Aires was also still very much part of living memory: it entailed the paradox of Britain endorsing an attack, in South America, that seemingly betrayed the very values it was claiming to defend from Napoleon in Europe. Thus, the third part of the puzzle was the potential, after the Louisiana Purchase and the 1812 British-American War, for a self-image of North America's superior 'destiny' to be projected upon Spanish America.

Epilogue, in Black and White

Afro-Latin Americans participated in and influenced political debates during the revolutionary period, at times leading the elites to acquiesce to radical measures they initially either did not contemplate or did so with ambiguity. When this fact is acknowledged it becomes clear that no consensus regarding racial equality was immediate. Not only did the white Creole elites have to overcome a colonial tradition that linked law and order to racial hierarchies, but they also had to declare racial equality without having a successful example to follow. As historians of the period often point out, the United States had already shown that a modern republic could coexist with slavery and racial inequality.

In the minds of many white Creoles, racial equality was associated with the unappealing image of revolutionary Haiti. Early republican race relations were charged with deep tensions. In the aftermath of the wars of independence, which saw the consolidation of a powerful black or brown political and military class – including generals, congressmen and senators – and the enfranchisement of a segment of the free black population in many parts of Latin America, free black and brown or *pardo* men and women had developed new expectations of freedom and equality and exerted political pressure in a way that the white Creole elite would have been foolish to ignore. In short, after independence,

the future of race relations was one of the most controversial and decisive problems of the post-colonial period in Latin America.[25]

★

On 7 March 2001 the *Washington Post* published a report on the results
of the 2000 US Census under the headline 'Hispanics Draw Even with
Blacks in New Census'. The story documented a profound shift in the
composition of the population of the United States. It also suggested
that the consequences of such a change would be far-reaching for the
political and cultural life of the United States in the new millennium. In
accordance with that report, the number of Americans who described
themselves as Hispanics grew by nearly 60 per cent in the 2000 Census
and totalled 35.3 million, about three million more than the Census
Bureau had predicted. The importance of these figures cannot be over-
stated, as the once-a-decade census affects the way in which congressional
district boundaries are divided, federal funds distributed and domestic
and foreign policy and market decisions are made in the United States.

In the US, 'Hispanics' or 'Latinos/as' are generally considered to be
people whose ancestors are from Spanish-speaking countries. However,
unlike Creoles or mixed-white mestizos in Spanish and Portuguese
America (nowadays, Latin America), 'Hispanics' cannot claim the
umbilical cord that still ties Latins, in South America, to Europe. This is
so because 'Hispanics' in the US, particularly after they were recognised
as a 'minority' in the 1970s, must first demonstrate their allegiance to
the American nation and claim such nationality for themselves. They
are thus latecomers in the Great History of the advance of Anglo-
American Spirit. Put simply, they are second-class Americans, whereas
Latin American Creoles or mestizos are second-class Europeans in the
sense that they are conscious of not being who they are supposed to be
– Europeans. Thus, for instance, Colombian intellectual Torres Caicedo
put forward the idea of Latin America in the nineteenth century in this
way: 'There is Anglo-Saxon America, Danish America, Dutch America,
etc.; there is also Spanish America, French America and Portuguese
America; and therefore to this second group what other scientific name
applies but Latin?'

Torres Caicedo was a Francophile who coined the term 'Latin America' in reference to a Spanish and Portuguese government, economy and an 'educated' civil society connected to the interests of the rulers of Europe, which turned its face to France and Britain, later on to the United States, and turned its back not only on Spain and Portugal but also on Afro-America and Indo-America. Afro-Latin Americans and Indians do not have the same problem. Their political consciousness emerged in the nineteenth century 'from not being considered human, not from not being considered Europeans'. In that respect, the *Washington Post*'s 2001 report elided the fact that 'Blacks' and 'Hispanics' are not necessarily separate groups. Not only it is true that by the end of the twentieth century Afro-Latin Americans outnumbered African Americans by three to one, that is, 110 million and 35 million respectively, but they also formed on average almost twice as large a proportion of their respective populations, 22 per cent in Latin America, 12 per cent in the United States. Perhaps most important is the fact that the political consciousness of Afro-Latin Americans and Indians in Latin America has much more in common with the political consciousness of African Americans and with Latinos who have cut their ties with Europe, in so far as both originated more in the spirit of prophecy and liberation that comes from 'not being considered human', than with the political consciousness of white mestizos in Latin America who still claim their second-class European membership of the exclusive club of globalisation.[26]

It was second-class membership of the club of globalisation that Bolívar rejected in the 1815 *Letter from Jamaica*. Under the reformed imperial system established by the Spanish Bourbon monarchy during the second half of the eighteenth century, a number of economic and political policies were introduced to stimulate manufacturing and technology in order to modernise Spain. In the colonies of Spanish America, this meant the establishment of a series of restrictions on competition through protection, subsidies and the granting of monopoly rights, increased taxation and reforms for the larger exploitation of the colonies' resources. The Spanish metropolis was not alone in following this path of economic development. In Britain, the Whig government of Robert Walpole had in 1721 introduced legislation essentially aimed at

protecting nascent British manufacturing and technology from competition, subsidising them, encouraging them to export, banning exports
from its colonies that competed with its own products and encouraging exploitation and production of primary resources in the colonies.
In trying to make absolutely sure that the colonies stuck to producing
primary commodities, both Britain, under the House of Hanover, and
Spain, under the Bourbons, compelled them to leave the most profitable
'hi-tech' industries in the hands of the 'mother countries'. The aim was
to ensure that the 'mother country' would enjoy the benefits of being
on the cutting edge of world development.

'At best we are simple consumers, clogged with repressive restrictions,'
said Bolívar to his British merchant correspondent. 'For example,' he says,
'the prohibition of cultivating European crops, the King's monopoly of a
wealth of products, the prohibition of manufactures which the Peninsula
itself does not possess, the commercial restrictions on even basic neces-
sities, the obstacles placed between provinces to keep them from inter-
course and commerce.'27 By 1815, however, the so-called 'mercantile
system' established by Walpole and the Hanoverians in Britain and by
the Bourbon crown in Spain was under attack. In 1776, Adam Smith had
published his masterpiece, *The Wealth of Nations*, arguing that the restrictions on competition and monopoly rights were bad for the economy. He
understood that Walpole's policies were becoming obsolete in the case of
Britain, since its industries had become internationally competitive, more
so than French, Dutch or Spanish industries (which, as Bolívar observed in
the *Letter from Jamaica*, never really took off). In that situation, protection
became less necessary and even counter-productive. Therefore, adopting
'free trade' was now increasingly in Britain's best interests.

By the end of the Napoleonic Wars in 1815, when Bolívar addressed
his letter to his British merchant friend in Jamaica, British merchants and
manufacturers were firmly established as the most efficient in the world
and British sea power guaranteed control over trade routes and expansive
commercial interests across the globe. Merchants and manufacturers in
Great Britain correctly concluded that free trade was now in their interest and started campaigning for it, as in the case of the move to repeal the
so-called Corn Laws that limited the country's capacity to buy grains and

foodstuffs abroad at cheaper prices. This is not to say that their attitude towards the colonies and other foreign competitors changed dramatically. The same British manufacturers and merchants campaigning for the repeal of the Corn Laws would be ready to insist on restricting trade when it was convenient, as in the case of the cotton manufacturers who agreed on the necessity of continued protection directed at keeping foreign competitors at bay. Some, like William Pitt the Elder in 1770, were unflinching in their conviction that 'the [North American] colonies should not be permitted to manufacture so much as a horseshoe nail'.[28] Other, later advocates of 'free trade', like Adam Smith, would recommend their recipe to the Americans advising them not to develop manufacturing industries of their own. Any attempt to stop imports of European manufactures would 'obstruct instead of promoting the progress of their country towards real wealth and greatness'.[29]

In spite of the apparent difference between Pitt and Walpole on the one hand and Smith on the other, the first two heartless mercantilists, the third a convinced free-trader, the result for the colonies of the Americas was the same. The advice was to concentrate on the production and exploitation of raw materials and leave 'hi-tech' industries in the hands of the 'mother countries'. Britain prohibited cotton textile imports from India, in 1699 had declared illegal the export of woollen cloth from its colonies to other countries through the Wool Act, and Walpole himself banned the introduction of slitting steel mills in North America and designed policies to encourage raw materials exploitation and production in the colonies. To set the record straight, at the time of Pitt the Elder British policies did allow some industrial activity in North America, just as the Bourbons encouraged small artisan and merchant activity among browns or *pardos* and poorer whites in Spanish America (thereby upsetting the caste system, much to the chagrin of the white Creoles, the sons of Spaniards born in America, who sat at the top of the colonial social ladder). In 1778, King Charles III of Spain issued a Decree of Free Trade that allowed the ports of Spanish America to trade directly with each other and with most ports of Spain, but, crucially, not with non-Spanish colonies or ports or with ships that were not Spanish. In this sense, the Decree is not dissimilar to the British Navigation Acts, which restricted the use of foreign shipping for trade between Britain and its colonies. Adam Smith, the patron saint of free-trade economists across the globe, praised the Navigation Acts as 'the wisest of all the commercial regulations of England', despite the fact that, like the Spanish Decree, it entailed the most blatant kind of 'market-distorting' state-regulated intervention. More than free-trade economists, Smith as well as the French economic advisers of the Bourbon Spanish crown were defenders of national interests in a historical and geopolitical context of contended and radically questioned colonial and neocolonial commercial relations.

The fact that many of the colonies of Spanish America were by the 1810s producing an abundance of resources that were vital to the British colonies in North America and the Caribbean, among others, meant that most of the trade was considered contraband, and was outlawed by the Spanish authorities. It is most likely that the relationship between Bolívar and his British merchant friend, the immediate correspondent of the *Letter from Jamaica*, developed within this context. Both of them were at the receiving end or the destination point of a global commercial relationship in which most of the advantage was concentrated on the other side, at the starting or departure point of the relationship. No matter how 'free trade' or 'mercantile', Bolívar candidly acknowledged before his British merchant friend that the result for them in the Americas would be the same: the repetition of an unequal system of global economic and political relationships.

He referred to the specific case of Spanish America under the Spanish system, but he did so because his British correspondent was familiar with the double-faced and paradoxical aspects of the global economy, and therefore could relate to and understand what he was talking about. This statement can be generalised for the case of a wider British and European audience, the intended audience of the *Letter from Jamaica*. The fact that in 1812 a London-based writer like Anna Barbauld would dare to make explicit what was, no doubt, a public secret in Britain – that the commercial expansionism of the United Kingdom, or potentially that of North America, was no different from the much vilified Spanish and Napoleonic imperialisms – shows this to be the case.

Bolívar could expect his audience to understand his point when he spoke of Spanish America as a storehouse of resources 'to satisfy the needs of that avaricious nation'. His immediate target was the declining empire of Bourbon Spain, but the bulk of his letter is dedicated to showing the wider consequences of the uneven character of the playing field upon which independent Latin America would make its entrance. Chief among these was the fact that under such a system 'which is perhaps now working more vigorously than ever before', Amerindians and Afro-Spanish Americans occupied no other place in society 'than that of brutes of labour', relative to the positions occupied by Spaniards from the Iberian Peninsula and their wealthy white Creole descendants born in America, including Bolívar's own family.

This entails recognising the fact that local race and racial tensions between Amerindians, blacks and brown *pardos* on the one hand, and white Spanish *peninsulares* and *criollos* on the other, and the tensions within these groups, are a consequence of the uneven playing field of global economic and political relations. In this sense, the interventions of Bolívar, Barbauld and others effected a division in world history and painted it black and white. More specifically, they realised that such divisions were a consequence of the active transformation of entire populations into brutes of labour by a global system that paradoxically depends on such destruction for the purposes of progress. This realisation also means that such tensions cannot be conceived simply as a local matter, but can only be solved also at the level of global relations.

Geopolitical relations, internal and external, also make sense within the context of paradoxical relations between the local and the global. An example of this is the internal tension between Jeffersonian visions concerning specialisation in the production of raw materials in relation to the potential for expansion after the Louisiana Purchase, over which he presided, and the Hamiltonian vision of the need for government protection over developing manufacturing and services industries in the United States, on the one hand, and the potential consequences of such tensions for the rest of the Americas and the world, on the other. It is also seen in the consequences of the Haitian Revolution and the establishment of a black republic on the island of Santo Domingo in 1804, relative to the concerns of caste and slave-based systems of raw material production in South America and in North America, in Louisiana and elsewhere, as well as in Napoleonic France.

As we shall see in the next chapter, racial tensions came to the fore during the period of political consolidation, including territorial expansion, and the establishment of the economic model of development of the former colonies of the Americas. The discovery of gold in California in the 1840s, for instance, would have a decisive impact upon the nascent political structure and economic make-up of Central America, Colombia and Panama. This impact would be most visible precisely at the level of racial relations: the relative political and economic rise of blacks and brown *pardos* in different parts of Latin America, as a result of the wars of independence, would clash with the emerging 'identity' of south-eastern American immigrants in Panama en route to California. This emerging American 'identity', in turn, was a result of the anxieties provoked by internal tensions between two different visions of development, which have been characterised above as Jeffersonian and Hamiltonian.

This includes expansionism, mostly driven not by governmental conspiratorial agendas but by private commercial interests that then impact upon political and state agendas. It also includes responses to such expansionism within and without the United States, in particular by Amerindian, black and *pardo* sectors in North and South America. Thus, this phenomenon also includes the consequences of the national defence of emerging commercial and industrial interests. The local context of these phenomena and tense relations, reflects, responds to and affects the global context, which, as Bolívar and his British counterparts knew well, would be dominated from their time onwards by the drive to progress and its paradoxical short- and long-term consequences. And as these characters in the drama of modern history also realised early on, at that level the dice were loaded from the very outset. The ensuing question would be: could the history of Latin America and the world be left to chance, to the throw of the dice, to the coming catastrophe, or could we, acting autonomously, overcome the sense of crises and create future environments?

6

Republic: The Sobriety of the Day After

Entering the Fray

When the British-American War broke out in 1812, as a result of the
introduction of trade restrictions by Britain to impede American trade
with France and of the impressment of American citizens into the Royal
Navy, but also because of the support given by Britain to the Amerindians
who were responding to the westward and southward expansion of the
American border, the United States Congress saw fit to double its tariffs
and restrictions on imports from the average 12.5 per cent to 25 per
cent. The war also provided the pretext and the space within which the
Hamiltonian vision of American economic development could finally
gain the upper hand. New industries could emerge as a result of the
interruption of the flow of manufactured goods from Britain and most of
Europe. Shipping and other related service industries also emerged and
sought new routes for trade transport and the mobilisation of peoples.
Since the ongoing (so-called) Indian Wars made overland westward
and southward transportation more difficult than it already was, Central
America became an attractive alternative. It also offered an additional
charm: the possibility of a direct trade route between the Atlantic and
the Pacific.

The new group of industrialists, who had now arisen naturally in this
context, did not take long to fully espouse the Hamiltonian vision of an
identity between the interests of nascent private industry and national
protective measures, and often saw their own private interests as the
interest of the nation. In their eyes, the destiny of the nation became
intertwined with their own forward march to progress, manifested and

confirmed by territorial and commercial expansion, and sometimes identified as a trait of the American character, its nature and even its singular
racial identification. After the war, this group of private entrepreneurs
actively lobbied for the protection of the state to continue and to be
increased. By 1816, tariffs had been raised even further, to 35 per cent and
even to 40 per cent in 1820. In this way, the vision set out by Alexander
Hamilton back in 1791, when he proposed that America should 'protect
its industries in their infancy', became firmly established. Early opponents of the Hamiltonian vision, Thomas Jefferson among them, did
not stop pursuing their preferred alternative view, more attached as they
were to the plantation economy, the specialisation of the country on the
production of raw agricultural and other primary products and cheap
imports, and, decisively, on the labour of black slaves and the forced
displacement of the Indians.

This is not to say that Hamiltonians were opposed as a matter of principle to slavery or to the ongoing extermination of the Native Americans
in the Indian Wars that ended in 1890, or that Jeffersonians were by definition expansionists and anti-abolitionists. The ambiguities of Thomas
Jefferson himself on this issue are still a matter for debate among historians. Both views were, in fact, responses to a rapidly changing international scene now modelled on the image of a race among peoples and
nations for wealth and progress, which often confused military might
with market forces in pursuit of openness for settlement and commerce,
further connectivity and/or protection. In this image, the way of life of
Amerindians and Africans forcibly brought to the Americas, based on the
priority of common access to resources and their responsible use relative
to long-term consequences, increasingly appeared less viable. It was being
replaced by further privatisation of land in the westward and southward
process of territorial expansion following the 1803 Louisiana Purchase,
presided over by Thomas Jefferson, but also by more abstract notions of
accumulation and investment of capital appropriate to the model of intensive industrialisation under safeguards and protections devised earlier by
Alexander Hamilton. The way of life of Amerindians, and Africans who
saw in their example a possibility for the future, was once more under
attack from the emerging world view of global commerce and universal

commodification, rural or industrialist. The result was, some might say, using a colloquial term, a veritable 'clash of civilisations'.

Clash of Civilisations

French writer and Nobel Prize-winner J. M. G. Le Clézio, who lived among the Emberá Indians of Panama and has written extensively about the stories of the Amerindians of Mexico and North America, prefers the expression the 'meeting of two dreams'. On the one hand there was the dream of gold, 'a devouring, pitiless dream, which sometimes reached the heights of cruelty [. . .] an absolute dream, as if there were something at stake entirely different from the acquisition of wealth and power, a regeneration in violence and blood to live the myth of El Dorado, when everything would be eternally new'.[1] On the other hand was the ancient dream, the dream foretold, which all Indians from the Viceroyalty of New Spain and the lands encompassed by the Louisiana Purchase knew about, and which Simón Bolívar remembered in his *Letter from Jamaica*: the return of the prophet of the forest. It had been announced, centuries before the arrival of Hernán Cortés and his men on the coast of the Mayan Yucatan Peninsula, that one day men from the other side of the ocean wearing shining armour and helmets, led by the departed prophet of the forest whom they called 'the Feathered Serpent', would come to rule over them once again. His arrival would bring about the end of days.

The *True Story* about the encounter was told by Bernal Díaz del Castillo. First an adventurer, later a chronicler, Bernal Díaz was with Cortés when the Spanish conqueror met the sorcerer priests of Moctezuma, ruler of the Mexica, in 1517.[2] After hearing from the high priests about the ancient dream of the Mexica, Bernal Díaz suspected sorcery and black magic. But where Díaz saw sorcery, Cortés sensed an opportunity. He could use the ancient tale of the dream to his advantage. Approached by the high priests, acting as ambassadors of Moctezuma, who asked if they could take with them his helmet, for it resembled those once worn by their ancestors before they disappeared into the forest, Cortés demanded in a fierce tone of voice that it be brought back to him filled with gold and gems, for gold was the only object becoming of gods. 'We are,' he told the priests of Moctezuma, 'gold-eaters.'

For the Indians gold was the metal of the gods, the excrement of the sun, or *takin*, as the Maya called it. They did not use it as money even though they understood the concept. Gold was reserved for the temples, for amulets for princes and for sacred jewellery. It was a sign of divine power. The Europeans' constant demand for gold simply confirmed in the minds of the Indians that these were in fact *teules*, the prophesied people from the east, the land where the sun rises. And, like most gods, these too were affected by an insatiable madness.

Without being aware of it, by giving gold to these foreigners the Indians gave them a mundane power they could never have anticipated, which became the instrument and cause of their end. The ornaments of the princes – the golden discs for healing that shamans contemplated for hours, the dazzling earrings and pectorals, the symbols of Moctezuma's father Axayactzin, the excrement of the sun and the tears of the moon – when melted down and turned into bars, then sent to Seville, Antwerp, Genoa, Venice and London, became collateral to finance further expeditions to Africa and the New World, and new lucrative commercial enterprises. Once the New World was reduced to submissiveness, the descendants of Hernán Cortés and Walter Raleigh 'set the stage for the conquest of the entire American continent, from Canada to the Tierra del Fuego', for African slavery, and for the modern world of commerce and unequal global trade. 'Without gold, without the raw materials, above all without the work of slaves, what might the fate of Europe and its "industrial revolution" have been?'[3]

When they received gold, the Europeans gave green glass stones in return. Perhaps Cortés knew that this was the colour of water and the centre of the world, revered by the Indians of the Americas. Perhaps he was simply laughing at the naivety of the Indians and took advantage of the good bargain. The clash between the dream of progress and the ancient dream of return got off to a good start, but only for one of the parties involved. A tale is told that after Cortés landed in Cozumel and Punta Mujeres a sorceress named Uiquixo came to the priests of Michoacán and told them that the mother of the gods had appeared to her in dreams. After being led to the house where all the gods lived, their faces covered in white paint and black masks, she delivered to

Uiquixo this message, which she communicated to the priests: 'leave off the sacrifice of men and bring no more offerings with you because from now on it is not to be that way. No more drums are to be sounded, split them all asunder. There will be no more temples or fireplaces, nor will any smoke rise, everything shall become a desert because other men are coming to the earth.'[4] If this encounter was indeed a clash of civilisations, which could be represented as a contest or a game, we would have to conclude that it was a game in which the dice were loaded from the start.

It is perplexing to think that, according to these sources, the dreams and the stories of the Amerindians already contained the tale of their own demise. But seen from a modern viewpoint, this notion of a moment when our expectations about the persistence of the present in time might fail can be a powerful tool. Nowadays, we know that the future that is announced as if it were written in the stars is in fact of our own making. But we tend to assume that what is today will be tomorrow. If someone announces or prophesises a terrifying occurrence, such as a new double-digit recession or a terrorist attack, we assume that these projections must be averted. In doing so, we place ourselves in the same position as that classical figure from literature: the seer who foretells a catastrophe in order to prevent it, but in doing so brings about the very disaster he was trying to avert in the first place. When we describe our present predicament as a paradox that involves the inevitability of progress or economic development, and at the same time an escalating energy and resources bill whose payment we must avoid or prevent at all costs, the result is the same.

In order to overcome the paradox, we may choose to follow the example of the ancient Amerindians. We know that our predictions are going to cause effects in the world, and instead of considering the possibility of a radical variation in the future as improbable, we acknowledge the catastrophe around us and change course, breaking a new path or creating a future environment. Put another way, the point is to acknowledge that history has no course, that our present condition is fragile and thus, rather than concern ourselves with restoring the lost past, we move to create the future.

This is what the Amerindians did every time they faced the brave new world brought about by their encounter with the Europeans. They embraced it as a new world, a new era different from what had been before, and struggled to make it their own. This is why there was no clash of civilisations, no contest between the archaic and the modern submitted to the rule of chance, the throw of the loaded dice. Instead, the very image that paralysed the Indians in the first place – the return of their departed gods – became thereafter the source of their tenacious resistance during the Indian Wars. These wars were fought throughout the Americas: in North America between 1600 – the year of the Sierra Gorda War launched by the alliance of the Zuaques and the Teguecos against the Spanish invaders in Mexico – and 1890 – the year of the massacre of Wounded Knee, which marked the end of the Indian Wars in the United States; and in the south of the Americas, between the indigenous insurrections in Chiapas, Mexico and Vilcabamba, Peru in the sixteenth and seventeenth centuries, the commoner (*comunero*) and abolitionist rebellions of the eighteenth and nineteenth centuries and the liberationist movements of the twentieth and the twenty-first centuries, including the 1994 uprising in Chiapas and the 2000 Water Wars in Bolivia.

Throughout these episodes, the idea of a recurrent time that contains catastrophic events, which are themselves by necessity moments of renewal, considered as a maxim for a practice of forecast and anticipation, remains central. It helps us understand the significant nature of the clash between the world view of the Indians and the Africans in the Americas, on the one hand, and that introduced by gold-seeking Europeans from the sixteenth century onwards, on the other. The former is based upon a forward-looking ethic that involves reading history as a cycle of destruction and creation, in which the creation of future environments remains our collective responsibility. The latter is backward-looking and contains its own delusion, an idea of regeneration in violence and accumulation, a self-reproducing drive to live the myth of El Dorado in a frozen present of permanent abundance and near-useless renovation. And if the future is simply more of the same, then nothing we can do would make the slightest difference. The result is irresponsibility and the spoiling of Nature, as well as a sense of social paralysis.

The Indian Wars were an outburst 'against the despoiling of the lands on the part of the Tarahumaras, the Mayos, the Yaquis, and the Seris, and against slavery and forced labour on the part of the Chichimeca peoples of the mining regions.[5] But it was an even greater outburst against the destruction of their future environments in the name of short-term gains, which would, ultimately, be disastrous for all. The rebellion of the Indians of the Cuinao valley, then the Mixton War, and the general uprising of the league of the Chichimeca nations were not only directed against the abuses, the pillaging of food reserves, and systematic slavery, but also expressed a rejection of the religious and socio-economic doctrine that was complicit with tyrannical power and their oppressive situation. The uprising of the Acaxees of the Sierra de Topia, for instance, was led by an Indian seer, a great speaker who called himself 'bishop', and who preached destruction in order to achieve liberation and promised rebirth after death in battle, stating that the guns of the invaders could no longer harm his people. A similar belief accompanied the 1585 revolt of the Indians of Nayarit, the Tepehuane rebellion of 1616, the 1644 uprising of the 'seven nations' and the rebel movements of Chiapas in the south-east, which resulted in the North American Indian Wars against the Yaquis of Juan 'Banderas' Jusacamea, and against the Apaches of Vitorio and Cochise.

These were rebellions supported by the desire to create a different future, in which the entire population participated, including women and children. They could be extremely violent, as in the case of the battles of the Peñol of Nochistlán and the capitulation of the Apaches in 1880. Facing defeat and deprived of water and food, the Indians of Nochistlán and the Apache threw themselves off cliffs. I remember visiting the site near Lawton, Oklahoma, where Geronimo, a leader and seer of the Chiricahua, threw himself off a cliff with his horse, Cadillac, after relentlessly fighting the Apache Wars, survived, and escaped. The town, named after Captain Henry Lawton of B Troop, 4th Cavalry, based at Fort Huachuca, Arizona, who led the expedition that captured Geronimo, is now a military base. It pays homage to Geronimo, the Indian warrior who was wounded many times in battle, but survived each time.

The Tepehuanes and the Chichimeca, the Pawnee and the Sioux, all faced the firepower of their conquerors convinced they could no longer harm them any more and that they were responsible for creating a future for their descendants. The holy war of the Chichimeca and the Tepehuanes continued in the Indian Wars of the Pawnee, the Sioux, the Pueblo, the Comanche, the Apache and the Seminoles in North America. It continued, too, in the *voudoun* ceremony at Bois Caiman presided over by the West African seer Boukman, which on 14 August 1791 launched the Haitian Revolution, and in the 1781 uprising of the Inca-Aymará Túpac Katari in Bolivia, which inspired the Katarista movement of late twentieth-century Bolivia. Inca-Aymará communities and Katarista activists reinvented the associative ethos that in 2000 motivated rural and urban populations to stand up to the exploitation of their commons and their resources, contrasting the long-term interests of their communities and the Bolivian nation with the short-termism of transnational corporations and remote international financial institutions. And in 2005 and 2009, the same ethos transformed these indigenous associations into an electoral success story, propelling former indigenous and union leader Evo Morales to the presidency of Bolivia. Since gaining power, the indigenous peoples of Bolivia, like the Zapatistas of contemporary southeastern Mexico, had focused their action on transforming the unequal nature of global economic and political relations. In this respect at least, they keep alive the spirit of the Amerindians and Afro-Latin Americans who, between the sixteenth and the nineteenth centuries, sought a new path to lead and rule the world: that to think like the original inhabitants of the Americas we should not set our sights on repeating the present or restoring the past but concentrate on shaping a world in which we all can have a future.

New Paths in the Nineteenth Century

While the Indian Wars followed their course in North America, the wars of independence in Latin America and the Caribbean had a different effect: the widening of opportunities for slaves and Amerindians to reassert their symbolic worlds and visions in local realities, within and against the global context of changing economic and political relations, or even adapt to and thrive in such changing conditions, as in the case of the ascension of a black middle class. Each of these transformations had taken place in the course of the wars for independence because of pressure from below. And their participation was in all cases decisive. Each reform, each concession, each declaration of equality responded to the actions taken by slaves, and from a much stronger social and economic position, those of the growing black and brown or *pardo* middle class. At the onset of independence, for instance, 400,000 free blacks and brown *pardos* and 200,000 Canarians, some of whom would be classified as *pardos* because of their mixed background, and mostly as *blancos de orilla*, or poor whites, dominated Venezuelan society numerically. In Brazil there were 1,305,000 free blacks and slaves, by contrast with 576,000 whites. In Cuba, Colombia, Puerto Rico, Santo Domingo, Costa Rica and Panama they were also the majority of the population.[6]

Until the early 1700s, the Spanish crown had generally supported and enforced the efforts of white artisans and merchants 'to maintain racial barriers in commerce and the trades'.[7] But in the late eighteenth century that position changed. Beginning in the late 1700s, the monarchy confirmed the right of non-whites to acquire militia commissions up to the rank of captain. In 1764, for instance, Sebastián de Miranda Ravelo, father of the Precursor of Independence, Francisco de Miranda, was appointed Captain of the Sixth Company of Fusiliers of the Battalion of White Isleños of Caracas. These colonial militias had been formed in Spanish and Portuguese America in response to the Anglo-French Wars and the British filibuster invasions of Cuba in 1762, and later on Puerto Rico in 1797 and Argentina in 1806. The appointment of Miranda's father caused a strong reaction among Venezuelan white Creoles who branded Miranda a mulatto. Now he could 'wear in the streets', they said, 'the same uniform as men of superior status and pure blood'.[8]

Later on the crown issued the *cédulas de gracias al sacar* decree, a legal procedure by which non-whites could effectively purchase or request from the crown certificates of whiteness. These allowed them to receive an education, marry whites, hold public office and become priests, while releasing them from official discrimination. The crown may have attempted to ease social tensions by allowing competition and some degree of social mobility, or infuse the economy with new energies, but whatever the reasons, these measures were firmly opposed by whites in all cases. In a caste society, they had the advantage and would not cede it willingly. Whites, already alarmed by the numbers, achievements and aspirations of free blacks and slaves, which they perceived as an 'insult' and a 'calamity', promptly expressed fears and anxieties intensified by the news of slave revolt in the Caribbean. The result was a paranoid style of politics, leading to the outright rejection of the Slave Laws of May 1789, which clarified the rights of blacks and slaves relative to their masters in the plantation.

Planters opposed these measures on the grounds that free blacks and slaves were prone to violence and French (i.e. Haitian) ideas of independence. Both parties claimed their point after the Coro Rebellion of 1795 and the La Guaira Conspiracy of July 1797, which appealed to 'liberty and equality', the rights of man, the abolition of slavery, Indian tribute and taxes, and had a Spencean-like plan of action that included land redistribution, the establishment of a constitutional government and pleaded for equality among whites, Indians and coloureds 'as brothers in Christ and equal before God', in language reminiscent of that employed by Dissenters, Methodists and other preachers of the Everlasting Gospel around the Caribbean. A similar rebellion had occurred, and nearly succeeded, in 1781 in eastern New Granada (Colombia) on the border with Venezuela. This was too radical for white planters and property owners.

The wars for freedom that took place between 1810 and 1890 intensified this state of affairs, to the point of making race, and other similarly 'imagined frontiers', the central issue of Latin American politics and the economy throughout the nineteenth and twentieth centuries.[9] Even today, with the rise to power of Amerindians and Afro-Latin Americans in Mexico, Venezuela, south-eastern Colombia, Ecuador, Bolivia, Paraguay and Brazil, it can be argued that race *is* the issue. From an economic perspective, the questioning of resource exploitation – mining, deforestation, oil and gas exploration, land grabs – and the establishment of export-oriented projects and economic models in the Pacific coast of Latin America and in the Amazon, often have a racial dimension.

For instance, much of the guerrilla and paramilitary violence that takes place in the coastal regions, mountains and jungles of Colombia is aimed at forcibly displacing peoples for the purposes of making space for the short-term profitable enterprises of mining or export-oriented agriculture. Forced displacement systematically affects Afro-Latin American and Amerindian peoples, particularly in the rural areas of the south-eastern part and the Pacific coast of the country. However, such violence is not limited to rural landscapes. On the one hand, processes of forced displacement such as the one taking place in Colombia have thrown the issue of latent race and racist issues in the faces of urban populations accustomed to thinking of themselves as tolerant of, or at least oblivious to, racial issues because of their mixed or mestizo background. On the other, the late twentieth century has seen the redescription, if not the invention, of new urban social categories along the lines of access to property rights or lack thereof that are often superimposed on and still resemble older caste lines.

This is the case, for instance, in the proposals of Peruvian economist Hernando de Soto. His distinction between 'informals', those lacking access to property rights, and 'formals', those in possession of their bundle of property rights and access to real state-based financial credit, does not follow a strict skin-colour code. And yet, most notions of race have rarely followed strict skin or proper biological or genetic lines of distinction. Indeed, when late-modern writers and commentators argue that to speak of race is nonsense, particularly in Latin America, since 'we are all mixed', they may be unwittingly conjuring up an image of disavowal and repression of the aspirations and identifications of indigenous and Afro-Latin American peoples. Such an active disavowal and repression of Amerindian or Afro-Latin American memory is at the very core of racialisation and racism in the continent.

Bearing in mind such contemporary attempts to silence once more the majorities of the Latin American continent, by turning them into some sort of cultural or economic 'minority', it is important to remember that the revolutionary legacy of Latin America is much wider and more varied. On the one hand, it antedates the wars of independence of 1810–90. On the other, the wars of independence forged new paths for free blacks and slaves, as well as Indians and poor whites, to pursue freedom. Free blacks and slaves were able to introduce political and legal changes that would eventually undermine the institutions of slavery and control over populations that for so long had been at the basis of their local and the world economy, and take advantage of those changes, producing some surprising developments in the process.

Thus, for instance, earlier in the colonial period, after African slaves and Indians attacked their masters they invariably fled into the mountains, the jungles and the rainforest, as in the case of the Incas of Vilcabamba or the *cimarronajes*, *palenques* and *quilombos*, Maroon settlements established by escapee slaves outside Kingston, Jamaica, in Dutch Guyana, Bahía in Brazil, or Cartagena de Indias in Colombia. But by the early nineteenth century, whenever they attacked they did little to hide their deeds and motivations. Instead, they insisted upon the paradox of having to fight, to die or to work the whole of their lives for the exclusive benefit of 'a man who is my equal'.[10] Living under constitutional systems based on equality and human rights, featuring electoral and liberal parliamentary systems that were the result of revolution, Afro-Latin Americans – *pardos* and Creole slaves in particular – as well as Indians 'had absorbed the rhetoric of egalitarianism and citizenship'.[11]

Inevitably, such rhetoric led to a larger questioning of the caste society that had been in place since colonial times. Colonial administrators sought to establish in the Americas a racially stratified society based upon a set of political institutions that would reserve for whites all opportunities for social and economic advancement, and relegated non-whites to an inferior legal and social status. However, as already suggested, to speak of 'racial stratification' in this case does not necessarily mean that there were clean-cut divisions along a skin-colour divide from the very outset. In the case of Spanish and Portuguese America, precedents for the caste system existed in the legal institutions of Spain and Portugal that governed people of 'unclean blood', that is to say, Arabs, Jews, Gypsies and Africans, in the Old World.

In this sense, it would be best to understand 'race' as a social and geopolitical notion derived from a specific geographical and philosophical conception of the world that distinguished at least three portions of the globe and allocated to each a particular climate, resources and a specific population. According to this old 'philosophical geography', the closer a part of the world was to a more extreme climate the less likely it was that its population would be composed of anything other than 'barbarians'. Conversely, if the geography of the place corresponded to the more temperate climates, the middle of the globe – where the Mediterranean was located – it was more likely that its population would be 'a perfect community'. This was the term coined by the father of international law and international relations, Francisco de Vitoria, when he invented the idea of 'nations' back in the sixteenth century. On the basis of this notion, Renaissance Europeans distinguished between four groups that could be associated with their places of origin: white Europeans (doing the classifying), yellow Asians, black Africans and red or lighter dark Indians in America.

However, as often happens, these apparently clear definitions were rough around the edges. In the very first colonial generation, race mixture had created three new mixed groups: Afro-European mulattoes, browns or *pardos*; Indo-European mestizos; and Afro-Indian zambos. With each subsequent generation, both the possibility and the reality of ever more complex mixtures increased. By the eighteenth century Spanish officials recognised no fewer than sixteen permutations of race mixture, while finer classifications increased the number to up to fifty-two such mixtures. And after twelve generations, by the time of independence even these counted for only an infinitesimal fraction of all possible combinations. In the face of such complexity, racial identities became more difficult to pin down. In 1815, the royal attorney and the Archbishop of Mexico clarified that in the ensuing disputes, priests 'rely on the word of the parties', and thus the indeterminacy of racial identities opened abundant opportunities for the 'awkward castes' – those who could use money and social leverage to make a case for whiteness – to try to escape their position in the social hierarchy.

The first years after the wars of independence, fought in the name of equality and freedom from slavery, brought with them new paths and new possibilities to escape and transform established hierarchies. For slaves and others throughout the Americas, national independence and chattel slavery were mutually exclusive concepts. 'If our liberal constitutions have any meaning at all,' argued the lawyer representing Juana Móniga Murga in Lima in 1826, 'it is the freedom of every man no longer to be a slave.'[12] In 1822, thousands of slaves gathered in the mining town of Ouro Preto and in Salvador de Bahía, in Brazil, anticipating that changing political circumstances would open up in Brazil the same possibilities that had emerged in former Spanish America. When those failed to materialise, slaves petitioned, switched allegiance and on some occasions decided to strike back. In Jamaica, Simón Bolívar himself was the target of an assassination attempt by a black servant accompanying him, named Pío. Some say this was the result of a bribe and a drunken night. Others speculate about deeper animosities related to Bolívar's initial misgivings concerning the role of *pardos* and slaves in the revolutionary army. Bolívar then sailed for Cartagena de Indias in an attempt to reunite the *pardo* and white Creole factions in the city, now a free republic. In Cartagena, *pardo* and black militiamen led by Afro-Cuban artisan Pedro Romero had forced the local authorities to declare full independence from Spain on 11 November 1811. Romero and his men demanded 'equal rights for all the classes of citizens', entrenched the following year in Cartagena's constitution.

Other *pardo* men like José Padilla from Guajira rose rapidly in the ranks of the navy of the new republic, which also included French privateers, Dutch mercenaries and Haitian seamen. The example of the Haitian Revolution and La Guaira Conspiracy of 1797 inspired them to envisage a nation without racial distinctions. Both La Guaira in Venezuela and Cartagena in Colombia formed part of a larger administrative unity known back then as the Viceroyalty of New Granada and later on as 'Gran Colombia', which also included Panama and Ecuador. Colombians joined Venezuelans in the patriot army and travelled back and forth from one part of the Viceroyalty to another. Thus, their ideas of racial equality had a common foundation in the wars for freedom and independence.

The centrality of abolitionism and racial equality on Colombia's patriotism can be explained by reference to the wider transatlantic context, but it is nonetheless paradoxical given the profound divisions between white Creoles and the other castes. In fact, the rapid insertion of race into the core of national patriotism may have heightened those tensions, as Bolívar and Padilla would themselves find out. Padilla and the other *pardos* constantly clashed with the white Creole authorities of the Cartagena republic, leading to bloody fighting between the two factions in 1815. Unity then became a crucial element in the emergent national-ist ideas of racial harmony. Equality was the first and most crucial notion, but since the aspiration of equality frequently led to the kind of faction-alism that erupted in Cartagena in 1815, the focus fell on unity not only as a matter of regional but also of racial integration. Bolívar's projection of the Isthmus of Panama as a meeting point for independent nations must be understood thus, not only as a bulwark against existing and emerging imperialisms but also as an attempt to contain factionalism.

Factionalism originated in the conflict between individual or particu-lar interests and society's interest, often magnified when people began to vote as members of factions, which represented the emergence of specific group interests and could ultimately lead to the destruction of the state. Since in Spanish America factions tended to form around caste lines it was all the more important to establish institutions that could include and contain the extremes of caste exclusionary privileges and race war. Panama would be the perfect site of a new set of political insti-tutions guaranteeing unity over factionalism, 'the capital of the earth', as Bolívar put it. This was due not only to its location and commercial potential, but also because that potential was directly bound up with the rise of free blacks and mulattoes and the overcoming of all barriers to equality among the different sectors of the population.

After two centuries of suffering the economic, social and psychologi-cal consequences of second-class citizenship and inhumanity, free blacks, mulattoes and slaves were starting to experience the benefits of equal-ity. In Panama there were 37,000 free blacks and 4,000 slaves, a total of 41,000 black peoples as opposed to 9,000 whites and 12,000 Indians. In Panama blacks represented 66 per cent of the population compared with only 12 per cent represented by whites. They were socially and sexually mobile. Free blacks in particular were more racially mixed than black, more American than African, and with equal numbers of males and females. While the slave population suffered constant demographic decline, made worse by the hardships endured during the wars of freedom and independence, 'free black and mulatto populations enjoyed rapid rates of increase', a function of large numbers and freedom.[13]

By 1800 Panama reflected a situation that was common throughout South America and most of the Caribbean: free blacks and mulattoes outnumbered slaves in every part of Latin America except for Brazil and Cuba. They became an important part of the military, commercial and political life of their communities. In Panama, for instance, they controlled the commerce and retail of fruit and other foodstuffs, as well as transportation and the burgeoning service industry that had emerged around the transit of passengers through the isthmus. The search for egalitarian social relations in Latin America, which continues today, can be traced back to the prominence of free blacks and mulattoes in colonial and early independent society and to their greater upward mobility in that society. This also helps to explain important differences in the make-up of Latin American and North American societies, and in particular the United States. When Americans started moving south and westward, motivated by the recent discovery of gold in California and the twin ideologies of 'Manifest Destiny' and white supremacy, they were shocked to encounter a black population in the Isthmus of Panama freer than anywhere in the former North American colonies, and ready to protect that freedom by any means necessary.

The Rise of the Monroe Doctrine

'Equality under the law is not enough in view of the [free black, mulatto and slave] people's current mood,' observed Bolívar correctly in 1825. Now that the nightmarish reality of second-class citizenship or none at all was over, the peoples belonging to what were formerly known as 'the lower castes' were insistent that it be '*completely* over'.[14] The impact of this universal prescription in the way in which national identity was shaped in Latin America cannot be underestimated. Not only is it a central part of a better understanding of the nature of Latin American nations, but also, crucially, of the relations between Latin America, Europe and the United States. Thus, for instance, it is clear that in both

the United States and Latin America patriot nationalism and cosmopolitan ideals exalted the differences between tyrannical European rulers in
the metropolises and American republican freedom. This was also the
case of European radicalism, as Anna Barbauld's 'Eighteen Hundred and
Eleven' demonstrates. Yet the place of race in the equation of freedom
depended less on patriots' notions of freedom 'than on where their colonial power stood on the issue of race. In other words, it depended on
whether racial equality was perceived as a colonial imposition or as a
patriot aspiration.'[15]

The military and political centrality of free blacks, *pardos* and mulattoes
during the wars of independence meant 'the motley crew' succeeded
in finding a place in the new Spanish American nations. This made
broader and more creative forms of identification, shared with sailors,
commoners and slaves in North America and throughout the Atlantic,
more concrete in the sense that such forms concentrated the forces thus
identified and provided them with a determined shape, from standing
militias to caudillo groupings and, crucially, party politics within the
political architecture of the new nations. Especially in Spanish America,
there was a clear tendency for powerful landowners and merchants –
those who had monopolised wealth and privilege during colonialism
and planned to continue to do so under republicanism – to gather in
'conservative' parties which stood for the preservation of as much of the
colonial heritage – including the religious, social and racial hierarchy –
as possible. Liberal parties, in contrast, although drawing support from
among merchants and landowners as well, appealed especially to social
groups formerly excluded from positions of political and economic
power. 'Liberalism thus spoke to economic elites from outlying provinces far removed from centers of power in the former colonial capitals
[and] to middle- and lower-class nonwhites.'[16]

In contrast, the motley crew that took part in the American Revolution
failed to find a place in the American nation. Unlike what happened in
Spanish America, in the United States racial equality became a precarious concept constantly subject to challenge. It did not become central to
patriot nationalism and, thus, cosmopolitan forms of identification, more
abstract by definition, were forced upon those who had instructed Paine

and Jefferson but were never counted among the middle- and upper-class revolutionaries. These forces were dispersed after the American Revolution, for instance in the African American diaspora that after 1783 would anticipate modern pan-Africanism by settling, with the help of advocates like Olaudah Equiano and Granville Sharp, in Sierra Leone. Their dispersal and defeat was similar to that of commoners and radicals after the English Revolution a century and a half earlier. The earlier defeat permitted the consolidation of the plantation and the slave trade. The latter allowed the slave system to expand, and the plantation and extractive economy to gain new strength, particularly in the southern states of the Union. Crucially, it also permitted the consolidation of a national identity, specifically in the United States, in which racial equality was only one among a number of equally important and more or less respectable positions, including the support of Back-to-Africa programmes.[17]

The struggle for racial equality in the United States was linked to potentially violent regional conflicts and not to a unified front against a common enemy. Instead, in the new nations of Spanish America the principle of legal racial equality was never questioned.[18] The resulting differences in the political culture and national identity of both regions help to explain ensuing differences in terms of their international relations. Few stories illustrate this conundrum as well as the so-called 'incident of the slice of watermelon', which took place in Panama on 15 April 1856. The story also introduces us to a new era in the history of armed entrepreneurship. From Pizarro to Sir Home Popham, privately funded military expeditions, or 'filibustering', had been a prime tactic by means of which governments would engage in expansionist endeavours while at the same time maintaining a certain distance from the darker realities of imperialism. But after independence, all the nations of the Americas had made explicit commitments against tyrannical imperialism. Empires were, after all, incompatible with republics.

In 1824, for instance, Simón Bolívar attempted to create a common front against imperialism by inviting the republican governments of Mexico, Peru, Chile and Argentina, first, 'to form a confederation', and then also the United States, together with some British observers,

'to convene at the isthmus of Panama . . . a congress of plenipotentiar-
ies from each state that should act as a council during periods of great
conflicts, to be appealed to in the event of common danger, and to be a
faithful interpreter of public treaties when difficulties arise'.[19] The initial
exclusion of the United States had to do not only with British susceptibilities. It was also related to the actual meaning of the non-colonisation
and non-intervention principle established in James Monroe's famous
Annual Message of 1823, for which John Quincy Adams, then Secretary
of State, was mostly responsible.

In July 1824 the government of Colombia approached the US
government with the intention of securing a treaty of alliance, alarmed
with intelligence reports of French interference in the wars for freedom
and independence. Monroe responded that the US government and
Congress would take action to support non-intervention but would not
enter into an alliance. Furthermore, he said, previous consultation with
European powers also supportive of non-interventionist principles would
be required before any action could be taken or any alliance considered
with Spanish America. That position cooled Spanish American enthusiasm for the Monroe Doctrine. However, it was not accepted as the
final word in US–Latin American relations by most leaders south of the
border. In fact, the nomination of Henry Clay of Kentucky as Secretary
of State in 1825, after Adams's presidential election, was viewed as a
sign of closer relations in the future of the two regions. Clay was the
most prominent champion of the Spanish American cause in the United
States, and his credentials were tested in the so-called Poinsett Pledge
Controversy during the congressional debates concerning the Panama
Congress of 1826.

Joel Poinsett, then United States Minister to Mexico, had referred to
Monroe's message as a 'pledge' to protect Spanish America. Members
of the US Congress vociferously demanded clarification of the government's interpretation of non-intervention. In his reply, Secretary Henry
Clay demonstrated that even from the standpoint of a fervent supporter
of an American system of independent nations, the Monroe Doctrine
was a pragmatic policy aimed first at protecting the national interests of
the United States. Unwilling to make a strong public statement about

the limited nature of the Doctrine, Clay's hand was forced by repeated questions from Congress, determined not only to show respect for the constitutional conventions concerning the powers of the US Executive in foreign affairs but also to embarrass both Adams and Clay. The result, as historians of US–Latin American relations have observed, was an unnecessary dash of cold water on the relationship between the United States and Spanish and Portuguese America. It would cast a long shadow over the future of US–Latin American relations, and especially on those of Mexico and America, and Mexico and Colombia, which included Venezuela and Upper Peru, what is now present-day Bolivia.

Only in November 1825, apparently at the behest of President Guadalupe Victoria of Mexico and Vice-President Francisco de Paula Santander of Colombia, did the Adams government receive an invitation to the Panama Congress. On 26 December 1825, Adams nominated Richard Anderson Jr of Kentucky and John Sargeant of Pennsylvania as delegates to the Congress and explained that the mission would focus on commercial and diplomatic advantages while avoiding allegiances. The message sparked renewed opposition in the US Congress and initiated a debate that in effect destroyed any possibility of beneficial results from the Panama Congress. The debate hinged upon the fear of over-commitment in Spanish American affairs, when no such course of action had been mandated or even considered by the US government. In fact, Henry Clay's interpretation of what became known as the Monroe Doctrine was correct since both non-colonisation and non-intervention were vital to the interests of the United States, and the pledge to resist European interference in the affairs of independent American nations was a matter of the United States' own consideration rather than an over-commitment to foreign powers. Thus, the main driving force behind the opposition's attacks was purely political. The consequences, though, were far broader and more enduring. The delay in dispatching the US delegates was critical: Anderson died in Cartagena and Sargeant arrived three months after the Congress had adjourned.

Furthermore, Clay's bold statement about the meaning of the Monroe Doctrine would win no friends or influence in the new nations of Latin America. On the contrary, it fuelled already existing expectations about the potential for US expansionism westwards and southwards, which explains Bolívar's misgivings about the United States being 'foreign to us and heterogeneous in character'.[20] Instead, the Liberator pointed a finger at Britain's decisive contribution to Latin American independence, made concrete in the interposition of the British fleet between Europe and America by people like Rear Admiral Alexander Cochrane and later by his nephew, Lord Thomas Cochrane. The risks of increased British interest in Spanish America, which inevitably counted far more to the greatest naval, financial and commercial power in the world than the United States did, appeared minimal *vis-à-vis* the efforts of the Holy Alliance and the now clear meaning of the Monroe Doctrine as a policy established exclusively in the potentially expansive interests of the *norteamericanos*. That potential would become actual in the following years during the Mexican-American War of 1848 and, no less important, in the wake of the new wave of filibustering military adventures, moving west and south from the United States, and impacting with particular force upon Central America.

Filibusters and Banana Republics

The Panama Congress had limited impact in the 1820s, but it stands as a forerunner of the sorts of tribunals and appeal bodies that have become so familiar to practitioners of international law, human rights activists, NGOs and the state secretariats and foreign offices of all countries in the world since the late twentieth century. Besides, the proposal for the Congress clearly entailed the establishment of what is now known as the right to self-determination in international affairs and also foregrounded the prohibition of the use of offensive force now contained in article 2 (4) of the Charter of the United Nations. In that respect, the proposal contained in Bolívar's 7 December 1824 letter 'inviting governments to a congress in Panama' had a wider and more long-lasting impact that goes beyond the recognisable projects for Latin American unity.

In contrast, the Monroe Doctrine received a great deal of attention in the 1820s from Spanish American nations as a possible basis for the sort of political and military alliance advanced in proposals like the Panama Congress. But in the years following Clay's interpretation of Monroe's address, enthusiasm for a possible common pledge between the United States and Latin America declined and a much more ominous reality started to appear before the eyes of Spanish American governments: the spectre of self-interested North American intervention, coupled with an even darker ideology of racial, cultural and institutional supremacy that became known as the 'Manifest Destiny' doctrine. Both would converge in the episode known as the incident of the slice of watermelon. These events symbolised the dawn of a new era in the Americas: the Age of the Filibuster, also the Age of Banana Republics.

There is a certain irony in the fact that the term filibuster entered into the English language from the Spanish *filibustero*, meaning a pirate or buccaneer. It is perhaps one of the earliest examples of Spanglish in the American idiom, and one of the most politically significant. Today it designates a legislative tactic by which members of the US Congress delay or prevent a vote on a proposed bill. But the term was first applied to US adventurers like William Walker, Philip Nolan or Bernardo Gutiérrez – characters associated with the westward and southward expansion of the former colonies. Gutiérrez, for instance, was a colonist in New Spain, present-day Mexico, who ended up fighting the English side by side with the Americans in Louisiana and later became the first governor of a free Texas. Most of these men came from what are now the southern states of the Union – Texas, Louisiana or Tennessee. Driven by the westward expansion that followed the 1803 Louisiana Purchase, and hugely invested in the southern way of life, they attempted to foment insurrections in Latin America as indirect, perhaps even unwitting, agents of American governmental endeavours or as freelance soldiers in conjunction with well-established economic interests.

Philip Nolan, for instance, was associated with a New Orleans merchant named Benjamin Morgan, while William Walker's rise and fall – an individual story that has become synonymous with the story of US–Latin American relations – cannot be separated from the interests of the New York shipping and railroad magnate Cornelius Vanderbilt. And although it is true that the expansionist dynamic and the continuity of slavery in the southern states must be treated as distinct affairs, when it comes to the actions and impact of filibusters or armed entrepreneurs in the political and economic structure, and in the very identity of North, Central and South America, as much as in the history of relations between the three regions, they cannot be sharply distinguished. Since these military activities did not or could not necessarily count on official support and authorisation, they often involved a great deal of secrecy and deception. Ultimately, these were the always clandestine and more or less private armies of more or less private economic and political interests that shaped a great deal of the history of the Americas and hence the world. For instance, in more than one sense, filibusters are the true forerunners of Halliburton, Dick Cheney, Blackwater and Plan Colombia – an arrangement between the US government and Colombia, which, since the late twentieth century, has decisively guided domestic and foreign policy in the two countries.

Back in the nineteenth century, US attempts to purchase or annex Texas to the Union were not only the occasion of the war with Mexico that exploded in 1848, but also resulted in the further acquisition of Alta California in the south-western Pacific, Santa Fe de Nuevo México and the opening up of an entirely new chapter in Anglo-Latin American relations. On the surface, the aim of these interventions was to thwart British commercial ambitions in the area and gain a port on the Pacific. Under it there were also internal political divisions: Southern Democrats in the US urged the addition of new territory in the hope of avoiding being outnumbered in the Federal government by the faster growing North. The southern belief in Manifest Destiny thus converged with the fears of abolitionists in the North concerning the emergence of a southern slave power. Race and politics were, once again, the crucial issue

The term Manifest Destiny made its appearance between 1839 and 1845, and was first coined by New York writer and publishing editor John O'Sullivan, a close friend of the author Nathaniel Hawthorne. The apparent contradiction between the fact that a southern belief was given a name by a northern writer is resolved if we understand it as an attempt to unite factional positions under the umbrella of republican nationalism. He put it like this: 'and that claim is by the right of our manifest destiny to overspread and to possess the whole of the continent which Providence has given us for the development of the great experiment of liberty and federated self-government entrusted to us'. Like Bolívar, O'Sullivan was projecting the conflict between republicanism and monarchist imperialism, represented in this case by the Americas and Britain, on to the canvas of world history. However, unlike Bolívar's assemblage of nationalism and cosmopolitanism, in the case of O'Sullivan race was not centrally linked to republican freedom and the advance of world history. This is why his conception of world history was retrospective: to him, world history was animated by Providence, a figure of necessity (hence the term 'destiny') that manifested itself through the apparently disjointed occurrences of the past history of men, in particular through the historical fact of the expansion of Christianity and its privileged defender, the white race, and thus provided it with direction.

In that respect, the upward mobility and advancement of free blacks and mulattoes first experienced by north-eastern and south-eastern American immigrants, including filibusters passing through Panama in the late 1800s, would have seemed unacceptable, even contrary, to providential designs. After all, the nations of Central and South America were supposed to be populated by poor peasants and lazy coloured peoples often under the control of some despotic caudillo or dictator, dependent on the goodwill of foreign governments for their protection, and ultimately backward. That image corresponded with and seemingly confirmed the picture of world history advanced by Manifest Destiny speculations. Later on, in the late nineteenth and early twentieth centuries, powerful tycoons and multinational corporations like the United Fruit Company – established in 1899 with the purpose of creating a giant trade network of fruit, especially bananas, between the Caribbean, Latin America and the United States – replaced the goodwill and sympathetic sentiments of foreign powers and helped shape this prevalent image of Latin America for a later age. It was the age designated by that most infamous of all terms used to refer to Latin America: Banana Republic.

Race War in Panama

After the discovery of gold in California in 1848, it quickly became apparent to many in the United States that the safest and quickest way to bring American labour to the south-west was through Latin America. New

York transport magnate Cornelius Vanderbilt, for instance, opened a route through Nicaragua in order to compete with the already popular Panama route. In Panama, the influx of transit passengers from the East Coast en route to the West Coast of America had largely benefited not only the transport companies but also the free black and mulatto workers labouring as muleteers in the overland part of the route and in the food industry around ports and markets. These *pardos* had gained economic power and mobility as well as political power, given the recent approval of universal male suffrage in liberal New Granada, (present-day Colombia), of which Panama was part in the nineteenth century. This resulted, among other things, in a change in the dynamic in negotiation between the railroad company that served the overland part of the route between the Atlantic and the Pacific oceans, the workers and the local government, particularly when Panamanian officials – always in need of mass support – took the side of black workers.

The liberal attitude of 'uppity' *pardos* did not go unnoticed among white US immigrants, who did not think much of this apparent reversal of the natural order of things. Bar brawls and street fights soon followed, putting further pressure on a police force already stretched thin while trying to deal with more generic crimes. There were also widespread rumours, both echoed and denied by the US editor of the *Panama Star*, that the organisation of a 'vigilante committee' and a private police force hired by the railroad company and led by a US immigrant from Texas, represented a sign that Panama would soon follow the path of recently annexed Texas. In fact, these organisations resembled the vigilante parties of the same era in California. They shared a common goal: carving out spaces within the sovereignty of other nations, reclaiming them as independent – pending annexation to the United States – and then using them as bases of operation for commercial or further military enterprises. This included a form of 'outsourcing': the contracting of filibusters or small private armies ready to liquidate the sovereignty of other countries altogether.

Fears of filibuster invasion and race war took a new turn when news arrived in Panama that William Walker, who had declared himself president of the northern Mexican state of Sonora for a while back in 1854, had invaded neighbouring Nicaragua in December 1855. Paradoxically, while he was editor of the New Orleans *Daily Crescent*, Walker had taken sides against expansionism. Back then he disagreed with the southern expansionists who had got it into their heads that slave labour could turn Latin American countries – backwards and riven by internal disputes – into giant and very profitable plantations, thereby adding to the power of the southern states, which were under pressure from the increasing production and population of the north. Grief-stricken by the death of his beautiful wife from cholera, Walker left everything behind; he took a ship to Panama and then the overland route, travelling to the west coast of Central America and Mexico before arriving in San Francisco to work at the *Daily Herald*. The once polite and private man became shrill and outspoken; he had become a 'war hawk', aggressively racist and pro-filibuster. In the wake of the failed López invasion of Cuba, he wrote: 'that which you [the liberal public in the US] ignorantly call "filibusterism" is not the offspring of hasty passions or ill-regulated desire: it is the fruit of the sure, unerring instincts which act in accordance with laws as old as creation. They are but drivellers who speak of establishing fixed relations between the pure white American race and the mixed Hispano-Indian race as it exists in Mexico and Central America, without employment of force.'

After a rigged election in July 1856, Walker pronounced himself President of Nicaragua. On top of having contributed to the introduction into Latin American democracy of the seriously flawed habit of preordaining electoral results, Walker's first act in office was to reinstitute slavery. 'Filibustering and efforts in the U. S. South to expand slavery were intimately related in the mid-1850s.'[21] 'This was the essence of filibustering,' says historian Joseph Cummins, 'the white race taking over and controlling the red, brown, and black races.'[22] Filibustering was about two things: land grabbing, often through violent means, and control over cheap mobile labour. These are two elements of the same equation. That equation, the result of which is 'money that begets money', also included power over international and transoceanic routes. It also allowed authorities formally committed to the principles of non-colonisation and non-intervention to claim little or no involvement in expansionist adventures, thereby retaining, at the very least, the semblance of republicanism. Hence Nicaragua. From the point of view of free black Panamanians, they were the next obvious candidate on the list.

The re-establishment of slavery in Nicaragua and the threat to the transit zone sent shock waves throughout the Americas, particularly among political liberals and the popular sectors of the population in Panama. It seemed to repeat a pattern already exemplified by California, where pockets of slavery had survived in spite of the package of five bills passed by US Congress in order to diffuse the confrontation between southern and northern states, known as the Compromise of 1850, aroused by expectations of further territorial expansion following the Texas Annexation of December 1845 and the Mexican-American War of 1846–8. The constitution of the new state of California had denied blacks and natives the right to vote or access to the witness box in court cases against whites; vigilante bands like the Rangers went around killing men, mostly Mexicans, Chileans, Peruvians and Indian, who violated the new Anglo-American order.

Such a state of affairs was in stark contrast to the situation in Panama and Colombia, where the right to vote had been guaranteed to all men regardless of colour since 1853. In Colombia, however, the political enfranchisement of coloured peoples, or *gentes de color*, was contradicted by economic disenfranchisement. Although at first *pardos* and other peoples of colour benefited economically from work associated with the overground part of the passage through the isthmus and the construction of the railroad, as soon as the work was done and labourers were turned away, an underclass of unemployed and increasingly impoverished people emerged. Alternative forms of livelihood were swept away by the surge in demand for transportation, the building of the road and the railway line, and the dismissal of workers, an action that would be repeated throughout Latin America. And as had once happened on board the slave ships, peoples who had come from many places found they shared more than a space in Panama. They also shared a memory of abuse at the hands of white immigrants and common stories of earlier struggles. Soon, these memories turned into a form of collective bargaining, resistance and self-definition.

The insistence on equality and 'popular republicanism' clashed once more with old colonial patriarchal patterns and new ideas about property and 'free' labour; the result was social unrest and conflict. In Panama, concerned citizens and the railroad company sponsored private armies and vigilante committees similar to those that had been set up in California. This made the threat of filibusterism more acute. Panama state governor Fábregas sent a letter to Bogotá describing the general climate in no uncertain terms: 'the examples of Baja California and Nicaragua offer us ample evidence of a new kind of enemy against which the weak Hispanic American nationalities must prepare to defend themselves'. Such fears materialised in early April 1856 when a steamship ominously named after Mexico's conquistador Hernán Cortés, owned by Cornelius Vanderbilt and manned by at least forty recruits for William Walker's filibuster army, turned up in Panama City.

In command of the mercenary force was self-styled Captain Horace Bell. An immigrant to California during the Mexican-American War that ended in 1848, as soon as he disembarked on the isthmus Bell boasted about having been a member of the vigilante force created by Governor John Bigler, known as the California Rangers. The Rangers had participated in the violent consolidation of Anglo-American power in and around Los Angeles, showing a particular zeal in the persecution of Mexican and Spanish American dissident workers and unwanted 'immigrants'. Many of these migrants had arrived in California through Panama from Peru, Chile and elsewhere. However, the majority were Mexicans and *Californios*. This means, as Mexican activist and musician Rubén Albarracín put it to me during a conversation in London, that in most cases these 'immigrants' had not crossed the frontier. Rather, the frontier had crossed them.

The Incident of the Slice of Watermelon: The Los Angeles Prequel

Among the many claims made by Horace Bell upon his arrival in Panama was his crucial part in the manhunt of Joaquín Murrieta, a legendary protagonist of the history of California during the Gold Rush, also known as 'the Robin Hood of El Dorado'. Murrieta's story is the inspiration behind the fictional character Don Diego Vega, better known as Zorro, from Johnston McCulley's pulp stories of the 1920s.

According to some accounts Murrieta and his family arrived in Alta California in 1848 from Villa San Rafael de Alamitos in Sonora, Mexico. According to others, he came from Chile. If the latter, he must have come through Panama, which is perhaps why you can still find people around the Canal Zone who tell his story. Whether Chileans or Mexicans, the Murrietas were seeking fortune like many others in the gold-mining zone of *veta madre*, or Mother Lode, in the Sierra Nevada of California. While prospecting for gold, the Murrieta brothers were assaulted by a band of white vigilantes: his older brother was lynched, his wife was gang-raped and Joaquín Murrieta was horsewhipped and left for dead. Legend has it that he went to the county sheriff to file charges against the vigilantes, only to be informed 'that in California it was not illegal for whites to rape Mexicans, nor was it illegal for whites to kill Mexicans'.

No law exonerating whites existed, but Mexicans could not testify against Anglos in court and there was no will on the part of the authorities to intervene in the all-too-frequent instances of racial or land conflict on the side of non-whites. Angered, Murrieta recruited his remaining brothers and some friends to go after the culprits. The rest of the story has been the basis of many films: from Antonio Banderas' 1988 *The Mask of Zorro* to Emilio Estevez's Billy the Kid in *Young Guns*. The band of brothers captured and killed at least forty of the men involved in the deed. They turned to robbery and killing, striking down only Anglos. Then the authorities branded them as outlaws and put a price on their heads. The infamous California Rangers – a vigilante group formed to hunt down and punish rebellious Mexicans and immigrants – claimed they killed Joaquín Murrieta. Horace Bell said he was among them, but ask anybody who knows in East LA and they would tell you the vigilantes simply got hold of some other Mexican, killed him, cut off his head and put it in a brandy jar to claim the reward and paraded it around California, charging $1 per viewer.

In an even more complicated twist to the story, it is said that there was not one but two Murrietas, one named 'El Patrio' – the dark-skinned

prospector-turned-outlaw of the original story – and another known as
'El Guerro' – this one tall, blond, athletic and blue-eyed. They may have
been brothers, or cousins, or just friends, who ran the band robbing,
killing Anglos and stealing horses together. The latter, says Humberto
Garza, a community organiser whom I met once in Houston, Texas,
'died of old age in São Paulo, Brazil. He was ninety years of age, still
very handsome and a bit of a ladies' man who left more than fifteen
children in the San Joaquín valley in California, in Mexico and South
America.'

Crucially, the story of the Murrieta brothers merges with the history
of land grabbing that fuelled the fears of Hispanic Americans everywhere after the 1846–8 Mexican-American War. Today, children in
America learn about the Treaty of Guadalupe Hidalgo but rarely hear
about the Agreement at Querétaro, an addendum to the Treaty between
the United States and Mexico, that finished the war in 1848, and which,
according to Garza and the Mexican American viewpoint, has a different
story to tell about US land takeover in Latin America. First, it suggests
that the actual border between Alta and Baja California is not the right
one, and, second, it refers to the invasions of Sonora, in which William
Walker and Horace Bell took part, thereby setting the context for
Walker's and Bell's later enterprises in Nicaragua and Panama.

The Incident of the Slice of Watermelon: A
Key to the History of the Americas

People like Walker and Bell were in the avant-garde of Manifest Destiny.
When they arrived in Panama, Bell's forces were in the middle of an
ongoing battle between William Walker and Cornelius Vanderbilt, and
the latter's competitors in the transport business Charles Morgan and
C. K. Garrison, over the control of the Accessory Transit Company,
which owned the right to operate the interoceanic route through
Nicaragua. Walker had revoked Vanderbilt's licence and given it to
Morgan and Garrison, whom he knew from his contacts in New Orleans
and who had actually sponsored his military escapade. This particular fact
illustrates a more general truth: the sovereignty crisis of the nineteenth
and twentieth centuries in Latin America was meshed with capitalist

competition among entrepreneurs in the US, and the coloured peoples were caught in the middle. This may be the key to understanding the modern history of the Americas.

The *Hernán Cortés*, like other ships owned by Vanderbilt, had been transporting men and provisions for Walker's army in Nicaragua; as a consequence of Walker's volte-face against the New York magnate, it had been prevented from landing in the Nicaraguan port of San Juan. That is how Bell and his men ended up in Panama City. Forty dreaded filibusters, just as in Murrieta's story, entered the city of Panama on 8 April 1856 with Horace Bell in command. Terrified, the Panamanians confused him with William Walker himself.

A few days later, on 15 April, the passengers of the New York steam-ship *Illinois* disembarked at the port of Colón. Unable to board the ferry that would have taken them immediately to a San Francisco-bound steamship, they decided to take the Panama Rail and by the afternoon had arrived at Panama City railroad station. Some of them, including a few women and children wishing to explore the surrounding area, crossed the small bridge that leads to the barrio of La Ciénaga. 'On the other side of the bridge, a man named José Manuel Luna awaited the passengers from behind a small stand,' writes Aims McGuinness, 'on his stand Juan José had laid out slices of watermelon that he hoped to sell to immigrants during the brief period between their arrival in Panama City and their departure.'[23]

At about six in the afternoon, three drunken passengers from the *Illinois* approached his stand and one of them had a taste of a slice of watermelon from Luna's stand. 'It's one dime,' said José Manuel in perfect English. The man tossed the fruit to the ground and left with his friends without offering anything in return. 'José Manuel got hold of his knife, like in Rubén Blades' salsa classic "Pedro Navajas", put it in the back of his pants and said to the gringo,' Héctor, a fruit-vendor friend from the market in today's Panama City, tells me, '"*No, joda*, this is not the United States. Pay me and we're even." The American pulled out a gun and replied, "Kiss my ass, nigger." To which José Manuel responded in a firm voice, "I guess you think you're much of a man because you have a gun in your hand. Well, I have my knife. Let's see who's more of a man."'

By then a small crowd had formed around the men, cheering on one and shouting insults to the other. Most of them were *pardos*, free blacks and mulattoes, others were Indians who had arrived from the Pacific coast of South America. Héctor says the other men just ran away, leaving their friend behind to face the increasingly fired-up crowd on his own. In other versions of the story, one of the drunken men offered Luna a silver dollar. In his own testimony, Luna says he had already turned his back 'and was returning to my stand' when someone from the crowd jumped on the man with the pistol and disarmed him. 'That's Miguel, the boatman,' says Héctor. 'He was an Indian from Colombia and he came to Luna's help.' Historians say he was in fact Peruvian, and his name was Miguel Habrahan, or Abraham. The fact that this is more likely to be his second name than his surname suggests he was not an Indian but actually a freed slave. The official US report identifies him as a 'light-colored native'. It is possible that he was Jewish.

In Héctor's account, Miguel stepped in front of the American when the latter seemed ready to fire at Juan and demanded he put away his gun. When the gunman pointed it at him, Miguel wrestled the gringo and his friends, got hold of the gun and ran off with it into the thatched houses of La Ciénaga. This version coincides with Miguel's own testimony, which was published in the pages of *Gaceta del Estado*. But according to the official US report, it was Miguel who robbed the passenger of his gun while he was putting it away and fired at him. In that report there is no mention of the filibusters who were in town. Habrahan is solely to blame. In contrast, the Colombian officials brought in to assess the potential repercussions for their country laid the blame on the strong feelings that arose from the presence of Bell and his men, and on the railroad company that brought people 'from the West Indies and other places as labourers on the rail-road and afterwards were turned adrift by the company to starve'.

The difference between reports reveals the conflicting politics that had divided Anglo- and Latin America in the late nineteenth century, not long ago united by the republican belief in the free pursuit of equality and liberty. Turned into the free pursuit of unending profit by whatever means necessary – including the unauthorised but tolerated use of force by private armies of filibusters – at the expense of the 'weaker races', that same drive had led up to this moment. Both reports coincide in pointing out that, after the incident of the slice of watermelon, the bell of the nearby church of Santa Ana began to call for people to flock around La Ciénaga, where locals engaged in a brawl with passengers of the *Illinois*. The latter tried to escape in the direction of the railroad company's wharf; those who could took refuge in the railroad station, where they armed themselves and loaded a cannon that was there to be used by the company's now disbanded private army. Outside, men from the inner quarters of La Ciénaga and Arrabal gathered and traded insults with the Americans inside. Rocks were hurled, shots were fired. The police intervened under orders from the state governor to take back the station building. In attempting to force their way into the building, the policemen were joined by members of the crowd wielding knifes, sticks and machetes. Only once they were inside did the policemen realise that these were civilians, and attempted to lead the passengers to the ferry and to safety; the crowd demanded of them a free pass to defend the city against attackers bent on destroying it, but the policemen denied their request. It would seem that anger against the company was joined by a clear belief that the city was under attack by filibusters.

According to the information provided afterwards by the state governor, many Arrabaleños and Cienagueros did not consider their actions to be unprovoked and gratuitous aggression, but, rather, as being motivated by the intention to defend themselves and their country from an ongoing foreign invasion. Indeed, it was one of the filibusters who had arrived almost a week earlier, a man named Joseph Stokes, who loaded the cannon and fired on the crowd after exorting the passengers inside to rescue those who had not made it into the building and were in danger of being murdered by the mob outside. Horace Bell himself, full of praise for Stokes' actions, recognised that gun and cannon fire from the passengers inside the station contributed to the confusion that night. By the next morning at least seventeen people lay dead.

Even a week after the events of 15 April there was a widespread belief that filibusters had been behind the violence. On 16 April men from Arrabal demanded that Governor Fábregas give them weapons so that they could organise the defence of the city against the incoming invasion. According to the 21 April edition of the newspaper *El Panameño*, the people of Panama had demonstrated on that day that 'they would not stand aside and allow filibusters and others from the United States to do with them as they had done with the people of Alta California, Sonora and Nicaragua'. This language expresses neither confusion nor xenophobia. It tells us how the working people of colour in Panama refused to submit to the sort of demands for racial subordination that in the United States had turned the doctrine to defend equality in the republic and the entire continent, into a belief in the manifest destiny of one race to dominate all others.

All this trouble for a slice of watermelon? How can that be so significant in a land of plenty where Nature can easily supply an entire store? The natural abundance that in the minds of many characterises Latin America is just part of the story. The other part, so often omitted from the usual accounts, is the life and work of men and women who cultivate, harvest, transport and market fruit and other natural resources. It is the story of how local peoples relate to their natural surroundings, to their past, to each other – their struggles and expectations – and to the wider world during the industrialisation period, when railroad, sea transport and fruit companies changed their surroundings and decisively challenged their achievements and aspirations.

In the process of defending themselves, their ways of life and their social and political conquests, the people of Panama City 'had also meted out just punishment to the railroad company', as *El Panameño* put it in 1856. 'In order to get to the filibusters, it was necessary to attack the station violently. The people had passed sentence on the company and saw it as an enemy.' Behind the filibusters and the belief in Manifest Destiny were the Vanderbilts, Morgans, and Garrisons of this world, the forerunners of Shell Oil and the United Fruit Company. By resisting the filibusters and attacking the buildings of the transport company, *el pueblo* was turning the tables on these demi-gods and making visible the invisible effects of their competition and their greed for power.

The refusal of the people of Panama in 1856 offers us a glimpse of a world without masters and without gods. It is ironic perhaps that

C. K. Garrison had in the past lived in Panama. Before joining Benjamin Morgan in the Morgan & Garrison Partnership that Vanderbilt swore to ruin, he organised a banking firm, perhaps one of the first in a long line of financial and trading institutions set up in Panama and elsewhere in the Americas. In a way, they are the actual embodiment of Manifest Destiny and the filibusters.

Banana Republic

The image of sleepy, tropical places being penetrated by global capital in the guise of a powerful overlord or a foreign company is almost synonymous with Latin America. It became widespread thanks to fiction and scholarly literature, especially in the 1970s when economists began to describe cities like Manaus, Brazil's world capital of the rubber business, the cacao fields of Carúpano in Venezuela, the cotton areas of Guatemala, Nicaragua or Peru, the sugar cane *haciendas* of the Dominican Republican or US-occupied Haiti and the banana plantations of Caribbean Colombia as enclaves, 'factories in the field' run by foreign bosses and worked by uprooted and passive workers.

'Macondo was in ruins,' wrote Gabriel García Márquez in *One Hundred Years of Solitude*, '. . . the houses that had been built with such haste during the banana fever had been abandoned . . . The wooden houses, the cool terraces for breezy card-playing afternoons, seemed to have been blown away in an anticipation of the prophetic wind that years later would wipe Macondo off the face of the earth.'[24] Miguel Ángel Asturias described the reign of Minor Keith – the US railroad, fruit and shipping magnate, later on vice-president of the United Fruit Company – over Costa Rica, Panama and Colombia, as the second coming of the conquistadors and a new wave of exploitation and plunder in his novel *The Green Pope*: 'Chicago could not help but feel proud of that son who went off with a brace of pistols and returned to demand his position among the meat emperors, the railroad kings, the copper kings, the chewing-gum kings.'[25]

The Koran mentions the banana among the trees of paradise, but, as part of the export boom brought about by the second industrial revolution that took place in western Europe and the United States, it supported the rise of wealthy regional and national elites whose governments were able to bring civil wars to an end and impose a central authority upon their divided societies, and the fall of ex-slaves and free blacks who until then had successfully demanded land, freedom and citizenship. For the latter, the new export economy, represented by bananas and coffee in Colombia, Costa Rica, Panama and Brazil, rubber in Brazil, meat and cereals in Argentina and Uruguay, sugar in the Caribbean and oil in Mexico and Venezuela, meant eternal damnation.

Between 1870 and 1912, the annual value of Latin American exports grew from $344 million to $1.6 billion, and by the end of the period six countries in the region – Argentina, Chile, Costa Rica, Cuba, Uruguay and Puerto Rico – were exporting more goods per capita than the United States. The influx of tax revenues brought about a change in the balance of power, which shifted for the popular and multiracial mass movements of the nineteenth century to export-based elites. The official nationalist ideologies built around the notion of racial harmony were undermined by the arrival of scientific racism and social Darwinism, cloaked in the prestige and status of western science and technological progress. Latin America's racial inheritance became a problem, associated with the challenge of how the elites could transform their 'backward' or 'underdeveloped' countries into 'civilised' nations on the model of Europe and the United States.

Cuban elites, state legislators in São Paulo in Brazil, Venezuelan intellectuals like Rufino Blanco Fombona and *Regeneración* politicians in Colombia, as well as upwardly mobile peoples of colour, responded to the question of 'development' with a vast plan of racial homogenisation of their nations. The new 'sciences' coming from Europe and America merely confirmed and conformed to Latin American elites' own firm beliefs, derived from three hundred years of colonial slavery and caste social organisation, that the inherent inferiority of black, Indian and mulatto populations was an obstacle in the path to civilisation. Furthermore, as the export economy surged in Latin America, on the back of plantation-based crops, wealthier landowners found the capital and the incentive to expand their landholdings at the expense of commoner Indian and black peasants. In Mexico for instance, the enclosure and privatisation of state-owned lands impacted with special force upon Indian and mixed peasants, setting the stage for the Mexican Revolution. It is worth remembering that in 1810, a massive rebellion led by Indian and mixed miners and peasants had made its way through the plantation and mining zones north-west of Mexico City. Father Miguel Hidalgo and the image of the Virgin of Guadalupe presided over a violent peasant and slave reaction to the plantation and mine systems that maintained its momentum even after Hidalgo's defeat in Veracruz province. These slaves continued their guerrilla warfare, launched from the forested hills and mountains even after the achievement of Mexican independence in 1821.

In other countries of Latin America, the process of enclosure, privatisation and whitening, or racial homogenisation, was equally as intense and widespread. In Cuba, for instance, Afro-Cubans retreated to Oriente province in the face of a landowners' advance and the operation of US firms in the 1900s. The province became a national centre for black resistance, first to slavery and Spanish rule during the three wars of independence fought on the island, and then to land dispossession and the interests of US sugar companies. The latter repeatedly begged Washington for protection and US Marines landed in the province, first in 1912, then again in 1917. Even though on the second occasion American forces occupied the island for five years, they did not succeed in putting down peasant rebels, who continued to operate in the Sierra Maestra. When Fidel Castro and Che Guevara arrived in Cuba in 1956, they found their first recruits among the descendants of those rebels still living in the mountains of Oriente. Large commons, or *terrenos comuneros*, were also enclosed in the Dominican Republic and in Colombia's Cauca valley and the surrounding areas of the Pacific coast, where the dispossession of black peasantry continues to proceed apace to this day at the hands of paramilitary forces, often in cahoots with local elites and the regular armed forces, in order to open the way for oil palm crops, mining and oil exploration.

When the United Fruit Company moved to Central America, the ensuing migration from the Caribbean was followed by a wave of anti-West Indian sentiment sweeping through the Dominican Republic,

Costa Rica and Panama. In the latter, immigrants from the West Indies took most of the jobs in building and operating the Panama Canal in the zone now under American control after the 1903 US-backed secession from Colombia. By 1912 American President William H. Taft had confirmed an interpretation of the Monroe Doctrine that had been dreaded throughout Latin America since the days of Secretary of State Henry Clay. As he put it, 'the day is not far distant when three Stars and Stripes at three equidistant points will mark our territory: one at the North Pole, another at the Panama Canal, and the third at the South Pole. The whole hemisphere will be ours in fact as, by virtue of our superiority of race is already ours morally.' West Indian immigration into Panama or Colombia and Haitian immigration into the Dominican Republic signified the negation of such fantasies, made difficult already by the extent of the mulatto national population. The result was resentment, not only among national elites but also among working-class Panamanians, Colombians and Dominicans facing economic competition. Those threats intensified during the Great Depression of the 1930s, sometimes as a result of the economic hardships provoked by the financial crisis, at other times because of direct provocation by caudillos and dictators like Rafael Trujillo in the Dominican Republic or Panama City police chief Nicolás Ardito Barletta, who went as far as to propose Nazi-style anti-Semitism as a model for how Panamanians should deal with the black population.[26]

Before banana cultivation began in earnest in Caribbean Colombia, the private ownership of land was scarce. When not fighting civil wars, the racially mixed people of Ciénaga in the Magdalena region of the country raised some export and mostly subsistence crops in the *ejidos* or common lands that encircled the town. The predominantly white inhabitants of the old port of Santa Marta jealously guarded their Old World pedigree as they competed against the entrepreneurial spirit of the new city of Barranquilla, located sixty miles to the west. All the while, in the inland area of colonisation around Aracataca, mixed peoples and descendants of the Chimila Indians shared *indivisos* – expanses of land similar to the commons. From 1890 to 1910 most *ejidos* were privatised, but the process did not lead to the concentration of land in a few hands, and in fact this situation continued throughout the banana period. The United Fruit Company was happy to sign banana purchase contracts with small and large producers alike. Large banana plantations emerged in the area of *indivisos* and *baldíos* (lands declared empty) around the towns of Aracataca and Fundación. The enclaves that were formed in and around the plantation areas were not isolated micro-societies like the *haciendas* of old, but, rather, connected to the rest of the Colombian and the wider Caribbean region, and, through it, to the world. Even before the banana company arrived, the region had been buzzing with Italians, Jewish traders from Curacao, Palestinians, Syrians and Lebanese. Such connections multiplied once the banana economy got under way, bringing it closer to neighbouring Barranquilla and the rest of the Caribbean, and also to Bogotá in the interior of the country.

As the United Fruit Company developed banana plantations in the region, it employed heavily from among the local black and mulatto peasantry, already in contact with organised dockworkers in the port of Cartagena, and the riverboat workers of the Magdalena. They planned so as not to succumb to the powerful 'magic' associated with the flood of money in the banana-producing areas. Those who got too close to it and became rich almost overnight were changed by the experience, sometimes in dramatic ways. A story is told of a man called Manuel Varela, dark-skinned and particularly ugly, who in the 1920s built one of the biggest mansions in Ciénaga. It was rumoured he had made a pact with the devil: for each year of prosperity, a year of his life was discounted. He became obsessed with technology, like one of the characters of García Márquez's *One Hundred Years of Solitude*, and bought an electric tramway and a whole series of mechanical inventions in the United States, including, according to some accounts, a mechanical servant with whom he would play chess and drink rum, isolated in his big mansion, which soon acquired the nickname *La Casa del Diablo*, the Devil's House. He would only go out, accompanied by his mechanical friend, to seduce the young poor virgins of the region and attract them to his house. They were never seen again. He could speak with snakes and find paths in the dark. When he died, his fortune vanished. And yet his spectre would return during floods and times of great tragedy. He was seen embedding needles in ripe bananas to incapacitate policemen and soldiers shooting striking workers during the massacre of 1928.

By the end of 1928, the banana workers, strongly identified with the popular left wing of the Liberal Party, were ready to confront the United Fruit Company over better living and working conditions. In early November they brought operations in the entire plantation zone to a halt. On the night of 5 December, police and armed forces opened fire on several thousand strikers gathered in and around the main square of Ciénaga. No one really knows how many people died or what happened to the bodies of the dead. As happened with a similar massacre that took place in Haiti in 1937, government troops removed the bodies before daybreak and buried them in unmarked graves or threw them into the sea. Officials reported nine workers killed that night and thirty-eight more in the weeks of repression that followed. Those reports were contradicted several months later in the Colombian Congress by the popular leftist leader Jorge Eliécer Gaitán who had received very different reports sent, apparently, by the telegraphist of Aracataca.

The best-known version of the massacre was told by García Márquez in *One Hundred Years of Solitude*. It epitomises the multiple dramas and conflicts of the boom and bust economy of the export years in Latin America. It sums up the causes as much as the consequences. As the export-oriented model collapsed during the Great Depression, the largely conservative republics were swept aside in one country after another, to be replaced by new regimes based mainly on the support drawn from the forces of organised labour and social movements. As they had done in the past, these movements sought inspiration in the multiracial and syncretistic political and cultural milieux of the times, rather than in the civilisations and cultural fashions of Europe. They turned to the task of constructing new economies, new systems of governance and new forms of political identity.

Rather than being examples of cultural imperialism, the passive, one-way reception of 'foreign' ideas and conceptions, these movements were always receptive to the contributions of other societies. As Ciénaga poet Javier Moscarella told Catherine LeGrand in 1996: 'We are open but not submissive. We copy, we assimilate, we recycle into something else. It is impossible to dominate us. Our culture has remained intact because our subsistence technologies, our forms of sociability, and our free-thinking beliefs are our historical roots: they center us, they make us who we are. The United Fruit Company had no concerted program of social change ... The only power the United Fruit Company had was the power of corruption and that was circumstantial. There was money to be made and some people here took advantage of the situation.'[27] Today, as Latin American countries embark once more on the historical task of constructing new economies, new forms of governance, new political, social and national identities in the wake of the most serious economic crises since the 1930s, the example of recuperation and invention set by these men and women remains an inspiring legacy.

PART THREE

7

Empire: Tales from Mañana–Land in Neocolonial America

Manifest Destiny

On 18 April 1856, the US consul for Panama City informed the US Department of State about the events that had taken place in Panama City on 15 April. The report, written by US Department of State special investigator Amos Corwine, concluded that José Manuel Luna and Miguel Habrahan's actions had signalled 'native negroes' to launch a premeditated and unprovoked attack on innocent passengers 'in connivance' with the authorities of Panama, which was then part of Colombia. His report alleged that the 'rioters' had committed atrocities, including the rape of American female passengers by 'colored men' and an attack on a mother with child. Colombian and Panamanian officials, including the minister of foreign affairs, issued a complete rebuttal of American accusations, presenting the actions of the people of Panama City, and more specifically Arrabal, as acts of self-defence. They placed the blame for initiating the conflict on Jack Oliver and other passengers as well as on previous acts of abuse directed at local inhabitants, but also, and crucially, on fears of filibustering among the local population, fears justified by previous attacks on other parts of Latin America by bands of privately invested, armed Americans, as well as the actual presence of armed filibusters in Panama on that April day, which the Department of State's report failed to mention. The Colombian rebuttal also blamed the railroad company, which the authors accused of being responsible for the destitution of the poorer immigrants and former rail workers from the West Indies and elsewhere, now living in the slums of Arrabal.[1]

Whatever the similarities and discrepancies between these two official accounts, both of them obscured important aspects of the politics of the people who gathered in La Ciénaga and outside the station during and after the argument between José Manuel Luna, Miguel Habrahan and the drunken passenger. These are the lessons that matter most to us; not just the demise of 'deference' to white Americans on the part of black Latin Americans and Amerindians, but also, importantly, the assertion of their political identity in response to the social costs of Panama's transformation at the hands of the railroad company, that is to say, the transformation of republican Latin America into a 'backyard' at the hands of private and often foreign commercial interests. This is why one recognises in the parties involved in the watermelon incident the protagonists of the historical drama unfolding in the Americas after independence.

On the one side were the men and women of Arrabal in Panama, people like José Manuel Luna and Miguel Habrahan. In 1856 Panama, men of African descent such as Luna possessed rights corresponding to nothing that existed in Texas or California. At the time of the incident, Luna was clear about the significant difference between Panama and the United States in this respect. He was a coloured man with voting rights. And although most Amerindians were largely excluded from electoral politics, Habrahan's name appears on a petition signed by boatmen presenting themselves as citizens with the right to appeal to an elected government that had a mandate to protect and defend the economic interests of its constituents.[2] Both men responded politically to the pressures placed on them by the activities of the Panama Railroad Company, which deprived them of an economic future. This local action mirrored regional and wider actions, similar to those that had occurred in other parts of Latin America in the wake of the Mexican-American War of 1848. The war had been fought over the consequences of the scheme facilitated by Moses Austin and his son, Stephen, bankers from Texas, in 1823, which ended in the secession of Texas from Mexico in 1836 and its annexation by the United States in 1845, and the armed filibustering expedition of John C. Fremont to California in the winter of 1845, which resulted in California's secession from Mexico and US annexation after the Sonoma Bear Flag Revolt of 1846. The conquest politics of California and Texas resulted in systematic efforts by US whites to exclude 'foreigners' from economic and political dominance or significant participation. And when William Walker completed the conquest of Nicaragua in 1855, he re-established slavery in order to attract the support of slaveholders in the American South. The people of Arrabal were conscious of the threat imposed by these events to the liberties and hopes they had fought for during the wars of independence. The Panama Railroad Company had already conquered their economic future; they would defend their political future at all cost.

On the other side were the industrialists and financiers who rose to power in the United States during the divisive years of expansion, conquest, economic consolidation and war, men like Cornelius Vanderbilt, Charles Morgan and C. K. Garrison. In the United States, the Mexican-American War was a partisan issue and a key element of the origins of the American Civil War. Whigs in the North and the South opposed it; most Democrats, particularly in the South, animated by popular belief in what the editor of the *Democratic Review* John O'Sullivan termed Manifest Destiny, supported it.[3] At their simplest level, such tensions reflected differing choices concerning the model of economic development and the political orientation of the United States.

The industrialists and financiers of the American North favoured the Hamiltonian model of protection of nascent national industry, which made their private interests identifiable with those of the nation. Slaveholders in the American South preferred the Jeffersonian model of export-oriented and extensive agriculture and extraction. Conquest and expansionism, in principle closer to the land-based premises of Jeffersonians, in fact provided the context within which these competing models would finally coalesce and complement each other. The California Gold Rush and its aftermath, for instance, provided new business opportunities for the likes of Vanderbilt, Morgan and Garrison, who provided funds and resources to back the brazen missions of conquest led by William Walker and his filibustering brethren. In that respect, the two models become united in their recognition of the need to sever all ties between the revolutionary spirit of the Constitution of the United States, on the one hand, and the agency of the people themselves, in general, and in particular the capacities of Amerindians and slaves, including their conception of the land as a commons, on the other, in response to the imperatives emerging from global exchange and the privatisation of all relations.

This process, which set the rapacious greed of international trading against the very foundations of the republic, was experienced internally in the expansionist drive to conquer the border, appropriate Indian land by means of exploration and 'discovery', and the development of the notion of community rights devoted, paradoxically, to the expansion and protection of private interests in the US Constitution. But it was also experienced externally, in the popularity of the Manifest Destiny ideology, the deeds of conquering companies of filibusters like William Walker's group and other armies on the West Coast and in Latin America, and the rise of the sort of discreet or faux imperialism exemplified by the Panama Railroad Company and the United Fruit Company in Panama, Costa Rica, Colombia and elsewhere.

The costs and transformations associated with this historical process were intertwined from the very outset with the refusal to recognise the capacity or even the right of Afro-Americans and Amerindians, and those like them at home and abroad, in Panama as well as other places, to take advantage of the principles of equality enshrined in the constitutions of Latin America following the wars of independence, and of the laws of supply and demand. That refusal is not surprising in the case of Jack Oliver, the main American protagonist in the watermelon incident, a white man who came from one of the few places in the Americas where 'slavery was still a legal institution in 1856'.[4] The drunken Oliver and the American filibusters came from a place where black men and natives were regularly deprived of the most basic rights, rights that Amerindians and Afro-Latin Americans had fought for and established during the wars of independence.

Moreover, this deprivation had been interpreted and justified by many in North America as one crucial element of the historical course and destination set by God or fate, or inherent and manifested in the entrepreneurial character and the economic and geopolitical mission of

America. This is the notion that came to be known as Manifest Destiny, which mediated the transformation of Henry Clay's interpretation of the Monroe Doctrine, and which established the principles of non-colonisation and non-intervention of European powers from the stand-point of America's national interest, into the expansive and far more aggressive interpretation put forth by US President Theodore Roosevelt. One year after the watermelon incident in Panama, the US Supreme Court would decide, bluntly, in the Dred Scott judgement of 1857, that a black man had no rights the white men were bound to respect. Forty-seven years later, in 1903, the fears of the black and Amerindian population concerning American intervention in the affairs of their land would be confirmed when Panama seceded from Colombia and opened the way for the construction of a US canal. The military and economic presence of the United States in Panama would last until at least the year 2000.

If Roosevelt was not directly responsible for the plot to incite revolu-tion and secession in Panama in 1903, it is clear that at the very least he was 'extremely well informed' as to the conspirators' plan. This is the conclusion drawn by Roosevelt's biographer, Henry Pringle, after careful examination of the available evidence. The Panama republic was born in room no. 1162 of the old Waldorf Astoria Hotel in New York. Bent on selling the French franchise to the Americans, Philippe Buneau-Varilla and William Nelson Cromwell spoke loudly about their connections in the White House, and of the fact that President Roosevelt recog-nised the emerging new order in terms of a new understanding of the Monroe Doctrine with 'indecent and unwise haste'. Pride in the canal later, and his view of the international order, caused him to declare, 'I took Panama and let Congress debate.'[5]

On Liberties

A way of charting the process that set the imperatives of international trading against the foundations of republicanism in the Americas and else-where is to look at the history and influence of Magna Carta.[6] Created in the thirteenth century in Britain as an armistice in civil war, restored as a basis of government in times of peace after the 1217 Treaty of Kingston, and established as the common law of the land between 1225 and 1297, the Charters of Liberties, known as Magna Charta and its companion Magna Charta de Foresta, gradually became the very cornerstone of the development of our most basic social and political institutions – church, town, family, government and commons. Magna Carta included in Chapters 47 and 48 a number of energy resources – and ecology-related principles of common right, access and use – extremely relevant to our current woes concerning the disastrous consequences of the paradoxical dynamic between progress and destruction.[7] Chapters 7 and 33 defined limits of privatisation. The Charter of the Forest (Charta de Foresta), in turn, protected common access to energy resources and established principles in relation to building and developing future ecologies.

Today, the language of the Charters resonates with the provisions of the UN International Covenant on Economic, Social and Cultural Rights, and with the intellectual and practical legacy of development economics and international politics in Latin America and elsewhere.[8] But in the sixteenth century, as commodity exchange and privatised relations replaced the many forms of communing at local, national and global levels, the Charters were largely ignored. After the Putney Debates in Britain in the seventeenth century, Magna Carta and the Charter of the Forest were separated, paving the way for the transformation of the former into a protector of negative individual liberties and free trade, and a companion of the legal fictions of 'discovery' and the passivity of natives in respect to their environments that justified expansion and empire.

As we have seen in previous chapters, the defence of the commons persisted in spite of these developments, adapted to urban conditions and became central to the struggles against racialised slave trade and unequal international trading, which fuelled the criticism of empire and the wars of independence on both sides of the Atlantic in the eighteenth and nineteenth centuries. The settler colonies of North America and the struggling peoples of Latin America and the Caribbean embraced the idiom of the 'free-born Englishman'. Peoples of African descent in the Caribbean and *comuneros* in mainland South America de-racialised it, connected it with the world view of Amerindians and gave it a universal dimension.[9] But after the eighteenth-century uprisings of slaves, commoners and Amerindians in the Caribbean and the mainland colonies of the Americas, the commoner and abolitionist uses of the language of the Charters were muted, while being introduced into the US federal Constitution. These latent sources of the Constitution would be reawakened after World War II, when President Franklin Delano Roosevelt proposed a second Bill of Rights for the American people. But during the eighteenth, nineteenth and early twentieth centuries, the language of the Charters, fundamental to law and the Constitution, coexisted with the grabbing of indigenous peoples' lands and resources, and the expansion of racial slavery and exclusion. This was in contrast to developments in Latin America and the Caribbean, for instance the abolition of slavery in New Granada and the granting of voting rights to men of colour.

This contrast, and the paradoxical coexistence of the foundational language of liberty contained in the Charters with the realities of slavery and Indian genocide, can be explained by the legal, political and geopolitical developments that took place between 1842 and 1903 in the United States, which profoundly impacted upon the Americas and the rest of the world. The first date corresponds to the decision of the US Supreme Court in the case of Martin v. Lessee of Wadell, on 9 February of that year, the second date to the secession of Panama from Colombia and the 'taking of Panama', as President Theodore Roosevelt put it, in reference to the construction of an American canal and its control over the isthmus, which would last until the beginning of the twenty-first century.

In the Martin case, Chief Justice Roger B. Taney, who came from a family of tobacco planters and slaveholders in Maryland, gave the opinion of the court. The decision turned on the meaning of the letters of patent given by Charles II in 1664 to his brother James, granting him New Jersey, and the subsequent proprietors' surrender to the crown of all powers of government while retaining the rights to private property. Specifically, the question concerned whether or not the common right to piscary belonged to the common people of England, to the king as his property or regalia, or to subsequent private proprietors. Judge Taney decided to uphold the principle of 'public interest' or 'community rights' when it conflicted with the monopoly of private property, arguing that a common right of royal regalia became a public good with the transfer of sovereignty to the people of the United States after independence. The decision is reminiscent of that in the Charles River Bridge case, also prepared by Judge Taney. Both decisions were regarded by many on either side of the Atlantic as a revolutionary attack on private property. But, in fact, they paved the way for the consolidation of the US model of economic development combining the drive forward of protected industry with the drive outward, westward and southward, under the imperatives of global commodity exchange.

This is why the crucial issue in the Martin case was the right of Charles II to make the grant in the first place. To this issue, Taney responded that the right was claimed not by conquest but by discovery. In answering the question of the ultimate title to land and resources in this manner, Taney unwittingly echoed the questions surrounding the 1492 *Capitulaciones* between the Catholic Majesties and Christopher Columbus, and the results of the debates of 1550 in Valladolid, Spain, when the Spanish emperor sought to establish the crown's right to the lands and resources of the New World over and against the native inhabitants. If claimed by conquest, then the defeated Indians would retain their property, while right by discovery regarded the New World as uninhabited – according to the fiction that established Native Americans as living in an eternal, unhistoried state, as passive recipients rather than actors in their own right and therefore incapable of transforming their surrounding environments. Another echo was that of the Putney Debates of the seventeenth century, when the rights to hold the land in private were separated from the common protections contained in the Charter of the Forest. Taney said that the right of the crown 'cannot at this day be questioned'. The time coincided, decisively, with the Indian Wars.

'These were the days of the Trail of Tears, the forced removal of the Cherokee, Chickasaw, Chocktaw, Creek and Seminole nations from their lands.'[10] In 1857, the same Judge Taney would deliver the infamous Dred Scott decision. Thus, the US Supreme Court notion of community and public rights outlined by Taney excluded Amerindians and African

Americans alike.[11] Crucially, in 1861 the recently formed Republican Party came up with a winning formula combining the Hamiltonian 'American System' of infant industry protection with the free distribution of public land sought by the western states. The 'American System' based on Hamilton's model was defended in that form by Henry Clay of the disappearing Whig Party, also the leading supporter of independence movements and revolutions in Latin America after 1817 and interpreter of the Monroe Doctrine. The formula allowed Republicans, and American industrialist protectionists, to win the Presidency in 1860 with Abraham Lincoln, a former protégé of Henry Clay, as their candidate. The Republican Party undertook to support the drive forward by raising industrial tariffs to their highest level in US history, giving as reason the expenditure for the Civil War. Tariffs on manufactured imports remained at between 40 and 50 per cent until World War I, and were the highest anywhere in the world.[12] It also responded to the drive outward of the US by promising 160 acres of land to any settler-coloniser ready to farm it for five years. To that purpose, it passed the Homestead Act during the Civil War in 1862, which became the largest programme of land reform in human history.

It is important to note in relation to this that the most divisive issue between North and South in the pre-Civil War climate was not in fact abolitionism – which, although influential, was not mainstream in the North – but rather the rise of the industrialist protection or Hamiltonian model and the issue of land redistribution.[13] But in spite of the differences, opposite sides knew well that whatever model imposed itself, it would do so on the basis of the alleged incapacity of Amerindians, Africans and their descendants to decide their own history and shape their environment. In the eyes of most Americans this meant all Latin Americans.[14] These were the days of Manifest Destiny, of the Mexican-American War, of the Spanish-American War in which Spain yielded control of Puerto Rico, Cuba and the Philippines to the United States, of William Walker's filibustering, the watermelon incident and the Panama Railroad Company. The paradox of the frequent use of the language of liberty in these instances and its dedication to the protection and expansion of privatised relations and property is therefore solved 'once it is understood that the reality was based on the destruction of Native Americans', and the underlying fiction of a land empty of mankind and its works.[15] This solution points towards a continuity of conquest, no less than expansion, linking internal phenomena such as the subjugation of Native Americans, the rise of Jim Crow segregation of Afro-Americans and progressive economic and political reform with external phenomena such as 'continental expansion', the filibustering expeditions of William Walker and the taking of Panama in 1903.

It is crucial to recognise that in the end it was not Walker's vision of conquest and Manifest Destiny but, rather, that of the Panama Railroad Company that would prove to be more indicative of the future of the United States at home and abroad. Together with other developments, chief among them the US Supreme Court decisions, the Indian Wars, the formation of the Republican Party and the financial consequences of the rise of protected industrialism in America – including the development of a market of 'futures' in 1905 – the growing importance of the railroad company's more discreet form of empire would firmly establish the predominance of the Hamiltonian model of development and its consequences, costs and transformations, decisively shaping the relations between the United States, Latin America and the world.

Our Man Flint

The paradox of the progressive drive forward and the destructive drive outward, apparently solved in the projected image of others as lacking any agency or capacity of their own, and the way it came to shape the geography of political and economic relations between the United States and Latin America, is exemplified by the story of Wall Street financier-turned-covert-operative in Brazil, Charles Flint. I first read about Flint's exploits in an essay written by California-based Steven Topik, an expert on modern Brazilian and Mexican trade and economic history, who specialises in the confused relations between market forces and military might. In 2009 I decided to go to Brazil, to Recife and Rio de Janeiro specifically, in order to find out more about Flint, and perhaps learn the Brazilian side of the story.

Charles Flint 'was a master of theatre, not a master of war'. 'So true,' says my friend Douglas, as we sit down for a beer in one of the hotels on Copacabana, in Rio de Janeiro. 'And yet, unlike William Walker and others like him, Flint was successful,' he observes. Walker ended up before a firing squad in Honduras, having managed to make enemies of some of the most powerful men in the United States, his erstwhile supporters, Wall Street tycoons Cornelius Vanderbilt and Charles Morgan. Walker fell into the custody of the British Royal Navy, which controlled neighbouring British Honduras, and was delivered to the Honduran authorities and executed in 1860. 'Instead, Flint was hailed as the saviour of the then nascent Brazilian republic when his armada entered Guanabara Bay, sometime in 1893,' says Douglas.

As we leave the bar and walk down the promenade toward Leblon, where our dancing partners await us, Douglas explains to me why Flint is significant in the history of Latin America–US relations: 'You see, Flint was a banker, but in 1893 he pulled out of nowhere a twelve-ship flotilla and headed for South America to support the ailing government of Marshal Floriano Peixoto, second President of the Brazilian republic.' In fact, Flint was a business associate of some of the biggest names in Wall Street – Jacob Schiff, August Belmont and J. P. Morgan. Like Vanderbilt and Morgan, he started in the shipping business, as a partner in Gilchrest, Flint & Company, which then merged with W. R. Grace & Company. The latter specialised in getting raw materials, including guano and sugar, from Peru and Chile to North America and Europe. William Russell Grace had founded the company in 1854 in Peru, working first as a ship's chandler to the merchantmen harvesting guano, the manure of bats and seabirds that the Inca called *wanu* and used as a fertiliser and soil enricher. With its high levels of phosphorus and nitrogen, guano can also be used as one of the main ingredients to make gunpowder.

People like Flint and Grace learned about the properties of guano from the Indians of Peru and neighbouring Chile, and then set up businesses in New York to exploit that knowledge in the form of finished goods like fertilisers for agriculture or gunpowder for the military. As happened with other cases of so-called 'process industries' – such as rubber, in which raw materials from a 'peripheral' area whose useful properties are known as a result of 'traditional' indigenous knowledge are first harvested locally and then transformed into finished goods elsewhere, in an industrial 'centre' – the locals and indigenous in possession of the original knowledge, and their countries, received few or no benefits at all once all the stages of the commodity chain or circuit had been completed.

Why? The principle that explains why this is so – why, in spite of the fact that both indigenous local knowledge and raw materials are as much a part of the global commodity chain as the work of harvesting merchants and industrialists who transport and transform them into saleable finalised goods, only the latter benefit, or benefit the most – is the same one that we saw at play in the previous section. It is assumed that 'traditional' indigenous knowledge and local materials are there for the taking. And that as allegedly happens with the land, since indigenous and local peoples do not 'work' the local environment and its materials, cultivate them or transform them – since 'traditional' land and knowledge form a local environment that is 'empty of mankind and its works', then the local environment, which can be treated as the peripheral point of a global commodity chain or network, is valueless. Thus, it can justifiably be taken by those with the capacity to transform it into something valuable, who then benefit from it.

A purely contingent disequilibrium between the 'peripheral' local environment and the industrial 'centre' in the global commodity chain, based on the fiction that the peripheral environment is empty of mankind and its works and therefore is valueless, becomes the 'original' or necessary form of the commodity chain and the reason that justifies the distribution of benefits and costs across different stages of the commodity circuit. Put otherwise, disequilibrium becomes the law. The disequilibrium between 'peripheral' environments and industrial 'centres', frequently but not always localised in different countries, is contingent in so far as it depends upon the limited information and objective uncertainty that in most cases affects commodity chains. The notion of a commodity chain is useful here because it highlights the connections between the supply of industrial inputs and demand for finished industrial products, which, taken together, help explain the degree of uncertainty in a specific market over time.

On the one hand, transformations in the supply and demand sides of the chain or circuit generate uncertainty and constrain actors at each point (which I have called, metaphorically, 'peripheral' and 'central') along the metaphoric commodity chain or circuit. 'Commodity chain' is, in this sense, a metaphor for the movement of materials, goods, ideas, money and capital across the globe. It is this movement in time and space that generates value. Value, in this sense, corresponds to the differences, in time and space, generated by the movement of all of these things, and in particular, by the difference in timing between points that possess 'advanced' technology and those in possession of technology considered 'backward', or who possess none at all. On the other hand, the global movement of all things is itself contingent, in that nothing guarantees it will continue into the future or that there is an ultimate reason for its actual existence and continuity, or that of its laws. In this sense, 'commodity chain' is the name for an entity that is neither 'original', in the sense of being timeless, nor necessary, in the sense of having within itself the cause of its own movement, or an ultimate reason why its laws – what I have called before the laws of disequilibrium – must be as they are and no other way.

I believe that one does not need anything as complicated as a 'theory' to understand the notion that the way things are in the economy and in society is contingent. I, for one, tend to adhere to standard conceptions of trade: distribution of materials and geographical conditions largely determine the location of production; risks and rewards tend to be distributed in competitive markets. It makes sense to think that even when one country produces everything more cheaply than another trade between them can occur. Although country X is more efficient in producing everything than country Y, it can still gain by specialising in things in which it has the greatest cost advantage over its trading partner. Conversely, even a country that has no advantage over its trading partner in producing any product can gain from specialising in the trade of products in which it has the least cost disadvantage. But this justification, which has formed the backbone of mainstream economics and free trade since its formulation by British economist and stock-market trader David Ricardo in the nineteenth century, only works if one assumes that the current levels of technology between countries is a given, that it is an 'original' and necessary fact of the global market. Only if one accepts that assumption does it make sense to repeat what at some point in the 1980s became the mantra of our times: that free trade benefits every country.

Maverick economists, looking closely at what I have called the laws of disequilibrium in the global economy, have pointed out that, although Ricardo's theory is absolutely right within its narrow confines, it fails when a country wants to develop or to acquire more advanced technologies so that it can do more difficult things and avoid falling into the trap of being branded 'empty of mankind and its works', which in turn would make it into a geopolitical entity that is 'up for grabs'. I have only added that there is no reason for assuming that uneven levels of technology are 'original' or necessary because there is nothing original or necessary about markets and global exchanges. In this respect, there are no necessary and unchanging laws of economics.[16] When the uneven state of technological advance that allowed Flint and Grace to profit from indigenous Peruvian knowledge is made into a law, together with its underlying assumption that in 'backward' places allegedly empty of mankind and its works everything is up for grabs, what is at best a historical achievement is taken as the proof of a historical destination and projected on to future events. I resist, however, the idea that the assumption concerning 'backward' countries or communities could in any sense be presented as a historical achievement. It is simply a mistake.

Moreover, the technology available to people like Flint and Grace, but not to the indigenous descendants of the Inca in Peru in the late 1800s, as 'advanced' as it may be, would have been of little or no use for the purposes of trade and industry if not because of the fact that existing 'local' knowledge had observed the properties of guano and put them to use in agriculture, which is itself a technological achievement. In fact, in the case of Flint and Grace's trade in Peru, it was the basic technological achievement upon which the American entrepreneurs managed to build their empires. As such, it was a component part of the commodity chain. Within that chain, its value as a commodity (a basic bit of information corresponding to the 'peripheral' point of the chain) is expressed only relatively by the value of another commodity (another basic bit of information corresponding to the industrial 'centre' in the chain). This is in contrast to the assertion that the 'peripheral' commodity has less intrinsic value or none at all, because, allegedly, no labour time has been expended in its production, whereas the 'central' finalised commodity has more intrinsic value because labour time has been expended for its production. This assertion, which is homologous with the idea that 'peripheral' areas are empty of mankind and its works, turns such areas into what Bolívar called in his *Letter from Jamaica* 'simple consumers', 'brutes of labour' or reservoirs of materials for the benefit of other nations. Furthermore, the assertion depends on imagining one of the parties to the exchange and speaking of it as if it were 'archaic' in the pejorative sense of being backward in time. It is the time lag or difference provoked by this manner of thinking and relating to others what produces value on one side of the chain and less value or none at all on the other.[17]

Put another way, Flint and Grace accepted the current levels of technology between Peru and the United States as given and sought profit on that basis. From their point of view, which is that of short-term gains, this is simply chance and opportunity. Good entrepreneurs like them expose themselves to the risks involved in seizing such chances and seeking opportunities where others see nothing of value. But from the point of view of Peru and other countries like it, the short-term gains of people like Flint and Grace result for them in long-term losses, since their 'backward' status is reproduced and even required as a condition for the intermediaries' short-term gains. The situation may be profitable, at least for Flint and Grace and probably also for the locals participating in the process, but it is socially harmful. In our time, banking and financial services find themselves in precisely that situation: being highly profitable and yet far from being socially optimal. This is precisely how Adair Turner, the chairman of the British regulatory body known as the Financial Services Agency, referred in 2009 to the financial services sector.[18]

Charles Flint was certainly not short of courage when it came to taking risks. Through his experience with Grace he made impeccable contacts in the business and political circles of the United States, Peru, Chile, and later on Brazil. 'He became an associate of finance tycoon J. P. Morgan,' Douglas tells me. 'Through his clients in the gunpowder business he created with Grace, exploiting Peruvian guano, he gained access to arms deals, becoming a dealer himself,' says Douglas. Flint served as an agent for the Peruvian government while at the same time providing weaponry to Peru's erstwhile enemy, Chile, and became the Chilean consul in New York between 1876 and 1879. He went into the rubber business in Brazil, a venture that was basically identical to the guano enterprise in Brazil but this time attached to the automobile and *chicle* industries. In 1892, he merged several rubber importing and producing companies to set up US Rubber. And in 1899 he repeated the achievement by merging Adams Chewing Gum, Chiclets, Dentyne and Beemans to form American Chicle.

All the while, he became actively involved in seeking support for the republican cause in Brazil after news broke that the London-based financier N. M. Rothschild, Brazil's traditional financial agent, might be siding with royalist rebels. At the time, the rich South American territory was emerging from a long period of stability between colony and empire, after João VI left Portugal for Brazil, and his son Pedro I, and his grandson Pedro II, decided to keep the imperial throne outside Europe. Relations between the US and Brazil grew close after the end of Brazil's monarchic period. In the past, Brazil's monarchy had maintained a long history of trade and gold exports to Britain, which had made the latter extremely influential in Brazilian affairs. Seeking to maintain the status quo, British interests sided with royalists during and immediately after the republican transition. But as a young republic, Brazil managed to shake off British influence by negotiating a commercial reciprocity treaty with the United States under the McKinley Tariff, which had set the tariff rate for imports to the US at 48.4 per cent. The treaty established the rising economic influence of the US in Latin America, but it also illustrated Brazil's success in pursuing a foreign economic policy independent of European influence.

Brazil's independence in setting a course for its foreign and domestic affairs was further established in 1893, when the government of Floriano

Peixoto demonstrated firmness and diplomatic skill in dealing with a royalist naval revolt, backed by British commercial interests. 'Some say that Flint's employment of Pinkerton detectives may have had something to do with news of the revolt reaching republican ears,' says Douglas. 'Although he was, at the same time, brokering a loan from the famous Rothschild banking family, who were allegedly behind the conspiracy. Flint was a sort of double agent,' he tells me.

Flint raised the penchant of earlier filibusters for deception, conspiracy and smoke and mirrors to a new level of art. A modernist in politics, he almost single-handedly managed to turn what were for John Quincy Adams mere 'irregular actions shrouded in doubt and suspicion' into the most effective means to make the illusion of power transmogrify into real power. Flint realised early on that carefully placed information and seductive propaganda could be weapons as powerful as a ship's cannon. Having acquired a controlling interest in the *New York Times*, he used the newspaper not only to advance the cause of the gold standard in America, thereby also attending to his Brazilian connections, but also to feed information to the general public at home and abroad, shaping its opinion. He courted the favour of US audiences over the seemingly exotic and faraway war effort in Brazil and captured their attention, setting the stage for President Grover Cleveland to establish a precedent for expansion in spite of himself.

Always the businessman, Flint made sure the press boasted about the might and state-of-the-art technology of the fleet he was amassing to defend his friend President Peixoto of Brazil. The fleet comprised 'the fastest vessel in the world', according to the London *Times*, 'the most luxurious and largest ship ever built in Norway', in the opinion of the *New York Herald*, and a cutting edge, almost fully submersible submarine capable of 'firing experimental underwater torpedoes', as explained in the 2 December 1893 edition of *Scientific American*. Flint even organised a luxurious train journey to the Technological Exposition in Chicago, accompanied by his propaganda bureau, in order to buy a number of torpedoes recently invented by Thomas A. Edison, aptly known as 'submarine terrors' according to the *San Francisco Chronicle*, and the spectacular 'pneumatic gun', capable of firing shells at a target three miles away and widely acknowledged in Europe as the next big thing in sea warfare.

Flint and his contact, the Brazilian ambassador Salvador de Mendonça, did little to hide the fact that they were profiting from the war preparations. But a no less pressing intention was, as Flint put it, 'to give the fleet so much prestige that no one would dare to fight it'. All the while, Flint was benefiting the burgeoning technological and military industry of the US at a time of economic depression, and providing the US Navy with a real-life laboratory for combat trials. This may have been, in fact, one of Flint's primary goals. 'Flint was not a quixotic warrior looking backward to past martial feats, but a modern financier-technocrat' looking to make gains in the short-term.[19]

Despite some initial setbacks, the propaganda apparatus and the fear invoked by Flint's fleet worked. The naval rebellion against President Peixoto in Brazil lost its nerve and Flint proved that private armies' unofficial methods, not to mention the use of publicity, disinformation and illusion, could be useful and even successful in the conduct of international affairs. The key to Flint's success was not the killing force of his mercenary squadron, but, rather, his powers of seduction. 'Did you know that President Peixoto built a monument to the Monroe Doctrine after Flint's armada entered Guanabara Bay somewhere in Rio?' Douglas asks me. 'I had no idea,' I reply. Noticing that our dancing partners are growing impatient, we decide to leave Our Man Flint behind, and head for the Zero Zero club for a night of samba.

The Laws of Disequilibrium

By 1911, Charles Flint – financier, man of the world and international agent – had completed another of his mergers to form CTR, or the Computing-Tabulating-Recording Company. In 1924, the company was renamed International Business Machines, better known as IBM. In the coming decades, IBM would be at the forefront of the information and computing technology (ICT) revolution. The use of distributed information and communications technologies would in time give rise to the Internet and hold the potential to usher in a new industrial and social revolution. The realisation of that potential is transforming the way we organise and manage time, information and communication, as well as energy systems which promise to increase our capacity to create new living environments and to relate to one another and to the world around us in entirely new ways.

But at the end of Flint's life, all this promise and potential was obscured by the onset of the Great Depression. Charles Flint would remain a member of the board of CTR-IBM until his retirement. Upon his death, and although *Time* magazine did not consider his last venture important enough to be included in his obituary, the man who had produced fertilisers and gunpowder out of indigenous guano from Peru, fitted out warships for Brazilian revolutionaries, negotiated the Wright Brothers' first sales of aeroplanes abroad, and helped to kick-start the information revolution was christened by the famous American journal the 'father of trusts'.[20] According to *Time*, Flint gathered a fortune reputed to be $100 million. His life and exploits, colourful as they may have been, also provide a lens through which one can examine the operation of the laws of disequilibrium of the global economy in the process that culminated in such accumulation. Flint lived long enough to witness the stock market collapse of 1929; he retired in 1930 and died in 1934. He did not witness the effects of plummeting commodity prices, capital flight, high interest rates and coercive trade treaties that shocked Brazil and the rest of Latin America, after having destroyed at least two-thirds of the economy in cities like Detroit in the United States.

Those shocking effects obliged many to reconsider the operation of the laws of equilibrium and disequilibrium in the global economy, in order to understand what had gone wrong and how to fix it. Among them, the name of John Maynard Keynes has long been recognisable. But among his contemporaries, few rose to the challenge with the tenacity, originality and wisdom of the Argentinean Raúl Prebisch. By the time of his death on 20 April 1986, those who knew him remembered Prebisch's stature as a protagonist of the scene of international relations throughout the twentieth century, a champion of economic justice and fair north–south relations. He was widely credited as 'the father of development', and *The Economist* referred to him as 'Latin America's Keynes'.

This was no small recognition for a man whom the FBI and the CIA had considered a subversive and a communist in 1953. Earlier on, during World War II, J. Edgar Hoover had taken an unusual step in the opposite direction, and wrongly listed him as a dangerous Nazi supporter. In 1947, after Prebisch had proven Hoover wrong and become a crucial figure in the Allies' diplomacy in South America during the war, Washington blocked his appointment to the then nascent International Monetary Fund (IMF), in spite of the fact that Managing Director Camille Gutt had already offered him a post as Senior Advisor. In the new climate of paranoid anti-communism extending over the US capital his use of such terms as 'core' and 'periphery' made him suspect.[21] After he had presided over the United Nations Conference on Trade and Development (UNCTAD) in 1964, *The Economist* called him the leader of an emerging force on the stage of global relations, the 'voice of the poor'. In 1973, Chilean newspapers, toeing the line of Pinochet's regime, attacked Prebisch's research institution ECLA/ILPES, associated with the United Nations, as having allowed 'leftist' elements to distort its UN mandate and holding him personally responsible for the economic policies of the Allende administration.

As one of the creators of the so-called Prebisch–Singer hypothesis, which argued that the terms of trade between primary products in 'peripheral' areas and finalised or manufactured goods in industrial 'centres' are not in equilibrium and deteriorate over time, and justified the notion that developing countries should reduce dependence on unfinished or primary commodity exports by developing their manufacturing industry and protecting it during its stages of infancy – which came to be popularised in many quarters as the Import Substitution Industralization (ISI) model – his name was put forward not once but at least twice as a contender for the Nobel Prize in Economics. He was first nominated for it in 1977 by a group of economists, among them Jan Tinbergen – the first winner of the Nobel Prize in Economics in 1969 – and fellow recipients Paul Samuelson (1970), Gunnar Myrdal (1974) and Wassily Leontief (1974). Tinbergen resubmitted Prebisch's nomination in 1978. Jan Tinbergen said that 'Prebisch's contribution was multidimensional and unique, comprising theory, institution-building, and policy – no other development economist of his generation could match his record of achievement.'[22]

In the 1980s, at the height of Reaganomics, he was vilified as the author of Latin America's downfall for promoting the Import Substitution Industrialization model,[23] as well as of the 1970s financial bubble and the ensuing cash-and-debt crisis. And yet, it was at about this time that he had warned everyone that easy money – of the kind obtained through credit and speculation – was not a sound basis for growth and could spell disaster not only for Latin America, but also for the world as a whole. In that respect, he correctly predicted that the 1980s debt crisis in Latin America – which was due not merely to internal mismanagement but also to 'external' factors related to the deficitarian bias of the international financial system, and was experienced as a banking crisis in the US – would be repeated on a global scale.[24] Supposedly out of fashion these days, the research of contemporary economists like José Antonio Ocampo, the former Under-Secretary-General in charge of the Department of Economic and Social Affairs of the United Nations, and a leading scholar in the field, has observed that the deterioration in the terms of trade for primary products and simple manufactures is discontinuous, with sharp deteriorations in the 1920s and 1980s followed by periods of stability, thereby confirming the cyclical nature of the global economy and its contingent nature. As he put it in 2008, by most measures 'world inequality is high and rising'.[25]

In hindsight, Prebisch should be vindicated. Not only because his early prophecy concerning the global danger of financial bubbles proved correct, but also because, confronted by the Reagan–Thatcher challenge in his later years, he returned to the radicalism of his student and early research days between 1943 and 1948 and redirected the focus of the conversation on 'equitable distribution, vigorous economic growth and new institutional patterns in a genuinely participatory democracy', at a time when such things were being dismissed as unfashionable by the younger generation. The latter considered the language of 'centre-periphery' and uneven relations an embarrassment, or sought refuge in the obscurity of post-modern 'discursive' vocabulary. In the meantime, the notions of converging north–south relations, multilateralism and global justice and governance became problematic in Washington. And yet, going – and thinking – against the grain in an age when most men were content with being called 'conservative', he stood his ground, stating that 'the free market and authoritarian governments have not solved the problem', throwing his weight behind renewed calls for integrationism (with Brazil and Argentina picking up in 1985 where they left off in 1941) and discussing poverty, consumption patterns, multinational enterprises, human rights, the risks of accepting North American or European models uncritically, and, most of all, defending the creed that, notwithstanding the fashion of the day, globalisation should and could be guided by reasonable policies, that the tendency for financial markets to bubble should be tamed at all costs, but that this could only be done if a new spirit of international cooperation – led by emergent societies in the south ready to go beyond the simple imitation of 'developed' capitalist models – motivated communities and their governments. That is his enduring legacy to future generations.

Already in 1947, after reading Keynes, Prebisch saw that the Grand Man of post-war economics had gone only half the distance in explaining the reality of the global economy, and specifically the heavy burden that the cyclical nature of business and trade relations throws upon the shoulders of countries outside the core economies. Keynes' contribution was crucial but not a qualitative leap beyond the stubbornness of mainstream economists fixated with equilibrium theory. 'For developing countries,' he said, 'there is always disequilibrium.'[26] The focus of research should not be on the problems faced by companies in developed economies like Europe or the US, as perceived from the periphery, but, rather, on the nature and causes of the differential impact of business cycles in the starting point of commodity circulation, or 'centre', and the point of destination, or 'periphery'.

This is the same spatial language used by storyteller Horacio Quiroga in the late 1920s and essayist Roberto Fernández Retamar in 1971, the metaphors of journey, travel, discovery and expansion seen through the lenses of the seemingly unending process of the circulation of commodities. Like his literary fellows, Prebisch reclaims the point of destination as the new beginning. In 1923 he had spoken about the impact of such differentials to an audience in Melbourne, Australia, underlining the negative impact of a dominant landholding oligarchy on the political and economic life of a country like Argentina. Although more urbanised and with a larger middle class at the time than its neighbours Brazil and Chile, it had inherited from colonial days a powerful oligarchy in charge of the state within a dependent agricultural export economy entrenched by neocolonial relations with Britain.

This dynamic, Prebisch said, resulted in extreme concentration and the failure to develop a land-reform programme comparable to those undertaken in the United States under Lincoln, or Australia. A necessary and reasonable process of land reform had proven impossible; whole swathes of the Argentine interior remained depopulated or isolated after the genocide of the Indians, and, instead of homesteaders creating a crucial rural mass market, as in the British dominions or the US, Argentina imported migrant labourers for work in rural areas and increasingly to the peripheries of the cities. Terms such as 'centre' and 'periphery', which start to appear in more developed form in his correspondence of the 1940s, designate in principle this local reality (which others termed 'internal colonialism') perfectly represented by the example of luxury in the midst of rural- and urban-peripheral poverty presented by the Argentine elite.

However, this local phenomenon could only be explained from a global perspective. Just as colonialism had been the driving force of global economic relations, with British–Argentine relations replacing those between the Spanish crown and the Viceroyalty of Rio de la Plata, so too Argentine elites imitated locally those relations. It was therefore crucial to discern that pattern of repetitions as much as the differences between each repetition. The need for such a global perspective was confirmed when, as part of the Argentine diplomatic delegation attending the much heralded World Economic Conference scheduled to begin on 12 June 1933, Prebisch opened *The Times* and read the first of four articles entitled 'The Means to Prosperity', written by John Maynard Keynes.

This first piece made a lasting impression on Prebisch, who thereafter reacquainted himself with the whole body of work of the English economist. The two never met, but Prebisch did cross paths with Keynes during the conference and divined from his expression the huge disappointment following the realisation that the prospects for an early end to difficult times with multilateral and decisive collective solutions to the Great Depression were remote. Neither bankers nor governments had learned the lesson, and had decided to continue with ad-hoc solutions, purely reactive and defensive measures, asymmetrical stimulus to import-substitution without support for export-oriented manufactures, and high rhetoric driven by the desire to serve private and short-term interests even at the expense of those at the bottom.

Nevertheless, upon his return from London, Prebisch knew that the economic orthodoxy was damaged beyond repair, and, working from his experiences as a bank manager, his earlier intuitions and research concerning business cycles, and his renewed interest in Keynes, he started to work on a book project challenging the conventional wisdom about equilibrium and comparative advantage in the international economy. He spoke of 'inward development' and the need to pursue industrialisation because countries like Argentina faced unequal relationships with its industrial trading partners, and he maintained that the terms of trade for agricultural commodity producers like his country were in historical decline and that a 'persistent fall in the international prices of exports' could be expected in the future. He based this argument on his observations and statistical research concerning wheat and beef trade markets.

Crucially, he focused on the operation of the business cycle, disagreeing with the mainstream notion according to which market mechanisms functioned equally in all countries, benefiting industrial and agricultural economies alike, with the business cycle regulating circulation in the international economy. He had already observed in 1921 that in the case of Argentina the cycle created an atypical boom-and-bust phenomenon because of the lack of assumed self-correcting mechanisms. Now, in the wake of the 1918 crash, the 1920s boom and the Great Depression, he generalised this conclusion. The international economic system operated, he said, with a permanent disequilibrium because the business cycle had different effects in an industrial/producer country like Great Britain and an agricultural exporter/consumer country like Argentina. For him, there were no self-correcting mechanisms inherent in the system. Strengthening the position of consumers was crucial, and this could only be achieved at the moment via industrialisation, vigorous intervention to control cyclical fluctuations and integration.

However, this meant neither unbridled state intervention nor protectionism. On the contrary, Prebisch demanded on the one hand 'an intelligent regime' using state powers without stifling private forces. 'Monetary policy serves little or no use if it suffocates private initiative and the spirit of enterprise,' he wrote, 'which absolutely requires the profit motive to promote an overall climate of confidence.' On the other hand, at the international level he emphasised the need for an open trading system free of coercion after the devastation caused by the breakdown of trade into 'watertight compartments', as he put it, and warfare, during and after the Great Depression.

Prebisch was not referring merely to the trading blocs that emerged during the Depression and the world wars, but also to the 'bad example' set by 'elite' players, from local oligarchs and those imitating them, to global political and economic interests hijacking the democratic process and the multilateral trade and credit system for their own benefit in the midst of mass destitution, and doing so in the name of 'free trade'. 'The snobbish character of night life, the jewels of the women, the generous flow of champagne in night clubs and the brilliance of our Buenos Aires' cosmopolitan ambiance,' he had told his Australian audience back in 1923, 'provoke exclamations by foreigners that it is the Paris of South America. Little consolation for the working classes, who drag out their lives between sweatshop and hovel!'

Such isolation and the apparent advantages that come with it, like the gains made by Britain or the US in a global agricultural market distorted by subsidies, protections and forced 'free trade' agreements, at the expense of other countries unable to compete in such conditions or coerced not to establish measures of their own in their attempts to set up common markets, are as dangerous and unjust in the local case as they are in the case of the international economic system. 'Autarchy,' he concluded, 'is as absurd as free trade.' Both have noxious consequences. Instead, he proposed a judicious combination of import substitution and export promotion – a mixture of safeguards, subsidies and regulation – rather than blanket protectionism, which is not entirely dissimilar to the 'Hamiltonian' model followed by the US but removing from it the 'drive outward' – short-term expansionism, to the detriment of other countries' long-term capacities – that allows rich countries to 'kick away' the ladder once they had climbed it and force free-trade policies on poor countries. In the following years, he developed this vision to include a call for a new set of rules governing the international economic system, the need to tame the dynamics and structure of global inequality and promote integration and common markets, similar to today's Mercosur and the Community of Latin American and Caribbean States.

In 1949 Prebisch unveiled in Cuba the so-called *Havana Manifesto*, on the occasion of the conference of the recently founded Economic Commission for Latin America (ECLA) led by him.[27] The *Manifesto* deserves a place of honour among other foundational documents of Latin America's modern spirit, such as Martí's *Our America* or Fernández Retamar's *Caliban*, with which it has much in common both in terms of its structure and its enduring influence. In it, he reformulated his belief that 'the cycle is the typical form of growth in the capitalist economy, and that it is subject to certain laws of movement quite different than the laws of equilibrium. In these laws of movement the disparity between the timing of the productive process on the one hand, and the resulting circulation of money on the other, plays a fundamental role.' Starting in the early 1940s, but now on surer ground, he had 'tried to introduce systematically the concepts of time and space in economic theory. It is precisely the concept of space which has allowed me to study the movement in the centre and periphery, not in the spirit of introducing formal deductions, but to signal functional differences of transcendental importance.'[28]

This means to introduce a shift of perspective similar to that which looks at the point of departure of previous theories, and reveals that its assumptions were in fact end results of the observation that what had already been achieved at the production/industrial end of the economic circuit, as a fact, would also be expanded and take place at the other (consumption/agricultural) end of the circuit. Where others, following David Ricardo, saw equilibrium and relative advantage in global terms of trade, or synthesis and harmony, Prebisch saw an antinomy:

as he put it in the *Manifesto*, you start with the claim of a unified world economy in which all states, industrial and developing, are linked in a single system or chain of exchanges and are affected by a common business cycle. Within this system, however, the rich producer or industrial countries play a different role from developing consumer agricultural countries. Rather than assuming that the latter will one day necessarily become like the former, Prebisch invites us to contemplate the international economic system as it *really* is, that is, *before* agricultural developing countries become central, and ask whether the assumption that free trade benefits every country still holds when a peripheral country wants to move to the centre by acquiring more advanced technologies so it can do things that few others can. As he says, the answer in this case is negative. His focus is on the time – and the space – difference provoked by different and contingent levels of technological advancement, which makes the accepted premise of a unified, harmonious and universally beneficial world trade economy appear problematic.

Since there is nothing strictly necessary about the fact that certain points of departure, or 'centres', benefit more in the business cycle than points of destination, or 'peripheries', one can conclude that this is merely the result of disequilibrium made evident by declining terms of trade, such as the ones that Prebisch had observed in 1943 and that German historical statistician Hans Singer had shown in his report *Postwar Price Relations Between Under-developed and Industrialized Countries*, written between 1947 and 1949 for the UN Sub-Commission on Economic Development. In this respect, 'development' is not a matter of evolutionary traits or metaphysical forces, secular or otherwise, but, rather, a function of the relative distribution of benefits between the two points in a relation over time. And since that distribution is unequal it follows that the relation is unequal. This result corresponds neither to some essential trait or characteristic of each of the termini in the relation nor to the realisation of some hidden purpose animating the relation. It corresponds only to the passage of time and the relative positions of each of the termini in the relation at the moment of encounter.

Crucially, such positions (that one is industrialised and produces manufactured goods, while the other is not and produces mainly primary products in return for manufactured goods) are not only relative but also contingent. And because they are contingent, in the sense that no sufficient reason explains them, beneficial positions derived from technological or industrial advantages at any given point in time are no more just than, say, the fact that Spanish conquistadors benefited from the fact that their weapons were deadlier than those carried by the Incas. That contingent advantage did not give the Spanish the right to benefit from, steal, extract and plunder the wealth of the Inca, not even if in the process a transfer of technology took place, which in the future may or may not make the relationship more egalitarian. Similarly, the relative and contingent position of industrial or 'core' countries, at any given point in time, does not justify their benefits over time relative to 'peripheral' areas. In that respect, the relationship is unequal. A benefit derived from a contingency is not justified as a right, but, rather, as a mere privilege. Moreover, if that benefit persists over time, the relation does not become necessary but, rather, necessarily unequal or unjust. Therefore, as a practical matter, it must be overturned. The only question is how.

As Prebisch put it, from the perspective of the periphery the business cycle only obeys the 'laws of disequilibrium' or contingency, which is to say that it obeys no laws at all. Herein lies the ultimate and shocking truth of Prebisch's contribution: that, before the event, there is no such thing as the iron law of the economy. Therefore, there cannot be a non-speculative science of economics, and particularly of economic development. There can only be observations after the fact concerning economic relations. But to turn these observations – and the relative and contingent facts contained within them – into a matter of necessity, is an error. Unfortunately, it is an extremely common error.

Prebisch confirmed this time after time, from the World Economic Conference of 1933, following the Great Depression, when he saw a long-faced John Maynard Keynes trying to manage the circus that had ignored his (Keynes') proposal to consider a global reserve currency, among others, to the many instances in which the contributions of his research think-tank ECLA, its very existence, the actions of the majority group of nations at the United Nations Conference on Trade and Development in favour of a 'new international economic order', or the integrationist proposals for common market in Latin America were questioned from the standpoint that what is, is all that can be. No wonder Prebisch was called a 'heretic' by many in the field.

Do these conclusions mean that economics has no future? The opposite is the case. Economics *only* has the future. This means that the only question worthy of consideration is how to overturn a system of unequal relations. But this is, of course, a practical problem, a matter of ethical choice and political organisation and not an issue of pure calculability or analytical reason. Another way to say this is that all the important queries in economic life are retrospective but the really crucial question cannot be anticipated.

Criticised but undeterred, Prebisch took his proposals to the next level. In 1963 he coined the term 'New International Economic Order' on the eve of the UN Trade and Development Conference, over which he presided, insisting that an unjust world of north and south was morally repugnant and politically unsustainable, that the destinies of both parts of the world were intimately connected in the new landscape of global relations, and that only by identifying a 'global strategy of development' and agreeing to the fair rules of a 'global compact' concerning the distribution of information, regulation and the use of energy and other resources, would a durable ethic of cooperation safeguard the international community in the long term. He was perhaps the first to articulate with any clarity and sense of purpose that to link economic prosperity with global governance was the way to reform the international economic system. In that aspect at least, Prebisch should be acknowledged as the true father of globalisation. Not as a gospel of inevitability but as the realistic prophecy that only the south, a disciplined and creative developing world no longer sheltering behind defeatist rhetoric, could take the north through the challenges looming ahead for both.

The Great Debates

Ultimately, Raúl Prebisch was trying to answer the only crucial question remaining once you have put to rest all retrospective observations about the state of the international economic situation: how to overturn a system of unequal relations? How to tilt the playing field so that it is beneficial to all, in the long term, rather than only to some, in the short term? In the climate of the 1950s and 1960s, Prebisch saw that two answers were emerging. One was revolution. On 1 January 1959, Fidel Castro, Ernesto 'Che' Guevara, Camilo Cienfuegos and the revolutionary army of blacks and peasants from Oriente province seized Havana, where a mere decade earlier Prebisch had launched his famous *Manifesto*. Some of his collaborators rejoiced over the fall of the Batista regime. Regino Boti and Juan Noyola, who were part of his team of researchers, returned to the island, the former as minister of economy, the latter as head of a United Nations–ECLA special mission sent to the Caribbean island. Felipe Pazos, one of Prebisch's protégés who was at the International Monetary Fund, abandoned it to resume the presidency of the Cuban Central Bank after an exile of seven years. Celso Furtado, one of ECLA's most brilliant researchers, put together a report focusing on Mexico and Brazil, countries in which the ISI model had delivered stronger economic growth (in Brazil there was talk of a 'miracle') but at the price of 'growing inequality'. The study suggested that a more dynamic and interdependent external sector, such as that of Mexico *vis-à-vis* the US, did not mean an end to persistent trends of inequality. The ISI model of development was well established in Mexico, as well as in Brazil and elsewhere in the region. However, building upon previous research carried out at Prebisch's UN think-tank by former colleagues Fernando Henrique Cardoso and Enzo Faletto, Furtado stated that new contradictions, external as well as internal, were emerging and that these new developments were fuelling the call for revolution.

The other answer emerging entailed a complete overhaul of the international economic system through diplomatic means. This was the road Prebisch took many times, in spite of the fact that he experienced repeatedly and frustratingly the unwillingness of those in power to cede to reason and pressure from below. In November 1959, Che Guevara replaced Felipe Pazos as president of Cuba's Central Bank, complaining that he was 'neither revolutionary nor radical', and initiating one of the most interesting episodes of the so-called Great Debates of the 1970s and 1980s, on the road towards the economic transformation of Latin America. Prebisch saw this as a sign of radicalisation and a symptom that his favoured route, and the influence of the UN Economic Council for Latin America (ECLA) in the region, had become more problematic. By 1958 the model that the Frondizi administration of Argentina had set up with the support of the IMF and Washington, based on a radicalised version of mainstream 'free trade' notions, had collapsed. It would be the first of many such catastrophes to occur in Latin America in the late 1970s and during the 1980s, at the height of Reaganomics, Thatcherism, dictatorship, the 'Chicago Boys' and 'neoliberalism'.

Two Latin American stories illustrate the destiny of the question about how to transform a system of unequal relations. One occurred in the context of the electoral victory of Salvador Allende in Chile on 4 September 1970. Allende's victory stunned and inspired the region, and sent the Nixon administration into a tailspin. Famously, after Allende's electoral victory, US Secretary of State Henry Kissinger snorted, 'I don't see why we need to stand by and watch a country go communist due to the irresponsibility of its own people.' The Chilean elite agreed. At that point, the fate of the first experiment with radical democratic transformation was sealed. What followed after the CIA-backed coup that brought General Augusto Pinochet to power was, in the words of Raúl Prebisch, 'a long, dark night'. When he left ECLA in 1963 most countries in Latin America were constitutional democracies; after the 1964 Brazilian coup, military dictatorships had spread to Bolivia, Peru, Argentina and now Chile. Latin America was growing apart rather than integrating, 'national security' discourses turned murderous practices into 'necessary counter-insurgency measures' and the dark night of neoliberalism – a reaction to the crisis of inward-looking development and the looming threat of revolution – set in.

The second story is that of the Great Debates about the model of economic development that followed after the revolution in Cuba. The newly appointed head of the Ministry of Industries (MININD), Ernesto 'Che' Guevara, initiated a debate that questioned the transformative power of the two innovative forms of governance and economic transformation that resulted from the Great Depression and the two world wars: first, the economic nationalism and Import Substitution Industrialization (ISI) strategy based on the principles proposed by the

Economic Commission for Latin America and the Caribbean (ECLA), and second, the economic management system developed in the USSR, known in Cuba as the Auto-Financing System (AFS).[29]

Like most stories, the tale of the Great Debate begins with an error. Most people believe that after the Cuban Revolution, the island turned immediately towards the Soviet-led Council for Mutual Economic Assistance and simply replaced one master, America, with another, Russia. In fact, for a while Cuba experimented with the strategies proposed by Prebisch's ECLA. The universal acceptance of the option opened up by ECLA analysts and policy-makers at the onset of the sixties was evident from the favourable echo elicited by Fidel Castro's proposal, made at the time in the name of a victorious Cuban Revolution, that the US earmark $30 billion for programmes fostering technological progress and social reform in Latin America. The initiative was taken up in Brazil by then president Juscelino Kubitschek and came to fruition in the Alliance for Progress sponsored by the Kennedy administration. ECLA's proposals were recognisable in the Alliance views concerning agrarian and tax reform, aimed at systems that had been designed in the past to favour the landed classes, which in effect condemned national treasuries to perpetual shortages.

Throughout March and April 1959, Guevara engaged in the preparation of the Agrarian Reform Law, responsibly but steadily shifting towards collectivisation and cooperativisation, especially where American-owned property was concerned. By 1960, land reform and increased state ownership, coupled with the effects of economic and military aggression from abroad, marked the end of the experiment with ECLA's reformist option. However, unlike what many assume nowadays, this did not mean a shift towards Soviet-style economics. After a 1959 trip to Yugoslavia, then a founding member of the non-Aligned group of countries, Guevara concluded that the Soviet solution involving the widespread use of material incentives, credit and interest in order to speed up industrialisation would in the end simply reproduce capitalist relations. Developing these observations in the early sixties, Guevara was one of the first to predict, correctly as it turned out, the return of capitalism to Russia.

Thereafter he became a staunch critic of the Soviet system and Marxist orthodoxy. Instead, he took to studying the accounting practices of American corporations, which used money as a means of accounting rather than as a means of payment, and proposed the nationalisation of central banking – just as non-Marxist economist Willem Buiter did in early 2009, after the global crisis. Guevara set out to profoundly transform the meaning and use of money, credit and interest, following the example of US big business. He observed that these companies did not send bills or issue payments to their own subsidiaries. Rather, they developed techniques of accounting, command-and-control, administration and analysis based on informatisation and computing, which relegated money to the role of simply recording the value of what had been produced. This was called 'money of account'. Guevara adopted this approach in the Budgetary Finance System with which he proposed to run the Cuban economy after the revolution.[30] He also emphasised the use of moral incentives and collective self-discipline in a way that seems reminiscent nowadays of some of the main features of the Asian style of development, or the forms of community-based self-organisation present among the indigenous political organisations of Bolivia.

Guevara adopted the approach of US corporations in order to redefine the role of money as money of account or as a means of measurement, thereby ensuring the goals set out in the economic plan functioned as the determinant of production and investment. It strengthened the mechanisms of administrative management, which emphasised accounting, supervision and inventory records. 'Under our system, [money] functions only as a means of measurement, as a price reflection of enterprise performance that is analysed by central administration bodies so as to be able to control such performance.'[31] Mixing the potential of the ongoing information technology and computing revolution with community-based action, or 'commoning', Guevara sought to transform the whole banking and financial sector into a public utility rather than a profit-driven speculator, and focused on increasing labour productivity through cost controls. This meant improving technology, avoiding waste, and, in general, monitoring the cost of production in real time through the use of mathematical analysis and computing to regulate the economy and achieve the best allocation of resources.[32]

A similar experience was under way in Allende's Chile: in July 1971, the general manager of CORFO (State Development Corporation), Fernando Flores, invited British cybernetician Stafford Beer to assist Allende's government in the application of cybernetic principles of communication and control to the regulation of the Chilean economy. In March 1972 Beer began work on a new suite of management tools known as Cybersyn. He thought managers should have access to the most relevant information, which facilitated the process of making informed decisions rapidly. Cybernet, one of the four sub-projects of Cybersyn, expanded Chile's existing network of communication including some four hundred firms from the nationalised sector. Although rudimentary, this was a tool for 'real-time' economic control.

Beer and his Chilean colleagues designed these tools according to principles adapted from biology and the study of the human neurological system. Although it never became fully operational, thanks in part to the coup of 11 September 1973, the cybernetic model for managing viable systems developed into a serious strand of the cognitive sciences best exemplified in the work of Chilean biologists Humberto Maturana and Francisco J. Varela, and Flores himself, among others. One of their most important contributions has to do with a phenomenon called 'recursive feedback': a viable system, one that survives, deploys feedback mechanisms to grow and learn, to evolve and adapt, to become more potent in its environment. These may explain a common tendency to extrapolate a present state of the system into the future. The latter has been found to be predominant in areas of social life that deal with the human heart, with our ability to forecast and project our expectations into the future, such as financial economics but also international relations, particularly in such sensitive areas as security, prevention, collective choice, risk-analysis and regulation.

A similar insight informs the efforts of so-called behavioural economists nowadays. The latter are profoundly sceptical about the assumed inherent rationality of markets. Behavioural economists were among the first to sound the alarm about trouble in the housing and other markets in the 2000s. 'In some ways, we behavioural economists have won by default,' Richard Thaler observed in relation to those true believers who used to deny the possibility of fundamental flaws in the efficient-market paradigm, 'because we were less arrogant.' In many ways, Fernando Flores, Stafford Beer and the members of the Cybersyn project in Allende's Chile can be seen as the unacknowledged fathers of a discipline that today represents the future of economic theory and practice after the global financial crisis.

To speak of a 'left turn' in Latin America makes sense only as an index of the richness in creativity and experimentation that has characterised the region from the 1960s to this day. Those creations and experiments appear more relevant now, given that the economic crisis has thrown into disarray our most commonly held certainties and assumptions. As we find a way out, and in the process enact a new world order, these legacies of the past may hold the key to our future. Indeed, their renewal in Latin America is already showing the rest of the world that another path exists, and that at the end of it we may find our redemption.

8

Revolution, or How to See
the Beginning in the End

Rebellions of Everynight Life

'Tonight we're not going to discuss the Cuban Revolution. Tonight, I'm going to tell you about another kind of revolution. It started in the Caribbean, moved to New York first and then to Miami, and it's about to change the face of America.' This is Celeste. She is Cuban American, lives between Miami and New York, where she freelances as a journalist and engages in her most cherished passion, salsa dancing. Nobody I know cares more about Latino music and culture in the United States than Celeste. I joined her in Manhattan's Lower East Side, where she has promised to show me some of the most significant places in the history of the rising Latino presence in the East Coast of the United States.

At the moment there are only four states in the Union where non-Latino whites, or Anglos, are in the minority. In America, these are known as 'minority-majority' states. They are California, Texas, Hawaii and New Mexico. It is expected that the 2010 Census will show that as many as ten or twelve states have passed that milestone. If this is the case, it is likely that by 2040 the United States will be a 'minority-majority' nation. The steady rise in the Latino population, coupled with a slow but steady increase in the Latino vote, will have dramatic consequences for the political future of America. On the one hand, it bodes well for Democrats in key states like Texas. On the other, as Latinos become more powerful in a stronger Democratic Party, it is likely that they will turn against a model of economic development in which access to common goods such as housing, health and education have taken the form of private debts. Furthermore, given the consequences of the 2008 financial crisis, only the provision of mortgage refinance funds associated with a common right to housing would restore value to the toxic derivative assets that are today poisoning the world banking system. In this context, claiming access to common goods in the form of a social rent rather than as private debts has become a local issue of crucial global importance. Latinos, who bear most of the burden of the crisis and, as the majority, have the chance to turn things around, will be protagonists in their own right. The United States are set to become the next Latino States of America.

'This is the place where the Hernández brothers, Rafael and Jesús, held their dances and political meetings,' says Celeste, pointing at the building in Brooklyn where legendary promoter Federico Pagani conspired with fellow tuxedo-wearing men of the growing Puerto Rican community in late 1940s New York. This is one of the places in the United States where the story of the political rise of Latinos started. 'Rafael and Jesús were first recruited by jazz bandleader James Reese Europe to join the US Army's Harlem Hell fighters musical band, the Orchestra Europe, during the First World War,' she explains. 'After the war they moved to New York City. Here, their sister Victoria opened what was probably the first Puerto Rican-owned record shop in town, which also functioned as a booking agency and a base of operations for the brothers. They say it was Victoria who introduced them to Pagani', so Celeste tells me while we rush to the Lower East Side.

'Rafael wrote his greatest work "Lamento Borincano" in the late thirties, not far from here if you wish to believe the legend, and also "Comanchero", which I'm sure you've heard in the reggae version. Because you love reggae, don't you?' Before I can say a word, Celeste explains that by 1947 Rafael was back in Puerto Rico, and the number one band playing the Palladium was Machito and His Afro-Cubans. The Palladium is where we are heading – or at least that is where we imagine ourselves dancing tonight – in celebration of the most famous dance hall in 1950s Manhattan. Pagani created the buzz that made Max Hyman's dance venue the Palladium, situated on 53rd Street and Broadway, the most sought-after Latino joint in the world. In the midst of the bebop boom, Machito and His Afro-Cubans started merging Cuban rhythms with the harmonies and counterpoints of jazz. The result was the famous 'Latin jazz', a creature of the musical director of the band Mario Bauzá. 'Another mistake,' Celeste contends. 'Latin jazz is a misnomer. What happened was that Pagani and Bauzá agreed that Machito offered the safest way of bringing the Caribbean to Broadway. The black Latino orchestra had been playing at the Concord Hotel in the Catskills, and had pleased the mostly white and Jewish dance audiences. They wouldn't mind mingling with the Latinos if it was just for a day in order to listen to Machito. So they agreed to open for the Hispanic community only on Sundays. It was the perfect alternative.'

Celeste talks while leaning on my shoulder to adjust her tight red dress and check that her heels are up to a night of dancing and romance. A Yellow Cab brakes in front of us all of a sudden, nearly causing an accident: '*chica, me vas a matar esta noche*, you'll be the death of me, girl,' says the driver. Celeste laughs. As in Rubén Blades' song 'Pedro Navaja', the salsa version of 'Mack the Knife' that goes back to the revolutionary concepts of the jazz trends of bebop that Machito and Chano Pozo, among other musicians of Manhattan in the fifties, invented, her smile sets alight the entire avenue. 'When it opened in 1947, it was for whites only,' she says. 'Because business was poor, Pagani convinced Hyman to book Latin music. He agreed, but, as I said, for Sunday matinees only. They called it "Blen Blen Club", because of a piece Chano Pozo had composed while playing the drums with Dizzie Gillespie's band. So, the Palladium became the first downtown dance hall to start a Latin matinee.'

We sit at the table I had booked three weeks in advance, warned that the place was almost impossible to get into. Celeste orders a bucket of ice, a few bottles of Coke, lemon juice, and Cuban rum. 'Havana Club, Gold, not Bacardi please,' she tells the waiter. 'I didn't know you could get Havana Club in the US,' I observe. 'They hold it for me,' she replies. The waiter returns balancing bottles, ice and limes in one hand, while masterfully concocting cocktails with the other. 'Not stirred, *como en las películas*,' he says. Celeste rewards his gallantry with a glance and a smile. The man melts. Since we came in, I have noticed most eyes are on her; not only those of the men, mind you. 'You're well known around here,' I say. 'Come,' she says, 'there's something you should see.' She takes my hand and whisks me across the dance floor to a wall covered in old photographs. 'That's Pagani, leaning out of the window of another famous venue in the fifties and sixties, El Palacio de la Alegría, the Palace of Happiness', she tells me. 'He might be inviting a friend to join the dance, or calling him to a meeting of the Puerto Rican Voters' Association. When the orchestras were silent, the Hernández brothers would use the place to gather with members of the Puerto Rican community and discuss the issues that mattered to them. It was a crucial time for Latinos in the United States. A feeling of community was being created through music. The brothers were associated with the Merchant Marines and the National Maritime Union. They were very active in the political struggles of the day.'

To attract more customers, places like the Palladium and El Palacio de la Alegría opened their doors to African Americans, Puerto Ricans, Cubans, and later on Chileans and Colombians. Soon after, the patrons were a happy mélange that included Upper East Side WASPs, Irish and Italians from Brooklyn. Class and colour seemed to melt away in the incandescent rhythm of the music. On the one hand, in places like this American entrepreneurs learned that keeping strict separations along ethnic and national lines was not good for business. A 'melting pot', as Americans say, does better. Entrepreneurs like Hyman learned that 'minorities' could be tolerated, not only because they were good consumers but also because diversity gave their clubs, restaurants and cafés a sort of universal vocation that was lacking elsewhere in the world after the ominous days of the world wars and economic depression. Diversity gave Manhattan the social fabric of bars, restaurants, clubs and chance encounters in the street that give life to a place. It became the model of global cities elsewhere, from London to Hong Kong and Sydney, and from Buenos Aires to Paris and Cape Town. On the other hand, the 'browning' of New York also reflected changes under way elsewhere in the Americas.

As both the export economies and the projects of white Creole elites to make Latin American countries 'more white' collapsed in the wake of the economic crisis of the 1930s and the wars of the 1910s and the 1940s, common citizens, as well as intellectuals and policy-makers in the Caribbean and in the rest of the Americas, responded by sharply shifting course. 'Instead of ignoring and rejecting the regions' Indian and African heritage and its history of race mixture, Latin Americans acknowledged both and even went as far as to propose them as the foundation on which to construct national identities.'[1] When Mario Bauzá founded Machito and His Afro-Cubans in 1941, through dance and music he was giving something else to the world, something new, the kind of heightened spirit and diverse experience we now commonly associate with the ambiance of the global cities of our fractured world. It took only a couple of weeks for the promoters at the Palladium to realise that Sunday dances were not enough. First they extended the Blen Blen Club hours to include Wednesdays; within a year, the Palladium was devoted exclusively to Afro-Caribbean music. The club and the music 'represented a perfectly fluid convergence of all the qualities that enlivened the city'.[2] It also gave Latin orchestras, for the first time ever in this part of the United States, the chance to be the stars rather than the secondary acts they had been reduced to by the mainstream American promoters of the time.

That position 'at the top' resonated strongly with the new ethic of egalitarianism and self-affirmation, a mixture of political assertion and almost mystic spirituality that in the nations of the Americas was replacing the elitism of white Creole fantasies about European essentialist belongings. During the export years, from the early days of independence to the 1930s, the idea of racial harmony and popular, or populist, politics took hold of the imagination of the subordinated classes of Latin America. Others felt it, too, lost and broken souls coming to the Americas in search of the spark that had been lost in darkened Asia and Europe. On 5 July 1936, the recently arrived French poet Antonin Artaud wrote in the newspaper *El Nacional Revolucionario* an article explaining what he had come to do in Mexico: 'In truth the question is this: Contemporary European civilization is fragmented. Dualistic Europe can offer the world only a frightful dusting of cultures . . . The Orient is completely decadent . . . China is at war. The Japanese

of today have proven to be the fascists of the Far East . . . The United
States have only succeeded in infinitely multiplying the decadence and
the vices of Europe. All that is left is Mexico . . . that precipitate of
innumerable races, [which] is like the crucible of history. It is from that
precipitate, that mixture of races, that it must derive a unique product
from which the Mexican soul will emerge.'

In the same essay Artaud concluded, 'I came to Mexico to look for
a new idea of man.' Perhaps Artaud's break with Europe was not yet
consummated, for his Mexican dream, which would eventually take
him to live, actually or in imagination, among the Indian people of
the Sierra Tarahumara, was born in part out of the fascination that
European artists at the time felt for the art and the cultures of the
Americas they called 'primitive'.[3] Josef Albers and his wife, from the
influential Bauhaus school of art and design, were inspired by the stone
monuments and the textiles of the Inca; Michel Leiris and George
Bataille paid close attention to the paintings of Wilfredo Lam and to
the musicological writings of Alejo Carpentier; Mexican writer Jorge
Cuesta had met in Paris the leaders of the surrealist movement and
had selected and translated into Spanish, in Mexico, the poetry of
Paul Eluard, while some of his friends did the same with the work
of Isidore Ducasse, the Marquis of the Other World, and with André
Breton's *Nadja*. Speaking of the consequences of the 1910 Mexican
Revolution, the long march of the Indian armies of Pancho Villa and
Emiliano Zapata for land reform and for the soul of the land, Artaud
gave a precise meaning to the word revolution: 'renaissance of the pre-
Cortesian civilisation'.

At more or less the same time, in New York, new man and the soul
of the land were no longer hidden but present in the essence of music.
And the dancers at the Blen Blen Club perfectly deciphered that hidden
code of Afro-Latin American man and Amerindian man, 'and the musicians, finally, could let themselves go'.[4] Dancers and musicians communicated with the gods of life and surrendered themselves to a vertigo of
sensuality and thought, in the marriage of jazz with Afro-Caribbean and
Indian music, the ecstasy of the parties on Wednesday and Friday and
Sunday nights in the Blen Blen Club, which were in fact the unexpected

equivalent of the magical solar theatre that Artaud had dreamt of in Mexico. When Antonin Artaud went to the Sierra Tarahumara, if he went at all, he was ill, weakened by drugs, speaking neither Spanish nor Tarahumara. How could he have talked to the shamans, let alone participated in the peyote rituals? And yet, the Italians, Irish, Jews and Anglos who spoke neither Spanish nor understood the language of the Yoruba gods, had no problem enjoying the music and participating in the multifaceted spirit that is the essence of jazz-like styles such as those perfectly Cubanised by Pérez Prado in México or by Machito in New York. They all danced to the *batanga* rhythms of Bebo Valdez, and the Puerto Rican *bomba* and the *plena* music of the Combo of Rafael Cortijo. And they did not need translators.

These were the years of José Vasconcelos' book *The Cosmic Race*, published in Mexico shortly after the Mexican Revolution, and of Gilberto Freyre's essay *Masters and Slaves* and Fernando Ortíz's most significant work, entitled *Cuban Counterpoint*, which followed immediately after the revolutions of 1930 and 1933 in Brazil and Cuba respectively. Finally, this period also witnessed the publication of Carlos Siso's *Formation of the Venezuelan People*, written after the end of the Gómez dictatorship in Venezuela in 1935, more or less at the same time Dominican musician Luis María 'Billo' Frómeta started to set the standards for the Venezuelan partying middle classes in the style of Cuban Son with his band Billo's Caracas Boys.

Some of these writers and musicians located this feeling of newness in world history in the genuine nature of the intercultural and multiracial societies of the Americas, born out of early anti-slavery sentiment, for it was in Haiti and Colombia, rather than in England and France, that slavery had been abolished for the first time in human history. Others appealed to the levelling impact of the egalitarianism characteristic of the wars for freedom and independence of the nineteenth century, in which blacks, Indians, browns and mestizos fought side by side to put an end to colonialism. Yet others emphasised the continuous nature of the struggle against colonial and neocolonial relations, and its expression in the *candomblé* music and dance turned into tango and milonga in Argentina, by then also a craze in France and in the United States, or into samba in

Brazil, no less popular at home and abroad, in the Cuban rumba and Son and in Dominican merengue.

Miami, Our Latin Thing, or the Return of the City-State

Given the overwhelming reception of the Cuban Son between the 1920s and the 1940s, among the underlying rhythms of jazz in the United States there is no doubt that the island is both at the beginning and at the end of the story of the global reach, and the social and political significance of Caribbean popular music. It had originated as a repository of the broken memories of black folk in the plantations and as a register of the travails of street life. Rumba, in particular, expressed a carnal connection with the land in Oriente province, the Sierra Maestra where runaway slaves never ceased to wage war to free themselves from the chains with which their white masters bound them. Like the Aztecs, when these rebels got together and swore to protect their *palenques*, their Maroon cities, away from the daily toil and the whip of the master, they swore in their own way: stomping the ground with their own bare feet following drum rhythms that were a language, licking the earth stuck to their hands and their feet. The Aztec called it *Ontlaqualque*, or 'earth eating'; the Africans mostly danced expressing their carnal connection with the earth and her rhythms. Tilling the soil with little or no rest, mining the depths of the earth to extract minerals, all these were serious acts and their consequences should be carefully considered.

For the Africans as well as for the Indians, each moment of life, from birth to death, occurred in respectful relationship with the earth. The plantation, the intensive and extensive agriculture, the mining, the incessant rhythm of work in the *hacienda* that prefigured the incessant rhythm of work in the assembly line or the office, were for them, as they were for the nomadic civilisations of north-west Mexico and the United States, an infraction of the laws of Nature. Amerindians and West Africans, on the one side, and Renaissance Europeans, on the other, found themselves furthest apart over the idea of landownership. Tecumseh of the Shawnee nation asserted in the nineteenth century that, regardless of their many differences, for all Indians 'an equal right to this land, as in the past, so it should be today'. At Bois Caiman, after dancing and 'confessing their resentment of their condition' to a woman, a priestess 'dancing languorously in the crowd, taken by the spirits of the loas', the slaves of Haiti swore to set all the plantations of the colony on fire, not only with the aim of freeing themselves, but, moreover, in order to free the earth, which had also been enslaved. And, once again, they expressed their commitment to freedom and to the limitless nature of the earth by making rhythmic music and dancing. Through agrarian ceremonies symbolising birth and destruction, through war and joyful dances, this attachment to the earth took on a cosmic significance. Dancing was, from the outset, an ecstatic experience, the experience of a global or even cosmic, connectivity.[5]

People went to places like the Blen Blen Club in New York to plot and preach political revolt as they stomped their feet on the ground, expressing a carnal relationship with the earth in a manner that resembled the dances of the Pueblos of New Mexico and the rebellious slaves of Santo Domingo. In cities around the world, New York, London, Shanghai, Mumbai or Rio de Janeiro, dancing continues to express a spirit or at least the memory of a deeper and more global connection, and at the same time it provides an escape from the daily toil of work and spiritual healing. In that respect, an underground club playing Jamaican dance hall and drum and bass in the East End of London today is not that different from the mélange of jazz-like rhythms, Cuban rumba and Mexican mambo played at the Blen Blen Club in 1950s New York. The resultant diversity and deeper connection, the 'easy life', and the levelling effect of these communal experiences is what gives global cities, the city-states which today are at the centre of our fractured but interdependent world, more so than nations themselves, their singular spirit.

In each case, however, be it Cuban rumba, Mexican mambo, Brazilian samba, Argentinean tango or Jamaican dance hall these days, a combination of commercial pressures and national or city-state and corporate support was crucial to the arrival of these once problematic, even prohibited genres and forms of expression, to the mass market, and to their transformation from black rural or street music into icons of national and global popular culture. On the one hand, this initiated a process of cross-breeding or 'crossover', a form of growth and evolution that has continued to the present day, giving rise to myriad genres and sub-genres – in a process that strangely mirrors that of the invention of races in colonial and post-colonial times – which have been embraced by diverse audiences in places as far apart as Japan, Europe, Africa, the United States and Latin America. On the other hand, with the 'nation-alisation' and, later on, 'privatisation' of black or 'ethnic' cultures, a para-doxical phenomenon occurred: while it is true that the situation meant a considerable improvement on the previous outlawing of ethnic cultures, it is also true that when a valuable resource is nationalised and privatised, its previous owners no longer control it. Unsurprisingly, by the 1970s and 1980s 'descendants of that culture's original creators were calling for a reappropriation, reimagining, and refashioning' of ethnic-based cultural forms and their deep attachments to land and soul.[6] That process continues to this day, with the global city-states of the world becoming the new battlegrounds of a veritable cultural war of liberation.

The best example of the sort of global, multicultural metropolis that in the opinion of internationalists like Parag Khanna will run the fractured world that is emerging before our very eyes,[7] and of the tensions that lie hidden under a surface appearance of global harmony and threaten to tear it apart, is Miami. If the model that later became the blueprint for the global cities of the world was born in the streets of Brooklyn in the early 1950s, one could say that it has been brought to perfection, for good or ill, in Miami, Florida. People refer to it as 'Hollywood East' or, more precisely, 'Hollywood Latin America'. This is due, for the most part, to the media and entertainment industries dedicated to Latin American and Latino US markets that can be found there in the sun, amidst the pensioners and the oranges.

On the surface, everything about Miami seems cosmetic: the beautiful, scantily clad male and female bodies strutting along Lincoln Road, the 24/7 nightlife, the music scene, the great food, the Cuban and Haitian ambience adding substance to the art deco forms of the buildings on South Beach, and most of all the undeniable fact that this is the one city in the United States where 'Hispanic' is king. But that first impression is deceptive: the so-called 'Gateway to the Americas', in the plural, is much more than cosmetic. In the 1920s and 1940s, Miami would have

been in the mid-level company of cities like Amsterdam and Berlin, or
Buenos Aires and Taipei. After the 1960s, when Havana started a second
life in Miami, it became a 'world city', a veritable city-state in a league
of its own, perhaps in the same niche as London, Shanghai or Barcelona.
It remains so to this day.

It is not just the concentration of banks, head offices, entertainment
and news outlets and corporations, and futuristic upscale quarters like
Aventura or Brickell, or the critical mass of advanced service industries
such as accounting, private security, marketing, news, music, banking
and law, most of them connected to the Caribbean network which has
existed at least since the Dutch, the English, the French and the Spanish
roamed these seas. What is different about Miami is the specific kind of
innovation in services that plays a central role in the shaping of today's
and tomorrow's world. And that is a direct consequence of the processes of 'modernisation' of ethnic cultures that took place in nationalistic form during the fifties and sixties and was privatised between the
1970s and 1990s. As Afro-Latin American music, dance and religion
were promoted and diffused on a global scale, but under specific demographic and political conditions in Miami, they brought joy, release,
enlightenment and solace to thousands, perhaps millions. Official and
commercial promotion of 'ethnic' culture also provided livelihoods, and
in some cases fame and fortune to musicians, dancers, composers, choreographers, actors, producers, painters and artists who before would have
practised their craft in obscurity and poverty, thereby converging almost
perfectly with the mythical 'American Dream'.

Miami, also known as 'the Magic City', grew from just over nine
thousand residents in the 1830s, the majority of them soldiers brought to
wear down and force the relocation of the Indian, Black and 'Spanish'
Seminoles, when it was finally incorporated as a city on 28 July 1896,
to nearly 5.5 million in just 110 years, between 1896 and 2006. But
a great deal of its magic is due to its successful appropriation of the
process of economic and political 'nationalisation and privatisation'
of ethnic cultures that characterised the 'browning' policies of Latin
American regimes in the wake of the Great Depression and the World
War II, between 1930 and 2000. The consequences of the 1959 Cuban

Revolution played a central role in this process of re-identification: it introduced re-Africanisation and Latinisation as the social basis of populist politics. During the 1960s and the 1980s this fitted very neatly with the renaissance of black cultural forms in the United States and the rest of the Caribbean, including Brazil, where the effects were even more deeply felt. 'Racial democracy' became particularly entrenched in the city, reflecting also the growing demographic importance of peoples of Latin American descent as well as the rejection of more radical reactions to the shortcomings of populism, which were becoming apparent already in the early sixties, especially the revolutionary road that had led to triumph in Cuba. Thus, in the 1980s and 1990s, when it became clear that state planning-based models had failed and that populist governments had been unable to eliminate the centuries-long heritage of racial prejudice from the workplace and from society in general, the valuable cultural resource that had been 'nationalised' in line with more moderate developments in the United States and, with particular force, with changes in the rest of the Americas, was now 'privatised'. This also reflected changes taking place throughout the Americas, the free-market reforms promoted there by the World Bank, the International Monetary Fund and other major lenders, but also a more powerful identification with the tenets of the 'American Dream'.

The privatisation of previously 'nationalised' ethnic cultures, along the lines of 'American Dream' free-market ideology and principles, gave Miami's service industry its specific characteristics. In a sense, Miami is the perfect model of state capitalism: populist, based on 'racial democracy', interventionist in the last instance and ready to lead growth, but always committed to principles of non-dirigisme and private initiative in the sense of the aspirational culture informed by the mythical, magical 'American Dream'. Crucially, the actual cases of musicians, dancers, composers, choreographers, actors, producers, painters and artists gaining fame and fortune, turning into entrepreneurs and philanthropists, artists who before would have been marginalised and left destitute, are what make the magic of the American Dream work. And this depends on the populist official and commercial promotion of 'ethnic' cultures.

The city that never sleeps? Forget New York. Don't get me wrong: New York is fantastic, but the spirit – the spirit of the 1920s and the 1940s – has moved on. Today it is Miami. In a comparative study of seventy-three world cities conducted by the financial services company UBS in 2009, Miami was ranked as the richest city in the US (out of four included in the survey) and the world's fifth richest city in terms of purchasing power.[8] In 2008, *Forbes* magazine declared Miami 'America's Cleanest City', for its year-round good air quality, vast green spaces, clean streets and ecological and recycling projects. And in 2005, the city experienced its largest real-estate boom since the 1920s. Latinos embody all that globalisation is supposed to be about: integration, open exchange, image and appearance, competition and populist culture. This is the place where the consciousness of the frequent flyer comes to rest, a dream come true, a paradise of multicoloured sex and culture. The Miami metropolitan area has a combined population of 5.4 million people, the fourth largest in the US. Of that population 65.8 per cent are Hispanic, 22.3 per cent are black Caribbean or African American, while only 11.8 per cent are classified as 'non-Hispanic White', and the rest are 'Pacific Islanders', 'Other Races', 'Asian' or 'Native American'. Here Latin America rules. If Parag Khanna's vision of a diffuse world ruled by regional leagues centred on city-states were to come true, Miami is where the capital of the Americas' Regional Union would be. And what fun that would be.

Missing from the glossy image of success, fame and fortune and the inclusiveness of all races and all classes, and from the documentaries about the magic and power of Spanish-language dance shows like *Caliente* ('Hot') in Miami Beach, are those who do the domestic work, the office cleaning by night – while the rest of us fill the restaurants and clubs – or the intensive labour involved in the restaurants, bars and clubs that give this city its very particular lustre. It is a glow that all other cities in the globalised world would like to share, just as we would all like to receive some of the magic dust that falls upon the shoulders of Enrique Iglesias, Ricky Martin and Shakira, just three of the city's more illustrious celebrities. In contrast with this lustre, most of the people from the barrios and those involved in the city's politics would tell you about racial strife among whites, Cubans, African Americans, Haitians, and, more recently, Salvadoreans, Nicaraguans, and black Colombians. 'Look,' Ramón Grosfoguel, an expert on ethnic relations who teaches at the University of California in Berkeley, says to me, 'it is a fact that dark-skinned Cubans continue to occupy the lower ranks of the social and economic ladder in Miami.' 'Some years ago,' he says, 'the *New York Times* published the story of two friends, Joel Ruiz and Achmed Valdéz, who had arrived in Miami from Cuba at the same time. Once the greetings of '*Liberados!*' and '*Abajo el Dictador Castro! Down with the Castro dictatorship!*' had ceased and the fiestas welcoming them to '*Free Cuba, Cuba Libre*' were over, the soulmates went to separate communities based on their colour. After a few years, the one who had joined the white Cuban community was doing pretty well for himself, while the other, who was incorporated into the black Cuban community, was still struggling.' 'I think the story is representative of a more structural phenomenon,' Ramón tells me. 'It's not just the Cubans in Miami, or my fellow Puerto Ricans in the north-east. These things are happening everywhere since competition came back with a vengeance in the 1980s.'

Between 1959 and 1989, Cuban social and economic policy almost ended class inequalities, and in doing so came very close to eliminating racial inequalities as well. But since the 'Special Period' following the collapse of the Soviet bloc, the Castro regime has been forced to scale back its commitment to social equality and permit the open functioning of a market economy. In the resulting scramble to seize the opportunities created by that emerging economy, 'white racial solidarity, and the exclusionary barriers by which whites maintain their preferred position, have resurfaced in Cuba'.[9] A similar phenomenon may be observed in Miami, as well as in the cities with which it is twinned elsewhere in the Americas: Bogotá, Managua, Buenos Aires, Lima, Port-au-Prince – the latter now once more under US military occupation following the 2010 earthquake – Santiago de Chile, Salvador in Brazil and Santo Domingo in the Dominican Republic. 'During the 1990s,' Reid Andrews says, 'journalists noted the rise of racist skinhead gangs in Brazil, Colombia, Uruguay and Venezuela . . . [In the latter] anthropologist Alfredo

Chacón observed that "racism has always had a broad presence ... and today [1998] that presence is much more general and normalized."' If racism has varied at all during the last fifteen years, it has become more acceptable, 'unconscious and normal', as he says. In Venezuela, after a decade of the government of *pardo* military officer and populist president Hugo Chávez, the veiled references to his race ('who invited the *peon* to this party', I heard a government official in Maracaibo say in reference to him, twelve or thirteen years ago, when Chávez was merely a spectral presence in oil-dominated Venezuelan politics) are becoming part and parcel of the increasingly vociferous criticisms against his excesses and the managerial shortcomings of his version of populism, and reflect a climate of reaction against his 'revolutionary' attack on capitalist competition that will surely take the shape of a racialised, class-based backlash. And in neighbouring Colombia there is no more evident hate figure than opposition leader and black female Senator Piedad Córdoba, who is often depicted as a Chavista sympathiser.

The other side of Miami's magic statistics relates to the more than 23,000 condos for sale and/or foreclosed following the crash of the housing market between 2007 and 2009. The Miami area now ranks seventh or eighth in the list of US cities affected by foreclosures, and the levels of poverty are climbing ever closer to those the city experienced in 2004, when, according to the results of the US Census Bureau, Miami became the third poorest city in the Union behind Detroit and El Paso. Even the populist-privatist style of government and management has been questioned, bringing back memories of 2001, when Miami became one of the very few cities whose local governments declared bankruptcy. The problems have started to affect the quality of local services, for instance higher education. At the end of 2009, it was clear to the members of staff of the public universities and community colleges I spoke to in the city that the future belonged to a sharply divided higher education system, in which well-off, mostly white and white Latino kids can gain access to higher degrees while the less well-off face a life without such opportunities.

These and other issues mark looming divisions in the supposedly harmonious multiracial community of the city of Miami. In talk-radio shows, more recent generations of Cubans and other Latinos complain that they have left authoritarian or sharply compartimentalised regimes only to be incorporated into different but no less hierarchical systems. Thus, for instance, the 'thriving Latino community' that emblematic publications like the *Hispanic Magazine* spoke of in its July/August 2003 issue, appears now clearly divided. So much so, that here the Latino voice 'that's loud and clear across the country', as the magazine put it back then, is identified more often than not with that of the very well-to-do Latin Americans, Cubans, Colombians, more recently Venezuelans and Argentineans, who at the first sign of social unrest in their countries, or of the success of a party that does not suit their political sensibilities or threatens their pockets with egalitarian measures, move their mansions, their families and houses, to the new capital of Latin America. Less is heard about the Haitians, the poor Salvadoreans, or the Colombians of black African descent. They do not thrive. They do not strut their stuff in 'the posh beach sections nearby which have become home to movie stars, bikini models and fashionistas'. Among the less well-off, women like Natalia, a young woman from Envigado, near Medellín in north-east Colombia, whom I interviewed in November 2009, have no qualms about what might take them to the dreamed heights. '*Estas,*' she says, while caressing her perfectly shaped breasts, covered by a most gracious polka-dot bikini which leaves just enough to the imagination. Who knows? She might make it. Natalia, that is her name, says she is saving, doing some modelling and other jobs she would rather not mention while studying journalism and attending TV auditions. She already has a degree from the Catholic Bolivariana University of Medellín. But the law degree seems less likely to be useful than her beautiful green eyes, tinted honey hair, generous lips and her other attributes. One of the most successful Colombian *telenovelas* running this season in Miami's Latino TV channels is called *Sin Tetas No Hay Paraíso*. It can be rendered as *No Boobs, No Paradise*. I could not think of a more apt title.

Latinos under Fire

Former Cpl Luis Arredondo opened up his laptop. 'You ought to see this,' he said, 'but I warn you, it will never go away.' Out of this twenty-first-century Pandora's box came thirty of the most disturbing images I have ever seen. In the first picture he is smiling. In the background, the golden sands of Kuwait. To his right, Cpl Abel de la Cruz, twenty-three years old, from El Salvador. To his left Felipe Suárez Solar, twenty-one, a Chiapanecan Indian from Mexico who had migrated to harvest tulips in Washington State. Luis Arredondo is Colombian, from the south Pacific coast. He's not supposed to have the images, let alone show them to civilians. But he needs someone to see this and share with him, even if is just for ten or fifteen minutes, the sheer horror of what he went through. He needs someone to know and to tell the rest of the world that this was not supposed to happen. When they joined, fresh from school, not really knowing what to do, three good kids from more or less traditional Latin American families determined to do something real for themselves and in the world, to get involved, unlike their friends back in Colombia who kept having it easy while the rest of the country went up in flames, they never dreamt they would become the newest heroes in the president's good war.[10]

He was in one of the first Marine Divisions to enter Fallujah. Among his laptop photos there are burnt-out cars on the side of the road with people in them, families that is, their eyes still open seemingly in disbelief; a mother in black robes lifts to the heavens the charred remains of her little daughter. 'She dumped her in our Humvee,' said Luis, '. . . and they said we would be welcomed as heroes; greeted with coloured rice and flower petals.' In another photograph, bodies are piled up in the interior of a house, shot through with bullets. All of them bathed in blood. 'I may have done that, I can't remember,' he said. In yet another, the severed head of a man, eyes wide open, lies abandoned in the middle of a street. 'One bullet from a Humvee gun does that to you,' Luis remarked. Those were the only words he said that evening. After that, we went for a drink at the local bar. We sat there, drinking Coronas, staring at our own reflections in the mirror for hours on end. 'Come,' he said eventually, 'I'll take you to the place where Geronimo jumped off a cliff and escaped.'

There were other pictures of him and his two friends. From the moment they landed in Kuwait to the moment they were ordered into

Iraq, they spent most of the time bodybuilding. They challenged one another to see who could lift the heaviest weights, and took hundreds of pictures of themselves half naked. You can see their arms and chest bulging up, shot after shot. What was the point of all this bodybuilding? 'We were getting ready to face the enemy,' Luis observed. I suspect they were also shedding their former skins, trying on a new identity. Is this what Samuel P. Huntington had in mind when he pointed out that 'people use politics not just to advance their interests but also to define who they are'?[11] After penning his highly influential *The Soldier and the State* and *The Clash of Civilizations and the Remaking of the World Order*, which provided the ideological framework for conflict in the post-Cold War period, Huntington followed in 2004 with *Who Are We? The Challenges to America's National Identity*. There, Huntington brings the paranoid vision of *The Clash of Civilizations* back home, capturing the national security zeitgeist of the post-9/11 era, and portraying Latinos as 'the single most immediate and most serious challenge to America's traditional identity'.[12] One question follows: how do you define yourself against your enemy when you yourself are being depicted as the enemy? Just before they left for Iraq, the band of brothers had turned into something out of *Universal Soldier*. I saw those bodies again on the beaches of Miami. Of the three men in these pictures, only Luis returned. Abel was killed in action. Felipe shot himself in the head. Luis was there when it happened.[13]

He said there were many like them, many who were proud to serve America but could not make sense of what was expected of them in this war. Wasn't this also a war against them? People like Luis and Felipe left their bucolic but troubled lands trying to escape the climate of increasing polarisation and militarisation in places like southern Mexico or war-torn Colombia. Luis, for instance, was troubled by the ease with which his lighter-skinned school friends in Cali would echo the media's widespread use of 'terrorist' as a catch-all term to portray dissidents and opponents to the policy of 'Democratic Security' set up by the new Uribe government, and the perpetual dance between right-wing paramilitary, left-wing FARC *guerrilleros* and shrewd politicians who, in the end, always seem to be the only real winners.

Felipe fled because of paramilitary activity in Chiapas. He used to make an average of $10,000 a year in the tulip fields of Skagit and Washburn counties. One day, recruiters for the US Army turned up. Their arrival brought back memories of war. It also renewed questions about the identity of Latinos and their place in the US. Across the country, says journalist Roberto Lovato, 'Latinos are being besieged by two very different armies, with often counterintuitive agendas.'

He refers, on the one hand, to US military recruiters intensifying efforts to conscript Latinos 'to defend their country' in the wake of the war in Iraq and the 'surges' there and in Afghanistan. On the other hand, he refers to the Minutemen Project, and to people like former Democrat Republican James Traficant from Ohio, former US Defense Secretary Caspar Weinberger, Samuel P. Huntington and George W. Bush's Secretary of Defense, Donald Rumsfeld. These people depict Latinos as 'immigrant terrorists', 'illegals' and a 'flood of refugees' who are the significant source of social, economic and environmental problems, as well as a threat to American identity, competitiveness and predominance in the world. They are also the reason for switching from the War on Terror to a global struggle against violent extremism that 'appears designed to extend the moral and politico-military reach of the United States throughout the Latino Americas', starting at home.[14]

Huntington makes the connection between the kind of 'unending war' that characterises the merging of security and development in the era of globalisation, military recruitment and the threat to national identity coming from Latino immigrants like Luis and Felipe: 'without a major war requiring substantial mobilization and lasting years . . . contemporary immigrants will have neither the opportunity nor the need to affirm their identity with and loyalty to America as earlier immigrants have done'.[15] It may seem that escaping war and a paranoid style of politics south of the border, and having survived their own experiences of war in El Salvador, southern Mexico or southern Colombia, it all caught up with them again up north, when they enlisted to fight the 'good war' in Afghanistan or Iraq.

This explains why more and more US Latinos are exercising their preferential options, and their strength in numbers, against the securitisation of everyday life at home and the militarisation of foreign policy abroad. The anti-militaristic traditions of US-born Latinos, especially Mexican Americans and Puerto Ricans, Lovato observes, are combining with the anti-militarism of more recent Latin American immigrants who have experienced the ravages of war and paranoid politics at home. 'This new politico-cultural sensibility is taking hold among Latinos,' he says, and was a crucial motivation for the marches of 2006 and, no less important, in the run-up to the presidential elections of 2008. Polls during the election campaign showed Latinos had developed a singular concern for the destiny of military intervention abroad, the Iraq War in particular, parallel to, and at times even over, concerns over the economy and immigration.

Latinos made up 13 per cent of new military recruits in 2004, up from 10.4 per cent in 2000. Under the qualifications required for entering the military in the US, Latinos have been overrepresented among enlisted personnel in relation to the civilian work force. In 2001 Latinos made up 8.2 per cent of the qualified civilian work force and 9.5 per cent of enlisted service members. Latinos' representation has been highest in the Marine Corps and lowest in the air force. In the fiscal year 2004, nearly 15 per cent of US Marine Corps enlisted personnel were Hispanic, compared with 6 per cent of air force enlisted personnel. Latino representation in the navy has been rising. By September 2006, they constituted 14 per cent of navy enlisted personnel, about the same as in the Marine Corps that year. Latino men traditionally constituted a larger percentage of enlisted men than Latino women, in keeping with assumed stereotypes of Latino culture.

However, this has changed: Latino women have caught up with and even slightly surpassed Latino men in their gender's representation in the military. Traditionally, African Americans have been overrepresented in the US military, especially the army, since the start of the All-Volunteer Force in 1973, and they have been dramatically overrepresented among women in the military. Recently, in contrast, recruitment of African Americans has declined. At the same time, Latinos, who constitute a growing segment of the US population (by 2025 one in four Americans will call themselves 'Latino', and this may be an underestimation) have been underrepresented, but their percentage has been rising sharply and with considerable speed. Despite the traditionally masculine culture of the military institution, and the assumed machismo of Hispanic culture, Latino women now make up a larger proportion of female military personnel than Latino men do of male military personnel.[16] These statistics help explain why Latinos in the US have taken an interest in foreign policy and interventionism abroad. The numbers reveal a sharp increase in the participation of Latinos in the US Army *vis-à-vis* other groups.

Enrolment in the army is a traditional vehicle for so-called minorities in the US to demonstrate their loyalty to America, as Huntington says. However, the migratory experience of peoples from the south to the north of the Americas was qualitatively different in comparison to the experience of other migrations into the United States. For it divided from within the predominant idea of Latin America put forward by white Creole and mestizo elites, based upon colonial and neocolonial traditions of masculinity, loyalty to the paternal figure of the nation and the founders of the nation and the insistence – born out of the tensions inherent to the wars of freedom of the nineteenth century – that racial harmony and equality already existed. In that sense, the development of a new consciousness accompanied the massive migratory movement from south to north. The Latino experience in the US can be described in terms of a reintroduction of the Afro-Latin American and the Indian elements cast out from the idea of Latin America formed by Creoles and mestizos in the nineteenth century. This is to say that what happened to Latinos in the US transformed their very being on the basis of a recovery of the cultural elements that had been excluded from nineteenth-century notions of the spirit of 'Latinidad' – mixed in blood but pure or 'European' in mind – such as that exemplified in José Vasconcelos' 1825 book *The Cosmic Race*.

In his book, Vasconcelos proposed the acknowledgment of the facts of miscegenation (*mestizaje*) but firmly contained within an Ibero-American frame of mind that allegedly determined the very spirit of Latin (American) nations. In that frame, there was no room for African dreams or Indian magic, and the mind (the 'spirit') was conceived as a blank slate upon which the European dream (or any other dream) could be inscribed unproblematically. However, the experience of the US taught Latinos about the need

for and advantages of self-affirmation and cross-racial political organisation, and thus of the need to step back in relation to the strictures of the
state and the masculine 'spirit of the nation'.

'I'm glad that the [US] army is no longer able to recruit as many
soldiers, and that more people are raising their voices against this criminal
invasion,' says Camilo Mejía, a Nicaraguan-born former staff sergeant in
the US Army who refused to return to his unit in Iraq after spending five
months stationed there in 2003. While Mejía declared himself a conscien-
tious objector, the United States deemed him a deserter and sentenced
him to nine months in prison. In 2004, 9,477 foreign-born residents of
the United States signed up for the US armed forces – 2,352 fewer than in
2003, according to official statistics from the George W. Bush administration. 'I didn't want to die in a war that isn't mine, a war that is unjust and
immoral. That's why I turned myself in to my superiors,' declared Mejía,
the soldier-turned-activist, who happens to be the son of Nicaraguan
singer-songwriter Carlos Mejía Godoy, whose music served as the sound-
track to the 1979 Sandinista revolution in the Central American country.

From the beginning of the occupation of Iraq in March 2003 until April
2010, a total of 4,388 soldiers from the United States have died there.
By 2006, the year of the Latino marches in the United States, almost 15
per cent of American military casualties in Iraq were of Latin American
birth or descent, according to figures gathered by the Guerrero Azteca
(Aztec Warrior) Project, a US-based group led by Mexican immigrant
Fernando Suárez del Solar that is demanding the return of the soldiers
sent to the Middle East. 'Notice that the proportion of Latino soldiers
who have died in Iraq, most of whom were privates, is higher than the
proportion of Latinos in the US armed forces as a whole', I heard him
saying at a meeting in California. 'We are, literally, under fire,' said a
delegate to that meeting, 'but we're coming out fighting.' As we will
see, that 'coming out' is changing the face of America and radically
transforming the shape of relations in the Americas and elsewhere.

Latinos on the March

The United States fully entered into the twenty-first century on 1 May
2006. That day millions of migrants, mostly Latinos, and their supporters,

went on to the streets across many cities in the United States to protest the proposed criminalisation of undocumented migrants in the country. I travelled the south west and much of the north east of America on the eve of the marches, invited by friends, activists and academics whom I had met over the years, partly as a reporter and also as a participating observer. The spirit of unity and purpose I felt among participants and organisers, the overwhelming majority of whom were very young, was something I had not seen since the student and popular mobilisations of the 1990s in Latin America.

Such a collective stance reflects another fact observed by Latino writers in the United States: 'the Latino experience in the US parallels the emergent critical consciousness of Afro-Andean, Afro-Brazilian, Afro-Caribbean, and Indigenous people throughout the Americas'.[17] The point is not that the expansionist and racial ideals of white American elites, imitated by white Creole elites south of the border, have disappeared. Rather, the effect of the mobilisation of Latinos in the north and Indians, Afro-Latin Americans and others in the south, reduce the political impact of such ideals.

At the time of the marches, in Europe and much of the rest of the world, the name of America was synonymous with a crass form of faux imperialism that had alienated global public opinion and created a climate propitious for the most extreme forms of anti-Americanism. Daily revelations about abuses in Iraq and Afghanistan, extraordinary renditions and torture abroad, which came to be associated with the Guantánamo Bay US base in Cuba, greatly damaged the already dented reputation of the United States as a champion of liberty and a beacon of progressivism around the world. The fact that all of these actions were systematically justified in the name of, precisely, the cause of liberty and progress, did nothing to assuage the suspicion that America had turned from concerned protector of freedom and equality into a nasty racketeer, mingling Halliburton's interests with its own at the expense of the rest of the world.

In addition to that, security concerns at home quickly turned on the risks posited by an 'open border' allowing 'massive influxes' of immigration. The trigger for the 2006 Latino marches in the United States was a proposed piece of legislation that would have turned immigrants and those who help or 'harbor' them, terminology borrowed from the rhetoric of the War on Terror, into criminal felons, 'immigrant terrorists' or 'criminals', as Minutemen Civil Defense Corps leader Chris Simcox put it during a Town Hall meeting I attended in El Paso, Texas.[18] Since pretty much every single Latino family in the US includes a member or a relation whose immigration status remains unsolved, the proposed measure would have turned a huge number of Chicanos, Latinos and Hispanics, potentially the majority of them, into felons. However, a more careful look at the protests reveals something else behind the marches, something other than the outcry against anti-immigration sentiment in the United States. The proposal was the culmination of increasing anti-immigrant rhetoric and practices by popular media outlets, ideologues and vigilante groups on the southern border and elsewhere who are trying to create a moral panic about increasing immigration from Mexico. The marches were historic, the largest in US history.

In April 2006, political demonstrations ensued across the United States, in thirty-nine states and more than 140 cities. The protests were highly visible in Los Angeles, New York, Atlanta, Seattle, Phoenix, Washington, DC, and Chicago. Estimates of their size ranged from 200,000 in Phoenix to more than one million in Los Angeles. Researchers Adrian Pantoja, Cecilia Menjíbar and Lisa Magaña, who tracked numbers and followed the organisation of the marches, explain that these numbers illustrate 'remarkable grassroots mobilization in a short period of time'.[19] A second wave of marches took place in May. According to CNN, in May 2006 about 300,000 demonstrators marched in Downtown Chicago, and predominantly Latino schools saw a 10 to 33 per cent drop in attendance. On that day, 600,000 marched in Los Angeles and many thousands in San Francisco, Washington and other major cities in the United States. But the numbers do not convey the magnitude of what happened. The real story is that many among the US's largest ethnic 'minority' are feeling the pressure to define themselves as black or white, and to choose whether they will struggle to achieve power, or serve it. Latinos are already the largest growing population and largest minority group in the US. 'Their numbers,' explain ethnic studies scholars Nelson Maldonado-Torres and Ramón Grosfoguel, 'are to a great extent responsible for estimates by the US Census of Population that by the mid twenty-first century people of color will constitute a demographic majority in the country.' They explain how the hysteria and anxiety provoked by the number of Latinos, and above all, Mexicans, in the United States, created the environment for the proposal of the criminalisation of undocumented migrants 'and the linking between their will to join the military or lack thereof, which tends to be high by the way, their presence in anti-war movements, which tends to be less than representative, and the supposed threat to American identity'.[20]

In these observations there is a template for understanding the America to come. Consider the state of Texas, a representative case. On average Texas's Latinos are younger than the Anglos and their men and women are having many more babies than anybody else. In 2007, just over 50 per cent of babies born in the Lone Star state were born to Latinas even though Hispanics make only 38 per cent of the total state population. If the border were closed tomorrow, as the Minutemen want, 'Hispanics would still overtake the Anglos by 2034,' reckons Karl Eschbach, Texas official state demographer.[21]

More than half the children in the first grade of Texas schools are Hispanic, 'and in the Houston public-district the proportion is 61%,' notes Stephen Klineberg from Rice University, cited by *The Economist*. This means education in the state is, by and large, a Hispanic issue. 'We are creating a majority population here that is limited in its skill set. It is up to us: if we don't act, we're heading for disaster,' says Trey Martínez Fischer, chairman of the powerful Mexican American Legislative Caucus (MALC). Founded in 1973, the Caucus is a non-partisan organisation that serves as an information clearing house to state legislators and votes together on issues of concern to the state's Hispanic community. Since Latinos represent the state's fastest growing political and economic sector, the power and importance of MALC is considerable.[22] Marc Zimmerman, a researcher at the Latino information project LA CASA at the University of Houston, explained to me that in this sense, the future of America is tied to the fate of its Latino population: if they turn into a majority population with no skills, this spells disaster in a globally predominant information economy. Policy-makers, Hispanic and non-Hispanic, have no other option but to change course, and greatly increase access for Hispanics to public education, capital, health and public transport.

Texas is not the only state undergoing these profound demographic and social shifts. As I pointed out before, at the moment there are only four states in America where Anglos are in the minority: California, Texas, Hawaii, and New Mexico. But those in the know expect the 2010 Census to show that as many as twelve states have now passed that mark. 'By the middle of the twenty-first century that will be the case everywhere,' says Ramón Grosfoguel. 'In 2040,' concludes Klineberg, 'America itself will be a nation in which the "minority" turns out to be the majority.' The most important consequence of this momentous transformation is political: if the United States wants to make it into the twenty-second century, conserving its position of importance in global affairs, given that its productive and social destiny is attached to a Latino population that has been badly served by a rather conservative model of development, it will need to change that model.

To do so, it will have to transform its political identity, and this will require many changes and active intervention and reform from the bottom up. Assuming that Latino candidates will be more willing, and perhaps more able, to change the course of the past, US political capital will have to go to the candidates Latinos prefer, presumably their own. Conversely, given that they are becoming, and to a large extent have already become, an electoral force to be reckoned with, a party determined to survive and acquire or stay in power will need to court the Latino vote by presenting it with candidates to its liking, presumably Latino candidates. This is good news for the Democrats, less so for the Republicans who threw away the advantage that George W. Bush's ability to court the Hispanic vote gave them, by rejecting his plans for immigration reform in 2005–6, and instead headed in the direction of Minutemen wilderness.

The steady rise of the Latino population, coupled with a continuous increase in their tendency to vote, indicates that this is the shape of things to come. In 2008 that tendency was 49.9 per cent, up from 47.2 per cent in 2004. This means a lot of work still has to be done to catch up with 66.1 per cent tendency to vote among whites. A great deal of that work is being done by the young organisers who featured so prominently in the 2006 marches and thereafter in the grassroots electoral mobilisation which elected Barack Obama in 2008. This spells good news on yet another front: Latinos need to produce a stronger, younger, more active political leadership, particularly within the Democratic Party, if they want to serve not only their own interests but actually those of the nation since they have now become one and the same. This means, in turn, that the tone of their ideology, politics and policy needs to move, from right-wing conservative to left-wing liberal. This is already happening in Texas: as they become more powerful in an increasingly stronger Democratic Party, there is every chance that Latinos will turn against a model that has left far too many of them behind. In fact, as I have already said, given the consequences of the financial crisis, it is in the national interest that they do so.

Journalists in Europe say that real news in the Old World boils down to matters of class, while important news in the New World boils down to matters of race. There is some truth to that statement, although things may be changing in Europe too, but the general picture in the Americas is more complicated: in America, race and class overlap. If a conflict is coming, it is not Huntington's clash of civilisations, but, rather, good, old-fashioned class warfare and cultural revolution. Hence the question, where are young Latinos, the future stars of the Democratic Party, going to look in order to learn the left-of-centre language that combines 'reformist' and 'radical' ways? The answer is, back home, in Latin America. Or in this case, the kids' 'second home'. That is, the home of their parents and grandparents. In this respect, expect American politics to look a lot like Latin American politics right now: populist or popular, polarised, issue-based, with parties connected to and responding or even reacting to cross-racial grassroots coalitions, putting pressure on local and central government to engage in redistributive policy-making or group-specific protectionist measures. It will move further left, outflank Chinese-grown 'pragmatism' (or even show the way ahead, along with 'New Left' elements already doing their own 'battle for the soul' in China), it will surprise European conservatives, and take us all into the next century. Counterintuitive as it may seem, Latin America, led by countries like Brazil and now including the United States, is poised to lead the way.

9

Crisis: The Rise and Fall of Global Capitalism

A Strange Story of Take-off and Bank Robbery

The next President of Brazil may be a half-Bulgarian woman who has been accused of bank robbery and preaching armed revolution. She dismisses such allegations as 'ridiculous' exaggerations. And, in fact, what exactly the presidential nominee of the Worker's Party of Brazil did during the 1960s has become the stuff of folklore and mythmaking. What is known is this: born into a middle-class family with an immigrant Bulgarian father in the Brazilian state of Minas Gerais, at age seventeen Dilma Vana Rousseff joined the Política Operária, or Workers' Politics Movement, a radical political faction originated in the Socialist Youth of the Brazilian Socialist Party that opposed the Communist Party of Brazil. Soon the movement split between those who supported the struggle for a popular Constitutional Assembly and those who favoured armed revolution. The latter, including Dilma, formed the Comando de Libertação Nacional (National Liberation Command – COLINA), an armed resistance group that sought to wage war against the regime that ruled Brazil for two decades after the military coup led by Field Marshal Humberto Castelo Branco in 1964.

In 1969, the group's activities included four bank robberies and two bombings, with no casualties. Dilma did not take active part in any of these military efforts, but became quite proficient in the use of weapons, how to confront and avoid police repression and soon became a notoriously skilful leader who managed to impose herself among men accustomed to giving the orders. After a confrontation with a police force raiding the group's quarters went badly wrong, Dilma, by then a student of economics at the Federal University of Minas Gerais, flew to Rio de Janeiro with Claudio Galeno Linhares, who was also a member of the group. Later, she met the lawyer Charles de Araujo and the two fell in love.

The remainder of the group merged with a dissident faction of the Brazilian Communist Party and another group called the Popular Vanguard, led by Carlos Lamarca. Galeno had been sent to Porto Alegre and Dilma stayed behind in Rio organising meetings and transporting weapons and money. Her defence of a political alliance with the workers, against the military-based tactics of Lamarca's Popular Vanguard, put her on a collision course with the guerrilla leader who accused her of being 'a stuck-up intellectual' who thought of herself as some sort of modern-day Joan of Arc. The accusation was echoed later on by the military regime's prosecutor in charge of the investigation against the organisation, who named her 'the Joan of Arc of subversion'. Mauricio Lopes Lima, a member of the armed forces unit in charge of torture and the collection of intelligence, declared during the prosecution that Dilma was the intellectual leader of the group, responsible for industrial action, bank robberies and terrorist activities. Those activities would have included the theft of $2.4 million on 18 June 1969 from the safe of former governor of São Paulo Adhemar de Barros, an extremely unpopular and corrupt politician who rejoiced in being called 'he who steals but gets things done'.

Dilma dismisses such comparisons, and former militants like Carlos Minc, who took part in the robbery, and Antonio Roberto Espinosa, who was the head of the faction, allege that her position in the organisation as much as her participation in the group's less savoury activities have been widely exaggerated, for she always remained in the political wing defending the worth of political positions before her more military-minded male colleagues. Tensions within the group came to a head between August and September 1969, when a major dispute erupted between those who supported armed revolution and those who argued for the priority of political work among the masses. As a result of such debates the organisation split into a paramilitary group and a group advocating popular politics. Dilma was in the second group, in charge of carrying out political activities.

On 16 January 1970 she was captured, almost by accident, while entering a bar where a colleague of hers named José Leite Ribeiro had been forced by the military, after torture, to assist in the capture of another militant. After he was arrested and the soldiers were preparing to leave, Dilma turned up unexpectedly. She was armed and the men took her to the headquarters of the infamous OBAN, the section of the Brazilian army in charge of intelligence collection for the military regime, which, five years after Dilma's arrest, tortured to death playwright and journalist Vladimir Herzog in the same place where she had been held. While in custody, Dilma too was tortured with electric shocks administered with car jump leads. She was condemned to serve six years' imprisonment by a military court and sent to the São Paulo Penitentiary.

After almost three years in prison, Dilma was freed in 1972. She had lost 20 pounds and acquired a thyroid disease, the first of many health problems to plague her to the present day. She resumed her political activism at the Institute of Social and Political Studies linked to the legalised opposition party Democratic Movement, where she organised debates and lectures with such influential scholars as Fernando Henrique Cardoso and Francisco Weffort. After the end of the dictatorship in the 1980s, her political activism would take her from the Brazilian Democratic Labour Party, which she helped reorganise together with some of her former colleagues of the years of resistance against dictatorship, to the Workers' Party of Luiz Inácio Lula da Silva. She had come to prominence, and gained the attention of the former shoeshiner and street vendor-turned-union leader and Workers' Party founder, thanks to her success as state energy secretary in Rio Grande do Sul at a critical time for the sector. Later on, she became Lula's surprise first choice as his energy minister and thereafter, having helped get his government back on its feet after it all but fell apart during his second term in office, she was promoted as the new Chef de Cabinet of Brazil.

After becoming a minister, Dilma defended a new industrial policy ensuring that the deep-sea oil exploration platforms of national company Petrobras, which operates at arm's length from the government, had a 'minimum domestic content', arguing that it was unforgivable that a country with the ability to produce ships and platforms would not take part in the construction of a billion dollar project with the potential of generating close to 30,000 jobs. By 2008, the shipbuilding industry employed 40,000 people compared to five hundred in the 1990s, and Brazil now has the sixth largest shipping industry in the world. She also proposed that the universalisation of access to electricity be considered part of the social inclusion programme known as Fome Zero, a set of social strategies aimed at eradicating hunger, poverty and inequality in Brazil, and that it focused on regions with the lowest Human Development Index and families with an income of up to three minimum wages. As a result, by April 2008 the traditionally less developed north-eastern region of Brazil had surpassed the more developed south in power consumption for the first time in Brazil's history.

Dilma Rousseff is now in charge of the 'Growth Acceleration Program' (PAC), which is part of Brazil's new model of development, with other policies of direct social investment and rent transfer such as Auxílio Gas, the Popular Restaurant, the Water Cisterns programme, the Program for the Acquisition of Small Families Agricultural products (PAA), the Continuous Benefit Payment for social assistance (BPC), and the flagship programme Bolsa Familia, administered by the new ministry of social development and struggle against hunger. Bolsa Familia, or Family Allowance, operates as a direct and conditional cash-transfer programme that benefits families with a monthly income of up to $70, and is managed directly and preferably by women acting as family and community leaders. In essence, it combines immediate poverty relief with the promotion and support of the exercise of family and community social and economic rights (mainly health and education), in order to build up their capacity to break out of the vicious circle that carries poverty over from one generation to another. At the same time, it recognises the right of access to common goods as a social rent, rather than in the form of private debt. Thus it assumes the general form of a redistribution of income.

In this respect, it applies to national economic policy the principle of starting from the bottom in order to reform the monetary system. It is an example of innovative financial action, with regard to all the other interventions aiming to confront and overcome the cyclical and uneven character of the global economy, made evident by the onset of repeated debt and financial crises, culminating in the 2008 Great Recession. Together, Family Allowance and Rousseff's Growth Acceleration Program constitute the backbone of Brazil's 'take-off' strategy and of the country's response to the global financial crisis. Dilma's PAC has a total budget of $301 billion to be invested in the strengthening of Brazil's infrastructure between 2007 and 2010, thereby stimulating the private sector and the creation of much needed additional jobs. To summarise Brazil's special approach to global economics and progress, rather than bailing out the banks it decided to bail out its people.

All this time, Dilma Rousseff was acquiring a reputation among businessmen and colleagues of different political persuasion as a tough but fair negotiator who wanted to transform the state – to make it more effective but not smaller, democratic but also more egalitarian, conscious of the challenges of interdependence in the wider economic world but never prepared to sacrifice its social goals and the rights of all in the pursuit of the spectres of progress. She describes herself as 'Brazilian, democratic, socialist' and thinks that an intelligent woman with a militant past is ready to be the next President of Brazil, the Latin American country that according to most estimates will become by 2014 the fifth largest economy on earth and thus one of the countries that will dominate the world.[1] Not bad for a former guerrilla fighter, alleged bank robber and a prisoner.

The Other Prisoner's Dilemma

The biggest prison in the Latin world – in the entire world, in fact – goes by the peculiar name of the Twin Towers Correctional Facility. It is located in the centre of Los Angeles, California, and, in spite of the ominous memories its name might conjure up, it has nothing to do with the Twin Towers in New York, so brutally attacked on 9/11. Nevertheless, the two peach-coloured buildings on 450 Bauchet Street may be no less significant. They stand as the very symbol of our times. Within the walls of the two towers there are two gigantic gymnasiums, a medical services building and the Los Angeles County Medical Center Jail Ward, complete with mental health wards and an ensemble of kitchens capable of serving 17,000 meals per day to as many inmates. These include violent criminals, male, female, non-violent offenders and people with mental health problems.

Every day, hundreds of offenders housed at the Twin Towers and the other half-dozen facilities run by the Los Angeles County Sheriff's Department are released on to Bauchet Street. Those who are not picked up, or have no money to return to their families or friends, end up in the homeless shelters and social protection providers of Skid Row, the notorious area that contains one of the largest populations of exposed people in the US, around eight thousand, less than a mile from the Twin Towers. A social aid organisation called Volunteers of America runs a shuttle bus from the jails to a drop-in centre located at 628 S. San Julian Street. Besides Volunteers of America, other social services and protection providers in the Skid Row area include Union Rescue Mission, Urban Connection, Downtown Women's Center, Frontline Foundation, Los Angeles Mission Community Clinic, Fred Jordan Mission and Midnight Mission.

Together with the security services and the forces of so-called 'urban gentrification', they are the visible face of neo-humanitarianism at work in the slums of America. Crucially, however, the new humanitarianism at work in Downtown Los Angeles may not be that different from the theory and practice which have informed the post-2003 reconstruction efforts in Iraq or the aid campaign after the 2010 earthquake in Haiti. The latter are in fact the exemplary culmination and the consequence of a form of governance whose emergence can be dated back to the late seventies, and which was perfected during the 1980s and 1990s in Latin America, where it was tried out for the first time. This is a phenomenon that is global as much as it is local. Let us call it the neoliberal government of global insecurity.[2]

A recent study conducted by the Los Angeles Downtown business group Central City East Association (CCEA) found that 21 per cent of 153 inmates surveyed at the release centre, or IRC, in Bauchet Street had no place to sleep the night of their release. In November 2005, Los Angeles Downtown News reported that state parole officers have helped house 110 sex offenders in the Downtown area of the city. Altogether

322 are in the area, including those who finished parole but must still register their whereabouts. As a result, the area has the highest concentration of sex offenders in Los Angeles. Former and current inmates join the homeless, the sex offenders, the parolees, the drug pushers and their transnational circuits, the state security services and the social service providers, in an area situated in the middle of one of the richest cities in the world, something Estela Lopez, Executive Director of the CCEA, calls 'an abomination'.

Twin Towers Correctional Facility, the building that looms over the area of Los Angeles that Lopez calls an abomination, represents what might be termed the darker side of globalisation. Indeed, the inmates' quarters could have come straight from some of the darker visions of Jeremy Bentham or Michel Foucault, heptagons with a single security guard in the middle surveying ninety-six cells at a time through glass doors and CCTV cameras. And yet, Twin Towers is not a rotting, decrepit pit. In fact, the Towers are new and gleaming, themselves part of the process of gentrification of Lopez's 'monstrous' part of the city centre. Inmates refer to them as the 'Hilton of correctional facilities'. Five stories high, each floor is connected via an enclosed area with a basketball hoop, a recreational area and telephone lines that allow for what one nurse calls 'an umbilical cord to the outside world'.[3]

In this respect, Twin Towers cannot be compared with other famous places of incarceration such as Alcatraz or Sing Sing, or even with the 'Hanoi Hilton' used by French colonists in Vietnam and later on by the North Vietnamese for American prisoners of war, much less with the Tower of London, Newgate or the Bastille. For they are not a world apart, but, rather, our world turned inside out. As the inmates suggest, the Towers have more in common with our luxury hotels, our shopping malls and our airports. And, crucially, with the places where we work. In fact, if there is any dominant ideology at Twin Towers, it would be the rhetoric of self-reliance, responsibility and individual success that is also predominant in the workplace. In Twin Towers, inmates are 'compelled to contribute financially' to the sustainability of their institution. In this sense at least they own the place just as much as they are owned, imprisoned, by it. Moreover, this 'compulsion' is not the result of sheer coercion but rather a combination of financial magic and the ideology of self-reliance.

Thus, there is no single logic at work here, capitalist or otherwise. Rather, capitalism itself has been transformed in its neoliberal phase: on the one hand, the most crucial conflicts take place in the marginal world of contingent labour, between guaranteed and non-guaranteed workers and capitalistic elites whose motivations matter, rather than merely reflecting structural or fixed positions that represent the dual forces of a larger and abstract system. On the other hand, these conflicts are not singularly local. Thus, for instance, the reach of the prison system extends well beyond the walls of the prisons themselves: millions of people in North America are subject to the surveillance of parole, facing systematic exclusion from jobs and the tracing of information about their past, left in police and other databases, forever haunting their prospects and expectations about the future.

But the same occurs to those of us who live outside prisons and have nothing to do with the parole system. The difference between the form of surveillance of the Twin Towers Correctional Facility in Los Angeles, with a single security guard surveying many sites at once with video cameras, and the 4.2 million security cameras in a country like the United Kingdom, is only a matter of degree.[4] Of course, not many countries in the world have as extended a network of video surveillance as Britain, and yet, the paradox of the way in which the grandeur and power of the state as expressed in surveillance, punishment and security measures has grown in recent years appears in various forms in most of our societies. Crucially, as 'central' areas of the global system of circulation and communication move into the 'peripheries', and as digital and computing technologies spread their reach, the effect is felt mostly at the same level in which the rhetoric of self-reliance has an effect, that is to say at the level of the formation and management of our individual and collective expectations.

The fingerprints, images, records and even the DNA of prisoners and parolees are stored in police and security services databases in America and elsewhere, as are the biographical and/or biometric details of citizens in Latin America, Europe, the US and elsewhere who acquire updated

ID cards or passports, or enter the US as visitors, or use their credit and debit cards. This extends to those who ask for mortgages, micro-credits and personal or corporate loans in banks or other financial institutions, or buy books from Amazon, or music from iTunes and other goods online, or share health information online and buy prescriptions or other non-sanctioned drugs, or use social network services such as Facebook or Twitter, or search engines and mobile phones worldwide. All of these traces of your preferences, your tastes, your fears, even your most intimate fantasies and optimistic dreams are stored somewhere and can or are being used in an almost magical way to shape your expectations, to calculate your trajectory and to establish ultimately who you are. In the end, that is the only dilemma left for us, the citizens and stateless peoples of this post-ideological and crisis-ridden world: who are we? Who are you, you who dare to have an opinion, on behalf of what or whom do you speak? What are you worth on the scale of what society deems valuable? In what category do you rank yourself? Are you worth anything, or nothing?

Hell Is Other People

It is not simply the case that the security state has taken over the welfare state, wherever it has existed, to control the populations at the margins of market economy.

The unifying security state that reduces to simple categories the complex multiplicity of populations and the indeterminacy of their expectations, as peoples all over the world are divided into peoples at risk on the one hand, and 'secured' peoples on the other, is a function of the situation of the global market economy.

In that situation we are all disconnected, as workers and consumers, from the manufacture and distribution of our goods, but also from one another. Our expectations about ourselves and others, about who we are and what we can become are shaped within us from without. They are responses to firmly established frames of reference. These frames, which function as snapshots of a desirable but highly speculative future, tell us what to consume, how to behave and what to expect in relation to the position we occupy or may come to occupy within an already established, *realistic* set of options. We admire those who seem to us to occupy 'advanced' positions, and envy them at the same time. Conversely, we despise those who seem to us to occupy 'backward' positions, and pity them at the same time. Women, the insane, homeless people, certain social sectors, the poor, dissidents in our midst, and 'developing' nations: all of them are deemed 'backward', guilty of being stuck in the past. We believe that 'advanced' societies have escaped from the clutches of the past and are propelled forward by the inevitable forces of progress. In fact, however, we do not look forward and do not assume ethical responsibility for the future that we always share with others. We tend to look backward, assuming from the vantage point of our present that what has been achieved in the past shows to others an image of their own future and justifies our position in the present. We wrongly conclude that everyone's future will resemble our present, or an improved version of it. Moreover, we tend to look at the past from the vantage point of the present and rewrite our own histories so as to make them more consistent with how we see ourselves today, rather than as they really were.

This is how we come to believe that we are subject to impersonal, inevitable forces emanating from Nature, some creative power, destiny or technology, and see no connection between *their* guilt and *our* progress, their fate and ours. Our error is thus twofold: just as we present our own history and our present position as a model for others to follow and achieve in the future, asking for their admiration at the same time as we unwittingly provoke their envy, so we delude ourselves into thinking that our present is the inevitable result of a past whose fateful narrative is in fact the result of constant yet often subconscious acts of rewriting and repetition. Over time, we may even recommend our own path to others in the honest belief that that was the route taken by ourselves, and our nation, on the way to progress and success. But in doing so we make the lives of those we are trying to help more difficult: we deprive them of means of their own with which to draw specific trajectories in the future. Furthermore, in doing so we also reduce our own future choices. For if ours was the one true path, once it has been realised – once history has come to an end – what then?

We tend to believe others are poor because, unlike us, they are lazy, backward and have outdated institutions. Therefore, they *ought* to become like us or remain segregated, distanced in space and time. But what if they are 'backward' and have outdated institutions because they are poor? What if that purported fate, the notion that they ought to become like us and share our culture, is in fact part of their poverty? Culture is a profoundly reactionary concept; it describes the world of peoples and languages as an archipelago of separate universes. As a concept of separate identity it stresses integration within a system, purity, adherence to shared values and conformity in conduct and outlook. In modern times, such a notion of culture, identity and tradition emerged together with acts of purposeful forgetting, denial of the unfamiliar and alien as our contemporaneous other and, conversely, the affirmation of the familiar in landscapes we have never seen before or of the ordinary in the extraordinary.

This entails the suppression of memory, as when we speak of freedom while practices of slavery underwrite our entire economic system, pray to Jesus while considering the historical fact of the spread of Christianity to be sufficient proof that it is the true religion, or preach the virtues of free-trade and free-market policies to poor countries as a way of kicking away the ladder we ourselves used to climb up or because of misguided self-righteousness. But, in fact, slavery is no longer a colonial institution, as it is related to the displacement of masses of black and Indian peasants in Africa and the Americas into an urban landscape of wage labour, the forced displacement of rural populations following the enclosure of the commons and industrialisation between the seventeenth and nineteenth centuries in Britain, commerce, non-guaranteed employment and the adoption of 'western' lifestyles often ridiculed as 'inauthentic'. To hold the belief of Jesus as Christ leads straight into the universal problem of achieving a synthesis between the finite, the observable and the familiar on the one hand, and on the other the infinite, what we have never seen before and is yet to come without any proof or guarantee. The true story of development shows that before their industries were strong enough to compete internationally, neither Britain nor the US were ever the homes of free trade; that no countries succeeded only through protectionism and subsidies; few without some such measure; that for so-called 'developing' countries free trade has rarely been a matter of choice without coercion; that opening up economies selectively and gradually tends to be the most prudent and effective approach; and that there is no point in proclaiming that sacrifices must be made for the sake of growth and progress if neither is achieved.

These double standards are not a matter of ill intentions or abstract immorality, but, rather, a practical problem derived from our inability to recognise the contemporaneous value of forward-looking practices in a multiplicity of landscapes, common practices and in the stories we tell each other to achieve self-understanding, or our tendency to pass too quickly from describing such landscapes, practices and stories to regulating and integrating them into a 'culture'. Such purposeful acts of memory-repression and memory-fixation, the enclosure of common or popular culture, and the regulation of desires and expectations on the basis of spatial and temporal distancing, constantly making the future a little less real, are what disconnect us from what we eat, what we wear and what we make. They account for our lack of orientation. It is peculiar that we refer to the result of such acts as our 'identity', since, in fact, understood in such a way, 'intellectually, politically and economically', identity becomes 'identity at the expense of others'.[5] In that respect, perhaps blindness is too easy a metaphor for what is in fact a sacrificial act and a denial of the contemporaneous character of others' history and the real but improbable future we all face. Against such sacrificial acts of denial stand the 'moments of clarity in action' achieved throughout history by such people as the Haitian slaves rising up against their masters, the Christians denouncing the Roman Empire and the poorer or 'developing' peoples of the Global South challenging creatively the one-size-fits-all model of regulation, progress and globalisation that the north insists on calling 'the only model' and the one true path.[6]

A Small Matter of Time

The human nobility of those who resist and create – the value of on-the-job-sabotage and outright rebellion, of those nations and those within the nations who have devoted their lives to revolting against segregation, apartheid and the suppression of memory, in the labour movement, in the global justice movement, in the struggle to overthrow a system of unequal economic relations at home and abroad – is not recognised because such things are considered signs of immaturity and childish behaviour. As such, they belong to the past. As for the future, we already have a reference for it, an image of what awaits us, which we must responsibly follow as we make our way across the border: that is the image of the present as embodied in what the journalist Thomas Friedman once called 'the golden straitjacket'.

That was his term for describing a set of economic policies that pretty much summarised the prevailing neoliberal orthodoxy of the late 1990s, not just as a set of economic policies but also as a model, not only a mode of production but a mode of regulation: 'Unfortunately,' he said, 'the golden straitjacket is pretty much "one-size-fits-all" . . . It is not always pretty or gentle or comfortable. But it's here and it's the only model on the rack this historical season.'[7] For naturalist philosophers like Mr Friedman, our practices and eventful histories can be arranged in stages that follow one after the other under observable natural rules or cycles. Circles or cycles conjure up the social connotation of a circumference containing people who share certain information, goods and interests in a situation of scarcity and constant peril. In short, an identity and a culture defined at the expense of others. Acting as one, such people would forge, grind and flatten and wage war or set its surrounding environment on fire, much like the figure of the automaton in Thomas Hobbes' *Leviathan*.

What Friedman is really saying is that there is one 'culture', which may not suit all, but is the one you ought to adopt if you want to win the race of globalisation and vicious competition in a resource-scarce environment. And what characterises that culture as an automated unit is, as in the sixteenth and seventeenth centuries, gold lust, but this time with an emphasis on the alluring powers of the golden fetish. However, if read within the context of the other power of *Leviathan*, it turns out that to don the 'golden straitjacket' is to prepare for battle in the outside world of brutish resource and economic competition. Hence Friedman's call for an 'energy technology' revolution, the race for a technology that would give us the edge in the coming energy wars. This concept of the international realm as the scene of a perennial state of nature and war, originating in the spatial and time distancing practices of colonialism and empire, is a persistent feature in some conceptions of international and economic relations. Such images are still with us: and so we race one another, not just on a rectilinear track but also in vicious circles. But if on the track we can never 'catch up', just as Achilles can never catch up with the tortoise, within the circle there is no 'take-off', for we keep returning to the same place: the periphery repeats the centre, and in the future we and others will achieve what has already been achieved in the past.

As we have seen in the previous chapter, this was the conundrum that occupied the lifetime's work of Raúl Prebisch. He recognised the basic assumptions of mainstream Ricardian trade theory according to which current levels of technology between trade countries are given, those who seek to acquire more advanced technologies are simply 'backward', and this situation justifies a form of exchange that guarantees they will remain so in the future. The basic assumption was that everything must continue to be in the future the same as it has been in the past. In economic theory, this most basic assumption, which effectively erases the occurrence of truly new and unexpected events in the future, was captured in a set of principles concerning the efficient operation of markets and the coordination of our expectations. But those principles conflicted with the potential embodied by information and communication technologies, and with the goals of developing countries concerning the distribution of resources, risks and rewards in the global economy with a view to building up capacities to create future environments.

And so, as Raúl Prebisch walked the shoreline road of Lake Geneva to the vineyards of La Côte, taking a break from the long and tiring sessions of the successful 1964 United Nations Conference on Trade and Development (UNCTAD), he pondered his own future. Two things loomed on the horizon: first, the not small question of his mistress and illegitimate son, both of whom threatened to unleash disaster as much upon his personal life as on the strict public relations life and code of the United Nations. Second, the life of his research institute in

Santiago de Chile known by the acronym ILPES (Latin American and Caribbean Institute of Economic and Social Planning, associated with UN-funded ECLA) was under threat. The reason for this was the work of a brilliant young researcher who had fallen out with the Brazilian government after the 1964 coup that heralded almost twenty years of military rule in the country. Roberto Campos, minister of planning in the regime of Field Marshal Humberto Castelo Branco and a favourite of Washington, made it absolutely clear that Brazil, a critical leader of the G-77 group of developing countries in UNCTAD and already a global and regional power, would cut Prebisch's institute funding if it continued to give refuge to and allow the work of renowned dissident sociologist Fernando Henrique Cardoso to criticise Castelo Branco's neoliberal model of capitalism.

It was clear to Prebisch, and perhaps more so to his associates, that the newcomers – especially Cardoso, but also Celso Furtado and Francisco Weffort, joined by locals Enzo Faletto and Aníbal Pinto, among others – were at the forefront of a badly needed effort to revise the old ECLA doctrine expressed in his 1949 *Havana Manifesto*. The *Manifesto* had firmly established in economic theory the worthiness of considering space and time in the study of international economic relations and, thus, the cyclical nature of business and trade and the unequal nature of relations between 'core' and 'periphery' based upon contingent segmentations and distancing in space and time. Cardoso had been examining in Brazil the changing nature of such relations. He studied patterns of slavery in southern Brazil and the relationship between the internal and international role of entrepreneurs, on the one hand, and their political ideology, on the other. This role had been decisively transformed by the emergence of what we now call MNCs, or 'multinational corporations'. The presence of MNCs, he argued, meant that the 'centre' had moved directly into the 'periphery', a phenomenon which heralded new facts of production, new facts of distribution and new transformations in the mass media and management practices taking place on the back of, principally, the revolution in information and communication technologies.

The latter is perhaps the aspect that has received less attention from those who have considered the discussions and arguments put forward by

Cardoso and others in the ILPES–ECLA weekly Development Seminar in Santiago de Chile in the mid-sixties. However, it is central, for it is one of the crucial points in answering Cardoso's question to the seminar, 'What is the result of the "centre" moving into the "periphery"'? It has to do with the consequences of such new technologies. The answer to Cardoso's question was this: the closing of the spatial-temporal gap between centre and periphery or the possibility of responding to crises in real time.

Real Time

The era following the Great Depression and World War II, which lasted from the 1950s until the late 1970s in Latin America, can properly be understood as the period of the 'Industrial Revolution in the Third World', during which, as developing countries pursued supposedly wrong policies of state intervention and selectively opened up their economies, per capita income grew by 3 per cent annually.[8] In contrast, during the free-trade period of British-dominated neocolonial relations and unequal treaties, between 1870 and World War I, Asia grew at 0.4 per cent per year and Africa grew at 0.6 per cent per year. During that period western Europe grew 1.3 per cent per year and the United States 1.8 per cent. At the time, Latin America had obtained tariff autonomy and successfully de-linked the use of force (or 'gunboat diplomacy', in the terminology of the nineteenth century) from its financial and economic relations with foreign investors, still driven by the spirit of the first wave of decolonisation represented in the so-called Calvo and Drago Doctrines, named after two Argentinean diplomats who expressed such a spirit in the language of international law. During that period, Latin American countries grew as fast as the United States. In the case of Argentina, for instance, its profitable commercial relationship with Britain continued even until the Roca–Runciman Treaty of 1 May 1933 between the two nations, which exemplified the new and distorted conditions of the post-Depression era.

Developmentalism – the challenge to peripheral economies in the Global South to move from commodity production to a more diversified industrial economy and lead the world towards a new international economic order – proved not only irresistible and durable, but also more successful than its enemies at the time and revisionist historians today would have us believe.[9] It was a way to re-enact the memory of the period of struggle for independence and freedom in the context of the generalised trade pessimism of the early 1950s. Documents like the 1949 *Havana Manifesto*, for all its appeal to reason and moderation, some may say to diplomatic argument, successfully conveyed a subtle but unmistakable message of indignation not only in Latin America but also around the world. Those were the days when development economics meant taking a stand.[10]

During the 'Third World Industrial Revolution', between the 1950s and the 1970s, per capita income in Latin America grew at 3.1 per cent a year, faster than the developing country average. The tail end of this period coincided with the potential of the information and communication technologies revolution, which for many held the promise that 'cycles' and 'crises' could be faced by better, more efficient and effective forms of command, control, coordination and anticipation.

For people like Fernando Henrique Cardoso the point was that the entire system of global economic relations could look at itself from the vantage point of the future, via forecasts, statistical analyses and mathematical modelling and coordinate its responses to cycles in core and periphery areas beforehand, so as to defer them or avert them. Cardoso and others participated in a rich and creative environment where discussions about the consequences of cybernetics and other approaches associated with the rise of advanced information and communication technologies never took the naturalist route. They were firmly rooted in what can be considered the most important insight of Latin American cultural production in the late 1960s: the primacy of politics over any sort of determinism – economic, providential, technological, historical, dialectic, materialist and so on.

Even hard-nosed cyberneticians and pioneer cognitive scientists understood from the very outset that the decisive consequences of the 'third wave' of the Industrial Revolution would follow from political decisions and unforeseeable events, rather than from presumed immanent forces. That was the case with people like British scientist Stafford Beer or physicians such as Humberto Maturana, Francisco J. Varela and Salvador Allende, and those who perceived early on the likely consequences of applying the new cybernetic principles – self-organisation, recursive feedback, and efficacy of action – to public and private management and industrialisation, like Chilean scholar and political activist Fernando Flores, who provided the link between cyberneticians and ECLA-based economists close to government in the Chile of the late 1960s, all of whom took part in these debates in one way or another.

It is no surprise, then, that economic sociologists like Cardoso emphasised the subjective and political aspect of such radical transformations. From his perspective, open markets, security agencies (the police, the military) and minimal states could be combined in order to respond to looming catastrophes and the outcome of such combination could be regressive as well as progressive. The direction taken by such processes would be a matter of practical choices and responsible definitions. Some of these men witnessed how the ability to forecast and announce disasters in order to avert them became the central task of a minimal 'security state'. In that respect, as Cardoso argued, the 1964 Brazilian coup was key to understanding what he called the internationalisation of the internal market. It was not just another military takeover: it heralded many similar authoritarian experiments of 'non-interventionist' governments in Latin America and elsewhere, and the dawn of a form of global governance in which the problems of development could be merged with the challenges of security. But it was also a time of practical progressive choices and transformation. All certainties were being replaced by a more general and objective kind of uncertainty: the infinite, the real future.

Fictions

Literary critic Alberto Manguel has observed that the second revolution of literary fiction in Spanish was marked by the publication of *Ficciones* by Argentinean writer Jorge Luis Borges. Borges' most popular anthology of short stories was first published by Editorial Sur in 1944 and then by Emecé in 1956 in Argentina. In 1962 it was translated by Anthony Boucher and in the same year a separate translation of Borges' materials into English, including some of his fictional work, was prepared by James E. Irby for the English reading public under the title *Labyrinths*, first published in the United States in 1964. That was the same year in which developing countries secured their right to include safeguards in trade agreements, thereby tilting the playing field of international relations. The third revolution, Manguel says, 'has not yet begun'.[11] I believe Manguel is right. In fact, I believe there will not be a third period of Spanish fiction for quite some time, at least not until we accept the challenge posited by Borges: that the world we presume solid and persistent in space and time is absolutely contingent. That there is no necessity in it other than the one we introduce ourselves when looking back at it from the vantage point of the present. That what seems merely the part, or the part of no part, can contain a whole and that there is no such thing as a whole or a universe, which can contain all universes.

This concept, which, as Borges put it, 'corrupts and upsets all others', is not Evil, 'whose limited realm is that of ethics', but, rather, the infinite. Borges introduced the concept, in, among other places, his short essay 'Avatars of the Tortoise', which appeared in the 1962–4 collection of fiction and essays brought together under the title *Labyrinths*. In the essay, Borges clarifies the structure he uses in many of his most famous stories, the discounted part that contains a whole. Such is the case of 'The Circular Ruins', in which a dream takes place within another dream; in 'Aleph', in which one discounted atom of the universe contains the actual universe, or famously in 'The Analytical Language of John Wilkins', in which a Chinese encyclopaedia enumerates a set of classes of animals which includes the set of 'animals included in this classification'.

This Chinese box structure, or *mise en abîme*, a term that describes an experience similar to that of standing between two mirrors, also refers to a phenomenon that scientists in the 1970s, people like Stafford Beer, Maturana and Varela, Flores and others in Chile, termed 'recursivity', looping or self-reflection. Such a phenomenon is the basis of the science known as cybernetics and is now present everywhere in our daily life wherever there is a computer, the Internet, an iPhone, a search engine or the 'cloud' that many predict will be the next frontier of politics and capitalism. Our virtual avatar on Facebook is a self-reflection, no less real because it is virtual and yet altogether false. The screen showing the ups and downs of the stock market and the Wall Street analyst looking at it as if he were looking at the nervous system of the world is another example.

But Borges was less interested in such mundane applications; he was keener to emphasise the perplexities of reason or the prodigality of the *regressus ad infinitum*, which is reason's very own *mise en abîme*. In 'Avatars of the Tortoise' he displays the prodigality of the *regressus* in front of his reader, from Zeno's famous paradox involving Achilles and the humble tortoise to Lewis Carroll's 'endless dialogue, whose interlocutors are Achilles and the tortoise. Having now reached the end of their interminable race, the two athletes calmly converse about geometry.' The dialogue strikes at the heart of logic, aesthetics and the problem of knowledge ('cognition is recognition, but it is necessary to have known in order to recognize, but cognition is recognition . . . Is [this] a legitimate instrument of investigation or only a bad habit?').[12] This is also the problem of memory, which we saw before being repressed and displaced by that of 'culture'. It is thus the question of time and history: where do we stand in relation to the future? Do we lack the proper orientation?

Borges' humble contribution is to recognise that 'we have dreamt the world. We have dreamt it as firm, mysterious, visible, ubiquitous in space and durable in time; but in its architecture we have allowed tenuous and eternal crevices of unreason which tell us it is false.'[13] This is no radical scepticism or nominalist stance, sceptical about anything in general except names, but, rather, the recognition of our objectively uncertain position between the past and the future and a description of the manner in which we may find a way to move on in spite of blindness. In his own way, he faced the same paradox that Cardoso, Flores, Beer, Allende and others confronted in Chile during the 1960s and 1970s. Like movement in the story of Achilles and the tortoise, development (that perpetual race between developed and developing countries) may be nonsense. For it is not a function of who acquires what technology first (and thus, the ability to 'run faster') but, rather, a matter of orientation, which is always a political and a practical matter.

In their own way, these explorers faced the question of historical orientation having first escaped from the clutches of providence, the forces of progress, technological determinism, the logic of the market or the iron laws of history. They found out that the crucial question was how to deal with the consequences of the massive influx of people from the rural areas to the industrialised cities given that such industrial infrastructures were not up to the task and that the different actors – new businesspeople identified with the emergent multinational corporations, more traditional captains of industry still attached to the world of the *hacienda* and the nation, the military, the popular sectors swinging between their memories of anti-slavery struggle and the demands of success or revolution – seemed incapable of collective, coordinated action.

Thus, for instance, Cardoso found that the emergent 'business class' of Brazil, composed of new industrialists, 'new money' manufacturers and merchants, old captains of industry and landowners had a tendency to disavow the fact that inflationary and other financial situations were to the benefit of industrial expansions and helped to save them from lack of capital. Instead, as has happened once again in our time, after the 2008 crisis, they took a typical middle-class attitude and condemned the workers *qua* consumers for their excessive desires. Furthermore, they kept pushing government to expand bank credit for business without recognising any connection between these phenomena – financialisation of the economy, economisation of politics, culpabilisation of consumers, lifestyle demands imposed on them by the new facts of production and urban existence, and cyclical credit crises – and the marginalisation of workers and their turn towards radical politics.

According to Cardoso, the lack of what he called 'a clear orientation', a vision, a proper fiction – one which includes its own falsity, as Borges put it – allowed industrialists in Brazil and elsewhere in Latin America to identify in a general way with the people as a whole and to feel that their own interests were the interests of the nation as a whole. In this way they in fact fabricated generic frames of reference that ought to be interiorised by all of the peoples of the nation and even all of the nations of the globe: thus, for instance, they emphasised as an article of faith that

industrial growth in general would be the basis of future jobs and prosperity for everyone. In particular, those who had risen more recently to
wealth found it easier 'to feel an identification with workers, since they
see themselves as workers who have become more successful'.[14] The
result of this lack of an adequate fiction within the industrial group was
that the growth of the industrial sector in fact never destroyed the political order of the pre-industrial era. Personal links between men of wealth
and politicians continued; industrialists accommodated themselves to the
status quo: the 'patrimonial' state survived, as Cardoso observed, even
under the apparently contradictory guises of the 'welfare state' or, nowadays, the 'security state'.

As for the diverse paths of development between Europe and the
US on the one hand and Latin America on the other, it is best to
follow Cardoso's suggestion concerning the way in which urbanisation
and mass society, in particular the emergence of the kinds of expectations associated with urbanisation and massification, emerged in Latin
America before the economy got very far. Mass communications and
modern consumption styles put great pressure on inadequate productivity, 'and the response [was] to seek state aid and foreign assistance
[including foreign debt and renewed dependency] to meet demands'.[15]

In the context of the debates on social planning, collective action,
communication technologies and economic modelling that started in
the 1960s, and which took place not only in the US but also in Latin
America in countries like Chile, Cardoso's point about 'a lack of orientation' could be construed in terms of two paths opened up for economic
theory and political science (and practice) as both disciplines strengthened their relations with mathematics, forecasting and modelling. On the
one hand this was a trend associated with neoclassical economics, from
Pareto to Schumpeter, and a more 'traditional' tendency for a naturalist
and highly abstract use of mathematics in theorising, at the expense of
interpretative history, behavioural analysis and literature. On the other,
it was a form of economic modelling, planning and anticipatory politics that kept alive its links with biology, cognitive science, aesthetics
(literature, in particular) and the exploration of 'irrational' behaviour.
The latter was the path followed in Chile, not only in theory but also in

practice during the years of the rise to power of physician and socialist
politician Salvador Allende.

At the time of the publication of Fernando Henrique Cardoso and
Enzo Faletto's *Dependencia y Desarrollo en Latino América* (*Dependency and
Development in Latin America*, 1969) under the auspices of the research
and development seminar held by ECLA-ILPES, where the Brazilian
researchers continued their work after the 1964 military takeover
obliged them to leave their homeland, their own work concerning the
effects of the third wave of the industrial revolution on the economic
and political landscape of Latin America converged with the research
that physicians Humberto Maturana and Francisco J. Varela had developed separately and in connection with US-based scientists such as MIT
biologist Warren McCullough, Jerome Lettvin and a circle that also
included MIT mathematician Norbert Wiener and University of Illinois
electrical engineer Heinz von Foerster. Maturana and Varela, who kept
their contributions to Chilean cybernetics within the confines of their
laboratory during the 1960s and early 1970s, moved in the same circles as
the charismatic British and management-level industrialist Stafford Beer.
Beer's reading of Wiener's groundbreaking publication *Cybernetics* had
changed his life and sparked in him a lifelong interest in the application
of cybernetic principles to the steel industry. On occasion, during the
late 1960s and early 1970s, Maturana would leave the confines of his
laboratory to advise Beer on the theoretical aspects of the system that the
latter built for the Chilean government in the early 1970s. Beer knew of
Maturana's work before Allende came to power and ended up providing
the connection between his and Varela's work and the Chilean government's familiarity with and application of cybernetics, and, through it,
with the discussions and debates taking place at Raúl Prebisch's research
institute, ECLA-ILPES.

This connection would not be complete until Beer's arrival in Chile
in November 1971. However, upon reading Cardoso and Faletto's
insistence on 'self-reflexivity' rather than 'adaptation to external stim-
uli' and 'impersonal forces' as the key contribution of their *Dependency
and Development in Latin America*, it is difficult not to venture that the
surrounding environment of the research and development discussions

at ECLA-ILPES was facilitated by Chilean forays into the intersections between biology, cybernetics and economics. Already in 1962, the director of Chile's steel industry had requested the services of SIGMA (Science in General Management), a French-owned consultancy company that applied operational research and pioneering cybernetics techniques to business problems, whose director was none other than Stafford Beer. Beer put together a team of English and Spanish SIGMA employees who travelled to Chile and started working on the steel industry applying new principles of management inspired by new information and communication technologies. Their work soon expanded to cover Chile's railway network. One of the students employed by SIGMA to do intern work was Fernando Flores. He devoted himself to mastering the nuts and bolts of cybernetics and operations research and became quite familiar with Beer's work. He was also very active in political circles and in 1969 established, with a group of other young Chilean intellectuals, the Movement of Popular Unitary Action that later joined the Popular Unity coalition (UP) of Salvador Allende, a strategy that played a major role in Allende's victory in the 1970 presidential election.

In recognition of Flores' political and technical competence, the Allende administration appointed the twenty-eight-year-old as general technical manager of the Corporation for the Promotion of Production – *Corporación para el Fomento de la Producción* (CORFO), the state-development agency in charge of the nationalisation programme of the Chilean industry under the auspices of minister of economics and ECLA-ILPES director of the Development Division, Pedro Vuscovic. After Allende's inauguration, the government started implementing an economic plan designed by Vuscovic following Prebisch's ECLA principles, aimed at increasing purchasing power and aggregate demand through redistributive measures, particularly the increase of salaries and public expenditure. Chile's per capita income was $5,293 when Salvador Allende came to power. Between 1971 and 1972 it rose to between $5,492 and $5,663.[16] In the government's first year GDP grew by 7.7 per cent, production increased by 13.7 per cent and consumption levels rose by 11.6 per cent. In contrast, after the military coup that deposed Allende in 1973, Chile's per capita income fell to $4,323 in

1975. It would recover until 1981 on the back of the eighties financial bubble, only to fall back to $4,898 after the 1983 financial crisis. Per capita income in Chile would only recover its pre-coup levels in 1987, when it peaked at $5,590. These facts contradict the bad press that the Allende administration usually receives from revisionist historians.[17]

However, the rapid pace of the government's nationalisation programme, coupled with the lack of coordination between the government's plan and the different sectors of the social and political system that would have to put it into practice, exacerbated the fearful expectations of small and medium-level businessmen, while also sparking a frenzy of seizures of control of various factories by their workers against the explicit plans of Allende. Foreign investors opposing nationalisation without the expected monetary compensation further complicated the picture. In July 1971 political opposition mobilised against Allende and the politically unwieldy situation was compounded by the management difficulties created by the rapid pace of nationalisation and a series of politically motivated management appointments. By July 1971, the gap between the expectations of new urban consumers and the inadequacy of the Chilean productive and decision-making structure had created an explosive situation: consumption outstripped production, inflation rose together with a government spending deficit exacerbated by shrinking foreign reserves and the refusal of credit lines abroad.

On 13 July 1971, Fernando Flores wrote to Stafford Beer asking him for advice on how to implement 'on a national scale – at which cybernetic thinking becomes a necessity – scientific views on management and organization'.[18] The aim of Flores' team was to solve the problem of communication, coordination, decision-making and command that was crippling the attempted reform of the Allende government. By November 1971 Stafford Beer was in Santiago de Chile, ready to collaborate with a small government team put together by Flores on an ambitious project to apply cybernetics to the nationalisation effort. Project Cybersyn was born.

Today, we would call the sort of problem that Project Cybersyn was designed to deal with a problem of regulation. And since so many agree that the 2008 Great Recession was caused, among other things, by a failure of regulation, we must then recognise the pioneering vision of those who worked in the project in Chile in the 1970s. We must also acknowledge that, in spite of our apparent technological progress, we are in no way near solving the problem faced by the unorthodox team assembled in Chile. Their idea was fairly simple, as it brings to mind the Chinese box structure of Borges' fictional work: 'recursively speaking, the Chilean nation is embedded in the world of nations, and the government is embedded in the nation . . . all these are supposedly viable systems,' said Stafford Beer. This was meant as an analogy with biological systems 'in which the whole is always encapsulated in each part . . . this is a lesson learned from biology where we find the genetic blue-print of the whole organism in every cell'.[19] He might just as well have used one of Borges' short stories as an example.

Having identified their computer hardware options, the team settled on an existing telex network driven by the idea of creating a high-speed web of information exchange. Coupled with the computers and an Operations Room that seemed to have come straight from the set of *Star Trek*, Project Cybersyn embodied one of the closest precursors of the Internet of today. One part of the system, known as CHECO (Chilean Economy), was an ambitious effort to shape the Chilean economy and to provide simulations of future economic behaviour and was appropriately termed 'Future'. The Cyberstride suite generated its first printout on 21 March 1972. During the producers' strike of October 1972, Cybersyn proved instrumental in helping the UP government coordinate its response and mobilise its limited resources in a way that greatly reduced the impact of the industrialists' action. The strike had negative consequences for Allende's government in the long run, among them the incorporation of three senior members of the military into the Cabinet, but, thanks in great part to Cybersyn, it survived the crisis.

Following the strike, the network enabled the government to create a new form of economic mapping, collecting data from all over the country into a single report delivered daily to the presidential palace. This achievement represented a considerable advance over the previous six-month lag in the collection of statistical data on the Chilean economy. Moreover, Cybersyn had a political slant. Beer said that cybernetics 'should not develop its own ideology; but it should attest to one'. He recognised the dilemma of a cybernetic toolbox capable of increasing capitalist wealth or enforcing fascist control, but also perceived how it could make the pursuit of social goals more efficient while at the same time realising that social goals provided a purpose for regulating social action. In more ways than one, the project embodied the transition from the 'mode of production' to the 'mode of regulation' and the decisive role of subjectivity that has become the central feature of social life today. It also prefigured the centrality of collective action, subjectivity and the recovery of memory that has charted today's Latin American politics.

'Does it take more courage to be a cybernetician than to be a gunman?' asked Beer,[20] confronted by the frustrations of attempting to make the revolution work through democracy rather than through war and violence. On the morning of 11 September 1973, the Chilean armed forces launched a military coup against Allende led by General Augusto Pinochet. By 2.00 p.m. Allende was dead, incinerated by the flames engulfing the presidential palace. After the coup, the military tried to make sense of the Cybersyn Project, but, in spite of their awe at the sight of the Operations Room, they failed and decided to dismantle the system. The episode was forgotten, and the memory of a different path for our still ongoing digital revolution was erased.

Nevertheless, Beer's question is still relevant, perhaps today more so than ever, particularly in Latin America, as we contemplate the embattled fortunes of Venezuelans and Bolivians, as organised sectors of the population that were yesterday discounted try nowadays to take their destinies into their own hands. It is unfortunate that, as governments in Europe and the US look frantically for ways to engage an increasingly apathetic or resistant population, the efforts of Flores, Beer and their colleagues in Chile seem to us the stuff of science fiction novels. I wonder what Borges made of it, if he even came to know about it. If stories like this did not exist they would have to be invented. But this one was real.

The Story of the Warriors of Water

Some might say that Che Guevara's mistake was to have arrived in Bolivia forty years too early. If he were to arrive today, he would do so not in the rural region near Catavi and Ñancahuazú, but, rather, in District 14 of Cochabamba known to its impoverished inhabitants as Villa Pagador. In April 2000, the indigenous peoples of Upper Peru gathered together with other communities from the marginal zones of the city and the countryside, who still speak the Quechua and Aymara language of their ancestors, and stood up against the multinational corporation Bechtel, which tried to charge them for the most common of resources: water.

The episode is known as the Water Wars, and those who took part in it are referred to as the Warriors of Water. Even a seasoned guerrilla fighter like Che Guevara could have learned a few political lessons from them. On 4 February 2000 the poor indigenous people of Bolivia took to the streets to reclaim their natural right to have access to water. In response, elected president and former dictator of Bolivia Hugo Bánzer declared martial law and sent in the police to hammer protesters for days with tear gas and rubber bullets, leaving 175 mostly young people injured, two of them blinded. Bánzer suspended civil rights, banned gatherings and severely limited the freedom of the press. 'We see it as our obligation,' said the former dictator, using the first person plural often reserved for monarchs in those countries that still have a monarchy, 'and in the common best interest, to decree a state of emergency in order to protect law and order.' Back then, the same white mestizos who now beat their chests in Santa Cruz, Bogotá or Washington every time Evo Morales flexes his muscle to wrestle the truth from an all-too complacent media, said nothing.

President Bánzer kept on confusing 'the common best interest' with the interests of Bechtel Corporation, the world's leading engineering company behind the international conglomerate Aguas del Tunari, which owned the recently auctioned water services in Bolivia, and mistaking their profit as the 'law and order' to be protected. Following the World Bank's neoliberal recipe of privatisation, deregulation and protection of foreign investment, and lending to transnational economic policy the heavy weight of local armed forces, the Bánzer government had turned water and other natural resources into mere commodities to buy and sell in the global market. In doing so, he divided Bolivians into those who have access to water because they can pay for it and those who cannot. The latter became 'disposable peoples', who are part of Bolivia but in the end are discounted from it.

The story about the division and exposure of entire populations is characteristic of neoliberal governments all over the world, but in the case of Bolivia, those who were supposedly worth nothing and counted for nothing in the real world had a moment of clarity. At that moment they acquired a vision, the sort of clarity and vision that can only be achieved in decisive moments of collective action. In this respect, the resistance of the poor peoples of Bolivia against the global designs of Bechtel Corporation stands as a key example of Latin America turning away from globalisation and discarding Thomas Friedman's golden straitjacket.

In 2000, the Aymara Indian population of Bolivia resisted President Bánzer, martial law and the global might of Bechtel Corporation. 'I am in awe at what we were able to accomplish together,' said Jim Schultz, an American who became part of the '*We, the people*' that the Indian majority of Bolivia assembled in order to do the unthinkable: kick out Bechtel, rid themselves of the World Bank's conditionality and denounce the globalist mantra that until then appeared to have written the last chapter in their long epic of suffering. For theirs is indeed an epic. In the thirteenth century the Inca extended their confederation to include the Aymara population of Upper Peru, today's Bolivia. Three hundred years later Francisco Pizarro captured and held for ransom the Inca ruler Atahualpa in Cajamarca, bringing the confederation to an end. Not long after, European conquistadors, governments, merchants and investors were accruing the benefits of the silver mines in Upper Peru. Aymara and Quechua Indians provided most of the slave labour that made it possible for Spanish America to provide the bulk of the silver essential to the functioning of monetary systems around the globe. According to the often cited 1811 estimations of Alexander von Humboldt, between 1492 and 1803 the total value of silver production in Latin America, most of it concentrated in Bolivia and Mexico, surpassed four billion pesos. The largest silver mine of all time, that of Potosí in Bolivia, produced large quantities of precious metals late in the sixteenth century with a total of some 13,000 forced labourers, all of them Indian. Their tasks included digging mine tunnels with pick and shovel, with the occasional help of powder explosives. The refining of the minerals extracted was carried out first by the smelting method but increasingly with mercury amalgamation, which entails exposure to poisonous fumes.

Formal independence from the Spanish Empire in the nineteenth century did not change their situation. As in the American west and south, they continued to be marginalised and discriminated against, robbed of their lands and obliged to work under different variations of the *mita*, *encomienda* and *hacienda* patrimonial systems under which they were systematically, even legally, classified as child-like, a cultural minority in thrall of 'idolatrous' and 'irrational' practices who were 'archaic' and 'backward', put in the care of 'wardens' who profited from their labour. By 1900, the hereditary elites who had presided over the Bolivian state since formal independence was declared were inventively creating new ways of regulating the life and expectations of Indians. The 1900 Census created a frame of reference in which race and location were also implicit signs of class: 'whites' referred to urban proprietors, established businessmen and absentee landowners; 'mestizos' included urban workers and emergent merchants and low-level employees; 'Indians' comprised the class of rural or mining workers and female domestic servants. There were also 'Negroes' and those who fell under the catch-all 'No Answer'. According to these categories, the Indian population of Bolivia represented 48.5 per cent of the total, that is to say a minority. However, as in Borges' fiction, here one must look for the total in the part. As the authors of the census explained, 'war and successive epidemics had decimated the Indian populations since 1879', which they considered doomed to extinction.[21] This social Darwinist 'scientific' interpretation framed their organisation of the data: according to that frame there could be no 'urban' Indians.

Half a century later, in 1950, occupational categories played a wider role and, as a result of the recognition of indigenous workers in towns, cities and mining centres, the percentage of those classified as Indians rose to 63 per cent. Two years later, on 11 April 1952, an armed insurrection swept the country. Its epicentre was the mining region, and at its centre were Indian peasants and mining workers. The new party in power, the Nationalist Revolutionary Movement (MNR), a loose coalition of miners, nationalised the mining industry and, in true populist style, allotted expropriated land to peasant and indigenous families. But it also neutralised the vitality demonstrated by indigenous social movements during the mobilisation by reducing the dynamism and creativity of their living memory to a matter of museum collections and subordinating their historical role to that of the past of the modern nation-state. In this way, Indians were once again discounted.

The populist state of 1952 was succeeded by a series of military coups that culminated in the 1971 putsch launched by Colonel Hugo Bánzer against the left-leaning government of President Juan José Torres. Torres's call for a People's Assembly with representatives of specific popular sectors, among them indigenous peoples, and the nationalisation of Gulf Oil interests in the country angered the already uneasy white sector of the population concentrated in Santa Cruz and, crucially, the Nixon administration in the United States. With alleged support from the US and the Brazilian military regime, Bánzer launched a successful coup that sent Torres into exile in Argentina. Once there, Torres was kidnapped and assassinated by death squads close to the Videla military regime of Argentina as part of the infamous Operation Condor launched informally in 1973 as a proposal 'to extend the exchange of information' between various Latin American intelligence services in order to coordinate efforts in 'the struggle against subversion'.[22]

Towards the end of Bánzer's *de facto* government, another national census, this time adopting a linguistic criterion to establish its classifications, revealed that 68.5 per cent of Bolivians spoke an indigenous language. The census underestimated those who recognised themselves as Indians even though they no longer spoke their native language. Self-identification became the main criterion of the 1996 United Nations Development Program survey, which revealed that only 16 per cent of Bolivia's population identified themselves as Indians. Combined at times with the 1900 criterion of locality, the 1996 survey succeeded in 'demonstrating' that Indians were the minority. In fact, what the survey demonstrated was the recursive effect between neoliberal reforms and people's expectations at the subjective level. At the time, as Aymara historian Silvia Rivera

Cusicanqui observes, 'it was assumed that the liberalization of the market, relocation and migration would precipitate a massive conversion of indigenous people into mestizo "citizens," though situated at the lowest levels of citizenship'.[23] This assumption informed policies of 'training' worth millions of dollars in international aid aimed at creating a sense of 'citizenship', however partial, among Indians, which would have consequences for their identification as indigenous peoples. Therefore, these are in fact acculturation programmes aimed at providing second-class citizenship.

The Essence of Neoliberalism

On the one hand the 1996 survey seems 'to corroborate the long process of acculturation and degradation of ethnic' recognition that has resulted from 'the advance of world capitalism and rural-to-urban migratory processes'.[24] On the other hand, surveys like this map out the varying responses of peoples in the periphery of the global economic system to its expansion from the centre, and to the various demands for reference posited to them by such a centre, which include 'positive' and 'negative' images. And since this is a matter of the imaginary, the range of phenomena that are being measured, perhaps unintentionally, include imitation, identification and sympathy but also, crucially, expectations. The economic challenge, neoliberalism, is thus internalised as 'the most likely avenue to social advancement' in relation to the given set of options. Unsurprisingly, in this context the choice tends to be 'individual perseverance and striving', rather than, say, collective mobilisation. For this is the part which, embedded in the whole, defines the whole. If the surface appearance of neoliberalism is competition, then in terms of self-perception and the realisation of expectations, what one needs to be is a persevering and striving individual, and this is its hard kernel and essence. To choose anything else just will not do.

And if from the point of view of Indians and Afro-Latin Americans, confronted with the challenge of living in a neoliberal world, this means going against the memory and practices passed on by those who came before them, then it seems rational to abandon the latter. Thus, as the Indian or black middle class continues to expand, those of its members who wish to express their *indigeneity* or their *negritude* may tend to do so 'not through political action but rather through the pleasures of consumption: more specifically, consumption of "black" [or "Indian"] clothes, music, hairstyles and art'.[25] In a way, these surveys offer concrete evidence of the argument according to which contemporary global capitalism takes place as a mode of regulation – the absolute frame within which we can order our preferences and shape our expectations – rather than as a simple mode of production.

The point is, however, that in presenting itself as the very limit of what is possible – or, to put it in literary terms, as a fiction without falsity – neoliberalism makes itself vulnerable to attack from an unexpected angle: the impossible, or what Borges called 'the infinite'.[26] The case of the Water Wars and the rise to power of the Indians of Bolivia exemplifies what is meant by 'the impossible'. In the strictest terms, from the vantage point of the results of the UNDP 1996 survey and the 1994 Indigenous Census of the Lowlands of Bolivia, also co-financed by UNDP, the results of the 2001 Census showing that a surprising 62 per cent of the population of the country identified themselves as indigenous, and the events that took place between these surveys and thereafter – the Water Wars, the massive mobilisations in El Alto and La Paz, the rise to power of Evo Morales's MAS, the People's Constituent Assembly and so on – were simply impossible, or at the very least unthinkable. They were, strictly speaking, improbable.

In 1996, the unquestioned hegemony of neoliberal thinking was expressed in the pragmatics of structural adjustment policies.[27] The structural adjustment policies advocated by the International Monetary Fund and the World Bank, often attached contractually as 'conditions' for loans, and thus imposed upon governments, were ambiguous. This is so in the sense that the privatisation of natural resources such as water or the criminalisation of coca leaf crops introduced new divisions into an already critical situation. And yet, as Silvia Rivera Cusicanqui says, 'the elites were still naively confident in IMF and World Bank recipes for overcoming the critical situation of the Bolivian economy'.[28] The elites bought the stories sold or imposed by the IMF and the World Bank as if they could not possibly be false, as the very limit of the possible, *as the very image of the future*. Consequently, their expectations about the future, their own future and that of Bolivia, were formed in response to such strict frames of reference. But then, when consumers did not get what they were promised (instead of 'more efficient' private water services they got unpayable charges and thus no water whatsoever) consumption became a political act, and something the elites could not have contemplated actually occurred.

Since consumption involved self-identification, the betrayal of their expectations revealed to consumers, the *real* majority, not only the temporary shortcomings of the policies of privatisation, but in reality the very falsity of the image of the persevering and thriving private individual. In an act of memory-retrieval, collective action became the only way ahead, however improbable it may have seemed in terms of the past. To put it in a way reminiscent of one of John Maynard Keynes' most famous quotes: the facts changed and people changed their minds accordingly. However, in order to understand correctly what happened in Bolivia between 1996 and 2000 we must also remember that there are two ways of establishing the facts: after the fact (*ex post facto*) and before the fact (*ex ante facto*). The latter are anticipatory judgements, of the kind that become possible when we contemplate an image of the future and its error, and in the face of such a contingency (which Borges called a falsity) we change course and keep going. What we discover in such occasions is that no certainty is written in stone. 'Such illusions,' says Rivera Cusicanqui in relation to the investment of Bolivian elites on the certainties propagated by the IMF and the World Bank, 'had evaporated by 2000.'

In the first mobilisation, the so-called Water Wars that took place between February and April 2000, an unprecedented alliance among factory workers, farmers on irrigated lands, coca growers, and the marginalised urban population of Villa Pagador, took place in the streets of Cochabamba to refuse the terms of the social and economic relationship between people and water proposed by Aguas del Tunari, the subsidiary of Bechtel Corporation. As Rivera Cusicanqui says, 'in the highlands the movement opposed to the law privatizing water . . . decreed a massive road blockade, which reached its climax on 9 April 2000'. That day, two leaders of the blockade who had gone to meet the army and establish rules of engagement with a view to avoiding casualties were assassinated in cold blood by the troops. In response, the Indians 'brutally lynched an army captain, provoking a wave of racist outrage and fierce commentaries in the media'.[29]

In the second mobilisation, which lasted almost a month between September and October, the routes that connected the main Andean cities of Bolivia were completely cut off. The interruption of supplies to the cities reached critical limits and indigenous memory and self-recognition in the cities of El Alto and La Paz became evident when the indigenous peoples of Bolivia declared that they rejected military conscription in the state army, formed an indigenous government in the regions in revolt and decreed a 'state of exception' in a vast part of the country, thereby prohibiting entrance for state officials and assuming control of local administrative affairs within the region. The actions were equivalent to a massive expulsion of colonial invaders. In the process, what was a 'residual' indigenous self-recognition became a self-affirming subjectivity with a political strategy with which to face what Rivera Cusicanqui calls 'the imposed burdens of corporate capital along with the cultural impositions of the Eurocentric elites and their neocolonial style of managing the country'.[30] This explains the results of the 2001 Census.

A Viable End to the War on Drugs

In between the 2000 Water Wars and the next unprecedented Indian uprising that took place in October 2003, following a massacre of Indians and poor people in the city of El Alto and on the outskirts of La Paz, stands a seemingly disconnected event: in 1988 the *United Nations Convention Against Illicit Traffic in Narcotic Drugs and Psychotropic Substances* introduced the notion of 'licit traditional uses' of the coca leaf.[31] The notion was legally established in order to protect what at the time seemed a purely residual form of coca consumption among some of the indigenous peoples of Bolivia, Peru and southern Colombia, soon to become extinct under the pressure of the 'westernisation' of coca leaf producers and consumers. These included such practices as the *mambeo*, or chewing of the coca leaf, the *coqueo* or *akhulliku*, similar to but not exactly chewing, the use of herbal teas, rituals, coca flour for culinary purposes and so on. However, as in the case of the expectations set by the 1950 and the 1996 censuses, rather than becoming extinct these traditional 'licit uses' continued and, in some cases, expanded.

In fact, under the regulation brought about by the 1988 UN Convention, the legal and quasi-legal market of the coca leaf widened and prices rose steadily, a fact that serves as evidence of the existence of an internal and transnational market that surpasses the usual notions of 'traditional consumption' in so far as it incorporates modern urban and new types of consumers in Bolivia, the north of Argentina and elsewhere. This includes forms of quasi-ritual or modern social consumption, part of the lifestyle associated with the gaucho life of Santa Cruz and Beni, validated through its associations with the middle- and upper-class Argentine white people who frequently visit the region, and also endurance-related consumption by sugar-cane workers and loggers who have adopted the habits of Amazonian indigenous groups, artisans and truckers and even young people using the leaf for another kind of nightlife endurance.

From Bolivia to northern Argentina, Peru, Ecuador and southern Colombia, an emerging industry of wines, soft drinks (including the indigenous brand Coca Sek, which is sold by the Nasa people of southern Colombia as an alternative to Coca-Cola), teas, breads, flours and energy drinks holds the key to a viable alternative to the deadly 'war on drugs' imposed on these countries, and now upon Mexico as well, right on the border, if not already within the border of the United States, with well-documented and undesirable consequences. 'Both the traditional and surplus producers of coca thus face a demand for coca leaf that is not only growing but ever-more stratified and quality oriented, and that could grow even more if it had the proper international legislation and state and private support,' says Silvia Rivera Cusicanqui. As she observes, this would amount to an alternative to the 'war on drugs', one that would 'remove the surplus coca from the grip of the illegal economy by opening a high-value legal market of an expansive, quality-oriented world market'.[32] As she says, in the era of new-age medicines, energy supplements and alternative body-and-mind health products, this could be both a viable solution and a defence against illegal uses of the cheap, low-quality raw material that has grown out of control in many areas of South and North America, Europe and elsewhere.

In the massive demonstrations and roadblocks in Bolivia in October 2003 expressions of a renewed Indian memory proliferated and were translated into the creation of a network of communal solidarities 'in which women, the rites, and *akhulliku* served as invisible . . . bonds of solidarity that opposed the homogenizing designs of the global market . . . and its model of individual citizenship'.[33] This is a modern *indigeneity*, which rediscovers the legacy of the immemorial inhabitants of the Andes and the Amazon in order to find orientation, collective as well as individual, in the face of an uncertain future. To speak of 'the rights of Earth Mother' in this context, as President Evo Morales does during his visits to Europe and the US, has nothing to do with archaic motifs but, rather, as in the case of the coca leaf, it becomes a way to seek alternatives, enlightenment, a programme in fact, an image of the future that contrasts with the less desirable prospects of a world in thrall to climate change, drugs and resource wars, and thereby goads us into action.

In October 2003, the popular revolt led by the Indians of Bolivia brought down the government of Gonzalo Sánchez de Lozada, a white mestizo who spoke Spanish with an affected English accent and had become the successor of former dictator Hugo Bánzer. Two years later, in December 2005, an Aymara leader from the Chapare region who led the local coca growers' union, now known to the world as Evo Morales from Bolivia, won the presidential election at the helm of an Indian-led coalition with almost 54 per cent of the vote. At the time, these events were almost universally regarded as unwelcome triumphs of regressive forces opposed to free markets and free trade that were standing in the way of the unstoppable forces of globalisation and represented potentially global security threats.

'The idea that in Bolivia the rural and urban indigenous people who led the October revolt [and the Water Wars] against the government . . . or voted massively for Evo Morales' Movement Toward Socialism (MAS) were "archaic" or "backward" – that they were resisting modern market discipline in a kind of cultural or racial atavism – is part of an unquestioned common sense among the elites, as much in Bolivia as in the developed world.'[34] There are now signs that such a common sense is beginning to break down. Following Evo's election, indigenous and peasant memory and knowledge has become a political force to be reckoned with, regionally and worldwide. It is as if, five hundred years after the genocide that took place in the Americas, we have all been given a second chance. Perhaps now, when the Indians of the Andes and the Amazon speak, we will listen.

10

The Solution to All Our Problems

Heroes and a City in Flames

When he arrived in Rio de Janeiro in 1991, economist Fernando Fajnzylber was full of optimism. It was early in the year, when low clouds and driving rain hide the surrounding backdrop of high-peaked mountains and only the lower slopes of the Sugar Loaf are clearly visible from the grand Bay of Guanabara. The sight is enough to fill one's heart with deep emotions. At least in that sense it has not changed much since Lord Cochrane, the Dauntless, entered the Bay from Cape Horn on 13 March 1822. Back then, Lord Cochrane sailed past the fort guarding the harbour's entrance and laid anchor among the ships stationed off the waterfront. He, too, felt elevated by the sight of Sugar Loaf Mountain, and the warm welcome given to him by the port officer and Prince Pedro's government. He was already quite famous, a frigate captain with a brilliant record, a fearless fighter with a penchant for radical causes, 'a friend of the oppressed and a champion of liberty'.[1] When Lord Byron read in the London papers about Lord Cochrane's participation in the liberation of Chile and Peru from Spanish colonial rule between 1818 and 1822, he wrote: 'There is no man I envy so much as Lord Cochrane.' Sir Walter Scott wrote a poem in his honour. In Brazil, Thomas Cochrane's story would become legend.

Something similar occurred to Fernando Fajnzylber. He was not a seaman and there are no poems about his life and adventures. But, like Cochrane, he was a shrewd strategist, a fearless fighter for radical causes and a friend of liberty and the poor. Like the famous English admiral, he was an adventurous innovator and a man of action, in many ways a romantic and a radical. And, like Cochrane, his actions in Brazil would have profound consequences, deep enough to outlive him and reverberate around the world. Just about every single line that has been written about politics and economics in Europe and the United States in the wake of the global financial crisis, as well as being argued in the debates that set 'New Right' liberal economists like Zhang Weiying against 'New Left' critics like Wang Hui in the China of 'the twenty-first-century miracle', can be traced back to the work that Fajnzylber and his colleagues at ECLAC, the UN Economic Commission for Latin America and the Caribbean, developed between the 1970s and the 1990s. Without them we would all be at a loss in the increasingly uncertain seas of globalisation after the Great Recession.

ECLAC had been born as ECLA, the Economic Commission for Latin America, before the word Caribbean was added to its name in the 1980s. The year was 1947 and the United States had taken its place as the dominant world power in opposition to the Soviet Union, following their joint triumph over the Axis forces in Europe, Asia, Africa and some parts of the Americas during World War II. On 15 February the US proposed in the newly formed United Nations the creation of two regional commissions within the UN Economic and Social Council (ECOSOC) to oversee the reconstruction effort in Europe and the East. 'Latin Americans were not happy with the regional favouritism, and the government of Chile, with the support of other developing and Latin members of ECOSOC (Cuba, Peru and Venezuela) introduced a resolution that the UN also create the Economic Commission for Latin America.'[2] As usual, they all forgot about Africa. Latin Americans argued that the region was exhausted after the war effort. The US, Britain, Canada and other industrialised countries including the Soviet Union balked at the proposal. After all, US delegate William Thorpe reminded his colleagues at the UN, the Pan-American Union already existed with its own Economic and Social Council. The resolution to the ensuing debate was so split on north-south lines that a special committee had to be appointed to study the merits of the case, a sign of things to come. Citing wartime use of capital equipment, the high cost of the economic losses incurred during the war and the need for transnational coordination to accelerate growth, the resulting report supported its creation.

ECLA was born officially on 7 June 1948 in Santiago de Chile. The shallowness of US support for ECLA became apparent when it used the IX Inter-American Conference in Bogotá on 9 April 1948 to recast the Pan-American Union into the Organization of American States (OAS) and issued a direct challenge by increasing its Economic and Social Council budget from $40,000 to $500,000, or equivalent to ECLA's entire projected budget.[3] The stage was set for a tense relationship between the new American-dominated OAS and the capacity of ECLA to forge an independent path of economic development that would become highly influential in an increasingly autonomous Latin America.

These events must be set in the context of an extraordinary period in international history. After World War II, with its industrial supremacy now unchallenged after decades of consolidation under the Hamiltonian model of economic development, the United States started liberalising its trade and championing the cause of freer trade. The United States' now proven military might, paralleled only (but not for long) by that of the Soviet Union, provided further impulse to America's rise to a position of global influence. While the new inter-American system was being created, largely to defend the interests of the United States, which had dominated the recent discussions about the establishment of the United Nations and even managed to move the meetings of the organisation from London to New York, President Harry S. Truman, who had taken the decision in 1945 to drop two atomic bombs on Japan,[4] 'had now declared a worldwide crusade against communism. The CIA had been set up in 1947 as part of the anti-communist struggle, and the Pope had tacitly supported the American line; Truman got himself re-elected on the strength of this position.'[5] The state of Israel had been founded, NATO had been established, the first salvos of the Cold War had been fired (including the USSR's own first atom bomb test) and the Chinese civil war that led on 1 October 1949 to Mao Zedong's declaration of the People's Republic of China was well under way.

In Latin America, the Cuban Revolution was only a decade ahead. The events of 9 April 1948 in Bogotá, now known as *El Bogotazo*, came close to realising America's fears of revolutionary contamination in its own 'backyard'. The main protagonist in these events, the popular leader Jorge Eliécer Gaitán, embodied such fears as well as the threat of economic autonomy and regional integration that an organisation like ECLA entailed. In the minds of those representing the American delegation attending the conference in Bogotá, and in particular General Marshall, there was a direct connection between the eruption of popular discontent of *El Bogotazo*, the autonomist stance of leaders like Gaitán and organisations like ECLA in Latin America, and the threat of revolutionary contamination to the US's recently acquired taste for freer trade. And so, although *El Bogotazo* shifted the attention of delegates and the public in general to more urgent matters, Marshall and others did everything in their power to make sure that the OAS was finally established in direct competition with ECLA. Whatever the immediate and apparent causes of *El Bogotazo*, the tensions that led to the creation of the OAS in a bid to undermine ECLA were lived out in the streets of Bogotá. Such tensions framed, and gave a wider significance to, what happened on the ground.

On 9 April 1948 in Bogotá, while the Pan-American Conference was busily establishing the OAS, local hero Jorge Eliécer Gaitán was assassinated. In the aftermath, a wave of fury and hysteria swept through the city. Days of rioting, looting and confrontations between the armed forces and the people in revolt followed, which then spilled over into a frenzy that covered the whole of Colombia in blood. To Colombians, 9 April inaugurated a period of indescribable violence that seemingly continues to this day. Back then they called it simply *La Violencia* (the Violence); today Colombians have no name for its contemporary reincarnations and many in fact deny that such violence still takes place, in spite of all evidence to the contrary.

Gaitán was the most charismatic and popular politician in twentieth-century Colombian politics and one of the most successful political figures of Latin America's long period of populist politics, 'an outstanding lawyer who had imbibed a potent political cocktail offered by the Mexican Revolution, Marxism and Mussolini . . . [and] the hero of the rising proletarian classes and of many lower-middle-class inhabitants of the rapidly growing cities'.[6] He first came to international attention in 1929 when he took up the case of the banana workers striking against the United Fruit Company, massacred by Colombian security forces in the Caribbean town of Ciénaga in December 1928. Twenty years later, the man his enemies among the Creole elites disparagingly called 'El Negro' ('the Black Man') had become a political force to be reckoned with. He denounced 'the political country', the emerging and vaguely formed class of politicians in thrall to landowners, captains of industry, new industrialists and transnational interests, as the aloof oppressor of 'the national country', the rural and urban rabble, disposed of by the thousands in the myriad civil wars invented by 'red' Liberals and 'blue' Conservatives to serve interests other than their own.

A member of the Liberal Party himself, Gaitán had risen to the top of the political pile on the back of his only weapon: his words. His speeches fell upon his enemies like lightning bolts and worked their prophetic magic among the crowds who filled the galleries when he appeared in court and followed him by the thousands in gigantic silent marches, lit only by torches, that paralysed the city at night. He spoke for them; he put their thoughts and feelings into words. He did not talk about national pride, order or delusions of empire, but against them. By the time of his assassination on 9 April 1948, Jorge Eliécer Gaitán was well on his way to becoming the first elected socialist president in the Americas.

Because of that, and because of his defence of the banana workers of Ciénaga, Santa Marta and Aracataca in *la costa* – as the Caribbean coast of Colombia was known to its inhabitants – Gaitán was well known to the then young university and *costeño* law student Gabriel García Márquez. On that April day García Márquez was sitting down to lunch in his *pensión*, a boarding house located in Florián Street, not far from where Gaitán had his law practice, situated on Seventh Avenue and 14th Street, when the latter was shot twice in the chest and once in the head at precisely 1.15 p.m. He was pronounced dead on arrival at the local hospital a few minutes later. A friend of García Márquez who had seen the dying leader's body lying on the floor ran to the boarding house and told the young writer and his other friends, who immediately rushed to the scene of the murder. When they arrived, the assassin had already been lynched by the mob and men and women wept inconsolably, the latter soaking their Sunday-best headscarves in the blood of the fallen martyr. Soon, Bogotá was in flames, the riots quickly turning into mass rebellion.

Another young Latin American, a delegate to the Youth Student Congress organised in opposition to the Pan-American Conference taking place in Bogotá, took to the streets with the intention of witnessing first hand what looked like a revolution in the making. Two days earlier he had interviewed Gaitán in his office. Apparently, the Colombian politician was so impressed by him that they had scheduled another meeting for that very day, at 2.00 p.m. The young student had expected Gaitán to deliver the final speech at the congress. His name was Fidel Castro Ruiz. Events unfolded, snipers positioned themselves in the buildings near the Presidential Palace, people joined in the rioting, Gaitán's followers accused the Conservative government led by Mariano Ospina Pérez of having orchestrated the assassination and called on the people to take up arms and marched upon Bolívar Square, outside the Presidential Palace.

The Palace, also known as Casa de Nariño, was attacked with bricks, stones and Molotov cocktails. The leaders of Gaitán's Liberal Party pleaded with the crowd to stop the violence; undeterred, the multitudes attempted to force their way into the Presidential Palace and were fired upon by the security forces. Many were killed. Most of them were homeless people who had come to Bogotá to escape Conservative political repression in the rural areas – peasants of indigenous and Afro-Latin American origin, artisans and workers from the Perseverancia and Egipto quarters to the east of the main square and the Presidential Palace, in the hills, or from the proletarian neighbourhood of San Victorino, to the west. Both forces converged on the city centre with the intention of seizing power.

The government responded by sending tanks to crush the rebellion, and the army to protect the house of one of the wealthiest Colombian families in the north of Bogotá where the hero of the US Pacific War and winner of the Nobel Peace Prize, General George Catlett Marshall, attending the Pan-American Conference, was staying. The president's

wife had sent their eight-year-old son to the American Embassy for
safety. With the Pan-American Conference bereft of a host government
and foundering, Marshall urged his aides to find a way to save it. On 10
April, while the riots were still going on, Marshall and his aides managed
to initiate an urgent meeting of the remaining delegates, rounding them
up with the help of a driver and a guard flown in from Panama during
the night. Every delegation, except the Colombian, attended the 10
April meeting at the Honduran Embassy, where General Marshall said
that 'under no circumstances should the Conference fail to draft the
Charter of the Organization of American States, for to do so would play
right into the hands of the Communists everywhere, who were now
taking credit for the attempt to destroy Bogotá'.[7] Marshall was referring to the radical leaders of the Liberal Party and other political groups
– among them Diego Montaña Cuéllar, Carlos Restrepo Piedrahita,
Jorge Zalamea – who had taken to the radio stations and announced the
establishment of a Revolutionary Council, while the more moderate
Liberal leaders attempted to find a compromise with the Conservative
president in his palace. The delegates to the Pan-American Conference
voted unanimously to continue the conference after Marshall's speech.
The Colombians moved proceedings to a boys' school to the north of
the city centre, and Marshall departed to safety in the United States.
Meanwhile, in Bogotá, the tanks rolled towards the Presidential Palace,
propelled, it seemed, by vast numbers of people, some of whom sat on
top of them, carrying red flags and shouting Gaitán's name.

But as soon as they arrived at Casa de Nariño the tanks turned their
guns against the people and fired on them.[8] The moderate wing of
the Liberal Party reached an agreement with the Ospina government
according to which some of them would join his Cabinet. Effectively,
the agreement left the Liberal Party out of power for another decade
and plunged the country into an even more savage era of violence and
repression. The events of the day, El Bogotazo, showed the upper classes
the dangers represented by the urban workers invoking their memories of rural suffering, liberty and political self-sufficiency. Never again
would a politician arise with such ability to speak for the masses and
stand with them. With every year that has passed since Gaitán's death,

'Colombia has moved further away from solving its real political problems'. Instead, 'it was the crisis following his [Gaitán's] death' which gave rise to the leftist guerrilla movements and far-right paramilitary groups 'that continue to compromise political life in the country until this very day', as Gerald Martin observes in his biography of García Márquez.[9]

General Marshall flew back to the United States convinced that the whole conspiracy had been arranged from Moscow. Subsequently, the Colombian government broke off diplomatic relations with the Soviet Union. A week after the events of 9 April, the young Colombian writer Gabriel García Márquez and the young Cuban agitator Fidel Castro Ruiz set off, as Martin has it, 'from Bogotá on different planes towards their different historical destinies'. Destiny would bring them back together later in their lives, forging one of the most crucial friendships in Latin America's history. What happened on 9 April 1948 in Bogotá left an indelible mark on both of them: García Márquez abandoned his law studies in the city, went back to his beloved *costa* and became the most successful writer of twentieth-century Latin America. Never again did he take the two ruling parties seriously. For Castro, these events would be as crucial in developing a concept of revolutionary politics 'as later events in Guatemala in 1954 [when the democratically elected government of Jacobo Arbenz was toppled] would be to his future comrade Che Guevara'.[10] The IX Conference continued and the OAS Charter was established along American lines. Partly, this was due to the fact that Marshall and his aides, and the delegates, managed to stay in contact at all times. The same went for the Colombian government and its loyal circles. Some say the revolution failed in Colombia because the rioters forgot one simple detail: they never cut the telephone lines.

The Long Story of Crucifixion Economics

Telephones can stop a revolution. They can also help start a new era in geopolitical and economic relations. They remind us of the power of modern technology: on the one hand advanced technologies save time and shorten distance. On the other, they create another kind of distance. Such is the gap separating peoples and countries that have advanced technologies from those that do not. The fate of our world rests on that gap. It may be strange to think that everything hinges upon a gap, a void, if you like. But as one of the characters in Samuel Beckett's *Waiting for Godot* says, there is never a lack of void. For what is the shape of such geopolitical and economic relations when one nation appears to others alone and exceptional?

So wondered Argentina's ambassador-at-large Carlos Brebbia in 1941 when he wrote a letter from Berne, Switzerland, to his friend and then director of Argentina's Central Bank, Raúl Prebisch. 'What will the Americans do,' he asked Prebisch, 'now that they have all the world's gold in their possession? I sometimes imagine it may be like a person who has collected all the telephones in the world and can no longer ring up anyone.'[11] He was referring to the fact that the German invasion of Poland had totally transformed the European financial scene. Afterwards, every western European government was consumed with the need to mobilise for war. Holland was putting two million florins a day into defence, Britain was investing £6 million sterling daily – leaving no cash with which to pay for its imports of beef and wheat from Argentina, thereby depriving the latter of its principal source of hard currency to pay for its imports from the US. As every major European country borrowed up to the hilt from the United States at whatever the cost, the direction of the river of gold and silver that until then had been flowing from Latin America to the Old World, now changed direction towards the northern part of the New World. New York was now the financial centre of the world.

How had that happened? How did the US all of sudden become the holder of all the telephone and financial lines of the world? You could say that the United States successfully borrowed and perfected an idea from their former colonisers, the British, who had themselves borrowed and perfected it from their previous foes, the Spanish, who in turn had chanced upon the idea (but never quite managed to perfect it) as they came to terms with the wider significance of the 'discovery' of the New World. In his book *A Plan of the English Commerce* (1728), spy, businessman, tax collector, political commentator, economist and, as if that was not enough, novelist Daniel Defoe described the rise of the absolutist monarchic state in Britain under the Tudors through their alliance with the emergent merchant and landowning bourgeoisie. Using protectionism, subsidies, distribution of monopoly rights and charters of incorporation, government-sponsored industrial espionage and piracy and other means of government intervention, including the sanctioning of the slave trade, Henry VII, Henry VIII and Elizabeth I developed England's woollen manufacturing industry, which was Europe's high-tech industry at the time. The industry was then concentrated in today's Belgium and the Netherlands, to which Britain had exported its raw wool in the past, making a reasonable profit, just as Argentina would do until the early twentieth century exporting its raw meat and wheat to Britain. Since those who do difficult things that others cannot do and take advantage of it tend to earn more profit, the Tudors sought to change the situation and establish an indigenous manufacturing industry.

It took nearly a hundred years more for Britain's 'import substitution industrialisation' model to work, defying the market 'truth' that it should remain as an efficient producer of raw wool. Further impulse to the model set up by the Tudors came first from Oliver Cromwell's and then from Robert Walpole's policies. The former decided during the republican period after the English Revolution to seize trade through colonisation, involving bankers, insurers and investors even more as financiers of revenue-generating enterprises, and consolidating British sea power while continuing to promote woollen manufacturing, thereby widening Britain's reach into the global market, its access to labour power and remodelling the institutions of the state so as better to represent the rise of the merchant class relative to both the aristocracy and the more radical democratic sectors of the commoner class. Robert Walpole, Britain's first Prime Minister, for whom Daniel Defoe spied, introduced legislation in 1721 aimed at extending the protection of manufacturing industries from foreign competition, subsidising them and encouraging them to export. At the root of such legislation was the principle of roaming the seas and the world to buy cheap and to sell dear, redirecting the flow of hard currency, technological innovation and people's labour power in your direction,[12] just as the Spanish had done as they established the basis for true global trade back in the sixteenth century. Walpole's policies, which built upon and perfected that basic principle, remained in place for the next century and gave

Britain the edge over its competitors in Europe – France, Holland and Spain – but also, crucially, over its colonies and neo-colonies such as the US and Argentina, condemning the latter to a destiny of underdevelopment as producers of primary commodities.[13]

And it took one former British colony, the United States, almost another hundred years, one Great Depression and two world wars to provide a counterbalance to Britain's strategy of climbing up first and then kicking away the ladder for everyone else, as German economist Friedrich List put it, by repeating and perfecting the 'old' principle of accruing value through difference in world exchange (buy cheap, sell dear). In 1791 the Caribbean-born Alexander Hamilton, the first US Secretary of the Treasury, submitted to Congress his thesis that a backward country like the United States should protect its 'industries in their infancy' from foreign competition via tariffs and import bans, nurture them through subsidies and the prohibition of exports on key raw materials and develop financial and transport infrastructures. His views were constantly at odds with the interests of Southern plantation owners, dominant at the time and until the Civil War, and it was only in the space provided by the 1812 British-American War, and later on during the Civil War, that Hamilton's blueprint for the US economy finally took hold. 'He also set up the government bond market and promoted the development of the banking system . . . It is no hyperbole for the New York Historical Society to have called him "The Man Who Made Modern America".'[14]

Following Hamilton's blueprint, the US became the most protectionist country in the world until the 1930s as well as the fastest growing economy. Although there were other conditions such as abundant natural resources or a large domestic market, which could be cited as reasons for the US rise to economic world power, the positing of a causal connection between Hamilton's 'infant industry' blueprint and its rapid growth gains strength from the fact that many other countries 'with few of those conditions also grew rapidly behind protective barriers', such as Germany, Sweden, France, Finland, Austria, Japan, Taiwan, Korea, China, India, and nowadays also Brazil.[15] Only after World War II, with its industrial and financial supremacy now unchallenged, did the US start championing the cause of free trade, and even then it did so only strategically. It never liberalised its trade to the same degree as Britain did between 1860 and 1932, it continued providing 50 to 70 per cent of funding to its research and development programmes between the 1950s and the mid-1990s, and between 1950 and 1973 it helped kick-start the war-torn European economies by financing the rebuilding of infrastructure in Europe and elsewhere through the Marshall Plan.[16]

War in Europe and Asia had impacted upon the countries in Latin America in different ways. Torn three ways between a crisis of political direction in Buenos Aires, the failure of the Southern Cone Accord proposed in 1940, and a potentially delicate trade deficit after Britain's decision to postpone its payments in sterling until the end of the war, Argentina lost its privileged position as the most important economy of Latin America. Brazil and Mexico, and to a lesser extent Chile, grew closer to the United States and became good candidates for top-dog position south of the Rio Grande. In the case of Mexico, the combined effort against the Axis powers and the closure of Asia and Europe provided an opening for new directions in economic development and US–Latin America relations, perfectly symbolised in Mexico's co-chairing of the 1944 Bretton Woods Conference, which created the World Bank and the International Monetary Fund (IMF), but also initiated trilateral negotiations for a US–Canada–Mexico North American free-trade agreement. US-based economists like Joseph Schumpeter or Gottfried Haberler were interested in Mexico and the Bank of Mexico, which was then recognised as a forum for debating new ideas and approaches to post-war monetary policy. Both Argentina and Mexico had responded to the Great Depression by abandoning Britain's gold standard and introducing a broad policy of state intervention. Mexico had defied common wisdom by defaulting on its debt and introducing radical policies of land reform, the nationalisation of the oil industry in 1938 and the creation of a development corporation. Argentina had ended its traditional rivalry with Brazil and together with Uruguay, Paraguay and Chile created a blueprint to revive the long-standing dream of the formation of a common market in the River Plate basin that would diversify any dependence on old or new powers. The projected Southern Cone

Accord promised a diplomatic revolution in Latin America in the spirit of the pan-Americanism of the independence era. Despite its reservations about the prospects of a custom union in South America, the US accepted these developments in the spirit of enlightened self-interest. If the Accord failed in the end to reach its objectives, it was not because of undue intervention or ill intentions on the part of the United States but, rather, because Argentinean political institutions were coming apart.

In all, like Mexico and Argentina, most other Latin American countries shared the notion expressed by the likes of Raúl Prebisch that enough experience had been gained during the years of Depression and war to succeed. To this spirit of optimism, innovation and adaptation to new geopolitical realities must be added the political signals given by the US during the war period and afterwards that a new era of cooperation was dawning. During the war, the US needed key raw materials from Latin America to feed its war machine and in the post-war environment the closure of Asia and Europe indicated there would be sufficient room for mutual understanding. To many in the region such initiatives as the Marshall Plan and thereafter the presence of Marshall himself at the 1948 Pan-American Conference meant that, although the United States was now a successful country, its enlightened self-interest dictated that it should not act as one. Sometimes, however, as in the cases of US opposition to the building of an oil pipeline from Mendoza in Argentina to the Atlantic, its manoeuvring to get Bolivia and Argentina to sign away their tin and tungsten reserves in the early 1940s and the mixed signals given by the Truman administration concerning the US promises of economic partnership made during the war, the inconsistency of the US approach left many Latin Americans uncertain.[17]

On the one hand US generosity, which marked the period between 1947 and 1979, genuinely allowed the developing countries of Latin America and elsewhere to use nationalistic policies under an international system more receptive to new ideas and to the new energies unleashed by decolonisation. On the other, some of these challenging initiatives ended up being trapped in the ensuing rivalry with the USSR and the Cold War. One can see both attitudes present in Marshall's attendance at and intervention in the IX Pan-American Conference in Bogotá in 1948, in the response from the Latin American delegations present at the Conference, in the opposition expressed by the young Latin American students also present in Bogotá at the time, in the circumstances surrounding the birth of ECLA in relation to other institutions within the OAS and even in the very personal dilemmas faced at the time by respected innovators like Raúl Prebisch – almost obliged to take charge of ECLA after his appointment as a senior adviser for the hugely important IMF was blocked by the US. In between such attitudes and from such interstitial positions the critique of mainstream ideas about the alleged equilibrium of the global system would be articulated and turned into an enlightened strategy whose results were on the whole, for Latin America and for the rest of the world, spectacular.

As a result of such initiatives as the Marshall Plan, the General Agreement on Tariffs and Trade established in 1947 and the creation of the regional economic commissions for Europe, Asia and Latin America in the same year, and also thanks to a more enlightened attitude on the part of the United States towards the potential for development of the world's poorer nations, the richer countries went through a period of economic recovery that has come to be known as 'the Golden Age of Capitalism' (1950–73), while the more 'peripheral' countries also performed well. Per capita income growth rate in Europe went up from 1.3 per cent to 4.1 per cent between 1870 and 1913. It rose from 1.8 to 2.5 per cent in the United States, while in Japan it shot up from 1.5 to 8.1 per cent. And in places like Latin America and other 'peripheral' areas, to use the terminology that became popular around 1945 thanks to the theoretical and political efforts of such people as Raúl Prebisch, while building upon and perfecting the sort of policies used in previous eras by Britain and the US when the latter were 'backward' economies, under new political conditions and under a more perceptive international system, during the 1960s and 1970s growth in per capita terms was estimated at 3 per cent.

The international financial architecture that emerged in the aftermath of the Great Depression and World War II attempted to conciliate national economic interests with a serious rethinking of the terms of global trade and international financial supervision. The IMF and the World Bank were a result of such efforts, but so too were genuine Latin American initiatives with a global resonance, such as ECLA and the attempt to go

beyond Keynesian economics in the recognition of the cyclical nature of
the capitalist economy and the real laws of movement 'between the timing
of the productive process on the one hand and the resulting circulation of
money on the other', quite different from the existing assumptions about
the equilibrium of the international system.[18] At the time, Raúl Prebisch
observed that the events of the post-war era had led to an increased
politicisation of finance. His point concerned the real laws of movement
of the international economy, and there were two aspects to this insight:
on the one hand was the set of assumptions concerning the alleged equilibrium of the international system, and on the other the reality of cycles of
'boom' and 'bust' and the global system of exchange as 'subject to certain
laws of movement quite different from the laws of equilibrium', laws of
'disparity', unequal exchange or difference.

This should not to be taken to mean that the intertwining of politics and global trade and the circulation of money is a new or recent
occurrence. The opposite is the case. Prebisch and others were in
fact observing, from the vantage point of 'peripheral' countries in the
post-war era, a phenomenon whose existence may be contemporaneous with the very existence of the global system of exchange. One
needs to be reminded that the starting point of the long history of
globalisation coincides with the amalgamation of absolutist state and
mercantilism prompted by the European 'discoveries' of the Americas
in the Atlantic – which thereafter established a constant flow of gold
and silver that fostered worldwide trade and credit – and of a passage to
the East Indies round the Cape of Good Hope. In that period the
treasuries of the monarchic European states were fairly limited. The
establishment of chartered companies by the monarchies thus enabled
the ailing economies of such emergent states to use private funds for
exploration and trade that would otherwise have been beyond their
means. In the process, world credit and world money, as we saw in
Chapters 1 and 2, were invented.

On Margins

Call it the Baroque drama of conquest and empire. A group of investors, usually merchants, insurers and bankers, agree to underwrite an

exploration and conquest scheme or a passage across the ocean with the expectation of future profit, or 'return'. The term already suggests a close relation between the austere idiom of money and the rich imagery of adventurous travel. Aristotle, for instance, borrowed from Homer's *Odyssey* the example of an anchored ship in order to illustrate the concept of metaphor as movement – transport, transference, translation – central to poetic imagery and to the very act of writing.[19]

In the tradition that extends from the Latin poets Ovid and Virgil to E. R. Curtius, writing is often compared with seafaring and with the promise of return.[20] The nautical metaphor is central to writing precisely because it opens up in the space of a given document a period of time subtended by the promise of return. The value of the piece – a poem, in modern times a novel, but also a letter of credit, a banknote, an insurance policy or a derivative – hinges upon the realisation of the promise of return or its seemingly infinite deferral, as in the *Odyssey*. The image of an act of transportation, transference or translation in which the point of arrival lies outside known or even conceivable limits is the exemplary metaphorical figure. It is also the very essence of finance.

What we now call risk is nothing more than the anticipation of the perils that may befall those who hoist sail in search of the unknown. And its containment, by means of insurance, for instance, is conditioned by the possibility of dividing the amount of time that passes between setting sail and the occurrence of an anticipated event that might hinder the prospects of return, *ad infinitum*. Credit, the promise of return, and debt, the promised return, can thus be protected, seemingly for all eternity or, to be more precise, against the odds. It is all a matter of calculating the odds – providing some anchor to the promise of return – or calculating them away, for if it is true that the odds of some chance mishap are minimal then the delivery of promised return is secured. And this security forecloses the cycle of time opened up by the promissory note or the beginning of the novel, thereby making return – upon which the value of the whole enterprise hinges – not just a promise, a mere possibility, but a necessity.

A double fiction is required for the anticipation of return and the necessity of return to become one and the same, so that there can be value. On the one hand is the hero who battles it out against all odds. In the Baroque age this hero was identified with the navigator and his merchant ship, his sextant, his cunning and his weapons – chief among them an interpreter – sailing from Palos de Moguer or Plymouth and returning with marvellous treasure and fantastic tales of the unknown. Today, he may be identified with the analyst departing from his cubicle in the City of London or on Wall Street, navigating virtual seas aboard his landlocked desk with the help of computers and armed to the teeth with Black-Scholes equations.[21] On the other hand is the all-seeing eye, able to stare back at the universe of all possible outcomes from the vantage point of the accomplished totality of time. In the past he would have been identified with God or His representatives in this world – the Pope, the absolute Monarch. Today that function corresponds to the state or the corporation, the executive 'decider' – which can be a CEO or a president.

It is no surprise that in the archival record these two characters, the hero and the all-seeing executive, keep turning up and changing names without ever coming anywhere near the end of their journey. In what is perhaps the first documentary evidence of their encounter, they appeared with the names of Christopher Columbus on the one hand and Their Catholic Majesties, Queen Isabella and King Ferdinand of Castile and Aragon, on the other. On 17 April 1492, near Granada, both parties signed a document known to us as *Capitulaciones de Santa Fe*. The text is a simple contract in which certain things are exchanged, some prerogatives are stated, a promise is made and a debt is created. And yet, it is a strange text, perhaps even the strangest ever. Most fantastic of all are the lines with which the text begins: 'The things you have supplicated from Their Majesties, which they give and present in satisfaction for what you, Christopher Columbus, by our command, with some of our vessels and men, have discovered in the sea-ocean, and as reward for the journey you are now going to undertake in the service of Their Majesties, with God's assistance, are as follows: . . .'[22]

What is extraordinary about the text is the apparent mistake it makes: it was written in April 1492, before Columbus embarked on his extraordinary journey, before any discovery was made. It was anticipatory. And yet, what was being exchanged, the object of this contract, had not been seen by anyone in Europe. It was just an expectation, no more than a promise of return. How can a contract exchange something that does not exist – at least not yet – and still be of value? The answer is in the nautical metaphor, which produces the image of movement through space and time as if one could contemplate that movement from the standpoint of its actual completion. The image includes the possibility of failure, in the concrete form of exposure to all sorts of dangers, or 'risk', and the ability to avoid them, thereby completing the journey and delivering what was promised.

In this narrative, for it is structured as fiction, value accrues from exposure to risk. Of course, the litmus test of this sort of enterprise is the actual moment of return, or 'delivery'. However, since one arrives there (it is a point in time or space) by avoiding the many perils that may befall one on the way, there is always the possibility that by constantly deferring such dangers one accrues value solely through exposure even if in fact one never gets to the end of the journey. This becomes possible by infinitely dividing the time that passes between the present moment and the actualisation of any risk. From the imaginary point of view that looks at the journey in its totality this would be akin to actually having completed the journey, given that the formal condition for this result is to expose oneself to danger without falling victim to an actual dangerous situation. For that point of view one has moved even though one in fact has not. This is the paradoxical structure of contemporary finance.

In the *Capitulaciones* between Columbus and Their Majesties, this paradoxical structure appears at the beginning of the legal document, with the two temporal uses of the term 'discovery' (having discovered/going to discover) opening up in imagination a time between departure and return which corresponds to an imaginary kingdom that has not been discovered yet but has been promised, and whose delivery is contemplated by all the implicated parties. In fact, what those islands and that Continent may really be is of little importance since what counts is its existence as a place, or a *topos*, for difference, however fantastic such a place may be (El Dorado, Manoa, the Spring of Eternal Youth, the kingdom of the Amazon, the mountain of silver that devours men, the cut in the land that will connect the oceans allowing 'money to beget money', the future in which all real estate will continue to increase its value, and so on). Value arises from the parties' exposure to the perils that may or may not take place in that period of time. If they are avoided, then the journey should be completed, at least in the imagination. And this means that to contain the dangers by deferring them may in itself be a form of producing value, by producing new margins of exposure or subdividing risk *ad infinitum*. Some might see here an unsolvable paradox; others will see opportunity and will take advantage of it.

In one of the English translations of the *Capitulaciones*, which tends to obscure the temporal paradox, the issue of exposure to risk comes to the fore as the justification for the rewards given or made present by Their Catholic Majesties to Columbus: 'For as much as you, Christopher Columbus, are going by our command, with some of our vessels and men, to discover and subdue some islands and Continent in the ocean, and it is hoped that by God's assistance, some said islands and Continent in the ocean will be discovered and conquered by your means and conduct, therefore it is but just and reasonable, *that since you expose yourself to such danger to serve us*, you should be rewarded for it.'[23] The unnamed translator fortuitously encountered the truth of the twenty-first century in a fifteenth-century piece of fantastic literature.

Pizarro & Co. Reloaded

Take Francisco Pizarro's expedition to Peru. The basic structure has by now become familiar: a group of investors, merchants, insurers and bankers agree to underwrite an exploration scheme and a passage across the ocean with the expectation of future profit or 'return'. The only tie binding these merchants and the half-mercenary, half-adventurous entrepreneurs – Pizarro, De Soto and so on – is the shared belief in their heads that profits will be obtained at some point in the future. In any other respect the endeavour remains uncertain, for they are in fact dealing in beliefs, stories about cities of silver and gold and astrological charts. Because of this, they need some sort of anchor, an imaginary authority that can give something that it does not have and that is not there. In Spanish the word for giving is *otorgar*, which literally means creating or making present. Such is the monarch.

The monarch then issues a charter, and the ensemble of merchants, bankers and mercenaries become a company. Their abstract expectation is thereby incorporated. Literally. It is given a body, with a legal existence of its own, a corporate body. It is in this sense that we speak today of corporations. The monarch, like God, creates bodies out of thin air and infuses them with life. In exchange for this act of divine creation, which anchors the expectations of subjects, citizens and soldiers – always citizens and soldiers – the monarch charges a price in the form of a rent or a tax such as a fifth of the future or promised profits of the company ·thus formed. This was the *quinto real* or 20 per cent of all gains in the case of Pizarro & Co.'s scheme and that of the Spanish crown.

But up to this point all we have is the expectation of profit by all parties included in the crown and the crown's power, which is derived from God. More concretely, the monarch also offers to back the deal with a threat of force, a threat that becomes more or less realistic only once the monarch has suppressed all his competitors, as well as any actual or potential invaders. This is precisely what had happened in April 1492 in Spain. The power of Ferdinand and Isabella came from the fact that they had succeeded in the *Reconquista* and expelled Moors and all other competitors. So, the threat is believable only after the monarch has laid down the law of the realm, based upon its actual monopoly over the means of violence. The deal and the expectation of profit are thus protected or secured by law. Americans rediscovered this basic scheme in 1905, when the US Supreme Court established the 'contemplating delivery' doctrine, and on the basis of it invented the credit and financial system that has underpinned their dominant economic and geopolitical position up to the present day.[24]

However, up to this point it is all once again smoke and mirrors: the shared belief in the heads of investors and entrepreneurs, the possibility of future profit, the potential threat of state force, the likelihood of war against a foreign invader, the fictitious personality of the company and its accompanying set of legal fictions (or, as economists today would say, regulation), the divine right of kings and the mirror-like relation that makes a man a king only because other men stand in relation to him as subjects. Granted, the scheme has gained some concreteness: the corporate body, the political body of the state, the charter of incorporation, the royal seal, the existing capital and the calculated profit and, lest we forget, the monopoly over the means of violence. We may even have a product, an actual product such as a Dyson vacuum cleaner, or a revolutionary design such as an iPod, or a biotechnology patent, or, as in the case of Pizarro & Co.'s fantastic information, a map, a route and the will to do whatever it takes in order to get there. And yet, it is really all still up in the air. Only if Pizarro's information makes a difference: only then will the company have produced something valuable. And thus, when Pizarro & Co. hijacked the Inca ruler Atahualpa in Cajamarca and obtained in exchange for the promise of his release a roomful of gold, it was then that they delivered value.

Both Adam Smith and Karl Marx, afterwards, saw a major turning point in world history in the European discovery of the Americas. They both recognised the momentous consequences of what had happened in Cajamarca that November of 1532. Francisco Pizarro and his men melted the gold goblets and the sun discs and the silver pectorals into bars and ingots and sent them back to Spain. Once there, silver and gold were used to pay investors their profit and bankers in Genoa, Venice and Antwerp got their loans back with interest. The Spanish crown accumulated its 20 per cent and could then use it as collateral in order to fund new expeditions, which yielded even higher returns. And, after paying the bankers and the state, Pizarro & Co., as Hernán Cortés before him, and many after both of them, were still filthy rich.

From the perspective of Pizarro & Co. they had made a fair profit thanks to their superior technology, and from the perspective of the Spanish state there was equal exchange and equilibrium because everyone got their just share – investors got their profits, bankers got their loans back with interest, taxes were paid, soldiers and cooks and sailors and even the priests were paid, too. However, the value of that gold and that silver could be delivered – thereby provoking the sort of equilibrium that would allow bankers to keep on lending, merchants buying and selling, and states and churches financing their wars and their missionary expeditions – only because of the difference made by the way in which men like Cortés and Pizarro, and the European bankers and insurers and tax collectors, captured the meaning of gold and silver in comparison with the meaning given to gold and silver by the Inca and the Aztec peoples.

J. M. G. Le Clézio observes that gold had symbolic value for the Indians: since it belonged directly to the gods, it was their treasure. By demanding it, the Spaniards proved that they were *teules*, gods. But also, by giving the Spaniards silver and gold the Mexicans and the Peruvians gave their conquerors a terrestrial power they could never have anticipated. Without knowing it, they initiated a vicious cycle that meant their own demise, 'for the white man never shares'.[25] He can only accumulate and distribute in imagination. From the standpoint of the nations of Europe and their offspring in North and South America all there was was a fair and equal exchange. But from the standpoint of the planet as a whole – the global standpoint that became possible only once the Americas were 'discovered' by Columbus – the difference between systems of value distant in space and time made, and continues to make, all the difference. The difference in time between the expectations of profit of Genoese bankers, Spanish crown tax collectors and the chartered entrepreneurs of Pizarro & Co., on the one hand, and the delivery of such profits in the shape of gold and silver ingots and bullion, on the other, coincided with the gap between the dream of the conquerors, with their horses and arquebuses and ships and accumulation, and the dream of the Indians, with their apocalyptic cycles, their returning gods, their ritual warfare and their golden ornaments.

The exchange between these two systems, prefigured in the encounter between Cortés and the ambassadors of Moctezuma, in which the former presented them with green glass beads and in turn received golden sun discs and precious jewels, or the event in Cajamarca in which Atahualpa refuses the Bible and in return is obliged to deliver a roomful of gold, was simply unequal. No transparent communication could have been possible in such a situation. Nor can it be possible in any other situation. In that impenetrable gap between the two systems of value emerged money as world money.

It is often thought that money as we know it appeared in the Renaissance as absolutist states learned to mint coins of the realm out of nothing, just as they learned to issue charters of incorporation and created persons out of thin air, obliging everyone to use them and stopping them from creating their own means of exchange. And so, just as the absolutist state monopolised the means of force and the resolution of conflicts, it also monopolised the means of exchange giving itself the means of its own continuous reproduction via taxes and succession. Then they expanded in space and did the same in every territory they annexed to their dominions.

However, the story we have revisited from that fateful day in 1532 in Cajamarca and the encounter of the silver mines in Potosí to the emergence of the silver peso and the gold standard, the post-war plan of General Marshall and the credit crises of our day, reveals something else. Global trade emerged in the late sixteenth century when all continents began to exchange products continuously, 'in values sufficient to generate crucial impacts on all the trading partners'.[26] And the one product most responsible for the birth of such planetary trade was silver, both in its role as a commodity and, crucially, as the Spanish American silver peso, the first world money. Later, that worldwide circle would be redrawn again with the establishment of the gold standard in 1821 by Britain as a consequence of a series of trade agreements with Portugal dating back to 1703, giving it access to Brazilian gold reserves.

Silver and gold always competed with other monies but were most esteemed because of the premium placed on metallic currencies that were not debased. Such currencies could then perform the proper function of world money, that of serving as the universal translator between essentially different systems of value. The proper analogy here is between the function of reserve currencies as world money and the practice of translation, in which the translator renders the meaning that one thing has in a specific context (a familiar context or a mother tongue) into the meaning that the same thing has in another context (unfamiliar, or foreign).

According to this analogy, the meaning of something (its price) manifests an equilibrium, a certain position that something has in relation to all other things that have meaning, and this manifestation is there for all to see in the same way as the meaning of a word in our modern tongue is almost instinctively manifest to us. But when a word is translated into another context and another language, even if it achieves the same meaning we say that something was 'lost in translation'. On the one hand, the value of the word is altered in the different system in accordance to its different relationship with other words. On the other, the new manifestation carries with it this loss and this difference even if neither the loss nor the difference is manifest in the other context or language.

The same happens with world money, with the silver peso and the gold or (silver) dollar standard, which indexes loss and difference, space and time or distancing even if it does not, indeed it cannot, make them evident. This is what Milton Friedman had in mind when he pointed out to his economics students the power of capitalism to bring together all the products from the different parts of the world to make a pencil, or to 'flatten' the world, as he put it. This is the power of money, world money as capital. However, Friedman's insight falls short of the mark because he focuses solely on the production side of the story; the other side of the story is that for a pencil to generate value it must be sold and it must be consumed, which is to say that the difference it carries within it has to manifest itself to someone else, as price. The important point to remember is that the pencil has a different value for the consumer – with respect to his frame of reference – than the wood, the graphite and the rubber may have in their places of origin, and also for the seller and the producer, and that this difference never disappears but is only transferred.[27] In this sense, world money is not like a universal language – there is no such thing as a universal language, and all attempts to establish one have failed so far. Rather, it is an index of foreignness.[28]

Creditors and Debtors

In the end, world capitalism will always boil down to a specifically modern distinction between creditors and debtors that historically came to be in the place of the classical distinction between the civilised and barbarians. Pizarro and Cortés invented capitalism not because they formed companies, got capital and invested such capital with a view to future profits, but, rather, because in doing so they captured the margin between different systems of value and took advantage of that margin. In that respect, one can say that capitalism was invented on 4 March 1517 when Hernán Cortés demanded gold and the Maya Indians of the city the Spanish renamed Great Cairo, on the coast of the Yucatán Peninsula, sensing the dangers associated with accumulation of the metal, diverted the strangers, saying only 'Colua, Colua!', 'Mexico, Mexico!' The decisive act of this Baroque drama was, of course, the capture of Moctezuma, which was the solid example of the capturing of difference between value systems. And later on, when Carib Indians diverted Pizarro & Co. by speaking of El Dorado in Peru, the decisive and most concrete act took place in Cajamarca with the capture of Atahualpa and the offer of his release in exchange for a roomful of gold around 16 November 1532.

On that day, motioning to one of the translators and to Pizarro, Atahualpa told the conquistador that he was well aware of the reason why the Spaniards had come to Tawantisuyu (today's Peru). He walked to one of the rooms of the temple of the sun and with a piece of chalk drew a line on the wall well above his head. Then he said: 'I, Atahualpa, ruler of the Inca, will present you with all the gold and silver objects you and your men may wish, and fill with them this room all the way up to the white line.' 'In exchange,' he said, 'you will release me.' From his standpoint and that of the Inca, this was for Atahualpa a gift subject to strict rules of reciprocity. From the standpoint of Pizarro – military leader, strategist, diplomat, CEO, terrorist and now hostage taker – to give was to concede graciously what somebody else supplicates for, if you are king (he was not, Atahualpa was the king) or, more precisely, to retain something taken from somebody else's rights or belongings. Because one retains what belongs to someone else one has to give it back or give it away. At stake is Pizarro's relation with his king and with Spain: he has received a favour (*gracia*) from the King of Spain, who has chartered his company, and has to reciprocate. And he can only do so by taking what Atahualpa offers. He is in debt to the King of Spain, but not to King Atahualpa. This is why he will not reciprocate the gesture of the ruler of Tawantisuyu.

The temporal structure of Pizarro & Co.'s debt is the same as that between Columbus and Their Catholic Majesties in the *Capitulaciones*: the verb 'to discover' was first used in the past tense because Their Majesties were rewarding Columbus for his (promised) 'return', but the value of that return would only be realised once the promised return takes place in the future, which is why Columbus, like Cortés and Pizarro, is obliged to give 'in return'. In the gap between these two timings there is risk: that time can be divided *ad infinitum*, infinitely deferred, and each new division would accrue new value. It is little surprise that immediately after these companies were chartered, the terms of the relationship between the entrepreneurs and the states were denounced: Columbus felt defrauded by Their Catholic Majesties, Cortés ended up severing his ties with the crown, one of the brothers Pizarro would threaten to do the same after the new laws protecting the Indians were issued by the imperial centre. The time of the centre is not the same as the time of the periphery: in the impenetrable gap one risks the infinity of debt, as Latin American countries would discover in the 1980s and 1990s, or not being paid at all, which is what creditors always fear. At this point, the stand-off between debtors and creditors seems unresolvable. The circle of the journey is never closed, and with each new division another form of value is produced which can be accumulated. Now history comes in cycles, a repetition of crises in which none is decisive.

In contrast, Atahualpa sought to close the circle. The strict laws of reciprocity, so ingrained in the soul of the Inca, remained hidden to Pizarro, as they did to Cortés and Columbus before him. In the *Capitulaciones*, for example, there is no mention of the inhabitants of the land that has been promised in return. The absence of the Indians on paper is a sign of things to come. They are expected to be absent from the land and so they will be made absent. In turn, the laws of infinite debt and value seemed to the Indians of Mexico, Peru, North America and the Caribbean sheer madness. Seeking only to keep Pizarro and his ilk at bay, Atahualpa did not see that his actions in fact encouraged their vicious circularity. For Atahualpa could not have known of the place that silver and gold occupied in Renaissance Europe in relation to the bankers of Genoa, Venice, Antwerp and London, or to the merchants doing business in the Levant or West Africa, and, most of all, in relation to the Spanish monarch and the relationship between the latter, his subjects, and the other European monarchs. In any case, even if he had understood it would have seemed to him exactly what it is: utter nonsense.

The fact that Pizarro was part of a company chartered by the crown, a supplicant in relation to it, and forever indebted to it and to the interests of creditors and investors, that he was not merely some ambitious individual, escaped Atahualpa. The same happens to us when we choose to believe that the bankers and intermediaries in the middle of the 2008 Great Recession were merely driven by greed, and that this (lack of morals) was the cause of the crisis. At least Atahualpa can be excused because he had no experience of financial crises, and, moreover, he was part of a society that consciously avoided the abyss of debt deferred forever. We do not have such excuses. The different expectations of Atahualpa and his captor were embodied, incorporated in the gold with which he, Atahualpa, filled the room of the temple of the sun in Cajamarca. In turn, silver and gold transformed such expectations, on the part of Pizarro & Co., and the states of Europe into a terrestrial power the like of which no one in the world had seen before. Such was the power of translation, which carried the difference – spatial and temporal – between the value system of the Inca and the Aztec on the one side and that of Europeans on the other. It can carry any other global difference, for that matter. In concrete terms, that is the power embedded in world money, and so, any state that combines the power to incorporate with the realisation of value via world money, emerges triumphant among other competing communities and states across the globe.

We have seen that process take place in at least three cases – Spain taking the place of the Roman Empire, England taking the place of Spain, the United States taking the place of England. After the failure of the Project for a New American Century led by the George W. Bush administration and in the wake of the Great Recession there is already talk about the next dominant power: will it be China? Or will it be Brazil? Those who trade in the constant repetition of history speak of such things, unaware of the insignificance of their meanderings. Instead, the true challenge is to break the vicious circle, the repetitive production of difference and the eternal deferral of debt. To break with that circle would be not just to rule the world but to change the world. Many in Latin America, the descendants of Atahualpa among them, are attempting just that. Their attempt is the real story of our times.

The Solution to All Our Problems

Thomas Cochrane should be as well known today as Francis Drake. Throughout his lifetime he managed to pack in enough drama, political intrigue and invention to shame both Admiral Nelson and Drake himself. Fernando Fajnzylber should be as well known today as Will Hutton or Joseph Stiglitz, for his economic initiatives are no less far-reaching, influential and exciting than those offered in our day by the likes of Willem Buiter or Anthony Giddens. In fact, there would not be a Joseph Stiglitz, a Dani Rodrik or an Anthony Giddens if it were not for the work that people like Fajnzylber and others, such as the Brazilian Theotonio dos Santos or the Venezuelan Carlota Perez, are doing in Latin America. Through the actions of people like them the histories of Britain, the USA and Latin America, the Global North and the Global South became inextricably wedded, even if that connection remains hidden to less observing eyes.

And like Cochrane, Fajnzylber was dauntless: 'Here is the solution to all of our problems!' he declared after arriving in Rio for the *Fórum Nacional* organised by then minister of development João Paulo dos Reis Velloso. A minister of the Médici government during the last days of Brazil's dictatorship and the beginning of the transition towards democracy (Brazilians call this period *descompressão*, decompression), Reis Velloso had overseen Brazil's own 'miracle'.[29] During the time of the miracle, Brazil was able to finance 90 per cent of the investment made annually in industry and infrastructure, using the remaining 10 per cent represented by external investment only as a complement. State-led monetary and credit policy established a set of efficient internal incentives to accelerate growth, maintain low interest rates, intervene in banks – a couple of concepts we are now familiar with – and stimulate exports through a credit system known as *crédito-prêmio*, or 'credit-award', allocated to the most innovative enterprises on the basis of their achievements without immediate repayment obligations. At the centre of the 'miracle' strategy of economic development attributed to Treasury minister Delfim Netto was what Reis Velloso refers to as a 'peculiar' Central Bank. 'It didn't just work on defending money and controlling price stability and infla-tion. It was also a promoter of development,' he observes. Paul Singer, one of the founders of Lula's Workers' Party (PT), defended that model of low interests and state-led bank incentives against those who were pushing for the fastest possible growth, in and out of the PT.

'In the second semester of 1979 and the beginning of 1980 there were those who tried to re-enact the miracle strategy and already it didn't work,' says Reis Velloso, 'the circumstances had changed.' As Fernando Henrique Cardoso had already observed in the early 1970s, two types of change were taking place: the first one had taken a long time, a long cycle in which agrarian and nomadic Indian and Afro-Latin American communities became dominated by absolutist monarchical states – Spain, Portugal, Britain, France – that conspired with the merchant class, monopolised the means of violence and exchange, and spread a form of debt and circulation (transport and translation) that in accord-ance with the reorganisation of the world in the model of the nautical metaphor was potentially infinite. The result of this long cycle was the marriage of state and capital. Cardoso was looking at its tail end when he studied the changes in the institution of slavery in southern Brazil and the patterns of migration of Afro-Latin Americans into industrialising cities. The second change, which Cardoso pointed out as he observed how migrants brought with them into the cities their age-old networks of mutual aid, had taken a shorter time, like a cycle within the cycle. It pertained to the marriage between nations and the state, driven by rapidly changing waves of revolutions in communication.[30]

Writers, sociologists and historians working in Latin American coun-tries with significant Indian and Afro-Latin American populations also observed and represented this process in their writings and theories. Fernández Retamar in Cuba re-enacted the drama of the Carib Indian and the former slave as they left their traditional communities and nations via the commodity economy, in the midst of industrialisation. García

Márquez in Colombia described communities being swept away by the storm of progress, as did José Carlos Mariátegui, Aníbal Quijano and Mario Vargas Llosa in Peru, Silvia Rivera Cusicanqui and Álvaro García Linera in Bolivia, decisively, and even the young Borges in Argentina. Rivera Cusicanqui and García Linera, who is now the Vice-President of Bolivia under Evo Morales, carefully distinguish between the laws of reciprocity in gift and return that characterised pre-Columbian Andean communities, the plundering and redistribution that defined their relations with discoverers and conquistadors, and the exchange by money and infinite debt that rule in our financialised world.

But they also emphasise the power of the association, based on mutual aid like that still found alive among 'traditional' communities in the highlands and the slums of Bolivia, Ecuador and southern Colombia, yet not as closed as the traditional forms of reciprocity, which are gone. Rather, they present to us associations as living networks of voluntary exchange organised by those who once left their more or less traditional communities and migrated to the city slums or the circuits of production and consumption extending into rural areas, such as the coca-leaf chains studied by Rivera Cusicanqui.

Moreover, they present to us the communal association as a principle of social and political organisation and an ethical and economic form that is viable, alive and well, and was active during the Water Wars of 2000 and the rise to state power of Bolivian *cocaleros* in 2005, as much as during the Latino marches of 2006 and, crucially, among the cyber-communities arguing today for peer-to-peer finance as a way to escape the 'permanent state of siege' that characterises life in the United States, the United Kingdom, France or China. These cyber-communities are already experimenting with forms of open money in Mexico, with currencies that do not transform into capital, like Michael Linton's LETS (Local Exchange Trading System), Douglas Rushkoff's peer-to-peer cards, or Eric Harris-Braun's OsCurrency (Open Source currency) in the United States, and with commodity-based global currencies, as in the case of the Ecuadorian proposal to solve climate change by leaving resources in the ground and the already 'old' Brazilian proposal to 'charge' globally for Amazonian air. These proposals create the space for exciting design and creative policy questions: can the poor in the slums of the planet trade using their own currency? Would it be useful and viable to re-establish the money-as-account proposals made by Che Guevara when he was president of the Cuban Central Bank in today's Venecuba? [31]

The community-based and technologically-enhanced association could very well replace the marriage of capital and nation-state if it takes the planetary shape of an association of associations, or, to put it in a language that takes into account the ongoing cycle of technological revolution, a network of networks. This form, which today is reshaping discussions about finance in the wake of the 2008 crisis as much as the life and politics of Bolivia – which was prefigured in the extraordinary explosion of collective life that attended *descompressão* and democratic transition in Brazil, as described by Suely Rolnik and Félix Guattari in their book *Molecular Revolution in Brazil* (1986), and continues to fuel what *The Economist* termed in December 2009 'Brazil's take-off', which is the very soul of the global movement of movements known as the World Social Forum, housed in Porto Alegre and Mumbai, which was prefigured even before in the Cybersyn Project of Chile's Allende government in the 1970s – is the gift of twenty-first-century Latin America to the world. And it is a gift given under no laws of return.

A second condition is required for the association-principle to fully unleash its potential: to tap into the current technological revolution. Cardoso had already noticed in the 1960s and 1970s that technology cycles-within-cycles had the potential to change forever the timing difference between 'core' and 'periphery' nodes in the global economic circuit and the longer cycle, which, as we have seen, started in 1492. His insight can be related back to Prebisch's model of industrialisation by import substitution and forward to the proposals made by Fernando Fajnzylber, and, more recently, by Venezuelan economist and technology analyst Carlota Pérez. As she says, Prebisch's Import Substitution Industrialization (ISI) model offered 'a dynamic [and successful] solution both to the problems of the main corporations of advanced countries and to those of the developing countries'. Moving final assembly 'of the main consumer products to such countries mobilized their economies at the same time as it expanded world markets by creating significant layers of new consumers. Replacing imports of final products with imports of capital goods and parts, and performing final assembly under strong tariff protection, did not greatly improve the balance of payments of the developing countries . . . but there was growth, employment and, above all, the process generated demand for construction, infrastructure and complementary services and created the need for a wide professional middle class and an educated workforce,' she explains.[32]

Like Raúl Prebisch before and economic historian Ha-Joon Chang in our time, Pérez argues that, while David Ricardo's nineteenth-century 'free trade' comparative advantage theory is correct in general (that is, accepting current levels of technology as given), it fails when a country wants to acquire more advanced technologies (that is, to develop) so as to close the vicious circularity of global commerce. Another way to say this is that there is no such thing as the much-vaunted 'level playing field' praised by neoliberals in our time, and that from Pizarro and Atahualpa onwards the players have always been unequal. Prebisch's political and theoretical activism in Argentina's Central Bank, first, then at the regional level through ECLA and ILPES, and finally at the global level in UNCTAD and other scenarios, was aimed at 'tilting the playing field'.

In principle, the notion of a 'level playing field' sounds more reasonable than that of a 'tilted playing field'. Neoliberals who preach the benefits of Thomas Friedman's golden straitjacket, the one-size-fits-all single path to success in the new global economy, also love to talk about the 'level playing field', arguing that developing countries should not be allowed to use subsidies and regulation because these constitute unfair competition. Developing countries using such policy tools are thus depicted as a cycling team happily sprinting downhill while their competitors, developed countries, struggle to climb in the opposite direction. However, this is not the appropriate metaphor by which to describe the relation between Latin American countries and Europe or the United States. Historically, the best metaphor for global capitalism is the nautical metaphor, which was also in actual fact its original metaphor.[33]

Aristotle's nautical metaphor, which provided the policy advisers of late medieval and Baroque absolutist monarchies with a model for

their relationship with merchant capital, as evidenced by the case of
the *Capitulaciones* between Columbus and Their Catholic Majesties, is
in turn a poetic version of Zeno's paradoxical tale of Achilles and the
tortoise. It is well known that in the latter, speedy Achilles – whom I
am tempted here to replace with Speedy González, the cartoon character that in American popular culture has stood for all Latin Americans
– never catches up with Old Tortoise. This is so because, given a head
start, the Old Tortoise will always move one step ahead before Speedy
can cover it. The distance between them can be regressively divided
logically and mathematically *ad infinitum*.

It follows that the only way Speedy González can catch up with Old
Tortoise is if he jumps over the infinite abyss. That is to say, if he has
crutches or rather a good pair of air-trekker jumping stilts! Extra policy
tools like subsidies and regulation are like jumping stilts. But they would
not work if Old Tortoise countries also use them, or the latest most
powerful version, against Speedy González countries. This would be
like putting Speedy González in a wheelchair and then denying him a
stairlift because it would be unfair to give him 'special treatment'. But as
the economist Ha-Joon Chang says, we do not think about stairlifts for
people in wheelchairs or Braille texts for blind people as 'special treatment' since, like Speedy González, they are no less human than people
who can see or run around on their two feet. To give different treatment
to people with different capabilities and needs is fair. The same goes for
countries with different needs and capabilities. This is fair and just. This
is the content of the much debated 'human right to development'.

It turns out that the only fair or 'level' playing field is in fact a tilted
playing field. Realist sceptics among us, left and right, would argue that,
given World Trade Organization (WTO) rules and IMF–World Bank
conditionalities attached to much-needed foreign aid and loans, as well as
the fear of being punished in the future by rich countries, it is unlikely to
have the playing field tilted. However, there is nothing inevitable about
WTO rules and foreign aid conditionality and there are good reasons for
arguing that the status of development as a human right trumps other
rules even if these are 'privatised' or consented to between parties in
bilateral or multilateral trade agreements, in the same way in which the

Human Rights Act 1989 in the United Kingdom has been construed by British judges as having superior or 'constitutional' status in relation to other Acts of Parliament and has an effect on relations among particulars. This means that certain instruments of international law – like the UN Charter or human rights universal declarations, and also those that allow us to speak of development as a collective human right – should be construed as having 'constitutional status' in global affairs.

To argue for the constitutional interpretation of the UN Charter or human rights seems like a heterodox position nowadays, but until recently it was in fact the very orthodoxy defended by the United States against – you guessed it – the Soviet Union. Between the 1950s and the 1980s the Soviets argued for a literal and purely consensual interpretation of the instruments of international law. They claimed this was for the protection of the country's sovereignty against 'imperialism'; in fact, they were arguing for the 'privatisation' of international law. In concrete terms, this would mean something like the contemporary fragmentation of international law and de-linkage from international institutions defended in the US by neocons and some neoliberals in recent administrations.

Back then the United States rightly resisted this position, and so did the majority of the members of the UN General Assembly, including the G-77 and 'non-aligned' countries of the United Nations, which were the majority of the developing nations of the world. The US position started to change when developing countries flexed their muscles as the majority force in the United Nations, especially after the call for a 'new international economic order' (NIEO) issued in the 1964 UN Conference on Trade and Development (UNCTAD). But, in fact, the continuous support of the United States for a more substantive rule of law in international relations would only be interrupted decisively during the Reagan and Bush administrations. And, even then, it did so only because self-righteousness took over from reason and enlightened self-interest.

Today, realist sceptics on the right and on the left are fond of pointing at the inflexibility of geopolitics and 'the national interest' as limits on the viability of rights-based arguments and reasonable constitutional

approaches to international law. They would have you believe that international law either does not exist or simply does not work – 'look at
Iraq, they got away with it', those on the left would say, 'empire-lite
is a necessary evil, or a cost-benefit good', would answer those in the
centre and on the right. Notice that there is no real opposition between
these two answers: they both argue that empire is inevitable. They are
both wrong. People tend to forget that in the 1964 UN Conference on
Trade and Development what was 'inevitable' became contingent and
what was improbable actually happened. George Woods gave a strong
official message of World Bank support for UNCTAD. Eric Wyndham-
White acknowledged a clear difference of mandate between his GATT,
the equivalent of today's WTO and principal presumed opponent of the
Conference, and UNCTAD, thereby effectively narrowing its focus to
lowering tariffs and steering away from all other areas – commodities,
manufactures, finance, regulatory institutions and regional questions –
which would be left to the more democratic UN forum. East European
countries like Hungary and Romania openly refused to accept Moscow's
leadership in international trade and the majority of developing countries,
gathered as the G-77, dealt as equals with the group of richest nations.

Although the US and West Germany seemed implacably firm, the UK
and Sweden, like the World Bank, were prepared to consider supplemen-
tary financing mechanisms and trade preferences for developing countries;
these are prime examples of 'jumping stilts' in the policy landscape of development. Belgium and the Netherlands were also ready to find common
ground. The French proposed that consumers in developed countries paid
to stabilise Third World exports earnings. This was not just some Damascene
moment of enlightenment; it meant the global extension of the way the
agricultural sector was treated in the developed world, which France had
already extended to its ex-colonies. There was an explicit endorsement of
'south–south' trade, shipping reforms, provisions to assist landlocked countries like Bolivia, support of western countries for regional integration, even
the lowering of tariffs concerning exports of manufactured goods from
First World countries and tariff preferences for Third World manufactures
were considered (although on a case-by-case basis, and only within GATT,
rather than in a UN forum like UNCTAD). Sure, there were problems:

internal divisions were rampant and polarisation between the increasingly united developing countries and the group of richer countries often meant deadlock, threatening to condemn the Conference to utter failure. One Indian delegate likened the proceedings to a zoo and asked Raúl Prebisch whether he was part of it. 'Yes,' he answered, 'I am the ring-master.' And yet, it ended in success. 'For all its frustrations, the Geneva [UNCTAD Conference] . . . could still be of historical significance,' said the exceedingly sceptical *Economist* in an unusually positive editorial of 6 June 1964. 'Prebisch and the countries he represents are no longer outsiders. A new force is the emerging leadership of the poor.'[34]

The 1964 UN Conference on Trade and Development stands in history as a testimony to what humans are capable of when they attend to their basic instincts of solidarity, mutual aid and fairness. To argue for such 'basic instincts' is to acknowledge reason as the most basic element of what we often call human nature. So is it to argue for human rights from the standpoint of the poor, including the right to development. In this sense we can speak of tilting the playing field of global economic competition in the same way in which we tilt the playing field in sports competitions. Having recognised that in general the players are unequal, we introduce such regulatory measures as age groups or league divisions, in baseball or football, and sometimes even minute distinctions in weight, as in the case of boxing. We are correct in concluding that a boxing match between heavyweight champion Muhammed Ali and legendary Panamanian lightweight boxer Roberto 'Mano de Piedra' Durán would be unfair. The same would be true for a match between the US and Nicaragua, were they to compete 'on equal terms'.[35]

Moral Luck

Fajnzylber and Pérez add to the recognition of the fairness and success of ISI, NIEO and the 'infant industry' strategies deployed in post-war Latin America and Asia what the latter calls 'an element of luck'. This is not a reference to pure chance but, rather, a recognition of the time-contingency constraints faced by development strategies *vis-à-vis* technology shocks. Che Guevara also recognised this in the 1960s when, opposing the model of development proposed by Soviet-leaning Marxists in Cuba, he urged the introduction of mathematical analysis, probability and computing aimed at forward-looking practice.[36]

Carlota Pérez calls such forward-looking collective practices 'vision' and believes that lack thereof is the main ingredient in all sorts of catastrophic economic recipes. On the one hand, she explains thus the shortcomings of the ISI model in Latin America: 'By the 1980s . . . the information revolution was already taking off, its paradigm was beginning to rejuvenate the mature industries . . . attempts at subsidized export promotion were only successful when there were real local capabilities involved [as in the case of] Embraer, the Brazilian airplane producer.' On the other, she refers to the forward-looking redirection of ISI in Asia in the following terms: 'there was an element of luck in that the Asian region . . . quickly understood the importance of ICT [the Information & Computer Technology paradigm] and the trend towards global markets. They [the Asians] constructed . . . clear and nationally shared "visions" for their economic development, and experienced a resounding success.'

The key explanatory element in her account is ethical and political, not the simplistic electoral variety but what she calls 'an element of luck' or 'vision', that is to say, disciplined and forward-looking collective action or association. In this respect, her explanation of Latin America's 'lost decade' and the debt crises that engulfed Latin American countries between the 1980s and 2000 also contains a political element: neoliberalism (structural adjustment programmes + the 'Washington Consensus' institutional framework) was uneven and destructive not because it was 'orthodox' (which it was not; if the story we have revisited in this book is correct, neoliberalism is actually an act of erasing memory that can reclaim no historical orthodoxy because in its historicism it actively denies all truth and history) but rather because it was backward-looking (it was projecting some achievements of the past on to future events), ideological (in the sense of passing certain facts as true in all circumstances, that is to say, as necessary) and it dismantled communal connections. Located between the successful and creative post-war period (1943–73) and the successful and creative post-millennium period currently unfolding in Latin America, the neoliberal hiatus appears in Pérez's account, which at this point acknowledges Fajnzylber's contribution, as a moment of paralysis and lack of vision tantamount to ethical misfortune. In contrast, Che Guevara's early opposition to the Soviet model of management and industrialisation, his attention to the trend towards global markets and the revolution brought about by ICT, made concrete in his studies of US corporations' management and account techniques, linear programming and computing, which he also attempted to introduce into Cuba's educational system, or Chile's Cybersyn Project, are evidence of vision, whatever one might think of their political slogans and even if one disagrees with their tactics and the human cost involved. As Helen Yaffe says in relation to Guevara, his enduring legacy is a theory and practice of transition and not the tactics of guerrilla warfare.

Efficiency 2.0

Formalised theories of the efficiency of markets, such as those that became dominant during the neoliberal period of the 1980s and 1990s, and remained so until at least 2008, fuelled the notion that markets would regulate themselves and financial innovation would always be a beneficial sign of progress. The most esoteric financial instruments invented by those brilliant minds on Wall Street and in the City of London had been built upon such a notion. At their basis is the idea according to which an assumption used in an act of inference supposedly holds in future situations. Thus, in their analyses of risk and their prospective models there was no place for entirely new situations; the latter were considered insignificant, unlikely and improbable, which is why they were discarded even after such new situations became apparent early in the 2000s, as in the case of the Argentinean financial debacle of 2001–2.

'The Argentine . . . debacle of 2001–2002 demonstrated the limits of the global financial roulette that had been played to the hilt in the 1990s.'[37] It also revealed the contradictory strategies of the United States and other creditors in Europe with respect to the management of Latin America's seemingly infinite foreign debt. Chief among them was the contradiction between the neoliberal view that governments should not interfere with thriving financial markets and speculation and the notion that they, in particular the US Treasury (in alliance with the IMF), should be obliged to rescue faltering markets. In the case of the Mexican bankruptcy of December 1994, brought about by the commercial deficit of over $100 billion as a result of the General Agreement on Trade and Tariffs in 1984 and subsequent negotiation of the North American Free Trade Agreement (NAFTA) in 1993 and the kind of financial Russian roulette played by President Carlos Salinas de Gortari until December 1994, the US and the IMF came to the rescue, leading to repayments by Mexico of over $14 billion to the US Treasury and $17 billion to the IMF until 1998. In the case of Argentina, the IMF, in consultation with the Treasury Department, decided that there was not going to be a rescue package. In so doing, the largest default in history began until the government of leftist politician Néstor Kirchner adopted an unexpectedly hard line with foreign bondholders, maintaining the default on half of the foreign debt until early 2005, when an offer for conversion of the bonds at reduced value was made to and accepted by the majority of international investor groups.

Although the image of the US–IMF ensemble as a fireman, rather than a neoliberal policeman, still obtains, after the negotiations of Argentina's debt, which Carlos Marichal calls 'a major turning point in . . . financial history', it is more likely that other debtor governments will likewise demand more equitable treatment from bankers, investors and financial markets.[38] The change has to do with increased awareness of the political foundations (or regulation) of world finance and with the politics of multilateral agencies. Without a 'strong fireman', policing of the foreign debt of developing countries by the G-7, the group of the seven richest countries in the world, will become more difficult. With the onset of the financial crisis hitting G-7 countries harder than developing countries in Latin America and elsewhere, the level of difficulty increases. Add to that the increasingly important role of networked political activists in debt-finance negotiations – think, for instance, of the lead taken by the ensemble between the Afro-Latin American Communities Process (*Proceso de Comunidades Negras*) of southern Colombia, the international Association for the Taxation of Financial Transactions for the Aid of Citizens (ATTAC) and the Committee for the Abolition of Third World Debt based in Brussels under the umbrella of the World Social Forum, which is responsible for keeping alive the so-called 'Tobin Tax' initiative now espoused by Britain's Prime Minister Gordon Brown – and the result is a realistic prospect of genuinely equitable negotiations posing a fundamental challenge to neoliberal doctrines organised around the metaphors of 'fireman' and 'policeman' of the world.

This 'increased awareness' corresponds to what Carlota Pérez calls 'vision', the notion that economic and technological transformations taking place in the core countries of the world, and in the leading corporations of the main industries, determine the context in which 'catching-up' processes can take place. Within that context movements, underground struggles and the taking of positions occur, which can actually transform the context and expand the range of what is possible. That is the very definition of development. However, this means going beyond any situation of 'static' or even 'dynamic' dependency since the goal, which will take time and will require persistence and effort, projected on to the future to be realised in the present as an ethical-economic principle, is independence. It is not just a matter of 'catching' or 'climbing' up (and of kicking away the ladder, once one has got there) but, rather, of transforming the shape of the track, escaping the vicious circle and replacing it with a virtuous one (Pérez speaks of 'positive-sum' strategies of development), or tilting the playing field decisively. Liberating ourselves from naïve beliefs on the self-sufficiency and self-reproduction of markets is both part of and an objective of such strategies. It is in this sense that Pérez deploys such mantras as 'globalization is an intrinsic feature of the ICT paradigm; liberalization is not', or 'return of the repressed' in relation to the explosive resurfacing of inner tensions in the sub-prime mortgage credit crunch, and the network-like character of governmental and collective action nowadays.

It is true that economists were no naïve believers in market efficiency. The new generation of maverick economists like José Antonio Ocampo, Fernando Fajnzylber, or Pérez herself among others, were claiming that the so-called 'efficient-market hypothesis' or the 'HOS theory' that revamped Ricardo's notion of comparative advantages for the 'flat world' era were full of holes; nevertheless, their warnings were largely ignored. It is also true that no economic theory suggests you should value mortgage derivatives on the basis that house prices would always rise. However, that assumption was built into the set of received ideas concerning the authority of a certain use of reason that was central to the rise to dominance of the efficient-market hypothesis, the HOS thesis and its related notions in economic theory and practice. Moreover, since such received ideas about the use of reason (probability, mathematical modelling) are to do with the relation between reason and established institutions of power, or in the more technical language used by scientists and philosophers, between theoretical and practical reason,[39] then the crux of the matter is the relationship between economic theory and established political institutions, including the economy itself, which defend a political path, the liberal path of competition, individual thriving and perseverance and the finite nature of humanity and its resources, as 'the only true path'.[40] And this question about the crossroads between economic theory and political ideology as a *real* necessity, a dogma, has not been posited, let alone been sufficiently considered, in the wake of the debacles of the 1990s in Latin America and the 2000s in the rest of the world.

What was neglected was the need to think strategically about development, equality and economic growth. Fajnzylber's contribution matters precisely in that respect. In the early 1970s he had authored a couple of reports for the Brazilian Institute of Applied Economics Research (IPEA) on national and multinational enterprises in Brazil, and another on export-oriented strategies.[41] In the early 1990s, he published an influential work on strategies of economic transformation and equality.[42] It was the fruit of a decade's work at ECLAC, which seemed to solve the challenges confronting the institution as it sought to mount what Fernando Leiva calls 'a credible response to neoliberalism's laissez-faire counterrevolution in development thinking'.[43] In a nutshell, after Fajnzylber, economists like Carlota Pérez, governments and policy-makers started paying much greater attention to social, political, technological and cultural variables – to time, space and history – criticising the political absolutism of the previous years and its cold-hearted devotion to the rule of the market. In the case of Latin America, this means that the establishment of a model of development of its own must start with the recognition that the brief window of opportunity exploited by Asian 'fabrication industries' concerned with electronics, electrical appliances, clothing and so on has now closed, and end in the recognition of the opportunities offered by a concentration on 'process industries' that use natural resources and energy with a view to a high-tech and high-growth future 'taking intelligent advantage of the current and, most likely, also future favourable prices of these products [natural resources and energy] in order to fund an effort in developing the technologies and the human capital related to those very products'. The continent could become the supplier of material inputs (e.g. in particular, finalised products and technologies associated with distributed energy resources, renovated buildings serving as 'power plants', health and lifestyle goods finalised through indigenous knowledge by indigenous peoples, and so on), food and other agricultural products (from the most standard to the most sophisticated) to the rest of the world'.[44]

The strategy refers to the direct transformation of raw materials by chemical, electrical and other methods of composition, decomposition and recomposition 'such as those used in making steel from iron and coal, paper from wood pulp, bottled tomato sauce from fresh tomatoes', migrating gradually towards higher and higher 'value-added products with greater and greater specialized and customized features and to establish strong networks of innovation . . . to sustain the effort in time'. This is not incompatible with implementing strategies in defiance of the market, thereby engaging in the manufacturing of electronics and electric cars or apps, for instance. Nor with inequality-busting strategies such as Brazil's Family Allowance, which effectively creates a common fund for the purposes of mutual aid and treats access to common goods as a social rent, Venecuba's solidarity-health programmes or Bolivia's cash-transfer programmes to children in the country's public schools, to the elderly and to pregnant women, provided such strategies are put into practice and do not take the form of quick top-down handouts in the absence of a more long-term strategy. In this respect, the strategy calls for, and in fact demands, bottom-up mobilisation and strong political leadership and initiative. These can only grow if there is a fertile soil of mutual-aid traditions like those found among indigenous or Afro-Latin American communities, combined with the opening and fabrication of genuinely democratic spaces, some of which may even operate at arm's length from the state. Here again, the association principle of peer-to-peer authentic connections (attention, reputation, 'thick' relations, not just between humans but also with non-humans such as the Amazon forest and so on, which in time can even be transformed into markets oiled with non-capital money such as LETS or OsCurrency made operative through mobile phones) has an important role to play in preparing for the leap in future technologies. As SUNY director of Globalization Studies Fernando Leiva puts it, in this respect the most important innovation of the new Latin American policy framework 'is the active promotion of forms of social coordination beyond those offered by market forces alone'.[45]

Critics of the Chinese model of development within China would find here plenty of food for thought. 'New Left' Chinese commentators like Wang Shaoguang and Hu Angang pointed out in the early 1990s that, although in terms of restricting personal freedoms the power of the Chinese state was second to none, when it came to running the country in an effective way 'China's state was one of the weakest in the world'.[46] Like their Latin American colleagues, Chinese thinkers like Angang showed how, without democratic accountability from below or fear of sanctions from above, provincial leaders would put their interests above those of the people, leading to corruption, overheating of the economy, bad investment, low levels of domestic consumption and so on. Shaoguang and Angang argued that China's model of development is unsustainable because there is a limit to what the rest of the world can buy, meaning the Chinese would simply need to spend more, fight inequality and therefore establish the sort of associationist networks required to undertake such a task. The fact that China lacks genuine democratic spaces at grassroots level and that those which do exist are being actively dismantled by government, places the giant tiger economy at a disadvantage in the long term.

The First World's Soft Superpower

'For those of us who have long claimed that the world's international financial architecture needed deep reform, the call for a "Bretton Woods II" is welcome,' said Colombian economist José Antonio Ocampo in November 2008. 'Of course,' he observed, 'similar calls were made after the Asian and Russian crises of 1997 and 1998, but were not taken seriously by the rich industrial countries. Now that these countries are at the center of the storm, perhaps they will be more serious.'[47]

By the time Ocampo made these comments, students, workers, peasants, Indians and Afro-Latin Americans had recognised that an international economy so destructive it was now capable of turning water into debt, debt into slavery and slavery into an infinite hell on earth, could not be, in any sensible meaning of the term, right. Between 1982 – the year of the first Mexican debt crisis that brought to a close the loan boom inaugurated by General Augusto Pinochet after the coup that overturned the government of Salvador Allende in Chile – and 1994 – the year of the second Mexican financial collapse and the launching of the Indian Zapatista rebellion that took a stand against neoliberal globalisation in Chiapas on 1 January 1994, which was planned to coincide with the day when the NAFTA 'free trade' agreement went into effect – it became increasingly clear to the peoples of Latin America that all this destructive creation was not some flaw in an otherwise efficient and self-correcting path.

Impoverished, seemingly powerless, abandoned to their own versions of purgatory by ruling elites dedicated to securing and protecting the small spaces they had managed to carve for themselves out of the 'brave new world' termed globalisation, they stood up and fought an unlikely second war of independence. And they won. It has taken the rest of the world, particularly the so-called 'Global North', Europe and the United States, almost two more decades to recognise that, behind calls in the Global South to curb the international financial system, get rid of enslaving debt and stop believing in the dogmas of the 'free market' as if the specifics of an intellectual system were religion, lay a universal truth and the promise of a more fundamental freedom. Nearly two decades of crises within crises, debt defaults, growing inequality, resource plundering, bankrupt countries, water wars, environmental disaster, failed drug wars, repression, historical victories signalling massive political shifts and one Great Recession the consequences of which are still unfolding, it would seem that the rest of the world is catching up.

'The fact is,' declared Lord Turner, chairman of Britain's Financial Services Agency in August 2009, 'that intellectual systems – the whole efficient market theory, Washington consensus, free-market deregulation system can become like a religion.' 'But now,' added assistant editor of the *Financial Times* Gillian Tett, 'there is a real sense of confusion. Over the past year I have been talking to former true believers and they're like a priest who has lost faith in the Bible, but still has to go to church, and the congregation is sitting there but he doesn't know what the Bible is any more.'

The story told in the pages of this book leads to one simple conclusion: do not despair. There may be confusion, but there are in the world peoples who do not sit waiting for some priest to tell them where to go. Gone the faith and absent the dogma, the clergy has become useless. A new sense of responsibility and collective discipline has taken their place. People everywhere in Latin America stood up and sought their own way ahead. You have to give it to them: they did it when everybody else was taking for granted that history was over and there was only the one true path to be followed, by whatever means necessary. They dissented before anyone else did, and summoned the courage to go out there and make things happen. These people belonged to the world of the poor and the oppressed, not to the 'educated' middle classes; they did not come from the centres or the core networks of the globalised world, but belonged to the periphery. They had nothing in them to show the way ahead but the sheer magnitude of their own poverty and the climate of institutional slavery within which they lived. There was no vanguard, no 'socialist camp', no clarion call to rebellion and no manifesto. They produced knowledge out of that situation and in the process created identities and strategies that strengthened them and modified their surroundings. If many around the world perceive in Latin America a newfound sense of confidence and autonomy, and new local tactics aimed at 'global challenges', that is because of the realisation among Latin Americans that, for all the conventional wisdom about 'global solutions for global problems', actually where you live is where you take a stand.

These peoples, their identities and strategies, encompass peasant and labour movements; mobilisations against military regimes, either those wearing green fatigues and dark shades or their business-suited successors, against economic policies and eternal debt; Christian-based communities; neighbourhood movements; guerrilla organisations, transiting from the Cuban model to the network model of the global village and replacing for a moment at least their AK-47s with laptop computers; human rights mobilisations; women's movements; environmental activism and ethnic movements. Issues, strategies and declarations that at first had no single socio-economic referent eventually referred to a common climate of institutional oppression that linked them not only to the dimension of oppression peculiar to mass poverty, but also to an image and a memory of the lost commons of their Indian and African ancestors.

These were the commons of the past, but there are also the commons of the present: water, the coca leaf, and oil and gas, which once seemed lost to the global enclosures fostered by transnational corporations and the governments and international financial institutions they influenced or dominated. Crucially, there are also the commons of the future, which they are building through elections, constitutional assemblies, Zapatista *caracoles*, regional and global institutions, set to replace those associated with the nostrum that prices are always right and that in the world of finance globalisation markets exert their own self-discipline and governments or people should not stand in the way. These are movements, social and political, that have emerged from the multiple manifestations of poverty.

This becomes clear in the arena when the story is told from the standpoint of human rights. The majority of the victims of human rights violations in Latin America and elsewhere belong to the underworld of the poor and the oppressed: half of those detained and disappeared during Argentina's military dictatorship were workers and two-thirds were wage-earners; 70 per cent of those who died or disappeared at the hands of the military and death squads in El Salvador were peasants; more than 80 per cent of the victims of human rights violations in Guatemala during the 1980s were indigenous peasants and rural or urban workers; similar statistics exist for ethnic and women's movements and even more scandalous figures accompany the rise of the right-wing paramilitary in Colombia, now allegedly demobilised but whose ideology and sentiment remain widespread among the middle and upper classes of that South American country.[48]

There are, of course, many 'global problems' that stand in the way of the reconstruction of the world order as we make our way to the next century. But in general they can be grouped into two related but different kinds of challenges:

1) The fragmentation of the social sphere and the weakness of collective response and action, a consequence of the attacks unleashed upon labour and other perhaps more traditional forms of dissent and collective politics, but also of the rise of individualist, liberal globalism, during the 1980s and 1990s.

2) The internationalisation of capital markets and economic competition, and the financialisation of the international economy, resulting in the 'swelling' of intermediary and services sectors well beyond what is socially optimal, becoming excessively profitable, and reintroducing intolerable income gaps in the economy and sources of conflict and instability in the social fabric. These constraints over progressive models of politics and global transformation were identified early on by researchers looking at the prospects of emergent political options in Latin America.[49]

In the tension between citizenship and people, Latin American movements seem to have found ways to answer the first challenge. They have also discovered that the second problem was closely related to the first. Why does it matter? Not just because this paves the way towards transformative politics; this is not an ideological issue. Rather, because there are times, and we may be living in such times, when transformation becomes an imperative. Paradoxically, the fact that we live within the systems that need to be radically changed and believe in their ultimate value, makes us reluctant to embrace alternatives because it means admitting that our chosen policies and ways of life have failed and will continue to fail. Moreover, at stake is what experts call 'intergenerational equity', or, simply put, the future. And we may lack the appropriate sources of motivation to think and act about the future, since we live under constant pressure to live the present. Secretly we perceive that, as John Maynard Keynes is supposed to have said, 'in the long term we'll all be dead'. If so, then why bother?

These are, put otherwise, the psychic reserves of our economic systems, so deeply engrained that we do not even acknowledge their existence. Take, for instance, climate change: ultimately, no 'top-bottom' approach, best represented by the 'flexibility mechanisms' at the heart of the Kyoto Protocol, would work. This is because what is required goes beyond mere economic logic and enters into the realm of coordinated collective action, from the bottom up. The problem is we seem to lack, precisely, the tools and resources for bottom-up coordinated collective action. Put simply, economic distortions, inefficiencies and market failures have gone into our brains. Among other reasons, Kyoto failed because it has stifled discussion of alternative policy approaches. It became a failure of imagination. 'As Kyoto became a litmus test of political correctness,' explain climate change experts Gwin Prins and Steve Rayner, 'those who were concerned about climate change, but skeptical of the top-down approach adopted by the protocol, were sternly admonished that "Kyoto is the only game in town".'[50]

As it happens in most cases when radical collective action is required, a little political incorrectness goes a long way. But for that you need to break away from the herd, not an easy feat to accomplish in the 'flat world' of Thomas Friedman or the 'walled world' of the Chinese leadership. What is required is best exemplified by the way indigenous peoples from Bolivia and Ecuador overcome institutional settings which in practice mostly work as tailor-made for white male Creoles, for those who have stable jobs, and for those who believe you can fix a problem with the system without changing the system. The forms of citizenship that make up the institutional framework of most of our societies in principle exist also for them, but are not just inaccessible but actually stifling and disabling. If so, then the only reasonable alternative is to withdraw from such relations and enter into new ones, more equal and enabling. In turn, such enabling relations build more equal and socially valuable institutional settings that work. If an institutional setting does not work, for instance the Kyoto Treaty's scheme to deal with global warming, the reason is that it is disabling, it constrains, rewarding those who are part of the problem and unduly punishing those who, already victimised, could be part of the solution.

EPILOGUE

The United States of Latin America

United Latin America

On 23 February 2010, thirty-two out of the thirty-five countries of the Americas signed the Cancún Declaration on the Unity of Latin America and the Caribbean. Dealing with some of the most crucial issues of our time, from the financial crisis to climate change, the declaration focused on the creation of a regional organism aiming to gather in one voice all the countries of Central America, South America and the Caribbean. 'We have decided the constitution of the Community of Latin American and Caribbean States as a regional arena of our own, which will unite all of our nations in one voice,' said Mexican president Felipe Calderón, acting as *pro tempore* Secretary of the Rio Group and host of the meeting.

The Community will begin to operate during the 2011 meeting of the Rio Group in Caracas. The Community of Latin American and Caribbean States will formally replace the *ad hoc* diplomatic setting of the Rio Group, as well as the Caribbean Community (CARICOM) and the Latin American and Caribbean Gathering for Integration and Development (CALC). It will function parallel to the Organization of American States (OAS). 'The challenge to build bridges among the different nations of our Latin America and the Caribbean, and unite our wills without discounting our diversity, will guarantee the success of this encounter,' had declared Brazil's president Luiz Inácio Lula da Silva in December 2008, during the preparatory encounter for the Cancún meeting. 'We wish to consolidate this proposal,' said Bolivian president Evo Morales after the meeting, 'as an instrument to achieve the complete independence of Latin America and the Caribbean.'

President Rafael Correa of Ecuador explained that the inefficacy of regional organisms such as the OAS justified the need for a unified bloc capable of more decisive and efficient action in defence of democracy and self-determination, even if this meant discounting the intervention of the two North American powers. He was referring to the inefficacy of the OAS and the US and Canada's intervention in the resolution of conflicts such as the coup that unseated elected President Manuel Zelaya of Honduras in 2009. Bolivian vice-president Álvaro García Linera hailed the Cancún declaration as an historic achievement in the advancement towards 'a united Latin America, without paternalisms or trusteeships'. The final shape and supra-national structure of the Community of Latin American and Caribbean states will be defined in the following months. 'It will provide our sovereignty and capacity for self-determination with further strength, before those who wish to continue to treat us as their backyard,' he said.

Bolívar's calls for unity in 1815 and 1824 were the historical precedents of the Cancún Declaration. Back then, Bolívar put forth a similar proposal for a league of Spanish American nations to be based in Panama. The proposal excluded Brazil, which was still an imperial monarchy, as well as Haiti and the United States because of their different languages, histories and cultures. Brazil is now a republic whose model of economic development is firmly based on the idea of equality, and is recognised in the region and elsewhere as an emerging leader in world affairs that in many ways outclasses other emerging countries such as China, Russia and India. Haiti has also been invited to become part of the Community, partly in recognition of its pioneering role in the search for independence and equality in the region. As for the United States, it is the aim of the Community to represent a united, autonomous and mature voice before the influential colossus of the north.

There is much that America and Latin America have in common. Both are continent-size geopolitical units comprising different states, with their own histories, nuances and differing political and economic outlooks. Both were colonised by small seafaring nations before gaining independence within decades of each other. Both gave origin to and developed republican democracies, more or less decentralised, in which state governments have considerable power. Their populations are made up of the descendants of their original inhabitants, early colonists and African slaves, complemented later on by European and then Asian migrants. Both would seem surprisingly religious to European eyes, with different denominations of the Christian faith competing for believers, while at the same time developing collage versions of western religiosity and culture mixed up with pre-Columbian symbols, African beliefs and enlightened home-grown secular voices. In fact, both contributed decisively to the birth and global spread of a form of Enlightenment that traversed cultures, languages and localities, in the process inventing new ideas of liberty, notions of human brotherhood based on empathy, and truly universal conceptions of equality that became a springboard for social, cultural and political experimentation.

They have both developed a culture all of their own, but look for inspiration to one another more than they do elsewhere, at least since the onset of the Monroe Doctrine, and in view of a constant exchange of goods, populations and even territories. Those same exchanges are the source of their stark differences. America is rich, while Latin America is comparatively poor. America fights wars elsewhere in the world. Latin America does not. Early American entrepreneurs like Charles Flint took advantage of a consistent 'Hamiltonian' model of development and benefited more from Latin American resources than did Latin American countries, and in the process created a technological divide. America successfully implemented an unprecedented programme of land reform in the mid-nineteenth century, while most of Latin America resisted it.

On the one hand, such resistance, coming from local elites inheriting colonial hierarchies, furthered internal divisions that in time affected the openness and efficacy of Latin America's political and legal institutions. On the other, Latin America's wars of independence did result in the entrenchment of egalitarian prospects and ideas over and against inherited colonial hierarchies. This is why Latin America's 'melting pot' is, if anything, even more successful than America's. In spite of repeated attempts from white mestizo elites in Latin America to impose a homogeneous model of 'integration', vigorously sustained efforts to resist the insistent argument according to which the relative underdevelopment of Latin American countries is the result of their heterogeneity, their own incompetence – the incompetence of Amerindians and Afro-Latin Americans, that is – or the inefficiency of its own institutions, have succeeded in producing path-breaking political phenomena such as the rise to power of indigenous peoples. Bolivia's indigenous president Evo Morales furthered that argument by reminding those present in the final session of the Cancún meeting of the value of autonomous political and economic institutions. He stated that, 'while the government of Bolivia remained under the control of the International Monetary Fund (IMF) and the United States, the country could not advance in the struggle against poverty'.[1]

Look closely, however, and some of these distinctions between America and Latin America begin to blur. For all his rhetoric, Morales' Bolivian government invests its cash surpluses in US Treasury bonds. When he was in Manhattan in the fall of 2009 for the annual UN meeting, Harry Belafonte planned a benefit in his honour, in Harlem. The newly formed Bolivian Evaporative Resources Enterprise, which devotes attention to exploring the possibilities of the country's allegedly huge reserves of lithium, which could become crucial in the emergent electric car industry, will have to come to an agreement with a multi-national corporation – most likely American – or figure out, imitating and 'borrowing' American technology, or on its own, how to mine its lithium treasure at a competitive global price and put it to good use. The old Bolivian city of Potosí, which in 1611 equalled London in size and importance, and was the place where globalisation started in earnest, is now one of the poorest places in what has long been one of the poorest countries of Latin America. But its story is not too dissimilar to that of Detroit, in the United States.

In fact, as America's middle class threatens to crumble under the weight of the economic crisis, it will find itself in political territory that would be familiar to many south of the border. All the while, the middle classes of countries like Brazil or Colombia seem more confident about their prospects for the future. Many of Brazil's younger businessmen and bankers hold postgraduate degrees from American business schools, while Harvard University students in America benefit from the work of

Brazilian social thinker and legal theorist Roberto M. Unger, who also collaborates with North American cosmologist Lee Smolin in advancing some of the most cutting-edge science concerning the nature of our universe. American hip hop is a staple of Amerindian and Afro-Latin American culture. And although Latin Americans do not tend to fight wars elsewhere, in South Africa I was constantly reminded of how important the presence of Cuban and other Latin American fighters was to the defeat of the apartheid regime based in Pretoria.

Checking the Facts: the Americas Then and Now

The statements of the Latin American heads of state present in Cancún, emphasising independence and equality, were not ideological. Morales, for instance, was referring to the fact that, after comparing the results of the IMF-led policies of the 1980s and 1990s, when the country was the poster child for the market dogmatism of the Washington Consensus, with the results of what Bolivians now call 'Evonomics', the contrast could not have been sharper. Back then, South America's poorest country swallowed the unsavoury 'shock recipe' whole: it sold off the state-owned airline, the trains, the phone company, the electric company and, infamously, the public water system of the city of Cochabamba to California's engineering giant Bechtel. It also handed over its lucrative gas and oil fields and pipelines to Enron and Shell.

The recipe, applied under the watchful eye of Washington, the IMF and the World Bank, was supposed to drive the country towards prosperity. Instead, public oil and gas revenues plummeted, trains stopped running, the airline went bust and the net effect was the transfer of wealth to a small number of foreign corporations and to the rich white mestizo elite concentrated in the Santa Cruz crescent. Afterwards, renewed attempts by elite governments in Bolivia to enforce an IMF-mandated tax increase on the poor, sky-rocketing water prices and selling off the oil and gas reserves at bargain prices, led to a stand-off between the grassroots, on the one hand, and the government and the armed forces, on the other. The latter appeared to be defending the interests of international corporations and financial agencies against the very citizens they were supposed to represent. A new sense of political subjectivity emerged among the urban and rural poor, led by the coca-leaf unions, Indian revivalist groups and globally networked movements that helped bringing Morales and García Linera to power in 2005.

Since then, thanks largely to Morales' policy of 'nationalisation' of the gas and oil industry (in fact, merely a renegotiation of the country's contracts with various companies, leading to an increase in taxes and a more active role for the public oil company YPFB and the government), together with the hydrocarbon price boom of 2005 and 2007, the macroeconomic performance of South America's poorest nation has been astonishing. Bolivia's GDP growth in 2008 surpassed 6 per cent while the developed world's economies shrank as a result of the Great Recession. Bolivia's foreign currency reserves increased to more than $8 billion. Increased taxes on foreign oil companies did not scare off investors but, rather, produced enough new revenues to eliminate the country's budget deficit and generate surpluses three years in a row. Bolivia's government saved some of the revenue and aimed the rest at the poorest, via a cash-transfer strategy similar to the one applied by Brazil's Lula administration under the Family Allowance scheme.[2]

The strategy, specifically targeting children in public schools, pregnant women and the elderly, realised two principles: first, that of the mutual aid characteristic of traditional communities, but without their closed identifications; second, the economic principle of the need to sacrifice certain short-term gains for the sake of laying the groundwork to raise long-term productivity. In this case, by providing an incentive for poor Bolivian families to keep their children at school rather than pulling them out to work, establishing some form of social security for the elderly, and supporting women. Clever, given the leadership of women in communitarian networks among indigenous peoples in Bolivia, which in turn could provide the social structure for viable and creative processing industries in the future, such as those derived from the alternative uses of traditional communitarian knowledge about the properties of the coca leaf. In the meantime, Morales' government has also invested in infrastructure: it has paved 840 miles of roads, built 545 clinics and health facilities, distributed more than 1,000 tractors among primary farmers and established water connections for over 821,000 people. Bolivia's infrastructure still has a long way to go, and the country will have to discover new ways of producing things, or imitate old ones, to go beyond the 'curse of natural resources'. However, it is crucial to understand that such damnation is in fact the result of a technological divide that is the consequence of economic and political choices made by advanced countries in their relations with developing ones, rather than some 'natural' given.[3]

Bolivia's 'Evonomics' has earned praise from some unlikely sources. In October 2009, Gilbert Terrier, Senior Adviser in the IMF's Western Hemisphere Department, said in a press release that Bolivia's prudent saving of 'part of the windfall during the expansion period' of hydrocarbon prices 'has allowed the country to apply a counter-cyclical policy [countering the effects of the financial downturn cycle] in 2009, including more public investment to support internal demand and the social protection network'.[4] The 'bail out the people' scheme of Bolivia resembles that applied in Brazil and elsewhere in Latin America in order to successfully counter the effects of the global economic crisis. The overall strategy and its consequences sharply contrasts with the mixed effects of the 'bail out the bankers' tactic applied in Europe and the United States. So far, although it helped such countries to avoid slipping into a second Great Depression, the Keynesian intervention to rescue the banking system in the developed world has proved less effective in relation to the goals of stimulating demand, curbing the most speculative practices of the banks and addressing global imbalances.

The 2008 Economic Crisis as a Political Short Circuit
The current global economic crisis can be seen, among other things, as a failure of political reality and imagination. Politically speaking, it was at the very least questionable to short-circuit collective action and prudent legislative process, invoking 'necessity' and 'emergency', in order to transfer vast amounts of taxpayers' money, $700 billion in the case of America, to the banks. In a telling moment of truth, US Congresswoman Marcy Kaptur from Ohio tells filmmaker Michael Moore that 'the people here [in Congress] aren't really in charge. Wall Street is in charge', and suggests that what happened in the United States

in December 2008 was not just theft of public funds on an unprecedented scale, but also a *coup d'état*.[5]

Paradoxically, the political short circuit that was characteristic of the
events of December 2008, when Executive 'deciders' in the US and the UK
concentrated all power in themselves to the detriment of the Legislative,
the rule of law and the people, and marched on while invoking the necessity of the times (to stop 'the sucker', that is the banks and the debt-based
economy, from 'going down', as George W. Bush famously put it at the
time) actually reveals that, in today's global system, the 'impossibility' of
collective decision is what paralyses global capitalism. There is a clear sense
today that both Washington and Westminster suffer from a deep-seated
paralysis, an inability to make decisions that has so far translated into public
electoral apathy, hung parliaments, a difficult first year for the Obama
administration, radical attacks on the federal government coming from
right-wing fringe movements, riots and strikes in Europe, and a strange
vacuum in foreign relations. That sense of paralysis in the institutions of
representative democracy could easily transform into popular discontent
and creative rebelliousness, as is the case in Brazil, Bolivia or Greece, or
else become a fertile ground for the kind of populism that in America at
least is being successfully harvested by such fringe movements as the Tea
Party and an increasingly vociferous GOP.

As journalist David Brooks said in August 2008, the dispersion of
power brought about by globalisation and its discontents 'should, in
theory, be a good thing, but in practice multipolarity means that more
groups have effective veto power over collective action. In practice,
this new pluralistic world has given rise to globosclerosis, an inability
to solve one problem after another.' This means that one of the unacknowledged effects of the global financial crisis of 2008 has been to
undermine the very notion of unilateral and multilateral economic and
political predominance.[6] This should lead to widespread recognition of
the need to explore new forms of planetary governance. Initiatives like
the Community of Latin American and Caribbean States are a step in
that direction.

The initiative specifically aims at redrawing the Bretton Woods–IMF
landscape with the objective of re-establishing the economic sovereignty

of nations and the symmetry of international economic relations. This would be achieved by tilting the playing field in favour of emerging and developing countries. For instance, by guaranteeing access to credit in the case of a liquidity crisis, establishing a system of collective insurance and self-protection in the face of the biases of the global monetary system, going beyond existing schemes of debt restructuring and abolition, weakening the degree of intellectual property rights protection, and helping developing countries establish targeted research and development initiatives with accompanying subsidies, perhaps through an international tax on patent royalties. Overall, the aim would be to radically reform the political architecture of international finance and economics, on the basis of replacing the 'one dollar, one vote' free-market principle for the more democratic 'one man (one person, one country), one vote' rule.

Governments in the developed world reacted in 2008 with a turn towards 'strong decision', sidelining democratic political process. This was in fact a variant of the 'one dollar, one vote' rule in which a 'Strong Executive' announces a coming catastrophe in order to avert it, while at the same time behaving as a committee representing the interests of Goldman Sachs, Merrill Lynch and Lloyds Banking Group. However, the need for a 'new Bretton Woods' was forced upon the major global powers. It was made concrete, to a certain extent, in the increase of $500 billion in the liquidity of the IMF, and the call for an internal redistribution of power from the US and Europe to the emerging countries decided by the G-20, rather than the more exclusive G-7, early in 2009. The crucial role of Brazil, India and China was recognised. But there is still a long way to go before the more essential transformations proposed by grassroots movements and governments in Latin America and elsewhere, and by the newer generation of maverick economists led by Joseph Stiglitz, José Antonio Ocampo, Carlota Pérez and others, take place.

Chief among such transformations are the removal of the convertibility obligation into a capital account from the statutes of a proposed new IMF, the balancing of the interests of intellectual property right holders with those of the rest of the world, the redistribution of world demand from the (developed) countries in deficit (an 'empire without credit', in the case of the US) to the ones in surplus (for instance, Brazil and China, but also Bolivia), which, as British economist Martin Wolf put it correctly in the *Financial Times*, the G-20 meeting in London did not even attempt,[7] and the institution of a real supranational currency. But also, crucially, the serious and renewed consideration of the political question concerning the right to social ownership of common goods raised, however incipiently, by the various bail-outs after the 2008 crisis, and, before it, by events such as Bolivia's 'Water Wars'.

That question has been posited at the centre of Latin America's agenda for the future by the principled stand taken by 'Evonomics' in Bolivia and 'Lulanomics' in Brazil, echoed by the Cancún Declaration, but also by Obama's proposed new 'New Deal' in America. 'The principle is clear,' says Swiss economist Christian Marazzi; 'begin from the base in order to reform the monetary system.'[8] He refers in particular to Obama's Homeowner & Stability Plan (HSP), a component of his overall economic revival plan that constitutes a historical precedent for a wider provision of mortgage refinance funds for American families. 'The plan anticipates saving about four million families from foreclosure on their houses, but in such a way that a concrete value of the derivative securitised assets is re-established,' he says.

If up until today access to common goods such as land and housing, or health and education, has taken the form of, as we now know, toxic private debt, then strategies such as Obama's HSP, Lula's Family Allowance and Morales' cash-transfer initiative raise the issue of the legitimacy to claim such access in the form of the right to a social rent, which in our societies often takes the form of redistribution. Social rent and redistribution can be articulated in many areas, but, crucially, in education, research and development, housing and health provision. These are examples of areas in which helping families and younger generations by establishing guaranteed rights to a social rent are also, in fact, 'a veritable investment in the future'.[9] Even at the cost of certain short-term gains, this sort of investment, coupled with intelligent plans for process-industrialisation of the sort described by Carlota Pérez or Silvia Rivera Cusicanqui in Latin America, and other forward-looking ways of defying the market, such as the Bolivian initiative to develop a lithium-based electric car industry,[10] can hold the key towards long-term prosperity. Significantly, if these actions have an important impact on future prospects, they also relate to space decisively, for strategies such as these can be described as *local* interventions that manage to reso-nate with decisive regional and *global* dimensions, which often conflict with one another.

As Brazil's minister of social development, Patrus Ananias, in charge of the Family Allowance programme, explained to me during a conver-sation in September 2009, in the local dimension these strategies inter-vene precisely at the level of (aggregated) demand where crises destroy incomes, job positions, social ties and peoples' lives.[11] To the extent that they aim at restoring economic value to financial instruments (mort-gages, in the case of America, debt-related instruments, bonds and sovereign funds in the case of Latin America) or commodities (gas, oil, lithium, water, air, biodiversity and so on) created to be immersed in the circuits of global circulation, there is a global dimension to such local strategies. And this articulation between local interventions, on the one hand, and regional and global dimensions, on the other, often tends to be the point where, in times of crisis, heightened internal divi-sions, instability, competitive devaluations or defaults, and protectionist measures to regain bits of markets by taking them away from others, including coercive interventions to protect or secure key resources, lead to international conflict and war.

To acknowledge the importance of this question is therefore crucial in order to understand what is at stake for the world in the battle that is looming in the Americas. The contest is between those who see in the principled stance described above the only practical action that will restore value and values to a clogged-up international system, and doctrinaire populists who, like the Tea Party in America and the radical wing of the GOP, *Uribismo* in Colombia, some sectors of the Mexican right or the *Cruceñista* movement in Bolivia, see instead a downward slippery slope to Soviet-style communism. In the specific case of the Americas, the battle for the soul of our societies will also take the shape of a battle for the soul of Latinos and Latin Americans, since the latter hold the key to majority power in the United States and to economic revival everywhere.

In that respect, the recent and coming contests in such arenas as the states of Texas and California in the United States (particularly immigration policy, after the historic approval of the Healthcare Bill in the US), the Community of Latin American and Caribbean States, Brazil's domestic and regional contest for leadership and the future of Venezuela or Bolivia, concern not only the destiny of the Americas but also that of the world. In the first of such contests, Evo Morales and Álvaro García Linera were elected to a second term in the government of Bolivia on 6 December 2009, with 63 per cent of the vote and overwhelming majority participation, almost three times as much as the nearest competitor, thereby setting a new record for a country in which presidents were regularly elected with less than 25 per cent of the popular vote.[12]

Checking the Facts: Mexico and Bolivia

Compare Bolivia's results with those of Mexico after more than a decade and half's partnership with Canada and the United States under the NAFTA 'free trade' agreement. Three new batches of economic data confirmed at the end of 2009 what many expected: it had been a very bad year for Mexico.[13] According to ECLA's 2009 balance report, almost 36 per cent of Mexico's population were now living below the poverty line, while about twelve million Mexicans were now indigent. Thus, poverty, extreme poverty and inequality had all grown faster in Mexico than in any other Latin American country.

The National Statistics Institute (INEGI) found out that the country's third-quarter GDP had declined by 6.2 per cent due to a drop in manufacturing output, 'which could be traced back to a 37% reduction in foreign direct investment', given that the country lacks an indigenous industrialisation model. Finally, Mexico's creditworthiness was downgraded by international bond rating agency Fitch Ratings from BBB+ to BBB on the basis of its continued dependency on variable oil revenues, unsustainable debt levels, inability to implement counter-cyclical fiscal and other policies in the face of the international crisis and, crucially, its dependency on an increasingly uncertain climate of US trade and investment, compared with the increased diversification of the global trade and financial relations of all of the other major economies of Latin America.

And while Bolivia's government can operate smoothly and achieve better results precisely because of its deeper connections and forward-looking prospects construed in collaboration with communal associations and civic movements, future Mexican governments need to do more to approach, and profit from, the grassroots energy of such movements as the Zapatista Army of National Liberation (EZLN) led by the Tzeltal-, Tzotzil- and Tojolabal-speaking Indians of rural Chiapas, and the urban Mexican Electrical Workers Union (SME) that has been opposing the liquidation of the Mexican public power company in recent times, citing the example of the workers of Chicago and Buenos Aires, where Latino and Argentinean workers willing to work 'recovered' their industries and have successfully operated them as cooperatives.

What must be avoided at all costs is the tendency to liken these grass-roots associations, in spite of their diverse histories, to the country's out-of-control drug cartels, and present them as the prime obstacle on the country's path to institutional order and free market-based growth. The corollary of such unfortunate analogies is that grassroots associations must be removed by any means necessary. This would entail, in fact, a repetition of the script that in the case of Colombia led to the institu-tionalisation of far right-wing paramilitary forces and the infiltration of Colombia's Parliament and Executive after decades of a failed war on drugs, on the one hand, and, on the other, to increased intervention from and dependency on the United States' military and intelligence community. Analysts have started wondering whether Colombia's history might repeat itself in Mexico and on the US border.[14]

Lessons for the Future

That scenario is too pessimistic. It is unlikely and I hope it stays that way. On the one hand, the current US administration has given some signs, incipient as they may be, of its will to rethink its strategy in the context of Mexico's drug-trafficking troubles and the global economic crisis. Mexico, on the other, is far too smart and nationalistic to allow international support to turn into intervention. However, it needs to be smarter. First, it must call for a renegotiation of the North American Free Trade Agreement in view of the increasing amount of data that shows it is not working. Second, Mexican politicians and grassroots movements need to come together in order to stave off the import of the Counter-terrorism/War on Drugs model that has caused so much damage in places like Colombia.

Luckily, there are those in America and in Latin America who now question the wisdom of a War on Drugs model whose consequences are at best mixed and, at worst, disastrous. They point out that the more damaging effect of our failure of political imagination regarding the drugs' problem in Latin America, 'comes from the U. S. emphasis on curtailing the supply abroad rather than lowering the demand at home'.[15] The consequence is a transfer of power from governments to criminals in a number of countries, since in many places the drug-trafficking market that criminals dominate is the major source of jobs, economic opportunity and money for elections. In countries like Colombia, for instance, not only the political establishment faces this problem, but also rebels whose oppositional stance and political will have been seriously weakened by their involvement in the drugs market. In both cases, power has been transferred to those able to achieve the short-term goal of raising money and acquiring resources to support military efforts and political survival, to the detriment of long-term political goals, and the wellbeing of the population at large.

These commentators also observe that the current global economic crisis will only intensify these trends 'as battered economies shrink and illicit trade becomes the only way for millions to make a living'.[16] Colombia, for instance, has one of the highest percentages of unemployment in the region, which analysts like the former minister of fiscal and economic affairs Salomón Kalmanovitz estimate at between 12.3 and 14 per cent in the major cities.[17] In Mexico, the $10 billion worth of drugs that American consumers buy from the country's cartels each year allows them to pay for a highly motivated army of 100,000 that almost equals Mexico's armed forces in size. This ascendancy of the drug cartels is a global problem, from Afghanistan, where the opium trade is equal to 30 per cent of the country's legal economy, to Guinea Bissau and Great Britain. Traffickers themselves or the recipients of their electoral contributions can become influential economic and political actors. In response to these prospects and facts, three of Latin America's most respected former presidents chaired in 2009 a commission that spent over a year studying the best available evidence from experts in public health, medicine, the military and economics, and came out in favour of drastic changes in current policy.[18] Their report calls for real alternatives beyond eradication, interdiction, criminalisation and incarceration, which can only be debated in a policy space different from that limited between absolute prohibition and wholesale legalisation.

The emergence of such a space for more intelligent policy-thinking is related to the construction of a geopolitical space willing to consider the redefinition of the international economic system. The Community of Latin American and Caribbean States can help bring about such a space. The recovery of economies in deficit such as that of the US, and the strengthening of economies such as Mexico's and Colombia's, is tied up with the redistribution of world demand to emerging countries featuring surpluses or mixed accounts, such as the mining- and commodity-exporting economies of Latin America. In turn, America will not be able to continue to exist in a world in which Brazil and Bolivia, for instance, 'could save much more than [they] invested and dispose of the excess savings in America', as China has done in the recent past.[19]

That scenario, which increases the internal indebtedness of the countries in deficit, is unsustainable. Massive liquidity influxes from emerging countries allowed American capital to rely in the past on internal consumption through the explosive debt of American families. That world is now gone. America needs Latin American countries, as much as China and India, to invest more and spend more. This requires important changes in the international financial architecture. The fundamental imbalance between emerging countries in mixed circumstances or export surplus, on the one hand, and developed countries in deficit, on the other, must be addressed. This includes the establishment of a real supranational currency, combined with the creation of regional reserve arrangements such as the one considered for Latin America in the Cancún Declaration, and a set of 'inequality-smashing' policies everywhere.

The aim is to correct, on the one side, the imperfections with which the Bretton Woods arrangements were born after the International Clearing Union, the proposal made by John Maynard Keynes to create a more symmetric system, was rejected. And on the other, to solve the inherent instability of an international reserve system based on a national currency, and the high demand for self-protection that developing countries face because of the 'cyclical' or unequal nature of international finance and trade. The best way forward would be to complete the expectations of the reforms originated in the United Nations Conference of Trade and Development (UNCTAD) of the 1960s. This would entail moving into a fully Special Drawing Rights-based IMF with a clear 'counter-cyclical' and egalitarian focus, as proposed by Colombian economist José Antonio Ocampo.[20]

In order to work, the strategy to revive the world's economy would also require, crucially, the reorientation of the productive structures of emerging countries and a decisive drive against inequality, both at home and abroad. In the case of Latin America this entails a reorientation towards 'process industries', the industrialisation of its natural endow-ment of resources and raw materials. In that respect, the assertion of Latin American sovereignty over its natural resources, including those of its energy resources, is reasonable not only in terms of its self-interest but also taking into account American interests. But the convergence of such local interests requires a specific political context, which is global: as has been suggested throughout this book, in order to overcome the crisis, the global system will have to be redefined in terms of national sovereignty, regional poles and the symmetry of commercial exchanges. Economists refer to this as 'tilting the playing field'. The point is that if the playing field of unfair competition and unequal finance and trade is not 'tilted', it becomes more likely that the present crisis persists for a very long time, or is followed by similar crises in the future.

The future in question involves Latin Americans living in and out of Latin America. On the one hand, since the strategy for an economic leap in the Americas has both local and global dimensions, the future of the Americas concerns us all. On the other, the United States also needs a new 'New Deal'. Investments in health and education represent by far the two best ways of generating major growth in employment. They are more effective than budget and tax cuts. While most other ways to get money to the economy have broken down in the United States, the health and education fiscal policy channel is still working. Taxpayers' money given to banks, businesses and households (unless the latter is tied up to education and health, as in the Bolivian and Brazilian schemes) is likely to be saved, having little or no stimulus effect, as economist Michael Mandel has observed.[21] Additionally, a focus on health and education would greatly impact on the sector of the US population with the highest rate of growth, Latinos, which, together with African Americans, will soon become the largest majority in the country.

But in spite of the fact that Latinos and African Americans are missing out the most on health and education, some states are actually introducing cuts in these two key sectors of the economy. In states like California, suggested cuts would flow to the bottom of the hierarchy. Latinos and African Americans would be hit the hardest. This sort of policy is a stumbling block on America's path to recovery. It needs to be overturned by a political culture that considers reform by starting with the base, not only because it is the fairest thing to do but also because it makes economic sense. In fact, given that Latinos extend their networks beyond the US border, what happens to them locally has regional and global effects. And, conversely, what happens to their relatives south of the border also has an important impact north of the Rio Grande. A principled stance in favour of redistribution and access to such basic common goods as health and education south of the border, together with an economic viewpoint that seriously takes into account the effects of the present crisis on our mainstream conceptions of property rights, private debts and social rights, could help create the right political climate up north.

If it is true that only by realising the principles of such a new orientation at home and abroad – social ownership and redistribution – will we be able to overcome the present situation, then the stakes in the battle for the soul of the Americas could not be higher. Thus, to secure a future for all Latin Americans is in the best self-interests of the US and Europe: on the one side, because only by displacing world demand from the countries in deficit to the ones in relative surplus, among them

Latin America, will the world be able to push through the ongoing crisis and make it to the next century. And on the other, because this is the way to stop future waves of immigration from taking place, perhaps revert present migratory currents, and in any case to dispel the potential destructiveness of the anti-immigration drive in northern countries.

This also relates to the question 'why cannot we be anti-American?' My response is this: we cannot be anti-American or anti-British, even in the case of such disputed issues as the Falkland, or Malvinas, Islands, because the relation between the local and global dimensions in the context of the ongoing crisis is all too clear. And also because our Brazilian, Ecuadorian, Bolivian, Colombian and Mexican sons, daughters, cousins, nieces and nephews either live in such countries or have themselves become British, American and Euro-citizens as well. To consider this reality becomes all the more important if one seriously takes into account the fact that the United States is set to become the next Latin American country.

Hence, also, the importance of the emergence of autonomous alliances and independent organisations in the south that can engage with the north. We need in both parts of the world diplomatic institutions able to make each other's principles and interests clear with independence and strength, and to have the capacity to produce forms of collective leadership ready to argue on behalf of such principles and interests. What we require is recognition of a common past, and of the centrality of common and independent choices in the present for the long-term purposes of a better future. The alternative to a redefinition of the international system, along such principles, has now become unacceptable. It is the very real possibility that the crisis will last a long time or will be followed by similar crises, leading to competitive devaluations, all-round protectionist actions, internal divisions, general instability and the closure of nation-states risking anything for their survival in the name of 'security' and 'public consensus'. We must avoid this alternative, for this is how wars break out.

South and North

When I was in South Africa in 2009, some good friends invited me to see *Nothing But the Truth*, the award-winning play written by John Kani. At the end of the play Sipho, the main character, frustrated by the failure of the now ANC-dominated government to help fulfil his lifelong dream of becoming Chief Librarian, firmly states that 'the problem with this fuck-ing country is that it does not recognise that it isn't about me; it's about justice!' His jibe, directed at the Truth and Reconciliation process that took place as part of South Africa's transition from apartheid, was similar to an argument made years before by Nobel Prize-winning playwright Wole Soyinka. Soyinka had argued that the beneficiaries of colonialism have a reason for accepting, and, indeed, demanding of themselves, a transfer of wealth for all the enslaved in Africa and elsewhere.

Soyinka and Kani invite us to ask, in imagination, why there should not be a general levy imposed for reconciliation, and defended in terms of a transfer of wealth to the populations that have historically suffered in the course of the struggle to free themselves, politically and economically, from the imposed fate of supposedly global inevitabilities. In the specific case of South Africa, such an economic transfer would have countered the consequences of the economic transfer that effectively took place from South Africa to Europe, when many of the most important and wealthy South African firms, which had profited from and during apartheid, were re-incorporated and registered on the London Stock Exchange.

In this case, as South Africa-based economist Patrick Bond explained to me, when individual national and private interests were threatened by the combined forces of internal pressure from below, and boycott-ing and other forces operating at the level of global market forces from the top, they demanded and obtained protection from the state, at the same time as appealing to national and cultural 'rainbow' identity. This 'protection' took the paradoxical form of a promise of institutional reform, which would include a set of redistributive measures under the Black Economic Empowerment initiative, on the one hand, and financial liberalisation, on the other, which allowed firms like Anglo American, De Beers, Old Mutual, SA Breweries and Didata, among others, to move offshore, many obtaining permission to relist financial headquarters on the London Stock Exchange.[22]

What were the consequences of securing the short-term interests of these firms? If you divide the population of South Africa into ten income deciles and consider their racial composition, it turns out that the richest decile, which gets 57 per cent of the country's income, comprises 56.3 per cent whites, 9.6 per cent Asians, 6.6 per cent 'coloureds', and 27.5 per cent blacks. You will find the majority of whites located in the two deciles that share the biggest percentage of South Africa's income. In contrast, the poorest decile, which shares a meagre 0.6 per cent of South Africa's income, comprises a whopping 97.6 per cent of black Africans and only 0.6 per cent whites. In the next decile, which shares 1.2 per cent of the country's income, you find 95 per cent black Africans versus 0 per cent white Africans.[23]

The numbers tell us who in fact rules the country. They also reveal what did not change: political liberation from apartheid in 1994 coincided with economic liberalisation in 1995, meaning the wealth accumulated during or as a result of apartheid remained in the same hands. There was no significant transfer of the kind called for by Kani or Soyinka. Those who benefited from the spoils of racism kept their profits, and continue to benefit from them even though apartheid is officially over. That is the deeper meaning of the talk you hear in urban townships in Johannesburg and Cape Town or in the rural areas near Addo, of the protests and social mobilisation, of the 'rampant crime and insecurity', of the debates about 'nationalisation' fostered by the ANC Youth League on the basis of the pledge contained in the Freedom Charter and in South Africa's consti-tution, and, crucially, of the racialising reality barely concealed behind 'rainbow' discourses about the 'right to difference' and 'recognition of the other' in post-apartheid South Africa.

The case of South Africa functions as a cautionary tale. When we take the disastrous consequences of excessive economic liberty into account we must also include nation and the state, against the mainstream line toed by 'free market' doctrinaires, revisionist historians and Bad Samaritans, according to which the market forces of inevitability will bring about the overall beneficial ends of free trade, and with them the disappearance of the state together with the planetary spread of a philos-ophy of 'modern' self-reliance. In this light, we should be much angrier than we are about the fact that financial liberalisation has rendered the egalitarian goals of political liberation so much more difficult to achieve, all the while methodically unravelling and destabilising the incremental improvements on unsatisfactory circumstances, achieved by past struggles for and the achievements of social democracy, and turning the latter into the last resort for the forward- and outward-driven nation-state's survival.

The promise of Black Economic Empowerment in South Africa, with its redistributive social-democratic undertones, was effectively made redundant by the massive 'capital strike' that took place around 1995. Much the same happened in Latin America in the late 1980s and early 1990s, when, in reaction to the increasingly evident disastrous consequences of neoliberalism in the region, leading towards further instability, increased conflict and civil warfare in places like Colombia, Mexico, Venezuela, Argentina or Bolivia, rights-based redistributive legislation and political opening were implemented and combined with forms of financial liberalisation. All this in the name of 'rainbow' or 'mixed' national cultural identity.

Since then, it has become clear to many in Latin America that rights and multiculturalism can be hollow promises if we do not take a serious look at what makes economic and trade relations unequal, both at the domestic and the planetary level, and illuminate our conclusions with the perspectives and potency of grassroots and global networks. Latin Americans concluded that without tilting the playing field of global economic relations, as suggested by Kani and Soyinka among others, and without devising and defending innovative financial actions in relation to the international monetary system, and our relationship with Nature and its resources, from the bottom up, the promises of social democracy and a deeper relation with Nature would forever remain unfulfilled. Or else, they would be nothing more than the romantic dreams of people who mainly reside in advanced industrial nations. Thus, the task ahead is not simply to preserve worthy institutions as a defence against worse options, or sympathetically guard some against the potentially catastrophic consequences of unfettered market forces; but also to add better institutions to those worthy arrangements that exist today, and actively seek for our children a better world than the one we inherited, while we recognise what is owed to those who came before.

Problems like climate change, for instance, cannot be adequately addressed from the standpoint of restoring an allegedly lost symbiosis with Nature, an idea that often has a racial tone about it – that indigenous peoples were somehow able to survive without touching their environments. As this book has shown, that idea is at the very basis of what makes unequal exchanges both possible and unjustifiable. Rather, an adequate standpoint must combine, at the same time, the potential of empathic relations with state intervention aimed at creating future environments where we can all find a way out of the vicious circuits that often lead nations to further resource competition, and to confuse resource competition with military conflict.

As this book has also shown, environmental and resource crises, which are in fact crises concerning access to common goods, often experienced as credit crises or as competition for scarce materials between technologically less and more advanced countries, have the very real potential to invite imperialist contests between states. Therein, industrial financiers and states will risk everything for survival, and peoples of all nations, despite their wishes, will be engulfed in their acts, presented as a matter of national (or 'democratic') security, national interest or public consensus. This is what happened during the Indian Wars in South and North America and with slavery; this is also what happened in the face of World War I. It is the way of unmaking history.

Making History

The Latin American decision to set up a Community of Latin American and Caribbean States, which also finds inspiration in the European dream of union, is crucial in order to understand the world order that will take us into the next century. This is because it acknowledges that the alternative – of this crisis lasting a very long time or being systematically followed by other crisis – is simply unacceptable. The Community of Latin American and Caribbean States has gathered around the goal of redefining the international monetary system in the name of national sovereignty and regional poles, on the one hand, and the philosophy of the equality of commercial and economic relations in and between societies, on the other. In this sense, it recognises that the growing inequality within and between nations, which generates broken societies and leads to conflict, cannot be allowed to continue.

Chris Bryant, British Under-Secretary of State for Foreign Affairs until 2010, has a better answer than any other British politician I know, Conservative or Labour, to the challenge posited by the Americas becoming far more intertwined, stronger and utterly Latino. 'International relations should recognise the role played by hopes and dreams, and the Latin American dream, the dream of independence – not to have one's fate decided somewhere else, and to vanquish poverty – is universal,' he said to an audience gathered at the Overseas Development Institute on 7 July 2009 in London. He focused on three challenges that Britain, and by extension Europe, America and the rest of the world, face together with Latin America: tackling the economic downturn, solving climate change and collaborating to ensure global security – particularly against forms of extremism, the growing influence of drug cartels in politics, state terror and hard-power reflexes. Bryant suggested that dealing with these issues would result in renewed empathy between north and south, and that more collaboration based on a clearer and more just philosophy at the international level would ensue. Crucially, he focused on the most important and often neglected part of the new agenda for international relations: the establishment of ends desirable to all, and achievable in the future. Equality is chief among them.

One example of an adequate and viable standpoint in relation to a global problem like climate change is the proposal made by the Ecuadorian government in relation to the oil reserves of the Yasuní region, a biologically rich area roughly the size of Massachusetts, in the Ecuadorian Amazon. In 2008, President Rafael Correa proposed a tax on every barrel of oil exported from OPEC member countries. The funds raised through the so-called Ecotax, would be used to finance conversion to other energy sources and to protect fragile ecosystems from oil drilling, of which Yasuní is a perfect example.

No matter how well the proposed market mechanisms for the post-Kyoto era work, the most intelligent commentators acknowledge that there is a role for direct regulation and targeted taxes, subsidies or levies. They can be successful when geared towards tackling specific market failures and where the costs of taking such measures correspond with a consistent long-term carbon price. The Montreal Protocol can be presented as a historical precedent of such an approach, and of the way in which the auction of permits contemplated for the second phase of the Kyoto agreement could credibly raise about one trillion euros per year, which could be allocated to pay countries that maintain their forests and other natural ecosystems in good condition, while at the same time raising their capabilities to acquire better technologies.

Ecuador's proposal shares this spirit. Moreover, it indicates a way in which oil-producing and oil-consuming countries could relate to their immediate political environments and use their position as leverage. The institutional framework of the initiative in Latin America is crucial to its success. This is yet another reason why the Community of Latin American and Caribbean States is an important step, not only for the region but also for the future of the world. Discussions have begun in Latin America about the establishment of the Single Unit of Regional Compensation (SUCRE) through the creation of the Bank of the South and a Southern Stabilization Fund. A common currency would facilitate trade within the region and spur a progressive de-dollarisation of inter-regional trade and financial relations. The SUCRE could pave the way towards a regional monetary and financial system with its own financial code. The Yasuní initiative could be a way of backing up this system. In the case of Ecuador, the common currency would be backed by the crude oil reserves in Yasuní National Park and the reserves would play a similar role to that played by silver and gold in the past, as a backing for national currencies.

This is an example of innovative thinking taken to the next level, bringing together what is best about environmental politics and development economics, the possibilities opened up by regional integration in the context of globalisation, and the strengthened position gained by Latin American countries relative to the world's major powers and the international financial system in recent years. It even makes financial economics sound fashionable again. In this light, Latin America and other progressive forces in the world should indeed 'apologise a little less for past shortcomings and speak more assertively of achievements' and innovative proposals.[24] On the one hand, the aim of achievements like the Community and proposals like the Yasuní initiative and the Ecotax is to solve rather than just defer, and perpetuate, the cycle of global crises and the repetitive emergence of neocolonial relations and the conflicts accompanying them. On the other, governments and social movements are addressing the issue of north–south relations in specific terms: the focus is on the political foundations of global finance, trade and competition for resources, which seem to pit some regions and cities in the world, which fare well, against others, which fare poorly. This entails engaging in a crucial debate about the nature and spread of material and social progress to all mankind.

In this sense, if the question of local political independence dominated our efforts during the long nineteenth century, in the light of the current crisis the crucial question for the twenty-first century is that of political and economic global justice. The latter has raised, at least incipiently, the issue of the right to social ownership of common goods. This is the context within which it is appropriate to ask the question 'what if Latin America ruled the world?' As members of a global society, we recognise in Latin America's historical efforts an exercise of the right, or the duty, to look critically at our world. But that is not enough. In its example, we also learn that the truest form of rule comes not from producing the most cars, selling and consuming the most goods, or harbouring the deadliest military weapons. And that it cannot be measured in terms of debt-to-GDP ratios. Rather, it concerns the human capacity to make new history.

Select Bibliography

Like everything else, books are always collective creations. In the writing of this one I have consulted many books, papers, articles, blogs and websites that are the result of other people's creativity and capacity to form global networks dedicated to the production of knowledge. What follows is a selected list of these sources. To make it easier for readers, I have subdivided these sources into relevant subject areas. The complete and detailed list of references and sources used in this book can be found in the notes to each chapter.

Books

On pre-Columbian America, discovery and conquest:

Anonymous. *The Chronicles of Michoacán*. Translated and edited by E. R. Crane and R. C. Reindorp. Norman, Okla.: University of Oklahoma Press, 1970

Boorstin, D. *The Discoverers. A History of Man's Search to Know His World and Himself*. London and New York: Random House, 1983

Collier, J. *The Indians of the Americas*. New York: W. W. Norton, 1947

De Alva Ixlilxóchitl, F. *Obras Históricas*. Mexico City: Porrúa, 1977

Díaz del Castillo, B. *Historia Verdadera de la Conquista de la Nueva España*. Madrid: Espasa-Calpe, 1968. There is an English edition titled *The Bernal Díaz Chronicles: The True Story of the Conquest of Mexico*. Translated and edited by A. Idell, New York: Doubleday & Co., 1957

Guaman Poma de Ayala, F. *The First New Chronicle and Good Government. On the History of the World and the Incas up to 1615*. Translated and edited by R. Hamilton. Austin: University of Texas Press, 2009

Le Clézio, J. M. G. *The Mexican Dream. Or, The Interrupted Thought of Amerindian Civilizations*. Translated by Teresa Lavender Fagan. Chicago, Ill., and London: University of Chicago Press, 1993

Mann, Charles C. *1941. The Americas before Columbus*. London: Granta, 2005

Marrero-Fente, R. *La Poética de la Ley en las Capitulaciones de Santa Fe*. Madrid: Trotta, 2000

Mignolo. W. *The Darker Side of the Renaissance*. Ann Arbor, Mich.: University of Michigan Press, 1995

Ponce, P. *El Alma Encantada*. Mexico City: Fondo de Cultura Económica & INI, 1986

Rumeu de Armas, A. *Nueva luz sobre las Capitulaciones de Santa Fe de 1492 concertadas entre los Reyes Católicos y Cristobal Colón*. Madrid: Consejo Superior de Investigaciones Científicas, 1985

Thumfart, J. *Die Begründung der globalpolitischen Philosophie. Zu Francisco de Vitorias 'Relectio de Indiis recenter inventis' von 1539*. Berlin: Kulturverlag Kadmos, 2009

Yupangui, T. *Instrucción del Ynga D. Diego de Castro Tito Cussi Yupangui*. Madrid: Ediciones Atlas, 1988

On the Americas, from the wars of independence to our time:

Beuchot, M. *Los Fundamentos de los Derechos Humanos en Bartolomé de Las Casas*. Barcelona: Anthropos, 1994

Brown, Dee. *Bury My Heart at Wounded Knee*. New York: Holt Paperbacks, 2001

Bolívar, S. *Simón Bolívar. The Bolivarian Revolution*. Edited and translated by Matthew Brown. London: Verso, 2009

Cárdenas, P. E. *El Movimiento Comunal de 1781 en el Nuevo Reino de Granada*. Bogotá: Tercer Mundo, 1980

Cordingly, D. *Cochrane the Dauntless: The Life and Adventures of Thomas Cochrane*. London: Bloomsbury, 2007

Du Bois, W. E. B. *Black Reconstruction in America: An Essay Toward a History of the Part Which Black Folk Played in the Attempt to Reconstruct Democracy in America, 1860–1880*. New York: Harcourt, Brace & Co., 1935

Foster, K. *Lost Worlds. Latin America and the Imagining of Empire*. London: Pluto Press, 2009

Galeano, E. *Open Veins of Latin America. Five Centuries of the Pillage of a Continent* London: Serpent's Tail (1973) 2009

Joseph, G., LeGrand, C. C., and Salvatore, R. (eds) *Close Encounters of Empire*. Durham, SC: Duke University Press, 1998

Las Casas, B. *Historia de las Indias*. Mexico City: FCE, 1986

— *El Pensamiento Político de Bartolomé de Las Casas*. Sevilla: Escuela de Estudios Hispano-Americanos, 1976

— *De Regia Potestate*. Edited by L. Perena. Madrid: Consejo Superior de Investigaciones Científicas, 1969

— *Tratados de Fray Bartolomé de Las Casas*. Mexico City: FCE, 1965

— *Opúsculos, Cartas, y Memoriales*, in *Obras Escogidas de Fr. Bartolomé de Las Casas*. Edited, by J. Perez de Tudela Bueso, VBAE, CX, Madrid, 1958

— *Los Tesoros del Peru*. Madrid: Imprenta y Editora Maestre, 1953

Linebaugh, P. *The Magna Carta Manifesto*. Berkeley, Cal., and London: University of California Press, 2008

Lynch, J. *Simon Bolivar: A Life*. New Haven, Conn.: Yale University Press, 2007

McGuinness, A. *Path to Empire. Panama and the California Gold Rush*. Ithaca, NY, and London: Cornell University Press, 2008

Martin, G. *Gabriel García Márquez. A Life*. London: Bloomsbury, 2008

Mignolo, W. *The Idea of Latin America*. Oxford: Blackwell, 2005

Morton, A. L. *The English Utopia*. London: Lawrence and Wishart, 1952

Múnera, A. *Fronteras Imaginadas. La Construcción de las Razas y de la Geografía en el Siglo XIX Colombiano*. Bogotá: Editorial Planeta, 2005 *El Fracaso de la Nación. Región, clase y raza en el Caribe Colombiano, 1717–1810*. Bogotá: Banco de la República & El Áncora Editores, 1998

Parker, Matthew. *Panama Fever. The Epic Story of the Building of the Panama Canal*. New York: Random House, 2007

Pratt, M. L. *Imperial Eyes. Travel Writing and Transculturation*. London: Routledge, 1992

Racine, K. *Francisco de Miranda: A Transatlantic Life in the Age of Revolution*. Wilmington, Del.: Scholarly Resources, 2003

— 'A Community of Purpose: British Cultural Influence During the Spanish American Wars of Independence', in English-Speaking Communities in Latin America. Edited by Oliver Marshall. London: Macmillan, 2000

Rediker, M. *The Slave Ship. A Human History*. London: John Murray, 2007

Rediker, M., and Linebaugh, P. *The Many-Headed Hydra. Sailors, Slaves, Commoners, and the Hidden History of the Revolutionary Atlantic*. Boston, Mass.: Beacon Press, 2000

Rolnik, S., and Guattari, F. *Molecular Revolution in Brazil*. Semiotext(e), 2008

Rosen, Dred. *Empire and Dissent. The United States and Latin America*. Durham, SC: Duke University Press, 2008

Geopolitical foundations of global economics and development, from the sixteenth century to our time:

Álvarez Nogal, A. *El Crédito de la Monarquía Hispánica en el Reinado de Felipe IV*. Ávila: Junta de Castilla y León, 1997

Chang, H-J. *Bad Samaritans. The Guilty Secrets of Rich Nations & the Threat to Global Prosperity*. London: Random House Business Books, 2007

— *Kicking Away the Ladder. Development Strategy in Historical Perspective*. London: Anthem Press, 2002

Cook, Richard C. *We Hold These Truths: The Hope of Monetary Reform*. Aurora, Colo.: Tendrill Press, 2008

Dosman, E. J. *The Life and Times of Raúl Prebisch, 1901–1986*. Montreal and Kingston, Ithaca, London: McGill-Queen's University Press, 2008

Duffield, M. *Global Governance and the New Wars. The Merging of Development and Security*. London and New York: Zed Books, 2001

Escobar, A. *Territories of Difference. Place, Movements, Life, Redes*. Durham, SC: Duke University Press, 2008

Fajnzylber, F. *Changing Production Patterns with Social Equity*. Santiago de Chile: Cepal, 1990

Ferguson, A. *An Essay on the History of Civil Society*. Dublin, 1767

Flynn, D. Morineau, M., and Glahn, R. (eds) *Monetary History in Global Perspective, 1500–1808*. Seville: Fundación Fomento de la Historia Económica, 1998

Griffith-Jones, S., Ocampo, J. A., and Stiglitz, J. E. 'Introduction', in *Time for a Visible Hand. Lessons from the 2008 World Financial Crisis*. Oxford: Oxford University Press, 2010

Kahl, J. A. *Modernization, Exploitation and Dependency in Latin America: Germani, González Casanova and Cardoso*. New Brunswick: Transaction Books, 1976

Leiva, F. I. *Latin American Neostructuralism. The Contradictions of Post-Neoliberal Development*. Minneapolis, Minn.: University of Minnesota Press, 2008

List, Friedrich. *The National System of Political Economy*. Translated by S. Lloyd. London: Longmans, Green & Co., 1841

Maddison, Angus. *The World Economy: Historical Statistics*. Paris: OECD, 2003

Mandelbrot, B., and Hudson, R. L. *The (Mis)behaviour of Markets. A Fractal View of Risk, Ruin and Reward*. New York: Basic Books, 2004

Marazzi, Christian. *The Violence of Finance Capital*. Los Angeles, Cal.: Semiotext(e), 2010

— *Capital and Language. From the New Economy to the War Economy*. Translated by G. Conti. Semiotext(e), 2008

Marx, K. *Capital*, vol. I. London: Penguin Books, 2004

Mies, M., and Benholdt-Thomsen, V. *The Subsistence Perspective. Beyond the Globalised Economy*. Translated by P. Camiller, M. Mies and G. Wieh. London and New York: Zed Books, 1999

Morineau, M. *Incroyables gazettes et fabuleux métaux: Les retours des trésors américains d'après les gazettes hollandaises, XVIIe–XVIIIe siècles*. New York: Cambridge University Press, 1985

Ocampo, José. A., and Vos, R. *Uneven Economic Development*. London and New York: Zed Books, 2008

Ocampo, José. A. Stiglitz, Joseph E., Spiegel, Shari, French-Davis, Ricardo, and Nayyar, Deepak. *Stability with Growth: Macroeconomics, Liberalization and Development*. New York: Oxford University Press, 2006

Pérez, C. A. *Vision for Latin America: A Resource-Based Strategy for Technological Dynamism and Social Inclusion*. Santiago de Chile: ECLAC Program of Technology Policy and Development in Latin America, 2008

Smith, A. *Inquiry into the Nature and Causes of the Wealth of Nations*. Edited by Edwin Cannan. London: Methuen & Co., 1961

Topik, S., Marichal, C., and Frank, Z. (eds) *From Silver to Cocaine. Latin American Commodity Chains and the Building of the World Economy, 1500–2000*. Durham, SC: Duke University Press, 2006

Yaffe, H. *Che Guevara: The Economics of Revolution*. London: Palgrave Macmillan, 2009

On the sociological, anthropological and philosophical foundations of geopolitics and global economics:

Aristotle. *Poética*. Trad. Cast. de V. García Yebra. Madrid: Gredos, 1974

Curtius, E. R. *Literatura Europea y Edad Media Latina*. Mexico City: FCE, 1955

Dussel, E. *Twenty Theses on Politics*. Durham, SC: Duke University Press, 2008
— *The Invention of the Americas*. Translated by M. D. Barber. New York: Continuum, 1995
Fabian, J. *Memory Against Culture. Arguments and Reminders*. Durham, SC: Duke University Press, 2007
Gordon, J., and Gordon, L. *On Divine Warning. Reading Catastrophe in the Modern Age*. Boulder, Colo.: Paradigm Press, 2009
Guardiola-Rivera, O. *Being Against the World. Rebellion and Constitution*. London: Routledge & Birkbeck Law Press, 2009
Hughes, D. *Culture and Sacrifice. Ritual Death in Literature and Opera*. Cambridge: Cambridge University Press, 2007
Karatani, Kojin. *Transcritique*. Cambridge, Mass.: MIT Press, 2003
Ralston Saul, J. *The Collapse of Globalism and the Reinvention of the World*. London: Penguin Books, 2005
Rifkin, J. *The Empathic Civilization. The Race to Global Consciousness in a World in Crisis*. London and New York: Polity Press, 2009
Wacquant, L. *Punishing the Poor: The Neoliberal Government of Social Insecurity*. Durham, SC: Duke University Press, 2009
Wey Gómez, N. *Tropics of Empire*. Cambridge, Mass.: MIT Press, 2008

On Latin American early experiments with cybernetics and cognitive science:

Beer, S. *Brain of the Firm*. New York: McGraw-Hill, 1974
— *On Decybernation. A Contribution to Current Debates*. Box 64. The Stafford Beer Collection. Liverpool John Moores University. 27 April 1973.
Maturana, H., and Varela, F. J. *De Máquinas y Seres Vivos : Una Caracterización de la Organización Biológica*. Santiago, 1973. Translated into English as *Autopoiesis and Cognition: The Realization of the Living*. With a foreword by Stafford Beer. Boston, MA, 1980

On ethnicity, Latinos in the US and the rise to power of indigenous peoples in Latin America:

Comaroff, J., and Comaroff, J. *Ethnicity, Inc*. Scottville: University of Kua-Zulu Natal Press, 2009
García-Linera, Á. *La Potencia Plebeya*. Buenos Aires: CLACSO/Prometeo Libros, 2008
Grosfoguel, R., Maldonado-Torres, N., and Saldívar, J. *Latinos in the World System: Decolonization Struggles in 21st Century U.S. Empire*. Boulder, Colo: Paradigm Press, 2005
Jung, C. *The Moral Force of Indigenous Politics. Critical Liberalism and the Zapatistas*. Cambridge: Cambridge University Press, 2008
Rondón, C. M. *The Book of Salsa. A Chronicle of Urban Music from the Caribbean to New York*. Translated by F. Aparicio and J. White. Chapel Hill, NC: University of North Carolina Press, 2008

Reid Andrews, G. *Afro-Latin America*. Oxford and New York: Oxford
University Press, 2004

Articles

On pre-Columbian and colonial America:

Adorno, R. 'Felipe Guaman Poma de Ayala: An Andean View of the Peruvian
Viceroyalty', in *Journal de la Société des Américanistes*, vol. 65, issue 65, 1978
Ravilious, K. 'Messages from the Stone Age,' in *New Scientist*, 20 February 2010

On rebellion, independence and dependency in the Americas:

Birns, N. '"Thy World, Columbus!": Barbauld and Global Space, 1803,
"1811", 1812, 2003', in *European Romantic Review*, vol. 16, no. 5, December
2005
Bruit, H. 'América en el Pensamiento Político de Bartolomé de Las Casas',
1998. Available at http://www.ciudadseva.com/textos/estudios/casas/
casas06.htm
Buck-Morss, S. 'Hegel in Haiti', in *Critical Inquiry*, 26, no. 4
Heinowitz, Rebecca C. '"Thy World, Columbus, Shall Be Free": British
Romantic Deviance and Spanish American Revolution', in *European
Romantic Review*, vol. 17, no. 2, April 2006
Lasso M. 'Race War and Nation in Caribbean Gran Colombia, Cartagena,
1810–1832', in *American Historical Review*, April 2006

On the sociological and anthropological foundations of geopolitics:

Fabian, J. 'How Others Die – Reflections on the Anthropology of Death', in
Social Research, vol. 39, no. 3, autumn 1972

Historical and geopolitical foundations of the global economy:

Flynn, D., and Giráldez, A. 'Born with a Silver Spoon: The Origin of World
Trade in 1571', in *Journal of World History*, 6, no. 2, 1995
Luthin, R. 'Abraham Lincoln and the Tariff', in *American Historical Review*, vol.
49, no. 4
Medina, E. 'Designing Freedom, Regulating a Nation: Socialist Cybernetics
in Allende's Chile', in *Journal of Latin American Studies*, 38 (Cambridge:
Cambridge University Press)
Ocampo, J. A. 'What Should Bretton Woods II Look Like?', in *Journal of
Turkish Weekly*, 12 November 2008, available at http://www.turkishweekly.
net/news/61157/what-should-bretton-woods-ii-look-like-by-jose-anto-
nio-ocampo-.html

Turner, A. in 'How to Tame Global Finance. A Group of Leading Financial
    Analysts Quiz Britain's Top Regulator on What Went Wrong and How to
    Sort it Out', in *Prospect*, September 2009
Sachs, J., and Warner. A. 'Economic Reform and the Process of Global
    Integration. Brookings Papers on Economic Activity, no. 1, 1995
Sen, A. 'Rational Fools. A Critique of the Behavioural Foundations of
    Economic Theory', in *Philosophy and Public Affairs*, 6, 1977

Latinos in the US and indigenous peoples in Latin America:

Lovato, R. 'Latinos in the Age of National (In)security', *NACLA Report on the
    Americas*, vol. 39, no. 3, November/December 2005, New York: NACLA
Pantoja, A. Menjíbar, C., and Magana, L. 'The Spring Marches of 2006. Latinos,
    Immigration, and Political Mobilization in the 21st Century', in *American
    Behavioral Scientist*, vol. 52, no. 4, December 2008
Rivera Cusicanqui, S. 'Colonialism and Ethnic Resistance in Bolivia. A View
    from the Coca Markets', in *Empire and Dissent. The United States and Latin
    America*. Edited by Dred Rosen. Durham, SC: Duke University Press, 2008
Vidal, J. 'We are fighting for our lives and our dignity', in *Guardian*, 13 June
    2009

Academic writings
On the Americas during revolution and after independence:

Múnera, A. *Failing to Construct the Colombian Nation: Race and Class in the Andean-
    Caribbean Conflict, 1717–1816.* Ph.D. diss., University of Connecticut, 1995
Scott, J. S. *The Common Wind: Currents of Afro-American Communication in the
    Era of the Haitian Revolution.* Ph.D. diss., Duke University, 1986

Notes

Introduction

1. Galeano, E. *Open Veins of Latin America. Five Centuries of the Pillage of a Continent* (first published in 1973 by Monthly Review Press. Present edition, London: Serpent's Tail, 2009): 1–2.
2. Galeano, E. op. cit.: 1.
3. In this sense, the problem with Galeano's emphasis on the fate of oppressed peoples in Latin America is that it obscures the fact of the existence of a common memory, born out of the common losses suffered by peoples on both sides of the Atlantic, prompted by the rise of mercantilist and capitalist world trade during the first waves of globalisation that connected the two sides of the Atlantic with West Africa and the East. For the history of the emergence of the associative, mutualist tradition in the hidden history of the revolutionary Atlantic see Rediker, M., and Linebaugh, P. *The Many-Headed Hydra. Sailors, Slaves, Commoners, and the Hidden History of the Revolutionary Atlantic* (Boston, Mass.: Beacon Press, 2000).
4. For the basis of this account of the 'official history of globalisation' and the 'real history of globalisation', see Chang, J-H. *Bad Samaritans: The Guilty Secrets of Rich Nations & the Threat to Global Prosperity* (London: Random House Business Books, 2007); and *Kicking Away the Ladder: Development Strategy in Historical Perspective* (London: Anthem Press, 2002). See also *An Economic History of Twentieth-Century Latin America*. Edited by E. Cárdenas, J. A. Ocampo and R. Thorp (London and New York: Palgrave Macmillan, 3 vols, 2001); and Griffith-Jones, S., Ocampo, J. A., and Stiglitz, J. *Time for a Visible Hand. Lessons from the 2008 World Financial Crisis* (Oxford: Oxford University Press, 2010). The classical reference in this historical-sociological approach to development and economics is List, F. *The National System of Political Economy*. Translated from the original 1841 German edition by S. Lloyd (London: Longmans, Green & Co., 1885). In the case of Latin America, it is crucial to deal with the lifelong work of Argentinean economist Raúl Prebisch. See his *The Economic Development of Latin America and Its Principal Problems* (New York: United Nations, 1950). I have also found the more challenging and contemporary work of Japanese philosopher

Kojin Karatani very useful. See his *Transcritique*. Translated by S. Kohso (Cambridge, Mass.: MIT Press, 2003).

5. Chief among them, economists Ha-Joon Chang, Carlota Pérez, Fernando Ignacio Leiva, Fernando Fajnzylber and José Antonio Ocampo, and historians and anthropologists Fernando Coronil, Arturo Escobar, Alfonso Múnera and Silvia Rivera Cusicanqui.

6. Former UN rapporteur and professor of development politics Mark Duffield has argued that, during the final years of the Cold War and thereafter, strands of counter-insurgency tactics and neoliberal discourse came together to form a strategy of global governance centred upon populations considered 'at risk' or 'becoming risks themselves', that fused the national and the international, amalgamated development aid and conditionality with conflict-resolution and conflict-prevention, and generated an emerging doctrine of humanitarian or pro-democratic intervention that was applied extensively across the globe, particularly after 9/11. Examples of this 'merging of security and development' include Mozambique, Afghanistan and the US-backed Plan Colombia in Latin America. See Duffield, M. *Global Governance and the New Wars: The Merging of Development and Security* (London and New York: Zed Books, 2001), and *Development, Security and Unending War* (London: Polity Press, 2007).

7. Marichal, C. 'The Spanish-American Silver Peso: Export Commodity and Global Money of the Ancien Regime, 1550–1800', in *From Silver to Cocaine. Latin American Commodity Chains and the Building of the World Economy*. Edited by S. Topik, C. Marichal and Z. Frank (Durham, SC: Duke University Press, 2006): 25–52, at 26.

8. At best, this judgement comes after the fact, and recognises that things are in the end the way they are and could not have been any other way, which is uninteresting. At worst, this kind of judgement risks projecting what was achieved as a result on to future events. Thus, for instance, the overall goodness of empire is proven for Ferguson by the historical fact that empire expanded and secured 'free trade' for everyone. See Ferguson, N. *Empire. How Britain Made the Modern World* (London: Allen Lane, 2003).

9. For income growth figures see Maddison, A. *The World Economy: Historical Statistics* (Paris: OECD, 2003): Table 8b. For average tariffs see Clamens, M., and Williamson, J. 'Closed Jaguar, Open Dragon: Comparing Tariffs in Latin America and Asia Before WWII', NBR Working Paper, no. 9401. National Bureau of Economic Research (Cambridge, Mass., 2002): Table 4. Britain first used unequal treaties in Latin America, starting with Brazil and then continuing with Argentina and Great Colombia. The larger Latin American countries obtained tariff autonomy around the late 1870s, before Japan in 1911.

10. See on this Marazzi, C. *The Violence of Financial Capitalism* (Los Angeles, Cal.: Semiotext(e), 2010): 96–7. See also Rifkin, J. *The Empathic Civilization. The Race to Global Consciousness in a World in Crisis* (Cambridge and New York: Polity Press, 2009): 533–42.

11. See on this, Grandin, G. 'Counterveiling Powers', in *Latin American Studies Association Forum*, vol. XXXVIII, issue I, Winter 2007: 14–16, at 16.

12. See Kozloff, N. *Revolution! South America and the Rise of the New Left* (New York: Palgrave Macmillan, 2008): 1–5.
13. Martinez Fischer and Anchia are cited by *The Economist*, 'Lone Star Rising. A Special Report on Texas', 11 July 2009, 10–12.

1 The Dream of the Indians

1. In Charles C. Mann's *1941. The Americas before Columbus* (London: Granta, 2005): 4–27, at 10. I decided on the trip after reading Mann's account, following an old habit of mine, to re-enact literary descriptions of crucial journeys, places, and in this case the experiences he described and the observations made by researchers like William Denevan and Charles Ericksson. However, I had heard about these places 'thick with the remains of an unknown civilization' (10), from a Peruvian anthropologist working with an oil company in the Andean-Amazonic area that stretches from Peru and eastern Bolivia to western Brazil in 1998–9.
2. See on this Ravilious, K. 'Messages from the Stone Age', in *New Scientist*, 20 February 2010: 30–34.
3. Morison, S. E. *European Discovery of America*, cited by Mann, Charles C. op. cit., 14.
4. This view is well represented in the passage of Adam Smith's *Inquiry into the Nature and Causes of the Wealth of Nations* (1776), in which he contends that 'every individual is continually exerting himself to find out the most advantageous employment for whatever capital he can command. It is his own advantage, indeed, and not that of society, which he has in view. But the study of his own advantage naturally, or rather necessarily, leads him to prefer that employment which is most advantageous to the society.' The 'necessity' in question is the result of assuming that everybody else would do the same and would continue to do the same in the future. This means that in fact there is no future, no radical variation and no absolute newness. This view of the universe is thus like a snapshot, frozen in time. For the sociology and economics of this sort, the long term matters little, since in the very long term 'we will all be dead', as John Maynard Keynes allegedly put it. See Smith, A. *Inquiry into the Nature and Causes of the Wealth of Nations*. Edited by Edwin Cannan (London: Methuen & Co., 1961): vol. I, 475.
5. Ponce, P. *El Alma Encantada* (Mexico City: Fondo de Cultura Económica & INI, 1986): 10. Cited by Le Clézio, J. M. G. *The Mexican Dream. Or, The Interrupted Thought of Amerindian Civilizations*. Translated by Teresa Lavender Fagan (Chicago, Ill., and London: University of Chicago Press, 1993): 204.
6. Galeano, E. *Open Veins of Latin America*: 1.
7. Rifkin, J. *The Emphatic Civilization*: 533–41.
8. Le Clézio, J. M. G. op. cit.: 57.
9. De Alva Ixlilxóchitl, F. *Obras Históricas* (Mexico: Porrúa, 1977): II, 7. Also cited in Le Clézio, J. M. G. op. cit.: 57–8.
10. For these and other reports see Vidal, J. 'We are fighting for our lives and our dignity', in *Guardian*, 13 June 2009: 26. All quotes taken from the article.

11. Our mainstream belief in the inherent simplicity and innocence of indigenous peoples, a colonialist belief if ever there was one, common to conservationist ecologists as much as to developmental policy-makers, is part of the problem. This image, positive or negative, relates to their putative lack of impact on the environment. In both positive images like that of the Noble Savage or negative ones such as that of the Indians as vicious barbarians, chronic warriors, thoroughly pre-modern ethnicities, or cannibals without redemption, they are talked about as lacking what social scientists call *agency*. This means that such peoples are represented as if they were not actors in their own right, but more like things, passive recipients of whatever windfalls or disasters chance and destiny – the inevitable march of the forces of history – put in their way. Crucially, both negative and positive images of indigenous and other peoples identified by their ethnicity (Afro-Americans and Latinos in the US, Indians, indigenous, and Afro-descendants in Latin America, minorities in Asia and Europe) have histories that refer back to colonisation, and date back at least to the writings of Henry David Thoreau, Jean-Jacques Rousseau and Bartolomé de Las Casas, amongst others. All of them were critics of the extremes of colonialism and the perils of progress; nevertheless, they all regarded indigenous peoples as existing in societies without change who never transformed their environment from its original state. In fact, belief in a 'state of nature' became implicit in modern notions of progress and development, and indeed in our very images of the globe. The new world was mapped in the imagination of discoverers, conquistadors and their successors in accordance with projections that blew up geometric centres and disguised ethnic ones. Christian T/O maps and Chinese nested squares were gradually replaced by an image of the earth divided into four continents, rather than into four corners, with a geometric mobile centre (from the Mediterranean to the Atlantic, with Rome beginning to be more centrally located than Jerusalem) and fixed savage margins. Colonisation did not entail the eradication of previous belief systems, but, rather, a reorganisation according to which belief systems that did not resemble or embrace those of the expansive centre were marginalised, and spatial marginalisation in respect of the metropolitan centres also meant backwardness in time. Integration by conversion meant, as Walter D. Mignolo puts it, 'moving people from the savage margins to the civilized centers' (1995: 247). This is how the idea of identifying the margin with the past began to emerge, and thus also an idea of progress particular to post-Renaissance Europe. Such an idea was a response to the need for the consolidation of differences and the integration of a fourth part of the world into European consciousness. The point was to measure experienced differences in terms of values, and values in terms of chronological evolution or ascent. That is to say, to judge the unknown and unfamiliar by what is actually familiar and well known. Thus emerges, out of the Renaissance imaginary, a certain idea of experience that still has profound relevance in such domains as geopolitics, the division of scientific labour and economics (developmental economics in particular). It starts with the invention of the Americas, the fourth continent, as a passive entity

existing in the middle of the ocean waiting to be discovered. Certainly the mass of land existed, but the idea that it was 'empty of mankind and its works' that allowed and continues to allow for the appropriation of land and its resources, and the marginalisation of native peoples, was a European invention. Thus, conceptions of progress, experience and a world reorganised by the integration (rather than recognition) of 'America' also impact profoundly upon the daily lives of countless peoples around the world. See on this Fabian, J. *Memory Against Culture* (Durham, SC: Duke University Press, 2007): 17–29. See also Mignolo, W. *The Darker Side of the Renaissance* (Ann Arbor, Mich.: University of Michigan Press, 1995): 219–313.

12. As Charles C. Mann informs us, 'these views, though less common today, continue to appear'. He then cites the 1987 edition of *American History: A Survey*, a standard high-school textbook written by three well-known historians, from where the lines cited in this paragraph have been taken. See Mann, Charles C. *1941*: 14.

13. For these quotes see Racine, K. 'A Community of Purpose: British Cultural Influence during the Spanish American Wars of Independence', in *English-Speaking Communities in Latin America*. Edited by Oliver Marshall (London: Macmillan. 2000): 3 and 5.

14. Foster, K. *Lost Worlds. Latin America and the Imagining of Empire* (London: Pluto Press, 2009): 11.

15. William Yale, cited by Buchan, J., in 'Bitter legacy', review of *Sowing the Wind: The Seeds of Conflict in the Middle East* by John Kay. *Guardian Weekly*, 3–9 July 2003: 14.

16. See on this Rediker, M., and Linebaugh, P. *The Many-Headed Hydra*. See also Rediker, M. *The Slave Ship. A Human History* (London: John Murray, 2007), and Linebaugh, P. *The Magna Carta Manifesto* (Berkeley, Cal., and London: University of California Press, 2008).

17. Foster, K. op. cit.: xv. Foster quotes Jimmy Burns' *Beyond the Silver River: South American Encounters* (London: Bloomsbury, 1989): xiv.

18. Foster, K. op. cit.: 12.

19. For all quotations and paraphrases in this paragraph see Foster, K. op. cit.: xiii–xv.

20. For the findings of the 'new' school of archaeologists – Haas, deFrance, Winifred Creamer, Álvaro Ruiz, Michael Moseley and others – the 'Maritime Foundations of Andean Civilisations' hypothesis, and backing evidence, see Mann, Charles C. *1491*: 174–91. Archaeologist Jonathan Haas posits the questions 'where does government come from?', 'what makes people decide to surrender some of their personal liberty to it?' and 'what did they gain from it?" To him, Norte Chico may provide an answer to such questions because here people experienced a phenomenon different from mere insecurity: the common creation of new environments.

2   The Dream of the Mountain of Gold

1. See Silvertein, J. 'Highway Run', in *Harper's*: 70–80, July 2006.

2. *General Song*, or *Canto General*, is Pablo Neruda's tenth book of poems. It was composed in 1938, consisting of fifteen sections, 231 poems and more

than 15,000 verses. It starts in the heights of Macchu Picchu and ends with an actual affirmation of subjectivity (I am!). In this, and possibly other respects (rhythm, a certain proximity to the lyricism of Romantic poetry, while utterly modernist/indigenist in its appreciation of non-figurative construction of forms in space), it remains an exemplar of a long tradition that also counts the much underrated 'Delirium on Chimborazo' by Simón Bolívar among its representatives, and possibly owes as much to the rhythmic pulsating environment that has defined life in this region since before the Inca, as it does to the critical excesses and dramatism of European Romanticism. The song has been intoned several times by different musicians, most famously in the version rendered by contemporary Greek composer Mikis Theodorakis. I prefer the 1975 version, comprising seven out of the fifteen movements, recorded live from Piraeus, near Athens, sung by Petrus Pandis and Maria Farantouri. For the drive, I recommend this version as well as the notorious rock version performed by Chilean band Los Jaivas.

3. In his 1570 *Instrucción del Ynga D. Diego de Castro Tito Cussi Yupangui* (Madrid: Ediciones Atlas, 1988: 128), Titu Cusi Yupanki reported how people from northern Peru described the Spaniards recently arrived to their lands as bearded men who talked to themselves while looking at pieces of white fabric, with a mixture of amazement and amusement. Also cited in Mignolo, *The Darker Side of the Renaissance*: 87.

4. Anthropologist Johannes Fabian from the University of Amsterdam explains that within the emerging paradigms of anthropology, evolutionism and diffusionism, which he calls 'the warring twins', recognition by travelogues was expressed in two major forms: subsumption and collection. The former is related, precisely, to the invention of the fetish as a category to classify peoples through the designation of things that were 'somehow striking themselves or appeared strange in the context in which they were found, objects whose function was not understood, or, if it was understood, not approved of'. This is no mere denial of other peoples and their objects, for 'there was always a rest of recognition in the sense that fetishes were experienced as "devilish" objects; they were dangerous and therefore to be respected as long as the European beholders lacked the power to destroy them'. Andean textiles and their associated tactile aesthetics and politics were subsumed in this manner, respected as museum-like pieces of writing or art, when not destroyed. But secretly feared, suppressed, because of their pulsating capacity to return. See Fabian, J. *Memory Against Culture*: 54–5.

5. For this observation see Mignolo, op. cit.: 84.

6. Here, I have provided a translation of the Spanish original that emphasises the meaning of the term 'guisar' as 'to weave', 'to organise' or 'to set in relation'; the term 'infinidad' in its geometric, diffusionist sense as a form of (tabular or circular) distribution within which objects and meanings are organised or valued, and differences circulate or are made equivalent; and the term 'significaciones' in a sense closer to the English term 'significance' meaning 'the range of values, the location of, or the extent to which something matters'. The original Spanish goes like this: 'Y en cada manojo de éstos, tantos ñudos y ñudicos, y hilillos atados; unos colorados,

otros verdes, otros azules, otros blancos, finalmente tantas diferencias que
así como nosotros de veinte y cuatro letras *guisándolas* de diferentes maneras
sacamos tantas *infinidad* de vocablos, así éstos de sus ñudos y colores, sacaban
innumeberables *significaciones* de cosas.'

7. See Fabian, J. op. cit.: 55–6.

8. Unwittingly or not, Fabian's evocation of socio-historical treatments of
   surfaces of inscription (Durkheim, Simmel, Foucault) and things circulating
   as fetishes and commodities, invokes the anthropo-economic theorisation
   of silver and gold in chapter 3 of Karl Marx's *Capital I*. It invites comparison, and in fact also the making of historical connections going back to the
   beginnings of colonialism and world exchange in earnest in the sixteenth
   century. See Marx, K. *Capital*, vol. I (London: Penguin Books (1976),
   1990): 188–244, at 229 (where he cites Columbus's letter), 231 (where he
   makes explicit connections between lust for gold, hoarding, and the situation of conquerors and conquistadors of new worlds) and 241 (where he
   refers to the silver mines of the Americas).

9. See on this Marx, K. op. cit.: 229.

10. For all sources, quotations and paraphrases see Wey Gómez, N. *Tropics of
    Empire* (Cambridge, Mass.: MIT Press): 40–43.

11. See on this Thumfart, J. *Die Begründung der globalpolitischen Philosophie.
    Zu Francisco de Vitorias 'Relectio de Indiis recenter inventis' von 1539* (Berlin:
    Kulturverlag Kadmos, 2009).

12. D'Ailly's 1410 treatise *Ymago Mundi* was one of Columbus's favourite
    sources of cosmographical information, and very influential to his plans.
    For this description of the western tri-partite idea of the world, quotes and
    paraphrases, see Wey Gómez, op. cit.: 50–51.

13. This is a rendition of testimonies taken from Dee Brown's *Bury My Heart
    at Wounded Knee* (New York: Holt Paperbacks, 2001).

14. Quoted in the introduction authored by Venezuela's president Hugo Chávez
    to the recent compilation in English of the writings of Simón Bolívar, in
    Simón Bolívar. The Bolivarian Revolution (London: Verso, 2009): xv.

15. See Álvarez Nogal, A. *El Crédito de la Monarquía Hispánica en el Reinado de
    Felipe IV* (Ávila; Junta de Castilla y León, 1997), for statistical information.
    For this and other sources of statistical evidence, and sources of quotes and
    paraphrases, see Marichal, C. 'The Spanish-American Silver peso: Export
    Commodity and Global Money of the Ancien Regime: 1550–1800', in
    *From Silver to Cocaine. Latin American Commodity Chains and the Building of
    the World Economy, 1500–2000*: 25–52.

16. Galeano, E. *Open Veins of Latin America*: 29.

3   The Dream of the Conquerors

1. Flynn, D., and Giráldez, A. 'Born With a Silver Spoon: The Origin of
   World Trade in 1571', in *Journal of World History*, 6, no. 2, 1995: 201–20, at
   201 and 214.

2. For the account of the 1741 uprising and the attack on Fort St George, plus
   quotations and paraphrases, see Rediker, M., and Linebaugh, P. *The Many-
   Headed Hydra*: 174–210.

3. Cited by Daniel Boorstin in *The Discoverers: A History of Man's Search to Know His World and Himself* (London and New York: Random House, 1983), 257.
4. Parker, Matthew. *Panama Fever. The Epic Story of the Building of the Panama Canal* (New York: Random House. 2007: 4
5. Burrough, B. 'Pirate of the Caribbean', in *Vanity Fair*, July 2009: 81.

4   The Dream of Revolution

1. Bolívar to Maria Antonia, Cuzco, 10 July 1825, in *Obras Completas*, II: 163. Cited in Lynch, J. *Simon Bolivar: A Life* (New Haven, Conn.: Yale University Press, 2007): 16.
2. All quotes from Simón Bolívar's *Letter from Jamaica*, 1815. Included in *Simón Bolívar. The Bolivarian Revolution*. Edited and translated by Matthew Brown (London and New York: Verso, 2009): 40–64.
3. For these statistics see Crow, J. *The Epic of Latin America* (London, 1992).
4. This would require a treaty signed by all the interested parties. Lascasian scholar Queralto Moreno describes it as an international treaty, while Brazilian historian Héctor Bruit conceives it as a federation or confederation that recognises some kind of centralised, largely symbolic, representative or head of state, in this case the Spanish monarch. The idea of a confederation would not have been unfamiliar to the indigenous peoples of North and South America: there were Indian confederations in what is now Colombia and in Peru, referred to by Spanish chronicler Pedro Cieza de León as *behetrías*, as there were in North America – the Haudenosanee Five Nations brought under the Great Law of Peace and communal ownership, for instance. Importantly, historians, activists and anthropologists have long argued that the framers of the US Constitution – among them John Adams and Benjamin Franklin, two of the three drafters of the Declaration of Independence which included the right to revolution – were pervaded by this and other Indian ideals and images of freedom. The insistence on personal liberty as much as on social equality among the indigenous peoples of the Americas has been pointed out by commentators like the French adventurer Louis Armand de Lom d'Arce and the essayist Michel de Montaigne, and by Bartolomé de Las Casas, among others. Either as a confederation or an international treaty, these pre-Columbian traditions, filtered through the consideration of arguments set forth by Bartolo Sassoferrato, Remigio de Girolami, Jean Gerson and William Ockham – all of them frequently cited by Las Casas – lit the imagination of people like Francisco de Miranda, the Precursor of Liberty in the Americas, and Simón Bolívar. Miranda's 1784 draft constitution for the Americas, for instance, included plans for an independent union of all former Spanish and Portuguese colonies led by a hereditary head of state, or *Inca*. These designs were explicitly modelled upon surviving traditions among indigenous peoples, set in trans-cultural relation to European models of constitutional monarchy and, crucially, the actual example of abolitionists in Britain and France, revolutionaries in North America (including the 1776 Virginia Constitution and the Philadelphia Constitution), the Caribbean (the

establishment of Black Republics with charters of rights in Santo Domingo, modern Haiti and Guadeloupe) and South America (including the 1781 Proclamation of the Inca leader Túpac Amaru as king, and the Capitulations obtained by the commoners of New Granada in June 1781). Bolívar's 1815 *Letter from Jamaica* should be read in this context. For Lascasian designs for a confederation see Las Casas, B. de, *Historia de las Indias* (Mexico City: FCE, 1986): vol. 2, L. III, Cap. XI, 468. For his take on a federative treaty see, Las Casas, B. de, *Los Tesoros del Peru* (Madrid: Imprenta y Editora Maestre, 1953): 120–38. For his political ideas see, among others, Las Casas, B. de, *Tratados de Fray Bartolomé de Las Casas* (Mexico City: FCE, 1965): vol. 2, 1063, 1245–69, 1267. See also *El Pensamiento Político de Bartolomé de Las Casas* (Sevilla: escuela de Estudios Hispano-Americanos, 1976): 297, 311, 313–21. For Las Casas's trans-continental federalism see Bruit, H. 'América en el Pensamiento Político de Bartolomé de Las Casas', 1998. Available at http://www.ciudadseva.com/textos/estudios/casas/casas06.htm. Last accessed 31 December 2009. For the Haudenosanee Great Law of Peace, see Mann, Charles C. *1491*: 329–37. For New Granada's commoners and their linking of North American constitutionalism, British abolitionism and the Andean insurrection of Túpac Amaru, see Cárdenas, P. E. *El Movimiento Comunal de 1781 en el Nuevo Reino de Granada* (Bogotá: Tercer Mundo): vol. 1. For present-day communal indigenous movements (in Bolivia) see García-Linera, Á. *La Potencia Plebeya* (Buenos Aires: CLACSO/Prometeo Libros, 2008): 193–330.

5. Cited by Silvio Zabala in Beuchot, M. *Los Fundamentos de los Derechos Humanos en Bartolomé de Las Casas* (Barcelona: Anthropos, 1994): 9.

6. Las Casas, B. de. *De Regia Potestate*. Edited by L. Perena (Madrid: Consejo Superior de Investigaciones Científicas, 1969): 17.

7. A permanent state of rebellion existed in the Andes between 1535 and the 1780s, which was then connected to the two cycles of Caribbean revolts (one starting in the 1730s and continuing into the 1740s, the other between the 1760 Jamaican Revolt and the British Honduras rebellion of 1773 and the Haitian Revolution in the 1780s), and the Spanish American revolutions of the eighteenth and nineteenth centuries (starting with the commoners rebellion' of New Granada in 1781, Túpac Amaru II's siege of Cuzco in the same year, and including the Spanish American wars of liberation led by Miranda, Bolívar, San Martín and O'Higgins). By November 1535 the Inca high priest Villac Umu was urging Manco Inca, the 'puppet king' established by Pizarro and Almagro after Atahualpa's murder, to 'rebel once and for all and die for our liberty'. In January 1536, the younger Pizarro brothers, Juan and Gonzalo, were busy trying to extinguish the now numerous sparks of native rebellion. Subsequent uprisings, which included the Great Rebellion led by Manco Inca with the help of numerous tribes from the Amazon and the Andes that had been opposed to Atahualpa's rule in the past and had collaborated with Pizarro, led to the establishment of a free Inca state in the Amazonian city of Vilcabamba. These events formed the backdrop of Las Casas's campaign in Europe against the enslavement of the Indians, and of his later proposals for the establishment of a commonwealth of independent

American states. The city of Vilcabamba became a centre for guerrilla-style attacks led by Manco Inca's son, Titu Cusi, and his brother, Túpac Amaru I, captured and executed in the Amazon jungle on 24 September 1572, thirty-six years after Manco Inca's Great Rebellion. Such events were carefully considered during the late sixteenth century and the early seventeenth century by Peruvian chroniclers of Indian origin like Titu Cusi, who led yet another rebellion against the empire out of Vilcabamba in the 1560s, and Waman Puma de Ayala. In 1615, Peruvian writer Felipe Waman Puma de Ayala finished his account of the history of these rebellions and of the rise and fall of the Inca empire, which he titled *First New Chronicle and Good Government*. This 1,189-page tract, housed in the Royal Danish Library since at least the 1660s, can be considered one of the first examples of global political philosophy and enlightened critique written in the American continent. As the title concedes, the tract included a series of arguments in which memory and reason – understood as the rekindling of the texts of the past for the purposes of imagining the future – were advocated as the primary source and legitimacy for authority, against the claims of divine authority, just war and empire. Contemporary scholars have linked such arguments with Las Casas's works, while also pointing out the important differences between the Lascasian 'theoretical' tradition and Puma de Ayala's reasoning, grounded in practice (see Adorno, R. 'Felipe Guaman Poma de Ayala: An Andean View of the Peruvian Viceroyalty', in *Journal de la Société des Américanistes*, vol. 65, issue 65, 1978: 121–43, at 122 and 129. See also Las Casas, B. de, and Santo Tomás, D. 'Memorial', in *Opúsculos, Cartas, y Memoriales*, in *Obras Escogidas de Fr. Bartolomé de Las Casas*. Edited by J. Perez de Tudela Bueso (Madrid: VBAE, CX, 1958): 466. In 1781, the memory of Túpac Amaru's rebellion was alive, and served to connect the spirit of the ongoing American and Haitian revolutions with the arguments and accounts of Las Casas, and other missionaries, both in Europe and the Americas. There was in fact a two-way street between the events unfolding in Peru, the Caribbean and elsewhere in the Americas, and the writings and transatlantic activism of people like Las Casas, his fellow Dominican and Jesuit colleagues, and others. This is demonstrated not only in the emphasis placed by Las Casas on his later writings on Peru, and on the political imagination of the indigenous peoples of the Americas – particularly on notions of autonomy, social equality, common ownership and their familiarity with the idea of a confederacy. But also, later on, in the development of an anti-slavery movement of transcontinental scope in Europe. The accounts of missionaries in France, and of former slaves like Olaudah Equiano and Ottobah Cugoano in Britain, were crucial to the formation of anti-slavery and abolitionist movements in such countries during the eighteenth and nineteenth centuries. These, in turn, were central to European Enlightenment.

8. See on this Collier, J. *The Indians of the Americas* (New York: W. W. Norton, 1947): 138. Cited by Galeano, E. *Open Veins of Latin America*: 38.

9. See Dunbar-Ortiz, R. *Roots of Resistance: Land Tenure in New Mexico, 1680–1980* (Los Angeles, Cal.: American Indian Studies Center, UCLA, 1980): 5. Cited by Linebaugh, P. *The Magna Carta Manifesto*: 247.

10. See Rediker, M. *The Slave Ship*: 4–5. All quotes are his. He cites W. E. B. Du Bois from *Black Reconstruction in America: An Essay Toward a History of the Part Which Black Folk Played in the Attempt to Reconstruct Democracy in America, 1860–1880* (New York: Harcourt, Brace & Co., 1935): 727.

11. See on this Mann, Charles C. *1491*: 133. All quotes are his.

12. Bolívar, S. *Letter from Jamaica*, 1815, op. cit.: 40–64, at 49.

13. Rifkin, J. *The Empathic Civilization*: 2. Rifkin explains the contemporary relevance of the global paradox in the following way: 'We now face the haunting prospect of approaching global empathy in a highly energy-intensive, interconnected world, riding on the back of an escalating entropy bill that now threatens catastrophic climate change and our very existence. Resolving the empathy/entropy paradox will likely be the critical test of our species' ability to survive and flourish on Earth in the future' (2).

14. Bolívar, S. op. cit.: 48.

15. See Bolívar, S. op. cit.: 40–64, at 48–9.

16. 'The philanthropic bishop of Chiapas, Apostle of the Indies, has left posterity a brief narrative, extracted from the legal documents found in Sevilla. The barbarism of the conquest as recounted by Las Casas is acknowledged by all people of consideration and eminence ...' (41).

17. 'Though Cuauhtemoc, Montezuma's successor as king of Mexico, was indeed honoured as a prince, and the crown was placed on his head, it was a mark of derision, not of respect, reminding him of his fall before torturing him. The fate of Catzontzin, the king of Michoacán, the Zipa of Bogotá and all the indigenous nobles and dignitaries who opposed the power of Spain, was similar to that of this unhappy monarch!' (46).

18. See Bolívar, S. op. cit.: 48.

19. It is also a figure of militancy. See on this Badiou, A. *St. Paul: The Foundation of Universalism* (Stanford, Cal.: University of Stanford Press, 2003). For St Paul's statement as future-oriented, a caesura in history, see also Dussel, E. 'Kairós'. Manuscript on file with the author.

20. See on this Bolívar, S. op. cit.: 48.

21. For this quotation see Ferguson, A. *An Essay on the History of Civil Society* (Dublin, 1767): 53.

22. See Bolívar, S. op. cit.: 42.

23. And he was derided for it, left and right. On the left, by none other than Karl Marx himself who clearly projected on his image of Bolívar the result of his studies on the rise to power of Louis Bonaparte between 1848 and 1851, for good and bad. On the right, by a seemingly unending cadre of politicians and commentators, starting with the followers and hagiographers of General Francisco de Paula Santander in Colombia, who would point out that the nature of his 'autonomous' Executive and the 'aristocratic' nature of the Higher Chamber are proof of Bolívar's authoritarian leanings. The debate is relevant today not only as a matter of scholarship but also because it is a debate on the nature of 'Bolivarianism', considered nowadays in relation to the political stance of Hugo Chávez, the President of the Bolivarian Republic of Venezuela. If Marx critiqued Bolívar as an authoritarian Solouque, the militant of the Haitian Revolution who ended

up being crowned as Prince-Emperor in the island, and whose name was widely used in Europe by critics such as Marx to disparage all sorts of politicians as fakes and phonies, among them Louis Napoleon, then how can twenty-first-century leftists like Chávez recover the memory of the Liberator as the basis of their ideology and actions? Is not Chávez also an authoritarian by association? On the opposite corner are those who defend the memory of the Liberator as a convinced republican. What then: republican or authoritarian? One should start by clarifying: neither one nor the other, but a nineteenth-century man, a revolutionary, and a 'third' figure in between the opposition republican/authoritarian that militated for these contending interests and in the process discovered the irrelevance of the representative figures of 'law and order' that supposedly sustain the necessary compromise of those represented. As a militant, he also suffered in his own life the terrible consequences reserved for those who approach reality (which escapes representation and compromise) without caution. See on this latter point, the penultimate chapter of Gabriel García Márquez's celebrated historical novel *The General in His Labyrinth*.

24. The reference is to Simón Bolívar's 1815 *Letter from Jamaica*. Like his predecessor Francisco de Miranda, known as the Precursor of Independence, Bolívar recognised the growing importance of Britain (and, potentially, of the former British colonies in North America) in a world reshaped by the crisis of Imperial Spain, the outcome of the Napoleonic Wars, and, crucially, the emergence of a global monetary economy. This explains its chief literary motif – the drama of human sacrifice, measured by the model of a monetary economy. This motif had become familiar to the British public since at least Shakespeare's *The Merchant of Venice* and *Titus Andronicus*. These works provided the bridge between the Lascasian tradition – centred on the sacrifice of the body of the Indians – and the literary, philosophical and political writings and arguments of British abolitionists and political economists in the minds of the letter's intended readers. The letter aimed to marshal British support for the cause of Latin American independence by appealing to its (economic) self-interest, or, at the very least, persuade Britain not to intervene on Spain's side in the wars of liberation. Those aims were achieved: Britain declared its neutrality and turned a blind eye to the recruitment of soldiers and mercenaries discharged after the end of the Napoleonic Wars. But it also went beyond them in pointing out that the new world, heralded by the rise of a global monetary economy, could itself become potentially sacrificial. In that respect, it should be read together with the Baroque and Enlightenment tradition that goes from Shakespeare to Karl Marx and the Shelleys, Wagner, Sigmund Freud, Thomas Mann and José Saramago, via Kant and others. This tradition revolves around the most fundamental question: what is a life worth?

25. See Bolívar, S. op. cit.: 41.

26. Ibid.: 41–2.

27. Ibid.

28. 'It would take a prophet to predict what policy America will finally adopt. I shall, however, be so bold as to offer some conjectures which are

dictated by reason and hope rather than by plausible argument', Bolívar says (48). Thus, his comments concerning the constitutional and political arrangements likely to develop in the different Latin American countries should not be taken as descriptions or calculated designs. They are 'conjectures' and belong to the language of visionary speculation. As such, they can only be validated by the consequences following their establishment in the future (in retrospective manner). Importantly, such consequences cannot be calculated or prevented from the present standpoint. In that respect, they escape such frameworks of 'plausible argument' as risk scenarios or prevention, which correspond to the model of a monetary society. Thus, they can also be seen as examples of what Jamaican phenomenologist Lewis R. Gordon and political scientist Jane Gordon have called 'divine warning' in relation to modern forms of reading and writing catastrophe. If this is the case, then the aims of the letter were not purely strategic but also militant and prescriptive. It warns its readers about an image of the future undesirable enough so as to move them into action, more or less in the same way in which contemporary indigenous leaders like Davi Kopenawa warned his British audience in June 2009 about the catastrophic effects of the continuous plundering of Latin America's resources for economic purposes. Other examples could include certain contemporary approaches to global warming, or in the nineteenth century the anti-slavery writings of African American scholar and activist Frederick Douglass. There is in fact a whole tradition of prophetic language central to American political life, including Cornel West and Barack Obama in the United States, or Evo Morales in South America. Crucially, prophets do not speak of their conjectures as mere possibilities, but as having the density of the real. Their message could be summarised thus: keep going! But always approach the real with caution. On the importance of visionary speculation in politics see my *Being Against the World. Rebellion and Constitution* (London: Routledge & Birkbeck Law Press, 2009). For modern readings of catastrophe, see Gordon, J., and Gordon, L. *On Divine Warning. Reading Catastrophe in the Modern Age* (Boulder, Colo.: Paradigm Press, 2009).

29. See Sen, A. 'Rational Fools. A Critique of the Behavioural Foundations of Economic Theory', in *Philosophy and Public Affairs*, 6, 1977.

30. See Bolívar, S. op. cit.: 60.

31. I owe this observation to Derek Hughes' very important study of the place of death and catastrophe in literature and opera. See Hughes, D. *Culture and Sacrifice. Ritual Death in Literature and Opera* (Cambridge: Cambridge University Press, 2007): 81.

32. Hughes, D. op. cit.: 83.

33. See Rediker, M., and Linebaugh, P. *The Many-Headed Hydra*: 145.

34. William Petty is recognised as the founder of 'political arithmetic', a blend of old cosmography, natural jurisprudence, astrology and mathematical probability, which is at the basis of what we now call economics. In 1637 he became a cabin boy or shipmate, but was set ashore after breaking a leg on board. After a period of study he joined the navy and

studied anatomy in Holland in 1643. An English professor in Amsterdam recommended him to become secretary to Thomas Hobbes, allowing him contact with the new mathematical, astronomical and geographical methods being developed by Descartes, Gassendi and Marsenne. After studying medicine at Oxford and teaching there, he joined the army. He served as physician general of the conquering army in Ireland in 1652 and cartographer of confiscated lands in the Down Survey of 1654. In 1686 he considered the differing rates of population growth in London and predicted a demographic crisis by 1842.

35. Thus, for instance, Petty argued against sceptics who complained that the earth did not contain enough matter to resource a general resurrection of the dead, by calculating that such a resurrection could be completely supplied from two moderately sized Irish mountains. He should know: as surveyor of the conquering army he took fifty thousand acres for himself in County Kerry, where he divided and organised the local population into hewers of wood, fishermen, quarrymen, lead miners and iron workers in a way that strongly resembled the Spanish systems of *repartimiento* and *encomienda* in the New World. In another instance of mathematical historical teleology, Thomas Culpepper the Elder and Sir Josiah Child, governor of the East India Company, argued that the Israelites flourished as God's chosen people because the ban on usury enforced zero interest rates. See on these, Hughes, D. op. cit.: 83.

36. Most of the information and evidence on the Brazilian trade during the colonial era is based upon the classical study of Michel Morineau, *Incroyables gazettes et fabuleux métaux: Les retours des trésors américains d'après les gazettes hollandaises, XVIIe–XVIIIe siècles* (New York: Cambridge University Press, 1985). See also Tepaske, J. J. 'New World Gold Production in Hemispheric and Global Perspective, 1492–1810', in Flynn, D., Morineau, M., and Glahn, R. (eds). *Monetary History in Global Perspective, 1500–1808* (Seville: Fundación Fomento de la Historia Económica, 1998). Both cited by Marichal, C. 'The Spanish-American Silver peso: Export Commodity and Global Money of the Ancien Regime: 1550–1800', in *From Silver to Cocaine. Latin American Commodity Chains and the Building of the World Economy, 1500–2000*.

37. See on this Galeano, E. op. cit.: 56.

38. See on this Bolívar, S. op. cit.: 51.

39. See on this Pratt, M. L. *Imperial Eyes. Travel Writing and Transculturation* (London: Routledge. 1992): 46. See also David Sinclair. *The Land that Never Was* (London: Review, 2003): 49.

5   Independence: An Exterminating Thunderbolt

1. *Sparagmos* is an ancient Greek voice designating the tearing apart of bodies, often in the context of classical drama.

2. 'But reduced to reason by a mixture even a mob may be better of conciliation and firmness, than by irritation and redoubled penalties.' Byron, Lord. Debate on the Frame-Work Bill. House of Lords. 27 February 1812. Available online at http://orion.it.luc.edu/~sjones1/byspeech.htm. Last accessed 14 January 2010.

3. Spence, T. *The Marine Republic* 1794 in *Pig's Meat*, 2nd edn, 2: 68–72; A. L. Morton, *The English Utopia* (London: Lawrence and Wishart, 1952): at 164–5.

4. Most biographers of Bolívar and historians of independence in the Americas emphasise the connection between Latin America's wars of independence and the particular understanding of the Enlightenment consciousness represented by British Utilitarians. There is no doubt about the importance of these connections. However, this emphasis tends to obscure the no less important fact that leaders like Bolívar derived from their immediate surroundings and from the people they struggled with – including not only white Creoles but also black and *pardo* soldiers and sailors – an argument for a right to revolution that is quite unlike anything that could be found in the writings of Utilitarians. The environment within which leaders like Bolívar lived was dominated by black and Indian concerns, shot through with prophetic and profoundly radical revelations about the consequences of commerce and global empire such as those made by trans-continental black thinkers like Ottobah Cugoano, the Haitian revolutionaries or the commoners of New Granada. The Enlightenment was not a particularly 'western' phenomenon, but a transcontinental event. In the case of the Americas, the fractured Baroque consciousness of Spanish Americans entered into new and unexpected relations with the fractured consciousness of Africans, Indians and forcibly displaced Europeans. The resultant enlightened consciousness was not only new, it was forward-looking and founded its hopes and motifs in the recognition of the darkness of the present, rather than looking backwards at the darkness of the past, the Middle Ages or the *ancien régime*. For an example of the sort of emphasis referred to in these comments see Lynch, J. *Simon Bolivar: A Life*: 31–8.

5. See on these links, Scott, J. S. *The Common Wind: Currents of Afro-American Communication in the Era of the Haitian Revolution*. Ph.D. diss., Duke University, 1986. See also Múnera, A. *Failing to Construct the Colombian Nation: Race and Class in the Andean-Caribbean Conflict, 1717–1816*. Ph.D. diss., University of Connecticut, 1995.

6. *The Axe laid to the Root*, no. 4, 1817. Quoted by Rediker, M., and Linebaugh, P. *The Many-Headed Hydra*: 301. See Chapters 8 and 9 for my sources on the lives of Wedderburn, Despard and Thomas Spence.

7. William Cobbett, the founder and publisher of the *Weekly Political Register*, was himself heavily involved in radical politics as part of the so-called 'Westminster Radicals', a reformist group that advocated parliamentary reform in order to free it from private interests and kingly influence. The group included, among others, the British naval hero and future figurehead of Latin American independence Lord Thomas Cochrane (whose political career Cobbett mentored), and had connections with the abolitionists led by Thomas Clarkson and William Wilberforce as well as with philosophical radicals such as Jeremy Bentham and James Mill, and with religious Dissenters like Joseph Priestley and the London parish of Newington Green (which included such important figures as Richard Price, Mary Wollstonecraft, and had vital contacts with America, among them Thomas

Paine, Benjamin Franklin and John and Abigail Adams). When the Venezuelan diplomatic representatives of the newly formed Caracas junta visited London in 1810, they were introduced into this circle of relations by Venezuelan pro-independence advocate and general of the French revolutionary armies Francisco de Miranda.

8. The political importance of these trans-cultural or syncretistic religious figures cannot be underestimated. For instance, the voudoun or 'bridging' ceremony at Bois Caiman that launched the Haitian Revolution consisted of the invocation and embodiment of the forces of the sun, the sky and the sea in order to guide the struggle against evil forces, the forces of slavery (represented in Caribbean Yoruba traditions, for instance, by Exu or the Devil, the Lord of the Crossroads and uncertainty). It was a pact 'against' the devil, not one 'with' the devil. Looked at closely, the ceremony at Bois Caiman represented a forward-looking leap of faith. In this sense, it is akin to the sort of rational judgement that philosopher Immanuel Kant called 'reflective judgment', a form of anticipatory judgement. This sort of rationality, which often takes religious form, is crucial to the kind of judgements that augment our knowledge of exceptional or unfamiliar phenomena. Political and ethical anticipatory judgements, or 'prescriptions', are basic to modern political and institutional design, particularly to constitution-making. The 'self-evident truths' of the American Declaration of Independence of 1776 are of this kind, anticipatory prescriptions that can be verified only on the basis of their consequences in the future. Bolívar also observed the importance of such political uses of syncretistic religion and anticipatory judgement. See on this Bolívar, S. *Letter from Jamaica*, op. cit.: 61. On 'reflective judgements' and synthesis, see Karatani, K. *Transcritique*: 188–90. On 'radically syncretistic modernity' and the constitutional documents of the Haitian Revolution, see Fischer, S. *Modernity Disavowed: Haiti and the Cultures of Slavery in the Age of Revolution* (Durham: Duke University Press, 2004): 225.

9. See on this, Reid Andrews, G. *Afro-Latin America, 1800–2000* (Oxford and New York: Oxford University Press, 2004): 29. All quotes taken from his book.

10. Cited by Reid Andrews, G. op. cit.: 31. See also Guardiola-Rivera, O. 'Sex, Laws & Rock 'n' Roll: On Music as a Radical Organising Principle', in *Being Against the World*: 220–34. In *Bury My Heart at Wounded Knee*, Dee Brown also describes the effect of such bans on dance, singing and gathering among American Indians in the reservations of nineteenth-century USA.

11. Consider the opinion of the Governor of Popayán, in south-eastern Colombia, then New Granada, about the 'negative' consequences of the Royal Instructions of 1798, in his report to the king. Slaves now treat their owners, he said, 'with a sort of disdain, paying them merely formal obedience and taking every opportunity to dispute their obligations and even daring to express their ideas concerning equality'. Even though the intention of such laws was not to convey any conception of the basic rights inherent in all peoples as human beings, they provided slaves, Maroons,

pardos, mulattoes and Indians with a language and rhetoric through which they could assert precisely such a revolutionising idea. However, it is crucial to understand that if the laws did not intend that result, it was the (collective) action of Africans and Indians that brought about that result. Put otherwise, because no such *universal* concept of equality existed in the laws and institutions of the time, they had to invent it. To do so, they proceeded in much the same way as they did in the cases of religion and music: they approached the language and rhetoric of their masters, almost mirroring its ruses, ambiguities and prolific meanings, and turned it back on itself. This procedure is akin to what anthropologists call 'sympathetic magic' or the 'double aspect' of the fetish. On the one hand, a fetish is a man-made artefact that portrays something and seemingly gives us power over that which it portrays. It is under our control, just as it gives us control, like any other tool. And yet, as happens with every other tool or piece of technology, there is a sense in which the object, the fetish, remains beyond our control; it reacts back upon us and affects us. This explains the duplicity of meanings that the term 'fetish', which originated precisely in Spanish and Portuguese America at the time of the slave trade and obsessive gold lust, nowadays has in anthropology, in psychology, literary criticism and even economics. It refers to forms of syncretism and mimesis, but with a twist, since the unfamiliar and the new seem to emerge from within predictable uses of language and situations. This transversal rhetoric can be found in the argumentative and literary architectures of, for instance, Byron's 1812 speech in the House of Lords on the Frame-Work Bill, in Mary Wollstonecraft's retort to Edmund Burke's criticism of revolutionary action in the early 1800s, in the ex-slave Robert Wedderburn's writings and transatlantic correspondence of the same period, in Bolívar's *Letter from Jamaica*, and in the popular religiosity and culture – hymns, songs, stories – carried by sailors, slaves and commoners throughout the Caribbean and the rest of the Americas. For the opinions of the Governor of Popayán, see Salmoral, L. *Sangre Sobre Piel Negra* (Quito: Centro Cultural Afro-Ecuatoriano & ediciones Abya-Yala, 1994): 84–5. In 1807, the Defensor de Esclavos in Colombia held slavery to be 'against the law of nature … a violent and odious condition that, instead of being favored and extended, should be restricted and harassed'. See Salmoral, L. op. cit.: 77. Both are quoted by Reid Andrews, G. op. cit.: 36 and 218. Notice, however, that there is nothing natural in the way in which a slave would take the Defensor's declaration and turn it into an argument for the universal equality of all mankind. Not even the declarations of the American and French revolutions would suffice, since, although republican in nature and expressed in the language of natural rights, such were examples of the way in which republicanism and rights naturalism could accommodate oppression, land enclosure and slavery. A step further was needed, one that had not ever been taken before: the concepts of 'the human race' and of 'equality' had to be invented, at least in their truly universal sense. It is not just a matter of extending them (or 'inclusion', as politicians say nowadays) since the one doing the inventing cannot be recognised as an 'other' belonging to the same class; she, the slave, is not even human, but is 'below' (the threshold of humanity). Rather than a (horizontal) extension, what is required is a (vertical) ascent – from Hell to the Coming Kingdom – and thus the re-enactment of the world.

12. In 1814 Thomas Spence wrote a spirited defence of the Cherokee lands, at least partially based on his knowledge of the trans-racial communities among the Seminoles of the south-eastern United States and the Mosquito Indians of Central America. It is likely that part of this information was given to him by people like Edward Despard, a former Royal Navy officer who had fought with Horatio Nelson in Nicaragua and commanded a settlement in British Honduras. During his time there, Despard learned from the organisational practices of the Mayan *milpa*s and the ecological knowledge of Indian groups who had welcomed among their people disenfranchised Europeans and runaway African slaves. After confronting the interests of loggers and mahogany exporters in British Honduras, Despard lost his commission and was discharged from the navy. Disillusioned, and now married to an African American woman named Catherine, he came back to London where, in 1802, he was central in the organisation of a conspiracy that sought to seize London and declare a republic. In England, he was thrown into a milieu where working-class people like the Sheffield cutlers had embraced the cause of abolition after listening to the likes of Olaudah Equiano and realised they shared a common situation. He was part of that environment. Despard and his co-conspirators were arrested in November 1802 at the Oakley Arms public house. He was sent to prison and executed. While in prison, he met Thomas Spence. See on this, Rediker, M., and Linebaugh, P. *The Many-Headed Hydra*: 248–86.

13. See Minute of Cabinet, 15 July 1806, HMC, Dropmore Papers, VIII, 236.

14. Letters of Admiral Cochrane to Miranda, 30 July 1806 and 11 September 1806. Quoted by Robertson in *The Life of Miranda*: I, 316–19.

15. Notes on the Caracas, 5 August 1810, National Archives, PRO, FO 72-106.

16. Resonances can also be heard in Anna Barbauld's poem 'Eighteen Hundred and Eleven', which deals with the fate of empires and with revolutionary Spanish America. Barbauld's poem has been closely associated with the writings of revolutionary Latin Americans such as Simón Bolívar. Bolívar's 1805 *Oath Taken in Rome*, Barbauld's 'Eighteen Hundred and Eleven', and Bolivar's 1823 'Delirium on Chimborazo' belong to the same category. Note also that Bolívar's conception of the sublime in his 1815 *Letter from Jamaica* is closer to Barbauld and Mary Wollstonecraft's meaning of the term, rather than Edmund Burke's.

17. Olaudah Equiano contacted Granville Sharp in 1783. In 1787, Sharp co-founded the Committee for Effecting the Abolition of the Slave Trade together with Thomas Clarkson and others. In 1789 and 1790 Clarkson toured the great ports and main cities of England, making a case for the Committee's cause and selling Equiano's written account of his experiences as a sailor and a slave. Another one of Clarkson's friends, the writer and Dissenter Anna Barbauld, wrote the poem 'Eighteenth Hundred and Eleven' in 1812. The poem focuses on Spanish American revolution, in the

wake of the British-American War and conflict in continental Europe, but differs sharply from the writings of more moderate radicals who supported the cause of Spanish America at the time. The poem is a highly critical piece about the fate of empires, including British imperialism, and the potential for Anglo-American expansionism prompted by the 1803 Louisiana Purchase. The poem is a testament to transatlantic radical political thought in the nineteenth century, which continues to be of relevance. While the Barbaulds were in France they had met Jacques-Pierre Brissot, the founder of the abolitionist *Amis des Noirs* in France, leader of the Gironde Party and personal friend of Francisco de Miranda. Sharp, Clarkson and others persuaded Wilberforce to adopt the cause of the abolitionists. In the second half of 1810 Miranda took Bolívar to meet William Wilberforce and his fellow abolitionists.

18. Lord Thomas Cochrane was the nephew of Rear Admiral Alexander Cochrane, who had agreed to support Miranda's 1806 filibuster adventure in Venezuela as commander of the British fleet stationed in the West Indies. An associate of William Cobbett, who mentored his political career as a 'Westminster radical' in the British Parliament, he would later become one of the great naval heroes of Spanish American independence, 'the boldest buccaneer ever to swagger across a British Navy quarterdeck', according to the *Literary Review*, thanks to his interventions in Chile, Peru and Brazil. He was the very epitome of the Romantic hero, celebrated by Lord Byron in 1824. In that same year, on 23 August, Simón Bolívar wrote to Lord Thomas Cochrane inviting him 'to come to cooperate with us on Colombia's Panamanian coasts'. See, on Cochrane, Cordingly, D. *Cochrane the Dauntless: The Life and Adventures of Thomas Cochrane* (London: Bloomsbury, 2007). Thanks to Bill Swainson for bringing to my attention this most accomplished biography of the real Master and Commander.

19. See Mill, J. 'Emancipation of Spanish America', in the *Edinburgh Review*, 26 January 1809: 277–311, at 304–5.

20. See on this, and for the citation, Racine, K. *Francisco de Miranda: A Transatlantic Life in the Age of Revolution* (Wilmington, Del.: Scholarly Resources, 2003): 207–8. Miranda's house in Grafton Street was not only the focus of Spanish American voices for independence in Great Britain, but also a true space for trans-cultural and intercontinental political formation. James Mill and Jeremy Bentham moved in the circle that gathered around Miranda's house, which included such notables as William Wilberforce and Charles James Fox. Anna Barbauld knew and respected Wilberforce and Charles James Fox as well as the Dissenting theologian Joseph Priestley, who influenced the philosophical and political work of both Mill and Bentham. Surprisingly, she did not get along well with William Cobbett, another member of the same political circles, who opposed, like her, the War of 1812. Although Barbauld's writings are far more radical than those of Mill and Bentham, she did not go as far as Lord Cochrane's political mentor; Cobbett publicly mocked British institutions and authorities. Barbauld is more concerned with lending a voice to those who stand up against all empires, and specifically with Spanish America as a privileged site

for such a voice. It has been argued that she wrote 'Eighteen Hundred and Eleven' in response to the Venezuelan Declaration of Independence from Spain in 1811, since news of the event was in the British press; she could have read about it in the pages of the *Monthly Repository*. This idea gains support when the fact that Francisco de Miranda was at the very centre of the circles within which all these figures moved is considered. This is the same circle that Bolívar would be introduced to by Miranda in 1810. It is not clear whether Miranda and Bolívar actually met Anna Barbauld through their common friends in London, but it is most likely they knew of her, and vice versa. She was very interested in Spanish American affairs and appears to have been better informed than most of the other members of the Grafton Way circle. Clearly, they communicated with the same people. It is certain that Barbauld knew of Home Popham's Argentine expedition, and she does refer to La Plata and to Potosí as being at the very heart of a globally exploitative system. She also mentions Chimborazo in her poem ('On Chimborazo's summits treads sublime') in connection with the motifs of time and the sublime, exactly the same motifs behind Bolívar's later poem 'Delirium on Chimborazo'. Furthermore, as Nicholas Birns contends, Barbauld deploys the figure of Christopher Columbus in her poem as a signal, using 'dramatic South American landscape to explicitly portray "manifest destiny"', and, therefore, Latin America appears in the poem as the precondition of an actuality that is in practice North American, the US. This may well be one of the sources (or confirmatory evidence) of Bolívar's well-known concerns about the potential for the westward and southward expansionism of the United States following the Louisiana Purchase. Did Bolívar ever get to meet Barbauld? Did he read her? See on this Birns, N. '"Thy World, Columbus!": Barbauld and Global Space, 1803, "1811", 1812, 2003', in *European Romantic Review*, vol. 16, no. 5, December 2005: 545–62. See also Heinowitz, Rebecca C. '"Thy World, Columbus, Shall Be Free": British Romantic Deviance and Spanish American Revolution', in *European Romantic Review*, vol. 17, no. 2, April 2006: 151–9. Some of the ideas expressed in these paragraphs can be found in these articles.

21. For these quotes, see Wollstonecraft, M. *The Vindications: The Rights of Men and the Rights of Woman.* Edited by D. L. Macdonald and K. Scherf (Toronto: Broadview Literary Texts, 1997): 44, 75.

22. Heinowitz, Rebecca C. op. cit.: 151–9.

23. Barbauld, A. L. *Eighteen Hundred and Eleven, A Poem.* London: Printed for J. Johnson & Co. St Paul's Churchyard, 1812. Available online at http://digital.library.upenn.edu/women/barbauld/1811/1811.html

24. Heinowitz, Rebecca C. op. cit.: 151–9.

25. For the source of quotes and paraphrases, see Lasso, M. *Race War and Nation in Caribbean Gran Colombia, Cartagena, 1810–1832.* Available online at http://www.scribd.com/doc/19241050/Race-War-and-Nation-in-Caribbean-Gran-Colombia-Cartagena-18101832-. Last accessed 14 January 2010.

26. For some of the ideas, paraphrases and data used in this paragraph see,

Mignolo, W. *The Idea of Latin America* (Oxford: Blackwell, 2005): 58–64. See also Reid Andrews, G. op. cit.: 3. For the coinage of the term 'Latin America' in the nineteenth century by Torres Caicedo and French intellectual Michel Chevalier, see Ardao, A. *Génesis de la Idea y el Nombre de América Latina* (Caracas: Centro de Estudios Latinoamericanos Rómulo Gallegos, 1993): 18–19.

27. Bolívar, S. op. cit.: 49.
28. William Pitt the Elder, then Earl of Chatham, is cited in List, F. *The National System of Political Economy*: 95. See also for this reference, and the next, Chang, J-H. *Bad Samaritans*: 49.
29. As Smith said, 'were the Americans, either by combination or by any other sort of violence, to stop the importation of European manufacture, and, by thus giving a monopoly to such of their countrymen as could manufacture the like goods, divert any considerable part of their capital into this employment, they would retard instead of accelerating the further increase in the value of their annual produce, and would obstruct instead of promoting the progress of their country toward real wealth and greatness'. In Smith, A. *The Wealth of Nations* (London: Random House (1776), 1937): 347–8. There is no space here to engage in the analysis of the consequences of the advice of European economists at the time, Smith or J. B. Say to the American colonies, or to consider what would have happened if the Americans followed such advice. Suffice to say they did not. Instead they embarked on exactly the opposite path to that advocated by Smith and Say, and succeeded.

6   Republic: The Sobriety of the Day After

1. Le Clézio, J. M. G. *The Mexican Dream. Or, The Interrupted Thought of Amerindian Civilizations*: 1–3.
2. The reference is to Díaz del Castillo, B. *Historia Verdadera de la Conquista de la Nueva España* (Madrid: Espasa-Calpe, 1968). There is an English edition titled *The Bernal Díaz Chronicles: The True Story of the Conquest of Mexico*. Translated and edited by A. Idell (New York: Doubleday & Co., 1957).
3. See Le Clézio, J. M. G. op. cit.: 24–5.
4. *The Chronicles of Michoacán*. Translated and edited by E. R. Crane and R. C. Reindorp (Norman, Okla.: University of Oklahoma Press, 1970): 57. Cited by Le Clézio, J. M. G. op. cit.: 15.
5. See Le Clézio, J. M. G. op. cit.: 151–2.
6. Only in Mexico, Chile, Paraguay, Uruguay, Peru and Ecuador were whites in the majority in relation to free blacks or *pardos* and slaves in Spanish and Portuguese America circa 1800. However, in Peru and Ecuador, Indians massively outnumbered whites. In Argentina there were 69,000 free blacks and slaves, 70,000 whites and 42,000 Indians. In Colombia there were 306,000 free blacks and slaves *vis-à-vis* 203,000 whites and 156,000 Indians. These numbers, and their geographical distribution, help explain the social, ideological and political divisions that ensued during and after the wars of independence. Indeed, it could be said that the political make-up of the different countries of Latin America follows these numbers and changes

with them. The revolutionary legacy of Latin America has to be understood together with the numbers and locations of the different populations that inhabit it. In the twenty-first century, revolutionary Bolivia and Venezuela, progressive Brazil and the 'paranoid style' of politics in Peru or Colombia are related to racial divisions within the population, their geographical location and their relative hold on political and economic power. Historian Alfonso Múnera has applied this hypothesis to the case of Colombia's 'failure to build a nation', as he put it. See, Múnera, A. *El Fracaso de la Nación. Región, clase y raza en el Caribe Colombiano, 1717–1810* (Bogotá: Banco de la República & El Áncora Editores). For a table containing the population number used here, see Reid Andrews, G. *Afro-Latin America*: 41.

7. See on this Reid Andrews, G. op. cit.: 47. For all quotes and paraphrases, refer to it.

8. See Racine, K. *Francisco de Miranda: A Transatlantic Life in the Age of Revolution* (Wilmington, Del.: Scholarly Resources, 2003): 5–6. See also Rodríguez Mesa, M. P. 'Los Blancos Pobres', in *BOLANH*, 80, 317, 1997: 133–88. The episode is narrated also in Lynch, J. *Simon Bolivar: A Life*: 9.

9. See on this Múnera, A. *Fronteras Imaginadas. La Construcción de las Razas y de la Geografía en el Siglo XIX Colombiano* (Bogotá: Editorial Planeta, 2005).

10. This was the opinion heard by a committee of São Paulo planters gathered to consider the case of a slave who had murdered his master in 1871. The planters at the time paid particular attention to the fact that by then slaves were overwhelmingly native-born. See on this and for the source of paraphrases in the paragraph, Reid Andrews, G. op. cit.: 81.

11. See Dean, *Rio Claro: A Brazilian Plantation Society, 1820–1920* (Stanford, Cal.: Stanford University Press, 1976): 127. Cited by Reid Andrews, G. op. cit.: 82.

12. See Blanchard, P. *Slavery and Abolition in Early Republican Peru* (Wilmington, Del.: Scholarly Resources, 1992): 117. Cited by Reid Andrews, G. op. cit.: 55.

13. See Reid Andrews, G. op. cit.: 43.

14. Ibid.: 91. As Reid Andrews points out, 'Bolívar went on to express the fear that, as part of that drive for equality, "they will demand that the darker skinned elements should rule. This will ultimately lead to the extermination of the privileged class" and "pardocracy": rule by the *pardos*. Such fears of black vengefulness and lust for power were widely held among the white elites', and partly explain Bolívar's confrontations with *pardo* leaders in the revolutionary armies such as Manuel Piar and José Padilla. Yet vengeance was not in the mind of most Afro-Latin Americans. As Reid Andrews says, 'Bolívar had it right the first time: free blacks and mulattoes were demanding full rights to citizenship. And in return for the promise of those rights they willingly accepted the obligations of citizenship, serving in provincial and national armed forces and taking part in the contentious party politics of the early republican years. In so doing they played a central role in shaping the new republics and in defining the contours of national politics' (92). Colombian vice-president Francisco de Paula Santander also expressed the

paranoid style of politics characteristic of elite republican politics when he wrote to the minister of the interior to create more 'effective' criminal laws dealing with blacks who were 'developing projects of domination'. For the early republican ideology, particularly from the Creole standpoint, race equalled factionalism and was thus a threat to the unity of the country. Bolívar's notion of 'pardocracy' represented the triumph of one faction over unity and stability. Thus, as Marixa Lasso says, 'the racial policies of this period need to be understood within this overarching goal of eliminating any cause for racial conflict and division, and fostering a nation of citizens, which is to say, a nation of men with equal interests and values'. This means that there were at last two uses of the language of equality: from the standpoint of free blacks and mulattoes 'equality' meant full and actual equality. That they become full citizens in the sense of having full capacities, and that their specific interests and values informed the universal aspirations of the nation (i.e. equality for all). This can be called 'a universalistic politics of the multiple', which refers to 'racial harmony', as well as decolonisation, as an incomplete project yet to be achieved. In contrast, from the white Creole standpoint, 'equality' meant a nation of citizens in which 'citizenship' subsumed, absorbed and assimilated all actual and potential differences within a homogenous political culture that would provide a secure basis for constitutional institutions, or excluded as 'internal enemies' those who refuse to be assimilated. This can be called a 'particularistic politics of the One', which refers to 'racial harmony' as if it had already been achieved. Once declared unnecessary, racial grievances and calls for further advancement in the path towards equality became dangerous threats against the public order. See Lasso M. 'Race War and Nation in Caribbean Gran Colombia, Cartagena, 1810–1832', in *American Historical Review*, April 2006: 336–60.

15. See on this, and for the sources of quotes and paraphrases, Lasso, M. op. cit.: 359–60.

16. See on this Reid Andrews, G. op. cit.: 92–4.

17. See on this Rediker, M., and Linebaugh, P. *The Many-Headed Hydra*: 245–7. See also Lasso, M. op. cit.: 360. Interestingly, Back-to-Africa programmes in the eighteenth century seem to announce the type of resettlement 'out of here' viewed as a solution in post-war Europe in the twentieth century.

18. The point is that the universality of this principle, its axiomatic character, was beyond doubt. This is true, even though there were conflicts about the realisation of this principle: gradual or immediate, extended to all peoples of colour or only to newborns or those with property and so on. Marixa Lasso points to the celebrations of independence in the United States in the 1820s and 1830s as illustrating the lack of connection between nationalism and racial equality. Blacks were harassed and expelled from the celebrations by those who argued that the 4th of July 'belongs exclusively to the white population', while many African Americans chose a British holiday, 1 August, West Indian Emancipation Day, as their holiday.

19. See Bolívar, S. 'Inviting Governments to a Congress in Panama, 7 December

1824', in *Simón Bolívar: The Bolivarian Revolution*: 164–8. At first Bolívar's invitation excluded the United States, in deference to British susceptibilities 'among other reasons', as John Lynch explains, Brazil as a monarchy and Haiti, like the United States, 'as foreigners to us and heterogeneous in character'. Later, American delegates were invited, as were British observers. In 1826 he established an agenda for the congress, including the establishment of a common law regulating international relations, the granting of powers of mediation to the league on domestic and foreign affairs, the establishment of a continental force that could intervene in cases of internal anarchy and external aggression, and of a charter abolishing the slave trade and establishing guidelines or rights aimed at countering social and racial discrimination. In inviting the British, and even going as far as proposing that the British be given South American citizenship, he hoped to contain Spanish animosity but also the potential for US expansionism, while also transforming America into a centre for British relations with the western hemisphere, with Europe and Asia. Hence the choice of Panama as the new 'isthmus of Corinth' and potential 'centre of the globe'. Both the ascent and egalitarianism of the black middle class predominant in Panama, and its 'equidistant' location (in terms reminiscent of the old tradition of 'philosophical geography') made it a worthy candidate to become the capital of the world. It also meant strong opposition from pro-slavery quarters in the US. Indeed, when US president John Quincy Adams asked Congress for funds to send delegates to the Congress of Panama, southerners argued so firmly against them that by the time money was actually appropriated, the Congress at Panama had ended. See Lynch, J. op. cit.: 213–17.

20. S. Bolívar to F. de Paula Santander, Arequipa, 6–7 June 1825. *Cartas Santander-Bolívar* (Bogotá: Biblioteca de la Presidencia de la República, 6 vols, 1988–90): vol. 4: 388.

21. See on this McGuinness, A. *Path of Empire. Panama and the California Gold Rush* (Ithaca, NY, and London: Cornell University Press, 2008): 17.

22. See Cummins, J. *History's Great Untold Stories* (New York: National Geographic, 2007).

23. See McGuinness, A. op. cit.: 127–31.

24. See García Márquez, G. *One Hundred Years of Solitude*. Translated by G. Rabassa (New York: Harper & Row, 1967–70): 336.

25. See Asturias, M. A. *The Green Pope* (New York: Delacorte, 1971): 134–5. See also his novel *Strong Wind* (New York: Delacorte, 1968).

26. See on this Reid Andrews, G. op. cit.: 140–42.

27. Cited by LeGrand, C. C. 'Living in Macondo: Economy and Culture in a United Fruit Company Enclave in Colombia', in *Close Encounters of Empire*. Edited by G. Joseph, C. C. LeGrand and R. Salvatore (Durham, SC: Duke University Press, 1998): 333–57.

7   *Empire: Tales from Mañana-Land in Neocolonial America*

1. This account of the events of 15 April 1856 in Panama is based on Aims McGuinness' *Path of Empire: Panama and the California Gold Rush*: 123–51. All quotes and paraphrases are taken from and belong to his work on the

significance of the relationship between Panama and the West Coast of the US for its rise to dominance in the continent and the world.

2. See on this McGuinness, A. op. cit.: 105.

3. To wit, O'Sullivan was based in New York, which means that popular belief in the 'Manifest Destiny' of the United States was principally but not solely southern. O'Sullivan articulated these views in the context of hopes that adding territory westward and southward would add impulse to the Jeffersonian model of economic development, based on export-oriented and slave-labour-driven agriculture and production, and balance the Hamiltonian model of protected 'infant' industrialisation of the faster-growing North. Thus, he stated that it must be 'our manifest destiny to overspread the continent allotted by Providence for the free develop-ment of our yearly multiplying millions'. As the quote reveals, the tension between the two sides owed less to irreducible opposition than to the difficulties of reaching an adequate balance between the two models of export-oriented economic development in the US and the abandonment of the mercantile-colonial model imposed by Britain. This difficulty was played out in the US Supreme Court decision on the Charles River Bridge, which meant the end of internal monopolies or privileges granted by the state to corporations and the onset of internal competition of companies protected against external or foreign competition, and which preceded the infamous Dred Scott decision by almost two decades, also written by Chief Justice Roger B. Taney. But also, in the actions and decisions of numerous financiers and tycoons from the North and the South associated with the transport industry, who greatly increased their fortunes servicing the migra-tion routes through Central America to California, during the Gold Rush of 1848, after the annexation of the state from Mexico. Some of them, like the shipping and railroad tycoon from Wall Street, Cornelius Vanderbilt, or his New York ally, Charles Morgan, proposed the construction of a canal across Panama or Nicaragua, which was closer to the United States. These financiers worked closely with armed bands of mercenaries or 'filibusters', like William Walker, whom they financed and transported.

4. See on this McGuinness, A. op. cit.: 150.

5. See on Roosevelt, 'Books: T. R.', a review of *Theodore Roosevelt* by Henry F. Pringle (Harcourt, Brace & Co.), in *Time* magazine, 23 November 1931. Available online at http://www.time.com/time/magazine/arti-cle/0,9171,742699-1,00.html. Last accessed 14 March 2010.

6. I will base this account on the work of historian Paul Linebaugh. See, in particular, his *Magna Carta Manifesto*.

7. See on this Mies, M., and Benholdt-Thomsen, V. *The Subsistence Perspective. Beyond the Globalised Economy*. Translated by P. Camiller, M. Mies and G. Wieh (London and New York: Zed Books, 1999). Also Rifkin, J. *The Empathic Civilization*: 512 and 593 ff.

8. *International Covenant on Economic, Social and Cultural Rights*. 1966, 1976, pt I, art. 1, chap. 2. See Chang, H-J. *Bad Samaritans*: 27, n. 16; 37–8. Chang's reference on p. 27, n. 16, relates directly to the school of development economics initiated in Latin America by the writings and international

politics of Argentinean economist and diplomat Raúl Prebisch, and the Economic Council for Latin America and the Caribbean (ECLAC), known as 'structuralism', and in its post-neoliberal reincarnation as 'neo-structuralism'. Contemporary economists linked with this trend, like José Antonio Ocampo, are nowadays associated with the maverick and influential school of economics led by Joseph Stiglitz, among others, but also with the more or less inventive positions taken by economists like Venezuelan Carlota Pérez, Brazilian Theotonio Dos Santos, Chilean Fernando Flores or Uruguayan Eduardo Gudynas. See on this, Leiva, F. I. *Latin American Neostructuralism. The Contradictions of Post-Neoliberal Development* (Minneapolis, Minn.: University of Minnesota Press, 2008).

9. See on this and Rediker, M., and Linebaugh, P. *The Many-Headed Hydra*: 223–4.

10. Linebaugh, P. op. cit.: 173–4.

11. See Steiner, B. *Life of Roger Brooke Taney* (Baltimore, Md.: Williams and Wilkins, 1922). See also, Swisher, C. *Roger B. Taney* (New York: Macmillan, 1936). Both cited by Linebaugh, op. cit.: 170–91, at 176.

12. See Luthin, R. 'Abraham Lincoln and the Tariff', in *The American Historical Review*, vol. 49, no. 4. Among the most important legacies of Lincoln's presidency are the land reform programmes of the 1862 Homestead Act and the Morill Act, which established the 'land grant' colleges that helped boost the country's research and development capabilities. In time, this would become America's most competitive tool. See on this, Chang, J-H. op. cit.: 54–5.

13. Here I follow the opinion of Ha-Joon Chang. See Chang, H-J. op. cit.: 53–4.

14. That view proved to be enduring, and would frame a great deal of the geopolitical exchanges between the US and Latin America. In 1924, for instance, American writer Harry Foster would describe, in his *A Gringo in Mañana-Land*, an account of his travels through Mexico and Central America, what he saw as the contradictory nature of the typical Latin American who 'like the Mexican, is both an idealist and a materialist, [as] he sees no inconsistency in being both devoutly religious and frankly immoral.' Speaking of the people of El Salvador, he referred to them as 'half-breed' and would represent Latin American women as a type, the 'peon girl without a partner', who is 'the daughter of a rather sensuous race, and of a race that is not inclined to work when an easier living is to be obtained'. Other Americans, unhappy with the result of those momentous years of transformation, disagreed. Travelling through Brazil in 1856, American philosopher William James, for instance, believed he had found 'the original seat of the Garden of Eden'. Having witnessed the American takeover of Cuba and Puerto Rico after 1898, James concluded that Americans 'had finally vomited the Declaration of Independence'. We should take his comment as a direct reference to the liberties of the Charters. See on this, Lears, T. J. J. 'William James', in *Wilson Quarterly*, vol. 11: 88–9. See also, for quotes and paraphrases, Foster, K. *Lost Worlds* (London: Pluto Press, 2009): 118–19.

15. Linebaugh, op. cit.: 176.

16. Since most people tend to think that mathematics is the language of necessity – a proposition with which I disagree although I do not have the time or the space here to explain my disagreement – another way of saying that there is nothing necessary about markets is to state that economic behaviour cannot be described, as a whole, by precise mathematical relationships. Benoit Mandelbrot, one of the great mathematicians of the twentieth century, has described how economists have ignored years of progress in the study of ecology, weather and other natural phenomena partly because those studies did not warrant the assumption that catastrophic disturbances are vanishingly unlikely to occur, which underpins conceptions of the self-corrective nature of markets, givenness and necessity. See on this Mandelbrot, B., and Hudson, R. L. *The (Mis)behaviour of Markets. A Fractal View of Risk, Ruin and Reward* (New York: Basic Books, 2004). See also Kaletsky, A. 'Goodbye, Homo Economicus,' in *Prospect*, April 2009: 46–9; and Chang, J-H. op. cit.: 46–7.

17. See on the production of time difference and its relation with value, Fabian, J. 'How Others Die – Reflections on the Anthropology of Death', in *Social Research*, 39: 543–67, reprinted in Robben, A. (ed.) *Death, Mourning and Ritual: A Cross-Cultural Reader* (Oxford: Blackwell, 2004): 49–61. His assertion at the end of the article, referencing anthropologist Claude Lévi-Strauss, according to which doing anthropology entails a form of conquest, is strictly homologous to my assertion that the production of value in modern exchanges involves a form of 'discovery' and conquest. I argue that what was at first a historically contingent event – the event of discovery and conquest – was first formalised in law (constitutional law, as in the example of Magna Carta in thirteenth-century Britain or the Martin case decided by Judge Taney in the US) and then as a formal law of exchanges in Ricardian and post-Ricardian theories of trade and economic value, which are still current. The problem, I contend, is that exchanges entail the sharing of time and space in what we call the global space of exchanges or a commodity chain, and demand that producers located in 'central' areas of the global space recognise the people with whom they exchange as their coevals; however – and this is where the contradiction arises – when the same producers in 'central' areas represent to their buyers what they have used and learned in their practices of production and marketing, mainly via prices and advertising, in terms that consistently place those whose knowledge and resources have been used and refined, in a time other than that of the one producing and marketing. This entails an active process of forgetting, which is practically equivalent to acts of 'discovery' and conquest. As for the criticism of Ricardo's theory of value and trade implicit in these paragraphs, it is similar to the arguments expressed in his time by economist Samuel Bailey. I have only added the simple fact that, as in the case of the anthropological exchanges considered by Johannes Fabian, also in the case of economic exchanges what is being exchanged – commodities – cannot be exchanged directly. In the case of the economy they are mediated by money *qua* general equivalent. The question then becomes: why can commodities not be directly exchanged with each

other? The answer is that between each other there is a 'symbolic form', and so value arises out of the difference between symbolic worlds and the attempt to translate from one to the other, which often involves placing one symbolic world in a time or a space 'other' from that of the one who translates. Merchants like Flint or Grace in Peru were, just like their conquistador forebears Pizarro and De Soto, intermediaries placed in the position of translators. And as we well know, translation can never be, strictly speaking, direct. Like Cortés before the Aztec, intermediaries like Flint or Grace in the late nineteenth and early twentieth centuries saw in that difference not just superstition or magic, but, rather, turned what they saw as 'backwardness' into a chance and an opportunity, and used it to their advantage.

18. The actual quote is 'I think the fact that the financial services sector can grow to be larger than is socially optimal is a key insight.' See Turner, A., in 'How to Tame Global Finance. A Group of Leading Financial Analysts Quiz Britain's Top Regulator on What Went Wrong and How to Sort it Out', in *Prospect*, September 2009: 34–41, at 36.

19. See Topik, S. op. cit.: 182.

20. 'Milestones, 26 February 1934', in *Time* magazine. Available online at http://www.time.com/time/magazine/article/0,9171,747065,00.html. Last accessed 15 March 2010.

21. The US had also changed its pre-war position towards the government of Juan D. Perón in Argentina. Then, Argentina was the most important market in Latin America and one of the most important in the world, and the US saw its position as replacing Britain as Argentina's foremost trade partner 'threatened by European expansion and the dollar shortage'. At the same time, Argentina's leadership in the hemisphere had begun to be questioned by Brazil, whose own sizeable market would soon displace Argentina's pre-eminent position in Latin America, and Chile, a second contender. Prebisch's appointment was thus 'caught up in a bilateral diplomatic reorientation, with the State Department arguing that US support for Prebisch in the IMF could pre-empt this promising development with Perón. Thrown out of the Central Bank [of Argentina] by the Perón-backed military government in 1943 against US protest, a man who had risked and lost his career for the Allied cause and had continued to work closely with the Federal Reserve after 1945, Prebisch was sacrificed six years later on the altar of US rapprochment with Perón.'

22. Dosman, E. J. *The Life and Times of Raúl Prebisch, 1901–1986* (Montreal and Kingston, Ithaca, London: McGill-Queen's University Press, 2008): 485–6.

23. Ibid.

24. See on this, and on Prebisch's ECLA as a gadfly to the International Monetary Fund and the IBRD-World Bank, 'Raúl Prebisch on ECLAC's Achievements and Deficiencies: An Unpublished Interview', in *CEPAL Review*, 75, December 2001: 9–22, at 19 and 21. See also Griffith-Jones, S., Ocampo, J. A., and Stiglitz, J. E., 'Introduction', in *Time for a Visible Hand*: 1.

25. Ocampo, J. A., and Vos, R. *Uneven Economic Development* (London and New York: Zed Books, 2008): 1. See also Griffith-Jones, S., Ocampo, J. A., and Stiglitz, J. E. op. cit.

26. Prebisch to Victor Urquidi, 28 November 1946. Prebisch asks 'if Keynesian economics does not explain the reality of [business] cycles, how does one explain the reality?' Urquidi responded with the observation about disequilibrium on 6 December 1946. Cited by Dosman, E. J. op. cit.: 219.

27. In 1946 the US proposed the creation of two regional commissions within the United Nations Economic and Social Council (ECOSOC), one for Europe and one for Asia, to help with post-war reconstruction. Latin Americans reacted by reminding everyone that the region had collaborated in the war effort with considerable capital and natural resources and, although it had not been as badly hit as a theatre for war operations as Europe and Asia, it too was exhausted and as much in need of a vehicle supporting accelerated growth as any other region n the world. The initiative to set up such an institution, spearheaded by Chile, culminated in the creation of the ECLA on 15 February 1947, with little evident support from the US, to be based in Santiago de Chile. After the IMF fiasco, Prebisch became its second and most decisive Executive Secretary.

28. Prebisch to Eugenio Gudin, 20 December 1948. Cited by Dosman, E. J. op. cit.: 226.

29. After the experiment with ECLA-supported reforms came to an end, and amid proposals to follow the orthodox communist road, Guevara became a staunch critic of the Soviet model, in fact accurately predicting its demise, and set out to create a different one. Many aspects of his proposed model have been vindicated by the model of economic development in Asia and by proposals for radical reform made in Europe and the Americas after the global crisis of 2008. See Helen Yaffe's hugely informative *Che Guevara: The Economics of Revolution*. With a foreword by Lord Meghnad Desai (London: Palgrave Macmillan, 2009): 45–69.

30. Yaffe, H. op. cit.: 57.

31. This was in contrast to the use of money under the Soviet-style AFS or economic calculus, in which money serves not only for the purposes of measurement and collective coordination 'but also acts as a means of payment, an indirect instrument of control, because without funds the production unit could not operate. Under such circumstances, the production unit's relation with the bank are similar to those of a private producer in the capitalist system who must exhaustively explain plans and prove solvency to his bank. Consequently, because of the way in which money is used, our [BFS] enterprises have no funds of their own. There are separate bank accounts for withdrawals and deposits. The enterprise may withdraw funds in accordance with the plan from the general expense account and the special wages account. But all deposits come automatically under state control.' The issue is one of regulation, which Guevara sought to formulate using the example of US corporations and the principles of cybernetics underpinning the ongoing information technology and communications revolution. In his opinion, information technology had the potential to

do away with capitalist categories such as 'profit' and 'value' since collective coordination could be achieved without the need for intermediaries. In that sense, the autonomy given to enterprises under BFS was premised on self-organisation, while the 'autonomy' given to enterprises under the Soviet-style AFS relied on managing privatised funds and investments under the determination of the profit motive. See Guevara, E. 'On the Budgetary Finance System', in *Man and Socialism in Cuba: The Great Debate.* Edited by B. Silverman (New York: Atheneum, 1971): 132.

32. See on this Yaffe, op. cit.: 61.

8   Revolution, or How to See the Beginning in the End

1. See Reid Andrews, G. *Afro-Latin America*: 165.
2. See Rondón, C. M. *The Book of Salsa. A Chronicle of Urban Music from the Caribbean to New York.* Translated by F. Aparicio and J. White (Chapel Hill, NC: University of North Carolina Press, 2008): 2–3.
3. See on this, and for Artaud's quotes, Le Clézio, J. M. G. *The Mexican Dream. Or, The Interrupted Thought of Amerindian Civilizations*: 166–7.
4. See Rondón, C. M. op. cit.: 2.
5. For an account of the ceremony at Bois Caiman, see Antoine Dalmas' *History of the Saint-Domingue Revolution* (1814), and for Tecumseh, MacLuhan, T. C. *Pieds nuds sur la terre sacré* (Paris: 1974), cited by Le Clézio, J. M. G. op. cit.: 203. The relationship between rhythm, carnal connection and rebellion is also depicted in popular culture. In the TV series *Caprica*, the connection between dancing, deeper connectivity and the spirit of rebellion is perfectly symbolised in the underground virtual club where the children of the eponymous city get together to plot rebellion against their fathers, the colonisers.
6. See on this, and for quotes, Reid Andrews, G. op. cit.: 171. He cites Moore, R. *Nationalizing Blackness. Afrocubanismo and Artistic Revolution in Havana, 1920–1940* (Pittsburgh, 1997): 80–86. See also Comaroff, J., and Comaroff, J. *Ethnicity, Inc.* (Scottville: University of Kua-Zulu Natal Press, 2009).
7. See Khanna, P. *The Second World. How Emerging Powers Are Redefining Global Competition in the Twenty-First Century* (London and New York: Penguin Books, 2008).
8. The other top five cities in order of ranking were Zurich, Sydney, Luxembourg and Dublin. Los Angeles came sixth, New York eighth, Chicago ninth, Berlin eleventh, London fifteenth and Paris twenty-seventh. The survey was conducted by UBS for the City Mayors' Economics website, which allows residents and non-residents all over the world to rate the performance of mayors across the planet. The study was done in terms of purchasing power. It is available online at http://www.citymayors.com/economics/usb-purchasing-power.html. Last accessed 31 January 2010.
9. See Reid Andrews, G. op. cit.: 194–5.
10. All the names and some of the situations have been changed at the request of those involved. I have compounded similar views expressed by some interviewees as opinions of one single character for the purposes of effect and expediency.

11. For the quote, see Huntington, S. P. *The Clash of Civilizations and the Remaking of the World Order* (New York: Touchstone Books, 1997): 21. The quote continues: 'We know who we are only when we know who we are not and often only when we know who we are against.' The point is also reminiscent of the arguments advanced by 1930s German internationalist Carl Schmitt, hugely influential among the military, constitutionalists and foreign policy-makers in the Americas in spite of his association with the Third Reich.

12. Cited by Roberto Lovato in 'Latinos in the Age of National (In)security', *NACLA Report on the Americas*, vol. 39, no. 3, November/December 2005, New York: NACLA, at 27.

13. In *The Soldier and the State*, published in the late 1950s and still used in military academies in the US, Huntington had described the professional soldier as an expert in 'the management of violence' along corporate lines. As a responsible expert, the professional soldier must contain violence, in both senses of the word: internalise it within, while circling the wagons to keep it without. The bodybuilding of Latino soldiers en route to Iraq seems a perfect embodiment of the resulting paradox: they must shed any other traces of memory, place and culture in order to acquire the rigid identity that is supposed to count as 'loyalty to America'. The process is particularly painful, practically impossible if you're a Latino trying to avoid being stereotyped as a 'non-assimilated' internal enemy, an 'immigrant terrorist', or a 'drug-cartel criminal', to cite the terms used by Minuteman leader Chris Simcox in Town Hall meetings across the country. At some point during our conversation, Luis intimated a similarly ensuing psychological crisis might have had something to do with the suicide of his friend. Reportedly, his last words were 'Who are we here?'

14. See Lovato, op. cit. at 28. He reports on a 2005 meeting of Latin American and Caribbean defence ministers, in which Rumsfeld outlined his view of the 'new' hemispheric threats and called for a switch from the war on terror to 'a global struggle'.

15. Cited by Lovato, op. cit. at 27. He quotes Huntington's *Who Are We?*

16. Source: Department of Defence. *Population Representation in the Military Services*. Fiscal Year 2004. Cited by Mady Wechsler Segal and David R. Segal in 'Latinos Claim Larger Share of U.S. Military Personnel', available online at http://www.prb.org/Articles/2007/HispanicsUSMilitary.aspx. For a detailed exposition and explanation of statistical trends concerning the representation of Hispanics in the US Armed Forces, see 'Hispanics in the Military', a report by the Pew Hispanic Center, March 27, 2003. available at http://pewhispanic.org/files/factsheets/6.pdf

17. See on this Mignolo, W. *The Idea of Latin America* (London and New York: Blackwell, 2007): 135 and 137.

18. The so-called Minutemen describe themselves as a 'citizen's vigilance operation monitoring immigration, business and government'. According to the Minutemen Project's spokesperson Jim Gilchrist, they must be distinguished from the Minutemen Civil Defense Corps (MCDC), a volunteer group headed by Chris Simcox, dedicated to preventing illegal crossings of

the United States border. The activities of the MCDC are controversial: according to *New York Times* journalist Anthony Ramirez, the group has been criticised as 'a right-wing militia'.

19. See Pantoja, A. Menjíbar, C., and Magaña, L. 'The Spring Marches of 2006. Latinos, Immigration, and Political Mobilization in the 21st Century', in *American Behavioral Scientist*, vol. 52, no. 4, December 2008, Sage Publications.

20. I've talked several times with Maldonado-Torres and Grosfoguel, both in Berkeley, California, where they live, in London, and in Latin America. I've learned a great deal from them, and consider them the thinkers to watch in the coming Latino States of America. Together with SUNY Professor Eduardo Mendieta, and CUNY feminist philosopher Linda Martin-Alcoff, they are the most promising young Latino public intellectuals currently working in the US. For the source of these quotations see also: Grosfoguel, R., and Maldonado-Torres, N. 'Latinos (as), Migrants, and the Decolonization of the U.S. Empire', in *Naked Punch*, summer 2007 issue (London and Lahore: NP): 34–9. Grosfoguel, R. Maldonado-Torres, N., and Saldívar, J. *Latinos in the World System: Decolonization Struggles in 21st Century U.S. Empire* (Boulder, Colo.: Paradigm Press, 2005). See also Maldonado-Torres, N. *Against War* (Durham, SC: Duke University Press, 2008).

21. Cited by *The Economist*, in 'A Special Report on Texas', 11 July 2009, at 11. In accordance with the report, Eschbach reckons that over the eight years to 2008, natural increase accounted for just over half the 3.5 million in the state's population, while migration from other states for almost half of the rest.

22. See for citation *The Economist*, 11 July 2009, at 10. The report calls MALC 'the body to watch'. Although self-described as non-partisan, MALC claims forty-four of the seventy-four Democrats in the Texas House of Representatives, and there is not one Hispanic Republican member, which is, as the report rightly remarks, 'a gigantic problem for the party'.

9   Crisis: The Rise and Fall of Global Capitalism

1. In 2003, economists at Goldman Sachs singularised Brazil, together with Russia, India and China as the economies that would come to dominate the world by the second half of the twenty-first century. At the time, most reactions to the forecast were sceptical about Brazil. Now, it has been accepted that while China leads the world economy Brazil too is 'on a roll', as *The Economist* put it in its November 2009 issue. See *The Economist*, 14–20 November 2009. See also *Programas sociales aseguran derechos. Brasil está construyendo su red de promoción y protección social.* Published in 2009 by the Ministry of Social Development and the Struggle against Famine. Some of the information is also based upon a conversation with Brazilian minister of social development Patrus Ananias in September 2009.

2. Some of the paragraphs in this section are based on the work of UC Berkeley sociologist Loïc Wacquant. See *his Punishing the Poor: The Neoliberal Government of Social Insecurity* (Durham, SC: Duke University

Press, 2009). See also the book's review 'Imprisoner's Dilemma', by
Kim Phillips-Fein, in *Bookforum*, September–November 2009: 17.
For the global side of the 'neoliberal government of insecurity', appar-
ent in the current merging of development and security, see the work
of former UN reporter Mark Duffield, especially his *Global Governance
and the New Wars*. See also my book *Being Against the World*: 187–219.
For the source of some of the statistics and quotations, see 'Lawmakers
Seek to Stem Flood of Inmates Into Downtown', *Los Angeles Downtown
News*, 5 December 2005. Available online at http://dist22.casen.govof-
fice.com/index.asp?Type=B_PR&SEC=%7B0A2790CD-E2A0-4AD1-
ADCC-79E9FBBF6544%7D&DE=%7B720733B4-BE91-461A-8C3A-
67F326A00A14%7D. Last accessed 30 January 2010. These statistics have
varied in recent years: due to the Safer City initiative to 'clean up' Skid
Row, enacted by the city and the Police Department in reaction to news
stories about law enforcement agencies and local hospitals transporting
homeless people in their care to the area, among other reasons, homeless-
ness and crime have dropped considerably, reflecting also the incoming
gentrification of surrounding Downtown Los Angeles neighbourhoods.

3. Cited by Phillips-Fein. op. cit.: 17.

4. The figure corresponds to an estimate published in 2002 by academics Clive
Norris and Michael McCahill and repeated in the media and in the resignation speech of British shadow home secretary David Davis in the UK.
The broad estimate was obtained on the basis of a survey of the number
of CCTV cameras in two busy south London high streets. Another estimate comes from the CCTV User Group, a UK trade association, which
contends with caution that there are around 1.5 million 'public' cameras.
The figure neither contradicts nor supports the 4.2 million figure. Part of
the problem is that there are no official or even unofficial statistics on how
many CCTV cameras there are in the United Kingdom, and the government has repeatedly told Parliament that such figures are not collected.
For now, the 4.2 million figure is considered the best-guess extrapolation
of the number of cameras in London, or at least in two representative busy
London streets a few years ago. The Scottish government is in the process
of reviewing how many cameras are north of the border with England.

5. See Fabian, J. *Memory Against Culture*: 60.

6. For the source of the reference to 'clarity in action', see Buck-Morss, S.
'Hegel in Haiti', in *Critical Inquiry* 26, no. 4, 821–63, at 851.

7. Thomas Friedman's 'golden straitjacket' summarises the following policies:
privatisation of state-owned companies, maintenance of low inflation at all
costs, running a surplus budget or if not a balanced one, liberalised trade
and deregulation of labour markets, financial markets and foreign investment, pension markets and no or as little as possible state intervention.
Crucially, however, the point is to understand that these are not just part
of another set of economic policies to be applied prudentially or selectively
in relation to other policies or questioned from more enlightened positions, but, rather, that they comprise the only available option, the only
enlightenment or, as Margaret Thatcher and Alan Greenspan would say,

that 'there is no alternative', no future outside the established frame of reference and that countries ought to adopt the model if they wish to enter into the exclusive club of Lexus car makers and abandon that of perennial fighters over 'who owns which olive tree'. As can be seen, Friedman's distinction in fact repeats in the twenty-first century the image of the Leviathan conjured up by English thinker Thomas Hobbes's seventeenth-century division between those who live in the civil state and those who live short, brutish lives in the 'natural state' of war. Although in Friedman's case the emphasis is on the cultural-religious side of Leviathan's power, with free-market and free-trade economics considered as an article of faith in the place of the new religion. This allows for the image of a reduced, less interventionist state. As for the 'novelty' of technology in Friedman's 'flat world', one must remember that Hobbes' Leviathan was a machine, an automaton. As is well known, Hobbes's distinction between interconnected 'civilised' communities and backward peoples condemned to a short and brutish life referred not only to the state of Britain after the English Revolution but also, decisively, to the indigenous peoples of the Americas, the proverbial 'barbarians'. This other reference is crucial to understanding the place of Leviathan at a time when Britain was launching its imperial enterprise: the first export to open up the global space to all other exports was warfare. United, the people move forward as one gigantic warrior flattening the surrounding landscape. This provides a different context within which to interpret Friedman's views. See his *The Lexus and the Olive Tree* (New York: Anchor Books, 2000): 105. See also his his more recent *Flat World: A Brief History of the Twenty-First Century* (New York: Farrar, Straus & Giroux, 2005); and *Hot, Flat and Crowded: Why We Need a Green Revolution – and How It Can Renew America* (New York: Picador, 2009).

8. See on these figures Chang, H-J. *Kicking Away the Ladder.* 132, table 4.2. For the 'industrial revolution' in the south, see Singh, A. 'The State of Industry in the Third World in the 1980s: Analytical and Policy Issues', Working Paper, no. 137, April 1990, Kellogg Institute for International Studies, Notre Dame University. Cited by Chang, H-J. *Bad Samaritans*: 27, n. 19.

9. For an example of such revisionism, which must be read as a mid–nineties straight criticism of the views popularised by Raúl Prebisch in the *Havana Manifesto*, see the following quote from Jeffrey Sachs and Warner: 'Export pessimism combined with the idea of the big push to produce the highly influential view that open trade would condemn developing countries to long-term subservience in the international system as raw materials exporters and manufactured good importers. Comparative advantage, it was argued by the Economic Commission of Latin America [sic], ECLA and others, was driven by short-term considerations that would prevent raw materials exporting nations from ever building up an industrial base. The protection of infant industries was therefore vital if the developing countries were to escape from their overdependence on raw materials production. These views spread within the United Nations system (to regional offices of the United Nations Economic Commission) and were adopted

largely by the United Nations Conference on Trade and Development (UNCTAD). In 1964 they found international legal sanction in a new part IV of the General Agreement on Tariffs and Trade (GATT), which established that developing countries should enjoy the right to asymmetric trade policies. While the developed countries should open their markets, the development countries could continue to protect their own markets. Of course, this "right" was the proverbial rope on which to hang one's own economy.' See Sachs, J. and Warner. A. 'Economic Reform and the Process of Global Integration. *Brookings Papers on Economic Activity*, no. 1, 1995: 17. This is misleading revisionism. The period is described as an era of economic disasters in the Global South, caused by the 'mistaken' idea that the countries of such regions could dare to defy market logic. As a result, they suppressed the economic activities which they were good at (agriculture, mineral extraction and cheap, labour-intensive manufacturing) and promoted 'white elephant' projects that were economic nonsense. The problem with this picture, and with Sachs and Warner's condemnation of the right to 'asymmetric protection' (which was in fact a right to include appropriate, selective and agreed upon safeguards in trade treaties, or to extend to all a practice well established already in the historical record of so-called developed countries) is that the disasters did not occur and the bad, suicidal days proved to be not as bad or self-destructive at all. Ditto, during the period of the 'Third World Industrial Revolution' per capita income in developing countries grew by 3 per cent annually, much better in comparison with their rates of growth during the free-trade days of the age of empire and not bad at all *vis-à-vis* the 1.5 per cent achieved by rich countries during the industrial revolution of the nineteenth century. In contrast, in the countries that adopted extensive neoliberal reforms after the 1980s, growth slowed down to 1.7 per cent. Growth also decelerated in rich countries from 3.2 per cent in the 1960s and 1970s to 2.1 per cent 'not least because they did not introduce neoliberal policies to the same extent as the developing countries did', says Ha-Joon Chang. See Chang, J-H. op. cit.: 26–7.

10. Chang also points out that the average growth rate of developing countries in the 1980s would be even lower if one excludes China and India, but insists that those two countries 'have so far refused to put on Thomas Friedman's golden straitjacket' (27). One should add to Chang's list the case of Brazil. Although Brazil's 'neoliberal period' got off to an early start after the military coup of 1964, the pace and extension of such reforms turned out to be much slower than in other latecomer parts of Latin America, like Chile, Colombia or Argentina, thanks in part to the influence of the ECLA economists so earnestly dismissed by Sachs and Warner, such as Celso Furtado, for instance, and their contacts with the Brazilian business 'class', but also to a specific political articulation – between entrepreneurs, corporations, the military and the growing numbers of people, mostly black, migrating from rural areas to urban sites to join popular sectors. That articulation resulted in military regimes trying to relaunch the state-directed national development project in order to secure their

legitimacy while at the same time containing the potential 'contamination' of popular sectors with socialist or communist tendencies. To this end they formed a political assemblage that included MNCs, local and diverse elites while setting up a quarantine zone around popular sectors, which worked only to a certain extent. The result was a confusing period, with 'economic miracle' cycles followed by 'unfavourable national economic cycles', well represented in the fate of the Geisel government of the late 1970s. This explains neoliberalism's 'late arrival' into Brazil, why the weight of neoliberal stabilisation fell upon the shoulders of former ECLA 'dependentists' like Fernando Henrique Cardoso or popular leaders like Lula, but also, crucially, why the more heterodox climate that prevailed in Brazil, economic as well as political, generated mostly by the creativity and vigour of popular sectors, allowed for the remembering and re-enactment of the memory of independence, social autonomy and international solidarity that today characterises the Brazilian project and sets it apart from that of China, for instance. See, on the paradoxical path of Brazil, Leiva, F. I. *Latin American Neostructuralism. The Contradictions of Post-Neoliberal Development*. Minneapolis, Minn.: University of Minnesota Press, 2008): 74–8. I share Leiva's critical spirit towards some of the shortcomings of the more recent ECLA interventions (which he terms 'neostructuralism') but less so his pessimism about the contemporary phase of the Brazilian project. In my view, it underestimates the role played by popular sectors in lowering the pace and extent of neoliberal reforms since the mid-sixties until today.

11. See Manguel, A. 'The Prophet Squeaks. A Review of Roberto Bolaño's Nazi Literature in the Americas', in *Guardian*, Review, 6 February 2010: 12.

12. Borges, J. L. 'Avatars of the Tortoise', in *Labyrinths*. Edited by D. A. Yates and J. E. Irby (London: Penguin Books, 1970): 237–43, at 242.

13. Borges, J. L. op. cit. 243.

14. See Kahl, J. A. *Modernization, Exploitation and Dependency in Latin America: Germani, González Casanova and Cardoso* (New Brunswick: Transaction Books, 1976): 151

15. Ibid.: 152. See also the work of Santiago Castro-Gómez on mobility, velocity and expectations of mobility in the case of Colombia between the 1930s and 2000. On this, Castro-Gómez, S. *Tejidos Oníricos* (Bogotá: Instituto Pensar & Fondo Editorial Javeriano, 2009).

16. Based on the value of the US dollar in 1990.

17. For these data see Maddison, A. *The World Economy*: Table 4c. See also Public Citizen's Global Trade Watch. 'The Uses of Chile: How Politics Trumped Truth in the Neo-Liberal Revision of Chile's Development', Discussion Paper, September 2006. Available online at http://www.citizen.org/documents/chilealternatives.pdf. Last accessed 1 February 2010.

18. Fernando Flores to Stafford Beer, 13 July 1971, Box 55, The Stafford Beer Collection, Liverpool John Moores University. Cited also in Medina, E. 'Designing Freedom, Regulating a Nation: Socialist Cybernetics in Allende's Chile', *in Journal of Latin American Studies*, 38 (Cambridge: Cambridge

University Press): 571–606, at 581. See also Maturana, H., and Varela, F. J. *De Máquinas y Seres Vivos: Una Caracterización de la Organización Biológica* (Santiago, 1973). Translated into English as *Autopoiesis and Cognition: The Realization of the Living*. With a foreword by Stafford Beer (Boston, Mass.: 1980).

19. Beer, S. *Brain of the Firm* (New York: 1974): 156 and 249.

20. Beer, S. *On Decybernation. A Contribution to Current Debates*. Box 64. The Stafford Beer Collection. Liverpool John Moores University. 27 April 1973: 6. Also cited by Medina, E. op. cit. 600, n. 102.

21. República de Bolivia, Oficina Nacional de Inmigración, Estadística y Propaganda Geográfica, *Censo general de la población de la república según el empdaronamiento de primero de Septiembre de 1900*: 41.

22. This is how Brazilian General Breno Borges Fortes presented the proposal to the X Conference of American Armies held in Caracas on 3 September 1973. On March 1974 representatives of the police forces of Chile, Uruguay and Bolivia met with Alberto Villar, deputy chief of the Argentine Federal Police and co-founder of the death squad known as Triple A, to implement collaboration guidelines in order to 'contain' the subversive threat represented by the presence in Argentina of a number of political exiles. In August 1974, the corpses of the first targets of Operation Condor, all of them Bolivian refugees, including former president Torres, started to appear in rubbish dumps in and around Buenos Aires. French journalist Marie-Monique Robin has attributed the paternity of the operation to Argentine General Rivero, a former student of French intelligence services. Indeed, the infamous 'death flights', widely used in Chile and Argentina in order to get rid of the corpses and the evidence, were used by the French during the Algerian War. On 22 December 1992 Paraguayan judge José Fernández stumbled upon a set of files in a police station in the Lambaré quarter of Asunción which thereafter became known as the 'terror archives'. These documents contained detailed accounts of at least 50,000 people murdered, 30,000 disappeared and 400,000 incarcerated as part of Operation Condor. They also revealed the involvement of other Latin American countries such as Peru, Colombia and Venezuela in the operation. On 6 March 2001 the *New York Times* published a 1978 cable from US Ambassador Robert White to Secretary of State Cyrus Vance, released by the Clinton administration under the Chile Declassification Project. In the document, Ambassador White reported a conversation with Chief of Staff of the Paraguayan Armed Forces, General Alejandro Fretes Davalos. The US diplomat was informed that the South American intelligence chiefs involved in Operation Condor remained in contact 'with one another through a US communications installation in the Panama Canal Zone which covered all of Latin America'. According to Davalos this installation was used 'to coordinate intelligence information among the southern cone countries'. Ambassador White expressed his concerns that the US connection with Operation Condor might be publicly revealed in the wake of mounting pressure to collect evidence during the investigation of the assassination of former Chilean minister Orlando Letelier and his American assistant Ronni Moffitt in Washington, DC. See on this, Dinges, J. *The Condor Years: How Pinochet and His Allies Brought Terrorism*

to Three Continents (New York: The New Press, 2004); Kornbluh, P. *The Pinochet File: A Declassified Dossier on Atrocity and Accountability* (New York: The New Press); Robin, M-M. *Escadrons de la mort, l'école française* ('Death Squads, the French School'). Book and film documentary (French, transl. in Spanish) (Buenos Aires: Sudamericana, 2002); McSherry, J. P. *Predatory States: Operation Condor and Covert War in Latin America* (London: Rowman & Littlefield, 2005); and Cezar Mariano, N. *Operación Cóndor. Terrorismo de Estado en el cono Sur* (Buenos Aires: Lholé-Lumen, 1998).

23. For the basis of this account of the changing self-reflection and image of the indigenous peoples of Bolivia, plus quotes, census data and paraphrases, see Rivera Cusicanqui, S. 'Colonialism and Ethnic Resistance in Bolivia. A View from the Coca Markets', in *Empire and Dissent. The United States and Latin America*. Edited by Dred Rosen (Durham, SC: Duke University Press, 2008): 137–60, at 140.

24. See Rivera Cusicanqui, S. op. cit.: 141.

25. See Reid Andrews, G. *Afro-Latin America*: 196–7. Reid Andrews is referring to the case of Afro-Latin Americans, particularly in Brazil. His observations can, however, be generalised to a certain extent. For the case of the Indians of Bolivia, see Rivera Cusicanqui, S. op. cit.: 140–41. The census data used in these paragraphs are hers.

26. This also means to say that 'Evil' is neoliberalism's expected angle of attack. Hence, the 'security state' that emerges together with neoliberal governance focuses on evil-doers, reproducing them as the means to achieving its own balance. This is the sense in which commentators like Naomi Klein speak of the recently acquired capacity of capitalism to profit from catastrophe. This also entails that 'Evil' is not a real problem for capitalism in its neoliberal phase. It can deal with it, by containing it and – in preventive mode – arresting its spread. In this sense, evil-doers do not constitute a political challenge to neoliberalism. Instead, they contribute to its legitimisation.

27. See Rivera Cusicanqui, S. op. cit.: 141.

28. Ibid.

29. Ibid.: 142.

30. Ibid.

31. See *UN Vienna Convention against Illicit Traffic in Narcotic Drugs and Psychotropic Substances*. Article 14, paragraph 2.

32. See Rivera Cusicanqui, S. op. cit.: 150.

33. Ibid.: 157–8.

34. Ibid.: 137.

10   *The Solution to All Our Problems*

1. See Cordingly, D. *Cochrane the Dauntless*: 1. Also for Byron's quote.

2. For the circumstances surrounding the creation of ECLA, see Dosman, E. J. *The Life and Times of Raúl Prebisch*: 235–8

3. See Dosman, E. J. op. cit. 236–8.

4. In Charles Pellegrino's book *The Last Train from Hiroshima* the author quotes the following account of the aftermath of the atom bomb attacks

by Tsutomu Yamaguchi, the only person known to have survived both explosions in Hiroshima and Nagasaki. Yamaguchi describes the victims as 'ant-like walking alligators' who 'were now eyeless and faceless, with their heads transformed into blackened alligator hides displaying red holes, indicating mouths ... The alligator people did not scream. Their mouths could not form the sounds. The noise they made was worse than screaming. They uttered a continuous murmur – like locusts on a midsummer night. One man, staggering on charred stumps of legs, was carrying a dead baby upside down.' In this way, the Japanese people, including the men, women and children of Hiroshima and Nagasaki, had been turned into monsters twice. First, in words. To the already widespread image of the Japanese as sub-human, which informed the practices of mutilation of the Japanese dead carried out by some US soldiers during the Pacific War, Harry S. Truman added these comments on the second day after the Nagasaki bombing: 'The only language they seem to understand is the one we have been using to bombard them. When you have to deal with a beast you have to treat him like a beast. It is most regrettable but nevertheless true.' Second, in practice. Estimates of total deaths as a consequence of the Nagasaki atom bomb by the end of 1945 range from 90,000 to 140,000, others state up to 200,000 by 1950 and from 1950 to 1990 it is estimated that roughly 9 per cent of cancer and leukaemia deaths among atom bomb survivors were due to post-attack radiation. At least eleven known Allied POWs died in the attack. In the case of Nagasaki estimates of immediate deaths range from 40,000 to 75,000 to 80,000 by the end of 1945, and as many as thirteen Allied POWs died as a result of the explosion. Other 'unintended' victims included Korean and Chinese workers, Malay students on scholarships and some 3,200 American Japanese citizens. In 1975, the Radiation Effects Research Foundation assumed the responsibilities of the Atomic Bomb Casualty Commission created by President Truman to discern the conditions and outcomes related to radiation exposure in the long-term. But perhaps the most telling consequence of the unimaginable devastation that the bombings of Hiroshima and Nagasaki brought upon mankind was the firmly entrenched anti-nuclear position taken by successive Japanese governments. Instead of following the often travelled path of reciprocity and pre-emptive acquisition of nuclear armament, the Japanese went down the path less travelled and have consistently refused to use their advanced technological capacities in the pursuit of such weapons of mass destruction. In a way, both Harry Truman and the post-war Japanese people represent the parallel roads of our time, both tragedy and farce. See *The Spirit of Hiroshima: An Introduction to the Atomic Bomb Tragedy*. Hiroshima Peace Memorial Museum, 1999. Harry S. Truman Library & Museum. *U. S. Strategic Bombing Survey: The Effects of the Atomic Bombings of Hiroshima and Nagasaki*, 19 June 1946. President's Secretary's File, Truman Papers. 2. Hiroshima: 1–51. Walker, J. S. 'Recent Literature on Truman's Decision: A Search for the Middle Ground', in *Diplomatic History* 29 (2). April 2005: 334 ff. For the various death toll estimates, see Frank, R. B. *Downfall: The End of the Japanese Empire* (London: Penguin Books, 2001). For dehumanisation during the Pacific War, see Weingartner,

J. J. 'Trophies of War: U. S. Troops and the Mutilation of Japanese War Dead, 1941–1945', in *Pacific Historical Review*, 61 (1) February 1992: 54, 67. The author attributes the Truman quote to Ronald Schaffer's *Wings of Judgment: American Bombings in World War II* (New York, 1985): 171. And for the long-term historical consequences of the atom bomb attacks, see Sherwin, M. J. *A World Destroyed: Hiroshima and Its Legacies* (Stanford, Cal.: Stanford University Press, 2003). See also the fictionalised analysis of such effects in Alan Moore's graphic novel (with artist Dave Gibbons and colourist John Higgins) *Watchmen* (DC Comics, 1986–7).

5. For the source of quotations and paraphrases in this and preceding paragraphs, see the outstanding book written by Gerald Martin, *Gabriel García Márquez: A Life* (London: Bloomsbury, 2008): 125.

6. For these quotes, see Martin, G. op. cit.: 105.

7. For this quotation, see Rubottom, R. R. 'Diplomat in No-Man's Land', in *Life in the Foreign Service*. Last accessed on 9 February 2010. Available online at http://www.dacorbacon.org/dacor/lifefs/dipnoman.html. Rubottom was part of the American delegation in attendance during the IX Pan-American Conference.

8. See on this Galeano, E. 'Muere Asesinado en Bogotá Jorge Eliécer Gaitán, 1948', in La Haine. Last accessed 10 February 2010. Available online at http://lahaine.org/internacional/historia/mueregaitangaleano.htm

9. See on this Martin, G. op. cit.: 109. I have added to his statement about guerrilla movements the emergence of far-right paramilitary groups. The latter, inspired in part by the far-right fiercely anti-communist ideologies of the 1940s and 1950s, took the form of an alliance between former members of the drug dealing Medellín Cartel (some of whose most prominent members, like Carlos Ledher, espoused an explicit neo-fascist outlook, while others, like Pablo Escobar, attempted to enter into politics through the populist side of the Liberal Party), landowners of the Antioquia, Córdoba and Atlántico regions (where workers in the banana, mining, agricultural and cattle industries demonstrated a great deal of organisation and political awareness), politicians, industrialists and members of the country's security forces. These groups mimicked the militant language and tactics of leftist guerrilla groups, and also the highly symbolic and brutal acts of violence of the time of *La Violencia* intended to bring about the complete dehumanisation of the enemy (mutilation, disembowelling, psychological terror and so on). Their successful infiltration of or integration with the country's security services and other political institutions, particularly in the legislative and executive branches of power, has been repeatedly denounced within the country and abroad during the second half of the first decade of the twenty-first century.

10. See on this Martin, G. op. cit.: 107–9.

11. Letter from Brebbia to Prebisch, 24 January 1940. Cited by Dosman, E. J. op. cit.: 141.

12. The principle of exchange value, as rewritten by Walpole, was stated through the King's address to Parliament, in which His Majesty George I said 'it is evident that nothing so much contributes to promote the public

well-being as the exportation of manufactured goods and the importation of foreign raw material'. Two things must be observed in this elaboration of the principle: (1) that the principle according to which what creates value is the exchange of difference has the world as its proper setting, and thus, the difference that creates value is the difference between systems of value around the world. This is what the Spaniards concluded from their dealings with the systems of value they found in the Americas and elsewhere. Value in import/exports is a matter of world comparison and difference. (2) That the direction of the worldwide flow of value in trade is mediated through states, in the concrete form of the ensemble between the monarch and the nationally incorporated bodies of private interest, or corporations. Hence the importance of the principle being stated in its eighteenth-century form by the efficient/dignified element of a mixed constitution, the British mixed constitution, which after the defeat of the radical members of the New Model Army during the English Revolution reformed the state into a political and legal form that contains (in the sense of keeping within and keeping at bay) the democratic principle. Walpole's 'import substitution' model takes this new political reality into account and turns it into the political foundation of a national economic system projected upon the world, which subordinates technological innovation to such economic drive.

13. As Ha-Joon Chang points out, 'in 1820, Britain's average tariff rate on manufacturing imports was 45–55%, compared to 6–8% in the Low Countries, 8–12% in Germany and Switzerland and around 20% in France'. These tariffs were combined with other worldwide measures facilitated by colonial and neocolonial control ranging from bans on advanced manufacturing activities in the colonies, prohibitions on competing exports from the colonies such as cotton textiles from India, encouragement of primary commodity production in the colonies, the provision of export subsidies and the abolition of import taxes on raw materials produced in the American colonies and, ultimately, an assortment of policies aimed at ensuring that the most valuable industries would be left in the hands of Britain so that it could enjoy the benefits of being on the cutting edge of world development. Famously, Adam Smith accused Walpole's policies of being an example of 'mercantilism', both entailing the repetition of the earlier mercantilist system of the absolutist monarchies of Europe in Britain's 'industrial revolution' model, and denouncing that they were becoming obsolete since, having become internationally competitive, maintaining protectionist measures would make such companies complacent and inefficient. At that point, adopting free trade was increasingly in Britain's best interest. British manufacturers started campaigning for it, and in particular for the repeal of the Corn Laws that limited the country's ability to import cheaper grain. In this case, the effect of the anti-corn 'free trade' move was double: on the one hand it cut production costs by lowering the wages of labourers buying cheaper food, which elevated their living standards and purchase ability (at the expense of the standards of workers abroad) and therefore raised profits and lowered the risk of social unrest,

and on the other hand it intended to halt the move to industrialisation in continental Europe by enlarging the market for agricultural produce and primary materials, thereby luring Britain's potential competitors back into agriculture. Only in 1860 would Britain's tariffs be more or less completely abolished. See Chang, J-H. op. cit.: 45.

14. See Chang, J-H. op. cit.: 51.

15. Ibid.: 55.

16. The Marshall Plan was announced by General George Catlett Marshall, then Secretary of State, in his address at Harvard University on 5 June 1947. It was started in 1948 and ended in 1951, channelling the equivalent today of $130 billion to the financing of essential import bills and infrastructure even in former enemy countries.

17. During the war, Latin countries had sold the materials needed by the US to feed the war machine at prices fixed by the Office of Price Administration and could not convert their dollars into goods. The effect was inflationary. At the end of the war, when US goods were finally available for purchase, Latin countries found that there were no price controls on these industrial exports while the prices for their primary mineral and agricultural products declined. At the end of the war single-commodity countries like Venezuela, Bolivia, Cuba or Chile faced the real prospect of a downturn in trade and serious economic crisis. Yet the Truman administration opposed the creation of an Inter-American Development Bank, rejected multilateral efforts to stabilise commodity prices and seemed unable or unwilling to stop mounting congressional opposition against ratification of the International Trade Organization treaty proposed in 1948 in Havana and hailed by John Maynard Keynes as the trade counterpart of the World Bank and the IMF. Disappointment among Latin countries became widespread as Washington focused its efforts on Europe and Asia, which explains Chile's initiative concerning the creation of ECLA and America's hostility towards the idea. However, only after the independent mobilisation of Latin American countries in the UN did the United States decided to make good its wartime promises of cooperation, sending Marshall himself to Bogotá in 1948 to squeeze out of the Latin American delegations an agreement for an Organization of American States, mostly beneficial to the interests of the US in exchange for renewed promises of cooperation and the commitment of increased sums of money to an OAS-based development agency set in competition against UN-based ECLA, which the US could not corner that easily. This is but a repetition of the old theme of US–Latin America relations: dashed expectations of mutual recognition and cooperation. By 1949, at the beginning of the second Truman administration, and now in the midst of a full-blown anti-communist crusade, a sense of injustice was boiling up as Washington's priorities continued to ignore Latin American concerns either explicitly (as Henry Kissinger would do later) or implicitly, through inconsistent policies.

18. Letter from Raúl Prebisch to Eugenio Gudin, 20 December 1949. Cited by Dosman, E. J. op. cit. 226–7.

19. See Aristotle, *Poetics*, 1457b. For this reference, *Poética*. Trad. Cast. de V. García Yebra (Madrid: Gredos, 1974): 1457b.

20. According to Curtius, the Latin poets compared the composition of a poem with travelling by sea: making poetry is *uela dare*, to set sail (Virgil, *Geórgicas*, II, 41) and the end of the poem is *uela trahere*, to lower the sails (Virgil, ibid. IV, 117). The hoisting of sails at the beginning of the poem opens up a period of time equivalent to the promise of return, which ends with the anchoring of one's ship. The success or value of the composition hinges upon the realisation of the promise of return, anchoring (Estacius, *Silvae*, IV, 89; *Tebaida*, XII, 809; *Ilias Latina*, 1063). The content of the composition is an anticipatory contemplation of the perils that threaten the navigator, the poet, between departure and arrival and the tale of the realisation or not of such perils. See on this, Curtius, E. R. *Literatura Europea y Edad Media Latina* (Mexico City: FCE, 1955: 190).

21. In the mid-1970s a few adventurous occupants of Chicago's option pits started trading with the aid of sheets of theoretically anticipated prices derived from an equation and a mathematical model created by economist Fisher Black. The strings of matrix-like numbers that resulted came to be known as the Black-Scholes model, which used share and bind prices to calculate the value of derivatives exchanged in the financial market. One result of the emergence of the Black-Scholes model to top-dog position was rhetorical and political: it helped legitimise a market that until then had been derided as a gambling den. Another was the further entrenchment of a number of probabilistic assumptions among the basic premises or 'laws' of economic theory and practice associated with the notion of equilibrium – chief among them the 'rational expectations hypothesis' and the 'market efficiency hypothesis'. Crucially, an argument of probability is applied to the 'laws' themselves, rather than merely to the events subject to these laws. It is posited that if the laws were contingent, in the sense of being modified frantically, frequently, then we would no longer know anything because none of the conditions for stable experience and observation would ever obtain. But since they obtain, one must conclude that the world regulated by such laws is as constant as the laws themselves as a result of some underlying necessity. Necessity here means constancy in all possible futures, not necessarily in reality or in an experiment but at least in the presupposed or modelic totality of all possible futures. In this model there is no room for a truly catastrophic event, unrepeatable and capable of dividing time decisively. In this model, Ulysses is simply being irrational (Can't he just plot a course and stop wandering around? What's up with the gods? They condemn poor Ulysses to a game of absolute chance) and the idea of a final apocalypse, as in the Amerindians' idea of the return of the wandering prophet, is superstitious nonsense. Both Ulysses and the Amerindians would point out that the analyst's hypothesis of a universe containing all possible universes which can be observed and surveyed is, at the very least, no less superstitious. It may also be wrong, they would say, for the mathematics of the Long Count (what we now call post-Cantorian infinity, set theory, topology and so on) does not warrant the existence of

a set of all sets. Small wonder that such 'modern' and sophisticated models want nothing to do with low-probability, high-impact events.

22. My translation, from the Spanish transcription by Rumeu de Armas. See Rumeu de Armas, A. *Nueva luz sobre las Capitulaciones de Santa Fe de 1492 concertadas entre los Reyes Católicos y Cristobal Colón* (Madrid: Consejo Superior de Investigaciones Científicas, 1985): 52. This translation is intended to provide the reader with an intimation of the problematic use of the term 'discovery' in both the past and the future tense in the original document, which has been the source of much debate among Columbus scholars. The latter have advanced all sorts of explanations for the paradoxical use of the term 'discovery', from Juan Manzano's 'secret pre-discovery' thesis to Rumeu de Armas' 'retrospective modification' thesis to Demetrio Ramos' 'black letter law' thesis according to which we must understand what it says in the 'natural and obvious sense' that avoids temporal contradiction. However, as Raúl Marrero-Fente observes, none of these interpretations are less rhetorical than the others and in fact they all point at the central issue: the rhetorical character of the text is not accidental, the presence of the past in the heading of the contract breaks with and breaks up the prospective character of all contracts, turning this one into a special case of circularity. Far from being literal, the text has the structure of a fiction: Their Catholic Majesties pretend to give (*otorgar*, make present) what they do not have and have not seen, for in fact the lands object of the contract have not yet been found by anyone and exist only in fantastic literature. This is the point, however: to transfer something one does not have, such as future profit, which acquires value in the very act of transfer. This is the essence of value in finance and elsewhere, and it is connected with a form of knowledge that appeared in the fourteenth century as a tool for government and administration, known as *visitatio* or *inquisitio*. The characteristic procedures of a *visitatio* form the historical basis of statistical gathering, mapping and modelling, widely used nowadays in the practice of government and finance. See Marrero-Fente, R. *La Poética de la Ley en las Capitulaciones de Santa Fe* (Madrid: Trotta, 2000): 55–6.

23. This translation of the *Capitulaciones* between Their Catholic Majesties and Christopher Columbus is available online on the website of Yale University Library's Avalon Project.

24. In 1905 the US Supreme Court issued a couple of decisions known as *Fullerton v. Texas* (196 US 192 [1905]) and *Board of Trade v. Christie* (198 US 236 [1905]) in which the so-called 'contemplating delivery' doctrine was established. The Court concluded that traders in 'futures' could deal on conceptual or 'possible' entities so long as they contemplated corporeal goods in their minds while doing so. The issue at stake was that of incorporeal exchange (of futures). The doctrine owes much to the work of Judge Oliver W. Holmes, a member of the Massachusetts Metaphysical Club, together with William James and other prominent members of Boston and Cambridge's intellectual community, for whom 'truth lives, for the most part, on a credit system', as James put it, '… you accept my verification of one theory, I yours of another. We trade on each others' truth. But beliefs

verified concretely by somebody are the posts of the whole superstructure.' Truth and error become in this scenario a matter of shared beliefs anchored by a practical setting of exchanges, which are seemingly self-sustaining, self-reproducing, and, for the most part, imaginary. That anchor could be the Chicago Stock Exchange, an institution which emerged in connection with these cases and other regulatory frameworks.

25. See Le Clézio, J. M. G. *The Mexican Dream. Or, The Interrupted Thought of Amerindian Civilizations*: 25.

26. See for this quote, Flynn, D. O., and Giraldez, A. 'Born with a Silver Spoon: The Origin of World Trade in 1571', in *Journal of World History*, 6, no. 2, 1995: 201–20, at 201. The authors refer to 'sufficient value', meaning 'sufficiently different value'. Regularity and quantity of products exchanged were important, but what really mattered is that this exchange took place between 'all important populated continents'. The spatial distance accounts for an irreducible difference between trading partners that is indexed by world money, different form equilibrium price, and accumulated as margin or value. Importantly, space also entails time: the time there is between the expectation or the promise of profit and the delivery on that promise, or between offering one's labour-power or products and selling them. Hence, the only event that really concerns capitalism is when contemplated delivery never takes place. That is when bubbles 'burst'. States' 'sovereignty' (its capacity to issue money, charter companies, collect tax and back it all up with the threat of force and collective belief) always intervenes to make sure this does not happen, ultimately by using monopolised and/or outsourced means of force in order to create distance, new territories and time differentials.

27. In fact, this is true of everything that is valuable: everything is a composite, it reaches out to everything else and its potential becomes realised in its identity or position in relation to everything else. In that respect every single thing is an effect of a network, and to know its value we must know (1) where it stands in relation to something different, and (2) where it stands in relation to something similar with which it can be compared. But it is also the case that things are never fully identical with everything else they may be similar with or different from. They are not mere effects of a network. The network effect is like fantasy or fiction, which provides a structure within which that which is manifest to me, ready at hand to be used, and the difference it carries within, the fact that it is plugged into everything else and not just there for my sake or for the sake of everything else, which is not manifest to me, encounter each other in motion, that is, in space-time. Within that narrative structure, space and time, the manifest thing and its hidden connectedness and difference are contained and composed. Think about space and time, though, not as a fixed background or a structure, for it is the movement of the elements that determines the coordinates of space and time. This is precisely the quality of fiction: it creates a containment field, by providing the elements within with a self-reflexive form of temporality that creates the overall illusion of completeness and composition. However, as in the example of Friedman's pencil,

this composition, this unity, which is real – illusions are never unreal, they are simply virtual – is an aftereffect of the work of narrative, fantasy and fiction upon elements that are, in principle, decomposed and unrelated to one another. And, as Jorge Luis Borges correctly pointed out, this means that the work of fiction – for all its capacity to bring separate things together, thereby creating an illusion of unity with effects in reality – is always full of holes. Put otherwise, it turns out that reality is a composite, a work of fiction, made possible by fantasy, which is affected by contingency and anticipation. And thus, it is a completion process that fails, at least partially. In this respect, reality (what is valuable considered as a whole) is changing and its laws and regularities change too, but not because of the participation of chance; rather, it is because in fiction the things that are manifest to us can split from their hidden and more fundamental qualities – what makes them comparable and yet dissimilar – leaving behind what may be undesirable to us, which then becomes distinguishable from what is, in the thing, more than it is already. This is why we find in Friedman's pencil more than it already is, not just a tool for writing but also the very 'presence' of capital's (alluring and awesome) power. The same could be said of your new car or that designer dress you have craved since last Christmas. But these are no mere 'projections' of your psyche or your desires upon an otherwise inert thing: Friedman's pencil does embody the power of capitalism to 'flatten' the world and that designer dress you crave is alluring. So, in order to know what is valuable we need to know (3) that it is alluring and has 'aura', and also (4) that for all its 'aura' and allure that something is, like everything else, fragile and failing. And this has nothing to do with logic, at least not with mainstream logic, but, rather, with aesthetics. Art critics and aesthetics professors might tell you that, since the advent of mechanical and now digital reproduction, all aesthetic objects, all objects in general, have lost their 'aura'. This is not the case; it is the case that 'aura' has now been captured and colonised, indeed it is accumulated, by capital-value. This is why art in our time may be defined by either its relation to capital-value (its capacity to deliver on its contemplated promise, or sales) or its self-conscious attempt to distance itself from that relation. And, indeed, this 'failure' is what makes the art of our times valuable both in respect of its relation with the future and the shadow it extends upon the past. In a different but related manner, art critics might tell you that an aesthetic object is valuable because it endures and withstands the passage of time. But that is not true; in fact, what we admire in Roman ruins or in *Don Quixote* is not just its 'persistence' and sameness through time (which is just an illusion, for to read *Don Quixote* today or even rewrite it word by word in exactly the same way it was written by Cervantes will always result in some loss) but more precisely because of their fragility and sense of loss. Truth and value, which are in this case a matter of aesthetics and not logic, are on the side of difference and the ultimate difference is, of course, extinction.

28. See on this Marx, K. 'Economic Manuscripts of 1857–58,' in *Collected Works*, vol. 28: 99. Karatani makes the point thus: 'Exchanging a commodity with money is not simply an occurrence between two things (the commodity

and gold) but it is equal to placing the commodity in relationship with all other commodities. The price of a commodity does not simply express an equivalent relationship with money, but aggregates the relationship with all other commodities. What is more, the price of a commodity varies in different systems. And the difference inextricably persists, even when an equilibrium of prices in individual systems is presupposed. If placed between different systems, an exchange – even at a price that does only equal exchange within individual systems – can generate margin.' See on this Karatani, K. *Transcritique*: 231.

29. In fact, the term was coined in the title of a document called *Métodos de descompressão política*, prepared by none other than Samuel P. Huntington at the request of Leitão de Abreu, chief of the *Casa Civil*, or the Civilian Cabinet, of Brazil's military regime in 1973. The document, part of a wider discussion on alternative forms of political transformation, was widely debated and criticised by Brazilian intellectuals and politicians. For the source of this story, and a first-hand account of Brazil's 'miracle' and ECLAC's involvement, see Reis Velloso, J. P. *Tempos Modernos. João Paulo dos Reis Velloso: Memórias do desenvolvimento*. Edited by Maria Celina D'Araujo and Celso Castro (Rio de Janeiro: FGV Editora, 2004).

30. It is not surprising that this transformation was mostly observed by anthropologists, historians, storytellers and psycho-analysts, who cherish nations and communities as superstructures – the spaces of sensibility and imagination – rather than economists, lawyers and Marxist economists in thrall to the laws of exchange of state and capital. There are nevertheless important exceptions, Peruvian essayist J. C. Mariátegui being the most important. I would also add the names of Alejo Carpentier and Edouard Glissant in the Caribbean, Mario de Andrade in Brazil and Horacio Quiroga in the southern cone, but an explanation would exceed the purposes of this work. Suffice to say, for now, that they all created the *persona* of the 'hero without character' who is neither Pizarro nor Atahualpa, lives in the traditional-national community and goes to the city, São Paulo for instance, the space *par excellence* of production and consumption (or the other way around in the case of Quiroga) and create new forms and spaces of representation. The latter do not exist in representation alone, which is why to speak of the nations of the Americas and elsewhere as 'imagined communities', as Benedict Anderson does, may be academically enlightening but ultimately simplistic. The nation as representation was certainly intensified by literacy, literature, newspapers and education, but underpinning this process were technological revolutions and patterns of diffusion determining changing contexts for nation-state development. It is no coincidence that among the writers I have named nearly all of them played with or gave origin to 'modernist' forms similar to those of Dada and the Surrealists in Europe, their writings and poetics being themselves examples of little communication machines, computing and communication technologies before the advent of telex and computers. The nation-state was indeed imagined but this image was and is still required by realities. I prefer to speak of the nation-state being fabricated through telephone lines, telegraphs (and nowadays computers),

as in the case of the telegraphist of Ciénaga and Aracataca informing Jorge Eliécer Gaitán in Bogotá about the massacre of Afro-Latin American and indigenous workers of the United Fruit Company by the armed forces, which gives you the image and the reality of Colombia.

31. Canadian physicist, computer programmer and MBA graduate Michael Linton designed LETS in the 1980s in response to the financial crisis wreaking havoc in Latin America. Its aim was to protect regional economies against unimpeded global finance contractions and expansions. Linton started by examining the various currencies tried out during the 1930s Great Depression, such as Silvio Gessell's 'stamp money', and developed an idea for money-based exchanges that do not transform into capital, and has been put into practice in Britain, Canada, France, Japan and, crucially, in Argentina during the financial debacle of 2001–2. On such occasions it demonstrated its viability and potential, but when assembled with the Internet and mobile phone global networks, that potential can be unleashed well beyond the notion of local money. For peer-to-peer finance and meta-currencies see: http://www.open-sourcecurrency.org/ and also http://openmoney.ning.com. Good reads on the subject include: Douglas Rushkoff's *Life Inc.: How the World Became a Corporation and How to Take It Back* (New York and London: Random House, 2009); Michael Linton's The LETSystem Design Manual, available online at http://www.gmlets.u-net.com/design/home.html; Marc Gauvin and Sergio Dominguez's 'Formal Stability Analysis of Common Lending Practices and Consequences of Chronic Currency Devaluation', available online at http://bibocurrency.org/Formal%20Stability%20Analysis%20and%20experiment%20(final)%20rev%203.4.pdf, and 'Formal Specification of the International BIBO "@" Currency Specification', also available online at http://bibocurrency.org/BIBO%20currency%20specification%20v4.6.pdf. Interesting reads on the subject include: Thomas Greco's *Money: Understanding and Creating Alternatives to Legal Tender* (New York: Chelsea Green Publishing), and *The End of Money and the Future of Civilization* (New York: Chelsea Green Publishing, 2009); Richard C. Cook's *We Hold These Truths: The Hope of Monetary Reform* (Aurora, Colo.: Tendrill Press, 2008). The term 'Venecuba', suggesting Venezuela + Cuba as an emerging sub-regional unity, was coined by Fidel Castro during a visit of Venezuela's president Hugo Chávez to the island in 2005. Chávez refers to it as a form of communal-socialist solidarity network opposed to US 'imperialism' that extends from common community-health programmes to telecommunications to security and defence policy. In 2007 the Italian journal of geopolitics *Limes* published a special issue on the Chávez–Castro rapport subtitled 'Venecuba Project'; see on this Canali, L. 'Amici e Nemici di Venecuba', in *Limes, Rivista Italiana di Geopolitica*, 2/2007. For a less sober, antipathetic take on the project, see '"Venecuba, a single nation', in *The Economist*, 13–19 February 2010: 56. For Guevara's proposal of money as 'money-of-account', based on the accounting practices of US corporations rather than Marxist-Leninist

orthodoxy (which he vehemently opposed in these matters), see Helen Yaffe's *Che Guevara*: 57–67.

32. See on this, Pérez, C. *A Vision for Latin America: A Resource-Based Strategy for Technological Dynamism and Social Inclusion.* Paper Prepared Under Contract with the ECLAC Program of Technology Policy and Development in Latin America, 2008: 5–6.

33. Not only is the nautical metaphor the original metaphor of our 'one world'. Since the nautical image is the metaphor for the very concept of metaphor, as all poets since Aristotle – from Virgil to Borges – have correctly argued, then it turns out that the nautical metaphor is the only metaphor! In this sense at least it is correct to say that there is no such thing as a 'level playing field'.

34. Cited by Dosman, E. J. op. cit.: 409. For the basis of my account of the 1964 UNCTAD see Dosman, E. J. ibid.

35. For this analogy and a version of the general argument see Chang, J-H. op. cit.: 218–19. He uses football and boxing, including the Ali–Duran imaginary (mis)match and the US–Honduras competition. Chang also points out that in golf we even use an explicit system of handicaps 'that give players advantages in inverse proportion to their playing skills'. Regulations concerning the regional composition of leagues and the exchange of players, among others, allow for the fairness and 'fun-factor' associated with the fact that the underdog can actually win in baseball and American football. Something similar occurs in FIFA level football (soccer to Americans) and is at the root of the crisis in major football/soccer leagues in England or Spain.

36. See Pérez, C. op. cit.: 8. See also Yaffe, H. op. cit.: 45–61 and 70–72.

37. See Marichal, C. 'The Finances of Hegemony in Latin America: Debt Negotiations and the Role of the U. S. Government, 1945–2005', in *Empire and Dissent. The United States and Latin America.* Edited by F. Rosen (Durham, SC: Duke University Press. 2008): 107.

38. Ibid.: 90–116, at 108.

39. See on this the work of logician Valerie Kerruish, 'On Re-staging the Universal: Butler, Hegel and Contesting the Closure of Logic', in *Dilemmatta. Jahrbuch der ASFPG*, I (Marburg: Der Andere Verlag, 2006): 23–60, at 43 and 51. See also Guardiola-Rivera, O. *Being Against the World*: 141–52.

40. This is a reference to the quote often attributed to US president Ronald Reagan in relation to the work of Peruvian arch-liberal economist Hernando de Soto, in particular to his book *The Other Path*. In that book De Soto develops a proposal for the 'formalisation', as a bundle of property rights, of the naked possession that the marginal sectors of the population have over their squats in the slums surrounding cities of the developing (and developed) world. Once their informal acts of possession have been 'formalised', the poor of the developing world could use them as collateral in order to obtain micro- or soft-credits from the financial system in order to use them as capital for start-up enterprises and lift themselves out of poverty. The scheme is in some ways similar to Margaret Thatcher's

policy allowing users of council houses in Britain to sell them or obtain credits against their real estate. At first, the availability of credit and capital coupled with the entrepreneurial capacities of the thriving individual seems a marriage made in heaven. That is, until one notices that the scheme proposed by De Soto (and Thatcher) is an exemplar of the sort of 'sub-prime' mortgage market that poisoned the entire financial and economic system in the early twenty-first century. At the very least, the scheme is built upon the very same set of assumptions – market efficiency, financial innovation, disregard for the improbable – which, coupled with liberal political 'faith' and the rise of exporter/importer China, produced the poisonous mixture of the late 1990s and early 2000s. What would have happened to Latin America and to the rest of the developing world, and to the world economy, if more governments had listened to and put into practice De Soto's formidable plan? See on this Esquirol, J. 'Titling and Untitled Housing in Panama City', in *Tennessee Journal of Law and Policy*, 4: 2 (Knoxville: University of Tennessee College of Law, 2008), 243–300, at 260–61. De Soto's best known work to date is *The Other Path: The Invisible Revolution in the Third World*, published in 1989 and then retitled in 2002 as *The Other Path: The Economic Answer to Terrorism*. The hidden reference is to Shining Path, the ultra-leftist armed group which was active in Peru in the eighties and nineties.

41. See Fajnzylber, F. *Estratégia industrial e empresas internacionais: posiçao relativa da América Latina e do Brasil; Sistema industrial e exportaçao de manufaturados: análise da experiência brasileira* (Rio de Janeiro: IPEA/INPES, 1971). During the so-called 'miracle' period that ended between 1973 and 1974, Brazil experimented with a form of asymmetric opening of the economy: protection of goods for consumption co-existed with low tariffs for intermediate products and equipment. Between 1969 and 1974, according to a World Bank study published in 1983 (entitled *A World Bank Country Study: Brazil's industrial policies and manufactured exports*), the expansion of internal demand accounted for 96 per cent of growth in industry, while exports corresponded to a mere 12 per cent. The reason why the total goes beyond 100 per cent is, as then minister of development João Reis Velloso explains, that import substitution was -8 per cent in the period. Frequently, observers of Latin American economic history refer to 1950–80 as the period led by the 'import substitution industrialisation' model associated with the work of the first generation of ECLAC researchers under the lead of Raúl Prebisch and opposed to any opening of the economy. However, as the Brazilian example shows, the fact that during the period of highest growth the rate of import substitution in Brazil was negative suggests a less simplistic picture. 'There was import substitution in certain lines of production, but this wasn't the case for most of them', concludes Reis Velloso. There was a reasonable openness towards direct foreign investment, even though the benefits of Instruction 113 – which allowed for further opening – were not available at the time. During the 'miracle' period exports increased around 25 per cent annually, but imports also increased around 28 per cent; hence Brazil lost its *superávit* in the balance of payments, which was practically in equilibrium in 1972–3.

No IMF funds were used, not even the standby line of emergency credit. Overall, the strategy entailed a more aggressive approach to exports (Brazil exported Ford car engines to the US) accompanied by reasonable pragmatism. The concentration on 'final' or 'durable' goods, explained by a low capital/product ratio, came under criticism as either short-termism or a cause of the concentration of economic surplus in few hands. At this point, critics like Celso Furtado or Theotonio Dos Santos focused the debate on the appropriation of economic surplus as an obstacle of development. See, for sources, Reis Velloso, op. cit., at 139–44.

42. Fajnzylber, F. *Transformación productiva com equidad* (Santiago de Chile: Cepal, 1990). Known in English as *Changing Production Patterns with Social Equity*, this document constitutes the founding manifesto of Latin American neostructuralism.

43. See Leiva, F. I. *Latin American Neostructuralism: The Contradictions of Postneoliberal Development* (Minneapolis, Minn.: University of Minnesota Press, 2008): 1.

44. See Pérez, C. op. cit.: 11–14.

45. All quotes from Leiva, op. cit., at xxi.

46. As put by Mark Leonard in *What Does China Think?*, at 37.

47. Ocampo was secretary general of ECLAC in the late nineties after having served as finance and agriculture minister, director of the National Planning Institute and chairman of the board at the Central Bank in his native Colombia. In 6 June 2003 he was designated UN under-secretary general for economic and social affairs. He has taught at Cambridge University, Universidad Nacional de Colombia, and currently leads the Program in Economic and Political Development at the School of International and Public Affairs at Columbia University. Among his friends, including US economist and co-author Joseph Stiglitz, he is mentioned as a future winner of the Nobel Prize in Economics for his work on post-crisis institutional design. He is, with Joseph E. Stiglitz, Shari Spiegel, Ricardo French-Davis and Deepak Nayyar, the author of *Stability with Growth: Macroeconomics, Liberalization and Development*, (New York: Oxford University Press, 2006). For the source of these quotations, see Ocampo, J. A. 'What Should Bretton Woods II Look Like?', in *Journal of Turkish Weekly*, 12 November 2008, available at http://www.turkishweekly.net/news/61157/what-should-bretton-wood s-ii-look-like-by-jose-antonio-ocampo-.html

48. These statistics are based on the work of Carlos Vilas. He is a researcher and professor at the Universidad Nacional Autónoma de México, and a pioneer of the study of Latin America's new politics and economics. In 1997 he published the classic study *The New Politics of Inequality in Latin America*, together with a group of political scientists and academics from the US. Some of the ideas expressed in these paragraphs are based on his work; for those and quotes, see Vilas, C. 'Participation, Inequality, and the Whereabouts of Democracy', in *The New Politics of Inequality in Latin America: Rethinking Participation and Representation* (Oxford and New York: Oxford University Press, 1997): 4–42, at 5–6.

49. See, for instance, Kenneth Roberts' 'Rethinking Economic Alternatives',

in *The New Politics of Inequality in Latin America: Rethinking Participation and Representation* (Oxford and New York: Oxford University Press, 1997): 313–36, at 314.

50. Prins, G., and Rayner, S. 'Time to ditch Kyoto', in *Nature*, no. 449, 25 October 2007: 973–5.

Epilogue

1. This and other quotes from Latin American heads of state and officials related to the Cancún Declaration were taken from 'Vicepresidente boliviano saluda a nuevo organismo latinoamericano sin EEUU', 'Correa confia en la recién creada Comunidad de Estados Latinoamericanos y Caribeños' and 'Crean Nuevo organismo regional en Cumbre de Rio'. Available online at http://www.telesurtv.net/noticias/secciones/nota/67312-NN/crean-nuevo-organismo-regional-en-cumbre-de-rio/. Last accessed 24 February 2010.

2. 'Bolsa Familia' (Family Allowance) and 'Fome Zero' (Zero Hunger) are the flagship programmes of the Ministry of Social Development and Struggle Against Hunger. The Ministry was created by the PT government in 2004. Its aim is to strengthen social development and its objectives are to articulate and execute the social policies of the federal government that embody its decision to frame the access to common goods (food, health, education) causing extreme poverty and social exclusion, as a matter of social rent, and a priority in the national long-term agenda. To this end, the ministry networks with other organisations, governmental and non-governmental, which together, are linking such tactics as cash transfers, food security and welfare channels to the overall strategy of ending social exclusion. The financial programme known as 'Family Allowance' (PBF) directly transfers income to families with a monthly income of $70 per person. The programme articulates three dimensions: immediate alleviation of poverty by direct rent or cash transfers; the strengthening of the capacity to exercise basic social rights – access to property rights over commons as social rights – such as health and education; and the provision to families of further tools to enable them to break from the vicious cycle of the reproduction of poverty from one generation to another. PBF reaches eleven million families in all Brazilian municipalities. In 2007 it invested close to $5,000 million in the long-term future of the country. Source: Ministério do Desenvolvimiento Social e Combate à Fome-MDS. 'Brasil unido para superar el hambre, reducir la pobreza y las desigualdades sociales.' 2007. A conversation with Brazilian minister of social development Patrus Ananias took place in Bahía Blanca, Argentina, in September 2009.

3. According to the historical record, countries that are now technologically advanced 'borrowed', imitated and routinely violated copyright prescriptions in order to acquire the technologies and industrial infrastructure they required in order to overcome the divide of the industrial revolution. Throughout the nineteenth century the copyright regimes of today's rich countries did not enforce foreigners' intellectual property rights. Britain, the Netherlands, France and the United States permitted the patenting of

'imported inventions'. Foreigners' copyrights were not protected in the US 1790 copyright law. It signed the 1886 Berne Convention on copyright only in 1891. Between the 1850s and 1930s no legal consideration would stop the likes of Charles Flint and W. R. Grace from appropriating the knowledge of the indigenous peoples of Peru concerning the properties of guano and nitrates, or would include some form of compensation. By then, the US was a net importer of copyright materials and would only protect American authors. Until 1988, the US did not recognise copyrights materials printed outside America. Famously, after the end of World War II America would benefit from a crucial technological transfer from Europe, as pioneering German and Austrian scientists were relocated to the US. Despite this history, rich countries now encourage developing ones to enforce the protection of intellectual property rights to a historically unprecedented degree, through so-called WTO-TRIPs provisions and clauses in bilateral agreements, while at the same time allowing the patenting of bio-technological material and knowledge taken from indigenous peoples. See on this, Lander, E. 'Eurocentrism, Modern Knowledges and the "Natural" order of Global Capital', in *Nepantla. Views from South*, vol. 3, issue 2 (Durham, SC: Duke University Press, 2002): 245–68. See also Chang, J-H. *Bad Samaritans*: 122–44.

4. Cited by Jim Shultz in '"Evonomics" Gets a Second Term in Bolivia', in *NACLA Report on the Americas*, vol. 43, no. 1, January/February 2010: 4–4, at 4.

5. In the documentary film *Capitalism: A Love Story*, directed by Michael Moore, 2009.

6. As Cristian Marazzi correctly points out. For the quotation of David Brooks' 2 August 2008 article in the *Herald Tribune* and the observation about the end of unilateralism and multilateral 'hegemony' see Marazzi, C. *The Violence of Financial Capitalism*: 88. For a development of this argument, from the perspective of long-term historical cycles, see Arrighi, G. *Adam Smith in Beijing. Lineages of the Twenty-First Century* (London and New York: Verso, 2007): 175–276.

7. Martin Wolf's 31 March 2009 article in the *Financial Times* is quoted in this context by Halevi, J. 'Il Summitt e i conflitti intercapitalistici', in *Il Manifesto*, 4 April 2009.

8. See on this Marazzi, C. op. cit.: 96.

9. Ibid.: 98.

10. On the potential and contradictions of such an initiative, see Wright, L. 'Lithium Dreams. Can Bolivia Become the Saudi Arabia of the Electric-Car Era?', in *New Yorker*, 22 March 2010: 48–59.

11. Conversation with Patrus Ananias, 25–29 September 2009, Bahía Blanca, Argentina.

12. For the source of quotes and statistics see Shultz, J. op. cit.: 4–5.

13. See on this *Balance Preliminar de las Economías de América Latina y el Caribe*. United Nations/ECLA-CEPAL, 2009. For other statistics, sources of quotes and paraphrases see Rosen, F. 'Mexico's fireworks of 2010', in *NACLA Report on the Americas*, January/February 2010: 3.

14. See, for instance, Gootenberg, P. 'Cocaine in Chains: The Rise and

Demise of a Global Commodity, 1860–1950', in *From Silver to Cocaine. Latin American Commodity Chains and the Building of the World Economy, 1500–2000*: 321–51, at 344–6. See also Naím, M. 'Wasted: The American Prohibition on Thinking Smart in the Drug War', in *Foreign Policy*, May/June 2009: 167–8; and Rosen, F. 'Mexico's Fireworks of 2010', in *NACLA Report on the Americas*, January/February 2010: 3.

15. Naím, M. op. cit.: 167–8.
16. Ibid.: 167.
17. Kalmanovitz, S. 'El legado económico de Uribe', in *El Espectador*, 7 March 2010. Available online at http://www.elespectador.com/columna191625-el-legado-macroeconomico-del-presidente-uribe. Last accessed 24 March 2010. He also estimates that non-guaranteed or 'informal' workers comprise now 58 per cent of Colombia's labour force.
18. It included Brazil's Fernando Henrique Cardoso, Colombia's César Gaviria and Mexico's Ernesto Zedillo. The commission's report is available at www.drugsanddemocracy.org
19. See on this Krugman, P. 'China's dollar trap', in *New York Times*, 3 April 2009. See also Wolf, Martin, 'Why President Obama must mend a sick world economy', in *Financial Times*, 21 January 2009, and Marazzi, C. op. cit.: 93–6. He cites both Krugman and Wolf on this point.
20. As he says, moving in this direction would involve two dimensions: 'the first would be to make counter-cyclical allocations of Special Drawing Rights (SDRs), which would represent, in the traditional terminology, "unconditional" liquidity. The second would involve financing all IMF lending with SDRs.' His proposal differs from that of the Chinese in two important ways: first, in that it contemplates moving into a fully SDR-based IMF, so as to eliminate the need for the IMF to manage a multiplicity of currencies, only a small fraction of which can be used for IMF lending, which is how the present partially SDR-based IMF works. Secondly, it involves the active use of SDRs with some mix of global 'inequality-smashing' features, such as the creation of regional reserve arrangements – the Latin American Reserve Fund contemplated in the Cancún Declaration or the Chiang Mai Agreement in Asia – or the UNCTAD-based scheme to allow the IMF to buy unused bonds from multilateral investment banks in order to finance the demands for long-term resources and 'collective insurance' by developing countries. See on this Ocampo, J. A. 'Reforming the Global Reserve System', in *Time for a Visible Hand*: 289–312.
21. See on this Mandel, M. 'The big job engines: education and health', in *Business Week*, 11 March 2009.
22. Conversation with Patrick Bond, Cape Town, 6 August 2009. Patrick Bond is an economist teaching at the University of Kua-Zulu Natal in South Africa. He bases his observations, which I have relied upon, on data gathered by the South African Reserve Bank concerning investment reactions to political liberation between 1989 and 2000, particularly after the removal of financial rand and exchange controls in March 1995. Bond also advises the Ecuadorian government on a financial scheme aimed at 'leaving resources on the soil', mainly oil and gas, thereby providing a potential

solution to global warming.

23. These statistics were compiled and provided for me by South African economist Solomon Johannes 'Sampie' Terreblanche, in the course of a conference on the state of South Africa's economy. The occasion in question was the Seminar Supper supported by the Ubuntu Project, University of Cape Town, 8 August 2009. My gratitude to Drucilla Cornell for her invitation to take part in this seminar and other related activities. Her work and uncompromising attitude is an inspiration.

24. Judt, T. op. cit.: 4.

Index

DATE DUE